当代国外语言学与应用语言学文库

Studies in the Way of Words
言辞用法研究

Paul Grice 著

顾曰国 导读

外语教学与研究出版社
哈佛大学出版社

京权图字: 01－2001－1517

图书在版编目(CIP)数据

言辞用法研究/(美)格赖斯(Grice, P.)编著;顾曰国导读.—北京:外语教学与研究出版社,2002
ISBN 7－5600－2580－3

Ⅰ.言… Ⅱ.①格… ②顾… Ⅲ.语言哲学－文集－英文 Ⅳ.H0-53

中国版本图书馆 CIP 数据核字(2002)第 006586 号

言辞用法研究
Paul Grice   著
顾曰国   导读
*　　*　　*
责任编辑: 陈　忠
出版发行: 外语教学与研究出版社
社　　址: 北京市西三环北路 19 号 (100089)
网　　址: http://www.fltrp.com
印　　刷: 北京外国语大学印刷厂
开　　本: 650×980　1/16
印　　张: 27.75
版　　次: 2002 年 3 月第 1 版　2004 年 11 月第 2 次印刷
印　　数: 5001—8000 册
书　　号: ISBN 7－5600－2580－3/G·1233
定　　价: 36.90 元
*　　*　　*
如有印刷、装订质量问题出版社负责调换
制售盗版必究　举报查实奖励
版权保护办公室举报电话: (010)88817519

当代国外语言学与应用语言学文库

出版前言

　　《当代国外语言学与应用语言学文库》首批54种自2000年9月问世以来，取得很大成功，首印5000套供不应求，10月份便开始重印6000套。能在短短的几个月内出版发行如此宏大规模的语言学著作，这在我国学术出版发行史上是不多见的。自出版以来，许多单位和个人争相订购，研究生和大学生把《文库》视为良师益友，教师无论老中青都把《文库》视为知识更新的源泉。实践证明，外研社推出的《文库》受到了国内语言学界和外语教学界的普遍好评，它将成为推动我国语言学教学与研究和外语教学与研究的一个宝库。

　　在成功出版《文库》首批54种的基础上，外研社现在又推出《文库》第二批58种。《文库》第二批具有五大特色：一、由58部英文原著组成，所覆盖的学科从首批的26个增加到现在的33个，新增学科包括语言学史、语言哲学、认知语言学、人类语言学、语言的起源、语法化学说等，能更广泛地满足读者的需求；二、收入了当代语言学大师索绪尔、萨丕尔、布龙菲尔德、韩礼德、乔姆斯基、奥斯汀、格莱斯、利奇等名家的最有影响的作品，具有更高的权威性；三、增加了牛津大学出版社、哈佛大学出版社等世界知名出版社出版的语言学经典著作；四、依然配有专家导读，专家的队伍比首批更为强大；五、世界著名语言学家乔姆斯基教授和我国著名语言学家沈家煊教授作序。

　　本《文库》是一个大型的、开放性的系列丛书，它将对我国语言学教学与研究和外语教学与研究起到积极的推动作用。今后，外研社还将继续引进，争取把国外最新的、最具影响的语言学和应用语言学著作不断地奉献给广大读者。

外语教学与研究出版社
语言学与辞书部
2001年8月

Contents

Contents

Preface by Halliday

Foreign Language Teaching & Research Press is to be congratulated on its initiative in making these publications in linguistics available to foreign language teachers and postgraduate students of linguistics in China.

The books are a representative selection of up-to-date writings on the most important branches of linguistic studies, by scholars who are recognized as leading authorities in their fields.

The availability of such a broad range of materials in linguistics will greatly help individual teachers and students to build up their own knowledge and understanding of the subject. At the same time, it will also contribute to the development of linguistics as a discipline in Chinese universities and colleges, helping to overcome the divisions into "English linguistics", "Chinese linguistics" and so on which hinder the progress of linguistics as a unified science.

The series is to be highly commended for what it offers to all those wanting to gain insight into the nature of language, whether from a theoretical point of view or in application to their professional activities as language teachers. It is being launched at a time when there are increasing opportunities in China for pursuing linguistic studies, and I am confident that it will succeed in meeting these new requirements.

M. A. K. Halliday
Emeritus Professor
University of Sydney

王宗炎序[①]

　　近年来，国际交往日益频繁，国际贸易急速发展，出现了一种前所未有的现象：学外语、教外语、用外语的人多了；研究语言学和应用语言学的人多了；开设这方面专业的高校也多了，语言学硕士生和博士生也多了。就是不以此为专业，学习语言学和应用语言学的也不乏其人。为了给从事这个专业的师生提供便利，同时又帮助一般外语教师、涉外工作者以及汉语研究者开阔思路，扩大视野，提高效率，我们献上这套内容崭新而丰富的丛书——英文版《当代国外语言学与应用语言学文库》。

　　文库首批推出 54 部外国英文原著，它覆盖了语言学与应用语言学 26 个分支学科。这批书是我们与各地有关专家教授反复研究之后精选出来的。出版这样大规模的语言学与应用语言学丛书，这在我国语言学界和外语教学界是破天荒第一次。

　　我们这样做，抱着什么希望呢？总的说来，是遵循教育部关于加强一级学科教育的指示，在世纪之交，推出一套书来给中国的外语教育领航，同时也给一般外语工作者和汉语研究者提供信息，拓宽思路。

　　我们希望这个文库能成为进一步带动外语教学改革和科研的发动机；我们希望它能成为运载当代外国语言学理论、语言研究方法和语言教学方法来到中国的特快列车；我们希望，有了这套书，语言学与应用语言学专业师生就能顺利地进行工作；我们希望，通过读这套书，青年外语教师和外语、汉语研究者能迅速把能力提高，把队伍不断扩大。

　　以上是我们的愿望，可是从广大读者看来，这个文库是否真的有出台的必要呢？我们想，只要大家看一下今天的客观情

---

　　①　此序为《当代国外语言学与应用语言学文库》首批 54 种而作。

况，就知道这套书有填空补缺的作用，是让大家更上一层楼的扶梯。

我们跟许多人一样，认为国内的外语教学和语言学与应用语言学研究是成绩斐然的，但是某些不足之处也无庸讳言。

在语言研究方面，有大量工作还等着大家去做。汉语语法研究，过去由于结构主义的启示，已经成绩卓著，可是现在虽则引进了功能主义，还看不出什么出色的成果。语料语言学是新兴学科，在我国刚刚起步，机器翻译从 50 年代就有人搞，然而其进展至今不能令人满意。

在语言理论方面，我们不时听到一些片面的、所见不全的论调。有人说，1957 年前西方根本没有什么理论语言学，其创始者是 Chomsky；也有人说，语言纯属社会文化范畴；还有人说，搞语言研究只有量化方法才是科学方法，定性方法不值得一提。

谈到外语教学，某些看法做法是分明不值得赞许的。有人以为交际教学只管听说，不管读写，也有人以为教精读课就是教阅读，不管口语。在分析课文时老师满堂灌，学生开口不得，是常见的；教听力课时老师只管放录音，对学生不给半点提示点拨，也并非罕有现象。

上述这些缺点，我们早有所知，现在我们更加明白，必须力图改进，再也不能安于现状了。为了改进，我们就得参考国外的先进理论，借鉴国外的有效措施。眼前这个文库，就是我们上下求索的结果。

在编辑这个文库时，我们在两方面下了功夫。

一方面，在选书时，我们求全，求新，求有代表性和前瞻性。我们不偏爱一家之言，也不只收一家外国出版社之书。语言学与应用语言学的主干学科固然受到了应有的重视，分支学科可也不忽视。语料语言学、语言统计学是新兴学科，我们收入了专著；句法学、语义学久已有人研究，我们也找到了有关的最新著作。

另一方面，我们邀请了国内知名的博士生导师、硕士生导师为各书撰文导读，为读者铺平道路。语言学和应用语言学专著包罗宏富，初学者读起来可能觉得茫无头绪。为了助他们一臂之力，本文库中每一种书我们都请专家写了一万字左右的导读材料。哪怕书中内容比较陌生，谁只要在读书前看一下导读材料，读书后把材料再看一遍，一定能弄清脉络，掌握要点。

在结束本文时，我们想向爱好泛读的人们提个建议。语言和社会生活息息相关；我们靠语言与他人协作；通过语言继承传统文化，接受外国先进思想和科学知识；利用语言来教育下一代，帮助他们创造美好的未来；语言又反过来表达着我们的个性和我们充当的各种角色。学一点语言学和应用语言学，有助于增强我们的语言意识，对我们的工作和生活都是有利的。我们不妨把此事作为一个项目，列入自己的日程。持之以恒，必有所获。

王宗炎

中山大学教授
博士生导师

Preface by Chomsky

It is about half a century since the study of language undertook a rather new course, while renewing some traditional concerns that had long been neglected. The central change was a shift of attention from behavior and the products of behavior (texts, corpora, etc.) to the internal mechanisms that enter into behavior. This was part of a general shift of perspective in psychology towards what became known as "cognitive science," and was in fact a significant factor in contributing to this development.

With this departure from prevailing structuralist and behaviorist approaches, the object of inquiry becomes a property of individual persons, my granddaughters for example. We ask what special properties they have that underlie an obvious but nonetheless remarkable fact. Exposed to a world of "buzzing, booming confusion" (in William James's classic phrase), each instantly identified some intricate subpart of it as linguistic, and reflexively, without awareness or instruction (which would be useless in any event), performed analytic operations that led to knowledge of some specific linguistic system, in one case, a variety of what is called informally "English," in another a variety of "Spanish." It could just as easily been one of the Chinese languages, or an aboriginal language of Australia, or some other human language. Exposed to the same environment, their pet cats (or chimpanzees, etc.) would not even take the first step of identifying the relevant category of phenomena, just as humans do not identify what a bee perceives as the waggle dance that communicates the distance and orientation of a source of honey.

All organisms have special subsystems that lead them to deal with their environment in specific ways. Some of these subsystems are called "mental" or "cognitive," informal designations that need not be made precise, just as there is no need to determine exactly where chemistry ends and biology begins. The development of cognitive systems, like others, is influenced by the environment, but the general course is genetically determined. Changes of nutrition, for example, can have a dramatic effect on development, but will not change a human embryo to a bee or a mouse, and the same holds for cognitive development. The evidence is strong that among the human cognitive systems is a "faculty of language" (FL), to borrow a traditional term: some subsystem of (mostly) the brain. The evidence is also overwhelming that apart from severe pathology, FL is close to uniform for humans: it is a genuine species property. The "initial state" of FL is determined by the common human genetic endowment. Exposed to experience, FL passes through a series of states, normally reaching a relatively stable state at about puberty, after which changes are peripheral: growth of vocabulary, primarily.

As far as we know, every aspect of language — sound, structure, meanings of words and more complex expressions — is narrowly restricted by the properties of the initial state; these same restrictions underlie and account for the extraordinary richness and flexibility of the systems that emerge. It is a virtual truism that scope and limits are intimately related. The biological endowment that allows an embryo to become a mouse, with only the most meager environmental "information," prevents it from becoming a fly or a monkey. The same must be true of human higher mental faculties, assuming that humans are part of the biological world, not angels.

We can think of the states attained by FL, including the stable states, as "languages": in more technical terminology, we may call them "internalized languages" (I-languages). Having an I-language, a person is equipped to engage in the "creative use of language" that has traditionally been considered a primary indication of possession of mind; by Descartes and his followers, to cite the most famous case. The person can produce new expressions over an unbounded range, expressions that are appropriate to circumstances and situations but not caused by them, and that evoke thoughts in others that they might have expressed in similar ways. The nature of these abilities remains as obscure and puzzling to us as it was to the Cartesians, but with the shift of perspective to "internalist linguistics," a great deal has been learned about the cognitive structures and operations that enter into these remarkable capacities.

Though the observation does not bear directly on the study of human language, it is nevertheless of interest that FL appears to be biologically isolated in critical respects, hence a species property in a stronger sense than just being a common human possession. To mention only the most obvious respect, an I-language is a system of discrete infinity, a generative process that yields an unbounded range of expressions, each with a definite sound and meaning. Systems of discrete infinity are rare in the biological world and unknown in non-human communication systems. When we look beyond the most elementary properties of human language, its apparently unique features become even more pronounced. In fundamental respects human language does not fall within the standard typologies of animal communication systems, and there is little reason to speculate that it evolved from them, or even that it should be regarded as having the "primary function" of communication (a rather obscure notion at best). Language can surely be used for communication, as can anything people do, but it is not unreasonable to adopt the traditional view that language is primarily an instrument for expression of thought, to others or to oneself; statistically speaking, use of language is overwhelmingly internal, as can easily be determined by introspection.

Viewed in the internalist perspective, the study of language is part of biology, taking its place alongside the study of the visual system, the "dance faculty" and navigational capacities of bees, the circulatory and digestive systems, and other properties of organisms. Such systems can be studied at various levels. In the case of cognitive systems, these are sometimes called the "psychological" and "physiological" levels — again, terms of convenience only. A bee scientist may try to determine and characterize the computations carried out by the bee's nervous system when it transmits or receives information about a distant flower, or when it finds its way back to the nest: that is the level of "psychological" analysis, in conventional terminology. Or one may try to find the neural basis for these computational capacities, a topic about which very little is known even for the simplest organisms: the level of "physiological" analysis. These are mutually supportive enterprises. What is learned at the "psychological level" commonly provides guidelines for the inquiry into neural mechanisms; and reciprocally, insights into neural mechanisms can inform the psychological inquiries that seek to reveal the properties of the organism in different terms.

In a similar way, the study of chemical reactions and properties, and of the structured entities postulated to account for them, provided guidelines for fundamental physics, and helped prepare the way for the eventual unification of the disciplines. 75 years ago, Bertrand Russell, who knew the sciences well, observed that "chemical laws cannot at present be reduced to physical laws." His statement was correct, but as it turned out, misleading; they could not be reduced to physical laws in principle, as physics was then understood. Unification did come about a few years later, but only after the quantum theoretic revolution had provided a radically changed physics that could be unified with a virtually unchanged chemistry. That is by no means an unusual episode in the history of science. We have no idea what the outcome may be of today's efforts to unify the psychological and physiological levels of scientific inquiry into cognitive capacities of organisms, human language included.

It is useful to bear in mind some important lessons of the recent unification of chemistry and physics, remembering that this is core hard science, dealing with the simplest and most elementary structures of the world, not studies at the outer reaches of understanding that deal with entities of extraordinary complexity. Prior to unification, it was common for leading scientists to regard the principles and postulated entities of chemistry as mere calculating devices, useful for predicting phenomena but lacking some mysterious property called "physical reality." A century ago, atoms and molecules were regarded the same way by distinguished scientists. People believe in the molecular theory of gases only because they are familiar with the game of billiards, Poincare observed mockingly. Ludwig Boltzmann died in despair a century ago, feeling unable to convince his fellow-physicists of the physical reality of the atomic theory of which he was one of the founders. It is now understood that all of this was gross error. Boltzmann's atoms, Kekule's structured organic molecules, and other postulated entities were real in the only sense of the term we know: they had a crucial place in the best explanations of phenomena that the human mind could contrive.

The lessons carry over to the study of cognitive capacities and structures: theories of insect navigation, or perception of rigid objects in motion, or I-language, and so on. One seeks the best explanations, looking forward to eventual unification with accounts that are formulated in different terms, but without foreknowledge of the form such unification might take, or even if it is a goal that can be achieved by human intelligence — after all, a specific biological system, not a universal instrument.

Within this "biolinguistic" perspective, the core problem is the study of particular I-languages, including the initial state from which they derive. A thesis that might be entertained is that this inquiry is privileged in that it is presupposed, if only tacitly, in every other approach to language: sociolinguistic, comparative, literary, etc. That seems reasonable, in fact almost inescapable; and a close examination of actual work will show, I think, that the thesis is adopted even when that is vociferously denied. At the very least it seems hard to deny a weaker thesis: that the study of linguistic capacities of persons should find a fundamental place in any serious investigation of other aspects of language and its use and functions. Just as human biology is a core part of anthropology, history, the arts, and in fact any aspect of human life, so the biolinguistic approach belongs to the social sciences and humanities as well as human biology.

Again adapting traditional terms to a new context, the theory of an I-language L is sometimes called its "grammar," and the theory of the initial state S-0 of FL is called "universal grammar" (UG). The general study is often called "generative grammar" because a grammar is concerned with the ways in which L generates an infinite array of expressions. The experience relevant to the transition from S-0 to L is called "primary linguistic data" (PLD). A grammar G of the I-language L is said to satisfy the condition of "descriptive adequacy" to the extent that it is a true theory of L. UG is said to satisfy the condition of "explanatory adequacy" to the extent that it is a true theory of the initial state. The terminology was chosen to bring out the fact that UG can provide a deeper explanation of linguistic phenomena than G. G offers an account of the phenomena by describing the generative procedure that yields them; UG seeks to show how this generative procedure, hence the phenomena it yields, derive from PLD. We may think of S-0 as a mapping of PLD to L, and of UG as a theory of this operation; this idealized picture is sometimes said to constitute "the logical problem of language acquisition." The study of language use investigates how the resources of I-language are employed to express thought, to talk about the world, to communicate information, to establish social relations, and so on. In principle, this study might seek to investigate the "creative aspect of language use," but as noted, that topic seems shrouded in mystery, like much of the rest of the nature of action.

The biolinguistic turn of the 1950s resurrected many traditional questions, but was able to approach them in new ways, with the help of intellectual tools that had not previously been available: in particular, a clear understanding of the nature of recursive processes, generative procedures that can characterize an infinity of objects (in this case, expressions of L) with finite means (the mechanisms of L). As soon as the inquiry was seriously undertaken, it was discovered that traditional grammars and dictionaries, no matter how rich and detailed, did not address central questions about linguistic expressions. They basically provide "hints" that can be used by someone equipped with FL and some of its states, but leave the nature of these systems unexamined. Very quickly, vast ranges of new phenomena were discovered, along with new problems, and sometimes at least partial answers.

It was recognized very soon that there is a serious tension between the search for descriptive and for explanatory adequacy. The former appears to lead to very intricate rule systems, varying among languages and among constructions of a particular language. But this cannot be correct, since each language is attained with a common FL on the basis of PLD providing little information about these rules and constructions.

The dilemma led to efforts to discover general properties of rule systems that can be extracted from particular grammars and attributed to UG, leaving a residue simple enough to be attainable on the basis of PLD. About 25 years ago, these efforts converged in the so-called "principles and parameters" (P&P) approach, which was a radical break from traditional ways of looking at language. The P&P approach dispenses with the rules and constructions that constituted the framework for traditional grammar, and were taken over, pretty much, in early generative grammar. The relative clauses of Hungarian and verb phrases of Japanese exist, but as taxonomic artifacts, rather like "terrestrial mammal" or "creature that flies." The rules for forming them are decomposed into principles of UG that apply to a wide variety of traditional constructions. A particular language L is determined by fixing the values of a finite number of "parameters" of S-0: Do heads of phrases precede or follow their complements? Can certain categories be null (lacking phonetic realization)? Etc. The parameters must be simple enough for values to be set on the basis of restricted and easily obtained data. Language acquisition is the process of fixing these values. The parameters can be thought of as "atoms" of language, to borrow Mark Baker's metaphor. Each human language is an arrangement of these atoms, determined by assigning values to the parameters. The fixed principles are available for constructing expressions however the atoms are arranged in a particular I-language. A major goal of research, then, is to discover something like a "periodic table" that will explain why only a very small fraction of imaginable linguistic systems appear to be instantiated, and attainable in the normal way.

Note that the P&P approach is a program, not a specific theory; it is a framework for theory, which can be developed in various ways. It has proven to be a highly productive program, leading to an explosion of research into languages of a very broad typological range, and in far greater depth than before. A rich variety of previously-unknown phenomena have been unearthed, along with many new insights and provocative new problems. The program has also led to new and far-reaching studies of language acquisition and other areas of research. It is doubtful that there has ever been a period when so much has been learned about human language. Certainly the relevant fields look quite different than they did not very long ago.

The P&P approach, as noted, suggested a promising way to resolve the tension between the search for descriptive and explanatory adequacy; at least in principle, to some extent in practice. It became possible, really for the first time, to see at least the contours of what might be a genuine theory of language that might jointly satisfy the conditions of descriptive and explanatory adequacy. That makes it possible to entertain seriously further questions that arise within the biolinguistic approach, questions that had been raised much earlier in reflections on generative grammar, but left to the side: questions about how to proceed beyond explanatory adequacy.

It has long been understood that natural selection operates within a "channel" of possibilities established by natural law, and that the nature of an organism cannot truly be understood without an account of how the laws of nature enter into determining its structures, form, and properties. Classic studies of these questions were undertaken by D'Arcy Thompson and Alan Turing, who believed that these should ultimately become the central topics of the theory of evolution and of the development of organisms (morphogenesis). Similar questions arise in the study of cognitive systems, in particular FL. To the extent that they can be answered, we will have advanced beyond explanatory adequacy.

Inquiry into these topics has come to be called "the minimalist program." The study of UG seeks to determine what are the properties of language; its principles and parameters, if the P&P approach is on the right track. The minimalist program asks why language is based on these properties, not others. Specifically, we may seek to determine to what extent the properties of language can be derived from general properties of complex organisms and from the conditions that FL must satisfy to be usable at all: the "interface conditions" imposed by the systems with which FL interacts. Reformulating the traditional observation that language is a system of form and meaning, we observe that FL must at least satisfy interface conditions imposed by the sensorimotor systems (SM) and systems of thought and action, sometimes called "conceptual-intentional" (CI) systems. We can think of an I-language, to first approximation, as a system that links SM and CI by generating expressions that are "legible" by these systems, which exist independently of language. Since the states of FL are computational systems, the general properties that particularly concern us are those of efficient computation. A very strong minimalist thesis would hold that FL is an optimal solution to the problem of linking SM and CI, in some natural sense of optimal computation.

Like the P&P approach that provides its natural setting, the minimalist program formulates questions, for which answers are to be sought — among them, the likely discovery that the questions were wrongly formulated and must be reconsidered. The program resembles earlier efforts to find the best theories of FL and its states, but poses questions of a different order, hard and intriguing ones: Could it be that FL and its states are themselves optimal, in some interesting sense? That would be an interesting and highly suggestive discovery, if true. In the past few years there has been extensive study of these topics from many different points of view, with some promising results, I think, and also many new problems and apparent paradoxes.

Insofar as the program succeeds, it will provide further evidence for the Galilean thesis that has inspired the modern sciences: the thesis that "nature is perfect," and that the task of the scientist is to demonstrate this, whether studying the laws of motion, or the structure of snowflakes, or the form and growth of a flower, or the most complex system known to us, the human brain.

The past half century of the study of language has been rich and rewarding, and the prospects for moving forward seem exciting, not only within linguistics narrowly conceived but also in new directions, even including the long-standing hopes for unification of linguistics and the brain sciences, a tantalizing prospect, perhaps now at the horizon.

Noam Chomsky
Institute Professor at MIT

沈家煊序

刚刚过去的一个世纪是现代语言学在我国诞生、成长和发展的世纪。发生这样的情形是跟我们学习和借鉴国外语言学的理论和方法紧密相关的。我国传统的语言文字学科是小学，进入二十世纪以后，这门学科吸收了西方语言学的理论，引进和发展了新的方法，在继承传统的基础上进行了一番更新改造，从而获得了新的旺盛的生命力，走上了现代语言学的大道。拿我国传统的音韵学来说，由于欧洲历史比较法和内部拟测法等方法的引进，加上采用效果良好的标音工具——国际音标，这门传统的学科有了重大的转变和进展，我们得以构拟出古音的音值，同时也更好地区别古音的音类。汉语语法的研究，众所周知，我国学者自己撰写的第一部语法著作《马氏文通》正是直接学习和模仿西方语法的结果。上世纪中叶结构主义语法理论和分析方法的引进，使汉语语法研究提高到一个更加精深的层次。至于实验语音学、计算语言学、心理语言学这些跟自然科学联系密切的语言学分支，它们在我国的诞生和发展跟学习和借鉴西方更是分不开。尤其是改革开放以来，我国语言学界解除了长期的思想禁锢，学术空气空前活跃，国外语言学理论和方法的引进也随之出现了繁荣的局面。在新的世纪里要发展我国的语言学，我们在继承传统遗产的同时还需要继续学习和借鉴国外好的理论和方法，这一点是无庸讳言的。

外语教学与研究出版社引进并出版《当代国外语言学与应用语言学文库》，首批54本自2000年9月问世以来，取得很大成功。许多单位和个人争相订阅，研究生和大学生把《文库》视为良师益友，教师无论老中青都把《文库》视为知识更新的源泉。这次引进和出版的第二批58部，覆盖的领域比第一批又有所扩大，新增加了语言学史、语言哲学、人类语言学、认知语言学、语言的起源、语法化学说、音系学的优选论等内容。

此外还增加了汉语研究的专著，如汉语方言的连读变调模式，汉语的形态学。《文库》第一批是导论书和教科书为主体，专著和经典著作较少；第二批增加了不少经典著作，包括索绪尔、萨丕尔、布龙菲尔德、乔姆斯基、奥斯汀、格莱斯等人的作品。另外还有一些重要的专著，如斯珀伯和威尔逊的《关联论》，舍尔的《言语行为》，泰勒的《语言范畴化》，韩礼德的《英语的衔接》等。第二批还增加了不少语言教学和测试方面的著作，语言教学和语言理论应该是一个互相促进的关系。总的来说，第二批的出版可以更好地适应不同层次不同方面的读者的需要，也说明我们引进工作的广度和深度都有提高。第二批依然配有专家导读，专家的队伍也更为强大。

引进和借鉴的目的是要结合我国自身的语言研究和教学而有所创新。西方语言学理论和汉语及国内少数民族语言的实际相结合，和我国的语言教学实际相结合，这是《马氏文通》以来中国语言学的一条基本发展道路。中外结合，任重而道远，问题还不少。王宗炎先生指出，对国外语言学的学习和借鉴"搜集采购之功多，提炼转化之功少"。汉语界和外语界两股力量的汇合，小有进步，成效不大。外语界的学人"搜集采购"功不可没，但是有不少人言必称外国，对国外的理论讲得头头是道，问到自己母语里的情形就一问三不知。近年来不少人在论文中也开始举一些汉语的例子，但是蜻蜓点水，不痛不痒，有的甚至削足适履，拿汉语的事实去迁就国外的理论。汉语界的学人由于语言的障碍，大多只能通过别人的介绍和翻译来了解国外的动态，了解谈不上全面深入，视野不够开阔，思路比较闭塞。另外就是把眼光过分集中于汉语，忽视对语言普遍规律的探究，有人认为这是我国语言学长期落后的一个重要原因，我十分赞同。因此《文库》的引进还只是第一步，今后还有艰苦的跋涉。

在阅读和吸收《文库》的内容时，我想提这么几点建议：一是要由浅入深，循序渐进。一般来说，教科书较浅显，专著较精深，但教科书和专著也都有程度深浅之别。二是要去粗存精，去伪存真。国外的东西要虚心学习，但是也不要迷信。一部书读下来，要静心想一想，哪些是真有道理，哪些是貌似有理，哪些是精华，哪些是糟粕。（现在还有另一种倾向，为了表明自己有独立的思考和创见，曲解别人的观点。）三是联系实际，融会贯通。只攻一点不及其余的做法当然不可取，但有的人面对国外林林总总五花八门的理论和学派，书是读了不少，却始终理不出个头绪来。其实就《文库》而言，其中许多内容都是互相贯通的。比如，"语法化"的问题是近来语言学研究的一个热点，它牵涉到许多方面。要真正对这个问题有透彻的了解，既要有历史语言学的一般知识，还要了解功能语言学、认知语言学、语用学、语言类型学的相关研究成果，最好还要知道生成语言学的理论背景。融会贯通不够的一个主要原因是联系语言的实际不够，因此阅读时最好能联系你最熟悉、语感最好的语言（首先是你的母语）进行比较和思考。后面两点说起来容易做起来难：我自己也不能真正做到，提出来希望和广大读者共勉。

我们正处在一个信息时代，语言是人类最重要的信息载体。新兴的认知科学又把语言作为主要的研究对象，因为语言是人类最高级最重要的认知能力。新的世纪我国的语言学正面临新的挑战，《文库》的出版可以说是迎接这个挑战的第一个回应。

沈家煊

中国社会科学院语言所所长、教授

博士生导师

导　读

顾日国

1. 引言

Grice 的《言词用法研究》是一部非常难读的书。一方面是因为它是哲学类书，另一方面是因为它不是一般意义上的专著，而是论文集。专著首先对前人的研究或学术背景作专章的交代，然后才是著者自己的研究或观点。这样安排有利于读者理解原文。论文集则不同。论文通常见于专业杂志，都是写给专业同行们看的，学科的背景知识一概省去，同时还假定读者对同行的研究是熟悉的。此外，论文还有时间性、针对性和论辩性强的特点。《言词用法研究》一书犹为如此。本导读考虑到这两方面的困难，加强了背景知识的介绍，同时还提供了同行对 Grice 的一些思想的研究论文目录，以便读者作进一步的研读。

2.《言词用法研究》其书

《言词用法研究》是一部日常语言分析哲学（analytic philosophy of language）方面的书。全书收录编者自己的论文和演讲稿共 19 篇，分为两大部分。第一部分题为"逻辑与会话"，有 7 篇论文。原先是编者 1967 年在哈佛大学作的 William James 系列讲座，其中的 4 讲修订后陆续公开发表过，按发表的年代顺序如下：

1. Utterer's meaning, sentence meaning, and word-meaning 见于 1968 年 *Foundations of Language* 杂志第 4 卷，pp.225-242
2. Utterer's meaning and intentions，载于 1969 年 *The Philosophical Review* 杂志第 78 卷，pp.147-177
3. "logic and conversation" 载于 1975 年 P. Cole and J.L. Morgan 编辑的 *Syntax and Semantics* 第 3 卷 *Speech Acts* 专辑，pp.41-58
4. Further notes on logic and conversation 载于 1978 年 P. Cole 编辑的 *Syntax and Semantics* 第 9 卷 *Pragmatics* 专辑，pp.113-128

其余 3 讲的讲稿在一部分学者中有传阅，但未公开发表过。

第二部分题为"语义学和形而上学探索",有论文 12 篇。其中公开发表过的有 6 篇,按发表的年代顺序如下:

1. In defense of a dogma,与 P.F. Strawson 合写,载于 1956 年 *The Philosophical Review*,第 65 卷,pp.141-158

2. Meaning,载于 1957 年 *The Philosophical Review*,第 66 卷,pp.377-388

3. The causal theory of perception,载于 1961 年 *The Aristotelian Society*：*Proceedings*,*Supplementary Volume*,第 35 卷,pp.121-152

4. Some remarks about the senses,载于 1962 年 R.J. Butler 编辑的 *Analytical Philosophy*,Oxford：Basil Blackwell,pp.133-153

5. Presupposition and conversational implicature,载于 1981 年 P. Cole 编辑的 *Radical Pragmatics*,New York：Academic Press,pp.183-197

6. Meaning revisited,载于 1982 年 N.V. Smith 编辑的 *Mutual Knowledge*,New York：Academic Press,pp.223-243

读者会注意到,编者没有按发表年代编排论文的顺序。第一部分中的有些论文位于第二部分中的论文发表之后。也就是说假如读者按书中的顺序读下去,可能会遇到背景知识不够所造成的困难。那些对 Grice 的思想有所了解的读者,或已经读过他的某些论文的读者,可以按书中现有的顺序读下去。那些第一次读 Grice 的读者,我建议按下面的顺序读,其效果会更好一些。(1)第 14 篇 Meaning;(2)第 18 篇 Meaning revisited;(3)第 5 篇 Utterer's meaning and intentions;(4)第 6 篇 Utterer's meaning, sentence-meaning, and word-meaning;(5)第 2 篇 Logic and conversation;(6)第 3 篇 Further notes on logic and conversation。其余文章阅读的先后顺序可根据读者个人的需要。

那些对 Grice 的思想有很好了解的读者则可采取有针对性的选择读法。选择可根据 Grice 在反思性后记里谈到的他致力于探索的 8 个主题:(1)感知分析;(2)分析命题与综合命题的区分问题;(3)常识在哲学思辩中的地位问题;(4)言辞意义与说话人的意义的区别与关系问题;(5)研究意义的切入点问题;(6)会话合作原则及其次则问题;(7)(8)是关于他对逻辑研究中现代派和传统派之间的分歧的看法。

本导读不可能就上面的 8 个主题作逐一介绍。侧重点将放在 3、4、5、6

四个问题上。

3. 日常语言分析哲学及其方法

日常语言分析哲学，通俗地说，就是从分析日常语言入手来研究哲学问题。英语里从 philosophy（哲学）这个词可以派生出一个动词 philosophize，这个动词的意思是对某个问题进行哲学性思考和分析，我们不仿把这个动词译为"对……作哲学思辩"。在英语里，所谓日常语言分析哲学就是对日常语言作哲学思辩。这个思潮的带头人之一就是牛津大学的哲学教授 J.L. Austin，随其后的有本导读的对象 H.P. Grice，以及 P.F. Strawson 等。这些哲学家的写作和教学活动正处在这个思潮的最活跃的时期（大约在 20 世纪 50 年代至 80 年代）。由于主要人物都是在牛津大学哲学系任教，这个学派常常冠以"牛津哲学"（Oxford philosophy）的称号。

从西方哲学史上看，对日常语言作哲学思辩不是什么新的哲学课题。早在古希腊时期哲学家对语言是否是人的区别属性就作过较深入的思考。那么当代的日常语言分析哲学又有什么特点呢？首先，日常语言分析哲学是分析哲学这个大潮中的一个分支。分析哲学所关心的一些核心问题如命题、真假值、指称、有定表述、分析命题、综合命题、预设等都是跟语言发生直接的关系。研究这些问题的哲学家因而不得不对相关的语言表达式作出分析。然而他们分析语言不是对语言本身感兴趣，而是为他们构筑哲学逻辑体系服务。哲学逻辑是一种高度抽象的、高度形式化的符号语言。日常语言对他们来说是不严谨的，模糊的，充满了歧义和谬误，这些给哲学思辩造成障碍。日常语言分析哲学家则认为，虽然日常语言有这些"缺点"，但是它毕竟是人类生活经验的结晶，有许多值得哲学家作出深入思考和学习的地方。正确的态度不是想办法踢开它，而是去认识它，分析它。

Grice 在 Postwar Oxford philosophy 一文里（本书第 10 篇）明确陈述了他的观点。

> ... it is, in my view, an important part, though by no means the
> whole, of the philosopher's task to analyze, describe, or characterize (in

as general terms as possible) the ordinary use or uses of certain expressions or classes of expressions.

以感知为例，如果从哲学的角度研究它，研究者就应该看一看日常语言是怎么谈论它的。Grice 接着指出：

... it is in my view the case that a philosophical thesis which involves the rejection as false, or absurd, or linguistically incorrect, of some class of statements which would ordinarily be made, and accepted as true, in specifiable types of situation is itself almost certain (perhaps quite certain) to be false; ... To reformulate my second proposition in another way: it is almost certainly (perhaps quite certainly) wrong to reject as false, absurd, or linguistically incorrect some class of ordinary statements if this rejection is based merely on philosophical grounds.

这实际上是对怀疑主义者的挑战。哲学上的极端怀疑主义者通过"哲学推理"居然得出象人是看不见树的，甚至连自己的身体也是看不见的结论，因此象"我看见树"、"我看见我的手"这样的话是不真实的假话。在 Grice 看来，这是荒唐的哲学推理，同时也表明对日常语言进行哲学思辩的重要性和迫切性。

我们知道研究日常语言是语言学家的任务，哲学家研究它，这跟前者的研究有什么不同之处呢？Grice 认为他们的研究特点是 conceptual analysis：

To be looking for a conceptual analysis of a given expression E is to be in a position to apply or withhold E in particular cases, but to be looking for a general characterization of the types of case in which one would apply E rather than withhold it. And we may notice that in reaching one's conceptual analysis of E, one makes use of one's ability to apply and withhold E, for the characteristic procedure is to think up a possible general characterization of one's use of E and then to test it by trying to find or imagine a particular situation which fits the suggested characterization and yet would *not* be a situation in which one would apply E. If one fails, after careful consideration on these lines, to find any such situation, then one is more or less confident that the suggested characterization of the use E is satisfactory. （本书第 10 篇 Postwar Oxford philosophy, italics original）

从语言学的角度看，Grice 在这里描述的"概念分析法"就是基于个人语感的、通过反例对理论模型不断进行完善的这样一个动态过程。在语言学里这不算什么新方法，而且其局限性也是人所共知的。然而 Grice 用这个方法对英语动词 mean 的研究，为意义研究开辟了一个崭新的天地，为语用学奠定了一个理论基石。其成就与其说是来自方法，不如说是来自他的独到的看问题的哲学视角。

4. 对意义的剖析

对什么是"意义"这个问题的研究，可以说有几千年的历史。在 Grice 的意义理论提出之前，关于意义的主流认识是，词义铸成短语义，短语义铸成句义，句义铸成篇章义，使用者在这个意义流程中只是根据自己的需要选择使用。词义、短语义和句义在使用者具体使用之前就已经存在。也就是说，意义跟对意义的使用是分离的。对这个主流认识语言学家和哲学家都有过批判。最有力要推 Wittgenstein。他的著名的口号是"意义就是用法"（meaning is use）。Wittgenstein 自己并没有把这个观点发展成一个完整的理论。这要等到 Austin 和 Grice。（关于 Austin 的理论我们在评介《如何以言行事》时已有交待，在此不必赘言。）

Grice 从区别自然意义与非自然意义入手，把阐释意义跟交际双方的意图、信念和目的联系起来，通过确定阐释意义的中心点，建立一个既能阐释自然意义，又能阐释非自然意义的、整一的理论框架，颇有独到之处，作出了开创性的贡献。

在介绍他的观点之前，我们需要记住 Grice 的几个惯用法。（1）英语动词 utter 通常指发声或发音（注：发声不等于发音），而 Grice 则用来指任何用于传达意义的行为，可以是发声的或发音的，也可以是手势、用标记等。（2）英语动词 utter 的派生名词 utterance 有两层意义，一是动词意义的名词化，二是指动作的结果。我们用汉语"说话"来指动词意义，

"话"指结果。(3)带双引号的话不同于不带双引号的话。前者指原话,后者指分析过的意义或命题。这些细微的区别对于正确理解 Grice 的思想是很重要的。

4.1 自然意义与非自然意义

我们先看自然意义和非自然意义的区别。在下面的三句英语话里,

1. "Those spots mean (meant) measles."
2. "Those spots didn't mean anything to me, but to the doctor they meant measles."
3. "The recent budget means that we shall have a hard year."

mean 的用法属于自然意义。比较下面这两句话:

4. "Those three rings on the bell (of the bus) mean that the bus is full."
5. "That remark, 'Smith couldn't get on without his trouble and strife,' meant that Smith found his wife indispensable."

这两句话是非自然意义。

那么自然意义与非自然意义的区别在哪里呢?Grice 用了五个测试方法。方法一是看 mean 的一般现在时和过去时的用法会不会改变句子的逻辑蕴涵值。以(1)和(4)为例。我们先看代表自然意义的例 1:

"Those spots mean measles."

"Those spots meant measles."

两句话都逻辑蕴涵命题 Those spot mean measles. 代表非自然意义的例 4则不行。

"Those three rings on the bell (of the bus) mean that the bus is full."

"Those three rings on the bell (of the bus) meant that the bus was full."

这两句话不能都逻辑蕴涵 the bus is full.

测试方法二是看是否可以通过 what is (was) meant by ... 得出结论 is (was) that-小句。不通过者为自然意义,反之为非自然意义。测试方法之三是看是否有"某人 meant that ... by ...",不通过者为自然意义,反之为非自然意义。测试方法之四是看是否容许改写成含有直接引语的

说法，不通过者为自然意义，反之为非自然意义。测试方法之五是看是否容许改写成以 the fact that 引导的主从句式，通过者为自然意义，反之为非自然意义。

4.2 句义、话面（或字面）意义、言外之意

下面我们来看 Grice 作出的另外几个重要区别。

非自然意义并不是一个单一的意义，它自身就包含好几种意义。我们用小写的 x 代表说出来的话，用大写的 U 代表讲话人。Grice 首先区分下面三种情况：

1. x 的意义
2. U 在某场合说 x 时他的话面意思
3. U 在某场合说 x 时他的用意

我们暂且把 x 的意义理解为离开语境的 x 所具有的一般意义 (nonrelativized)。讲话人 U 在某具体场合说出 x，这就赋予 x 一个用于这个具体场合的、相对于讲话人 U 的话面意义 (relativized)。有时话面意义还不是讲话人在那个场合想要表达的全部意义。讲话人还有其他用意。举例说明。某学生想跟 Grice 教授学哲学，Grice 向这个学生原来的老师询问有关情况。老师对 Grice 没有说别的，只是说："他的书法很好。" x 的意义可以转述为"一男人的字写的很好"。在这个具体场合讲话人（即老师）的话面意义可以转述为"他的学生（某某某）写一手好字"。Grice 可以推出老师讲出这句话的用意，那就是"这个学生恐怕是长于书法而学不了哲学"。

那么，这三种意义哪个是最基本的呢？也就是说，我们可以用这个最基本的去阐释其他的两种或更多的意义。传统的做法是把 x 意义作为最基本义，再用它去解释其他意义。Grice 则从意义来自使用这个观点出发，认为讲话人在某场合通过做某事产生出来的意义是最基本的，用 Grice 常用的表达式说，这个最基本意义就是 By uttering x U meant that p（直译为"通过说 x 讲话人 U 表达意思 p"）.

早在 1957 年（本书第 14 篇）Grice 首次对"通过说 x 讲话人 U 表达意思 p"作了阐释。当说出来的话用的是陈述句式时，"通过说 x 讲话人 U 表

达意思 p" 为真, 当且仅当讲话人说出 x, 意图让听话人 A 相信 p, A 由于看到讲话人的意图而产生相信 p 这个信念。后来在 William James 讲座里 (本书第 5 篇), Grice 采用了下面这个直观性更好的表达式:

"U meant something by uttering x" is true iff, for some audience A,

U uttered x intending:

(1) A to produce a particular response r

(2) A to think (recognize) that U intends (1)

(3) A to fulfill (1) on the basis of his fulfillment of (2).

Grice 研究意义的这个思路有两个鲜明的特点。一是他通过讲话人的交际意图和目的, 以及听话人作出的反应来定义意义, 而不是用意义来定义意义, 这避免了旋环定义的毛病。二是他是通过使用来阐释语义。

4.3 俗成义、语义、讲话人的语用义

上一节介绍的 Grice 关于意义的几个区别是他的早期思想。在其后的十几年里 Grice 一直进行更深入的研究。上一节我们说过, Grice 通过讲话人和听话人之间的交际活动来阐释意义。那么这是不是说词语本身没有任何固定意义, 完全是由说话人和听话人双方在交际现场临时决定的呢? 对这个问题的回答是 Grice 不同于 Wittgenstein 和 Austin 的地方。Grice 比他们更重视词语本身所具有的俗成意义。简要地说, 我们可以把未放在具体语境中去的词语所具有的意义叫俗成义, 或叫语义, 被使用到具体语境中去以后叫语用义。语用义实际上就是讲话人的意义。我们之所以要区别语义和语用义, 是因为 (1) 语义最早源于语用义; (2) 在实际使用中两者时常不同。

Grice 在 Utterer's meaning and intentions (本书第 5 篇) 一文中对语义和语用的区别作了较详细的分析。他以英语句子 "If I shall then be helping the grass to grow, I shall have no time for reading." 为例。面对这个句子, 我们可以做下面这几件事。

(一) 原句我们可以理解为 (1a): "If I shall then be assisting the kind of thing of which lawns are composed to mature, I shall have no time for

F30

reading." 我们也可以理解为："If I shall then be assisting the marijuana to mature, I shall have no time for reading." 这两种可能的理解都是对"完整话语类型"(complete utterance-type) 而言的。Grice 把这种理解称为对完整话语类型的"脱时意义"(timeless meaning)的"具体化"(specification)。此外，(1b) 原话里的 grass 一词可以理解为 lawn-material，或指 marijuana。这叫做对不完整的话语类型的脱时意义的具体化。

（二）鉴于完整话语类型可能有多个脱时意义，当我们处在某一个具体的语境中时，我们就要针对这个语境选择其中的一个脱时意义。Grice 称这个操作为对"应用性脱时意义"(applied timeless meaning) 的具体化。同样，我们还有对不完整的话语类型的应用性脱时意义的具体化。

（三）某一讲话人 U 在说出上面这句话（或言词）时，他的意思可能是："If I am then dead, I shall not know what is going on in the world," 甚至还有 "One advantage of being dead will be that I shall be protected from the horrors of the world."① Grice 称这个具体化意义为"话语类型的某场合意义"(occasion-meaning of an utterance-type)。

（四）在上面的三个具体化过程中我们都用了引号，即用的是直接引语形式。第四种具体化用的是间接引语形式。Grice 用直接引语形式和间接引语形式来区别讲话人对他所讲的话的"当真"(commitment) 的程度。即使讲话人真的有上面（三）里分析的那个场合意义，讲话人也不会真的去死，只不过是暗示而已。Grice 称这样的具体化意义为"讲话人的场合意义"(utterer's occasion meaning)。

Grice 认为，讲话人的场合意义可以用来阐释其他三种意义，上文 4.2 节中讲到的"通过说 x 讲话人 U 表达意思 p"则可用来阐释讲话人的场合意义。在 Utterer's meaning, sentence-meaning, and word-meaning 一文里（本书第 6 篇）Grice 作了这方面的尝试，我们在此从略。

---

① 原话里 help the grass to grow 跟 push up daisies 不同，后者已经是成语，由单个词语的本义"推起雏菊"引申到"死亡"，而前者不是成语，没有死的意思。Grice 用 help the grass to grow 是要说明在这个特定语境里讲话人的语用义不是来自成语的意义。

5. 会话合作原则、会话含义和俗成含义

我们的语言直觉告诉我们，有时人们想表达的意思超出说出来的话的字面或话面意义。这就是 Grice 说的讲话人的场合意义。让我们先看以下 Grice 编的一段对话：

    A：Smith doesn't seem to have a girlfriend these days.

    B：He has been paying a lot of visits to New York lately.

A 对 B 说 Smith 这些日子好象没有女朋友，B 却答道他最近经常去纽约。从 B 的话里我们（包括 A）可以听出 B 暗示"Smith 在纽约可能有个女朋友"这个弦外之音。

那么这个似乎是多出来的弦外之音是怎么来的呢？首先它是一个推理的结果。其次这个推理不是按形式逻辑的规则进行的。这个推理所依据的基本前提就是 Grice 所说的会话中的合作原则。A 假定 B 作应答时 B 跟他是合作的。所谓合作，具体说来，就是：（1）说真话，不说假话；（2）提供适量的信息；（3）提供与谈话目的相关的信息；（4）说话清楚明了。Grice 把这四条分别称为质准则、量准则、相关准则和明了准则。在上面的对话里，由于 A 假定 B 作应答时 B 跟他是合作的，B 的应答在表面上似乎不相关，也就是说 B 似乎是违背了相关准则，而实质上他并不是真的在违背这个准则，他这么做是因为他缺乏足够的证据提供准确的相关信息。

通过表面上违背某项准则而引发的弦外之音 Grice 称之为"会话含义"（conversational implicature）。

会话含义只是含义中的一种。我们看下面这几句话：

    (a) She is poor but honest.

    (b) She got pregnant and married.

(a) 有把贫穷与诚实进行对比的含义。这个含义是由 but 这个词引发的。试比较:She is poor and is honest。But 换成 and 之后对比意义消失了。(b)有个先怀孕后结婚的先后顺序这个含义，这个含义是由 and 这个词引发的。试比较：She got married and became pregnant。先后顺序变了，意义也随之变了。Grice 把这类含义称为俗成含义(conventional implicature)。

至此读者也许会感到 Grice 总是在忙于区别各色各样的意义。他确实是这样。我们在看到这些区别的同时，要看到 Grice 的一个完整的宏伟的蓝图。他志在攻克的是各种交际中的意义问题。我们可以用下图来概括他的整个计划。

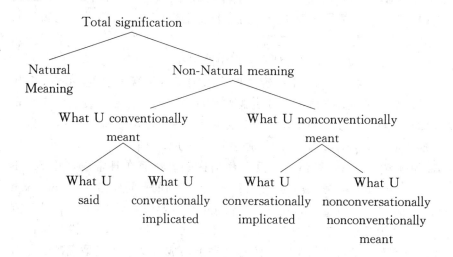

（注：此图主要根据 Neale，1992：524 绘制）

读者只要仔细研读《言词的用法研究》就可以得到 Grice 关于这些意义范畴的要点。

6. Grice 对日常语言哲学的贡献

与日常语言哲学家 Austin、Grice、Strawson 同时代的哲学家，如 Russell、Karl Popper 等对日常语言哲学持否定的态度。在他们看来，对日常语言的意义的阐释是雕虫小技，根本不是哲学家应该做的事。有人问 Popper 对日常语言哲学有何评论时，他说：

I am not interested in philosophizing about the meaning of words, partly because I think that even animals can learn the meaning of words. But human language begins with the *descriptive use of sentences*: or to put it in a less dry manner, it begins with story-telling.

...

Worrying about words and their meanings is one of the oldest pastimes in philosophy.（Magee，Bryan，1971．*Modern British Philosophy*．Herts：Paladin，p.103）

历史证明，正是热衷于日常语言语义问题的哲学家们的垂顾，才使得语义学和语用学研究有了长足的进步。Grice 在这方面的突出贡献是他的会话含义理论，为解决语义、语用和自然语言逻辑问题指出了一条道路。我们知道，罗素要通过逻辑分析清除日常语言的用法对哲学和逻辑带来的消极影响。逻辑运算功能符像"∧"、"∨"、"∩"、"∪"（∀x）、（∃x）、（ιx）等被用来定义日常语言中的"和"、"或"、"如果"、"全部"、"任一个"、"某一个"。不合定义的则表明日常语言有缺陷。Grice 则相反，他想通过对日常语言的分析找到其自身的特点，然后再找到它跟哲学的结合点。例如，上文提到的英文句子"She is poor but honest"以及"She got pregnant and married"用逻辑来分析即为 p∧q。从逻辑上讲，p∧q 跟 q∧p 是完全等值的，没有任何区别。然而在日常语言里 She is poor but honest 与 She is honest but poor 是不同的；同样 She got pregnant and married 与 She got married and pregnant 也是不同的。Grice 的处理方法不是去说日常语言里的 but 和 and 不纯洁、不可靠，而是说日常语言中的 but 和 and 等于是逻辑上的 ∧ 外加上俗成含义，也就是说逻辑分析只能解决日常语言中的一部分语义问题，多出来的部分需要通过新的途径（如语用学）来解决。这样做的优点是显而易见的。一方面可以充分利用逻辑语义学的成果，另一方面也抓住了自然语言的语用特点。这样既确立了语义学和语用学各自的研究范围，也指出了两者之间的联系。

7. 关于 Grice 的研究

导读，顾名思义，引导读者读，它只能起个引见作用，如此而已。要把 Grice 读懂读透则完全靠读者自身了。为了帮助那些有志仔细研读 Grice 意欲获其真谛的读者，我们在此附上研究 Grice 的一些参考书目：

Bach, K., 1994. Conversational implicature. In *Mind and Language* 9：124-162

Davis, Wayne, 1992. Speaker meaning. In *Linguistics and Philosophy*，15：223-253

Gazdar, G. 1979. *Pragmatics*：*Implicature*，*Presupposition and Logical Form*. New York：Academic Press

Grandy, Richard and Richard Warner, eds. 1986. *Philosophical Grounds of Rationality*: *Intentions*, *Categories*, *Ends*. Oxford: Clarendon Press

Gu, Yueguo, 1993. Pragmatics and rhetoric: a collaborative approach to conversation. In H. Parret, ed. *Pretending to Communicate*. Berlin: Walter de Gruyter, pp. 173-193

Leech, G. N., 1983. *The Principles of Pragmatics*. Longman

Levinson, S., 2000. *Presumptive Meaning*. The MIT Press

Neale, Stephen, 1992. Paul Grice and the philosophy of language. In *Linguistics and Philosophy*, 15:509-559

Recanati, Francois, 1989. The pragmatics of what is said. In *Mind and Language*, Vol. 4, No. 4 295-329

Schiffer, S. R., 1972. *Meaning*. Oxford: Clarendon Press

Sperber, D., and D. Wilson, 1986. *Relevance*. Oxford: Blackwell

Walker, Ralph C. S., 1975. Conversational implicatures. In S. Blackburn, ed. *Meaning*, *Reference and Necessity*. Cambridge University Press

还有三本哲学方面的书可读,以加深对哲学背景的了解。

Mage, Bryan, 1971. *Modern British Philosophy*. Herts: Paladin

Strawson, P. F., 1963 [1952]. *Introduction to Logical Theory*. Methuen & Co Ltd

涂纪亮,1987.《分析哲学及其在美国的发展》中国社会科学出版社

Preface

It will be appropriate for me to say something about the layout of the present volume. Of its two main segments, the first (Part I) consists of a revised version of the William James lectures which I delivered at Harvard University in the first part of 1967. These were entitled "Logic and Conversation," and in this volume they form a centerpiece around which other offerings are arranged. There are a number of connections between them and the other papers in this volume, and a case could have been made (and indeed was made by Jonathan Bennett) for dividing the original William James lectures and regrouping them by topic with other essays which appear in this volume. I have resisted this temptation, partly because the scope and content of the lectures has long been fairly familiar to many philosophers, some of whom may well have been awaiting an opportunity for a continuous perusal of the material, and partly because, though my discussion in these lectures of the problems with which they are concerned is for the most part neither my first word nor my last word on these matters, it does present a synoptic view, representative of a particular period (the 1960s), of an important and closely connected group of issues in the philosophy of thought and language.

The main focus of the William James lectures was on the nature and philosophical importance of two closely linked ideas (theme A), which may be loosely characterized as that of assertion and implication and that of meaning; these ideas form the topic of the lectures. But besides the topic of the lectures, another theme (theme B) is persistently discernible in the contents of this volume. This is a methodological or programmatic theme, which is manifested in a recurrent endeavor on my part to approach philosophy through a study of language, in particular of *ordinary* language. With the exception of Essay 19, the papers contained in Part II fall into five groups each of which is related to one or the other, or to both, of these themes.

The first group contains Essays 8–12; all of these papers relate to theme B, namely the role of the consideration of ordinary language in philosophizing; Essays 10–11 address this theme fairly directly, Essays 8–9 address the closely related topic of Common Sense, and Essay 12 moves in the same direction more indirectly in its discussion of the place of certainty in philosophy. Essay 13 deals with the analytic/synthetic distinction, the acceptability or unacceptability of which is crucial to the study of meaning, which is one part of theme A (the problems which form the topic of the William James lectures).

Essays 14 and 18 are discussions of meaning, one of the elements in theme A; Essay 14 is a precursor of and Essay 18 is a later development of the discussion of that topic in Part I. The first part of Essay 15 contains an earlier version of, and Essay 17 discusses an important application of, the notion of conversational implicature, which is an ingredient in theme A. Finally, the second part of Essay 15 and Essay 16 deal with fundamental questions in the philosophy of perception; their place in the volume is ensured by the double character of Essay 15. Essay 19 deals with a distinct topic, namely the province of metaphysics. The organization of the essays in Part II, because of its departures from the chronological order of composition, suffers the disadvantage of not providing an immediate picture of my philosophical development; but this defect is, I think, more than compensated for by the perspicuity of the presentation provided by this mode of organization.

The book concludes with a Retrospective Epilogue, written in 1987, in which, with the benefit of hindsight, I provide a commentary on a number of aspects of the papers collected in this volume. This commentary will most suitably be read after the papers on which comment is made; I hope that it will not be passed over, since in my view it contains new material, carefully but not exhaustively worked out, which is both of more than fleeting interest and also closely relevant to the original papers.

The essays in this volume appear in virtually the same form as that in which they were originally published or delivered as lectures, with the exception of a few places where I have chosen to rewrite them.

Part 1

Logic and Conversation

1

Prolegomena

There is a familiar and, to many, very natural maneuver which is of frequent occurrence in conceptual inquiries, whether of a philosophical or of a nonphilosophical character. It proceeds as follows: one begins with the observation that a certain range of expressions E, in each of which is embedded a subordinate expression α—let us call this range $E(\alpha)$—is such that its members would not be used in application to certain specimen situations, that their use would be odd or inappropriate or even would make no sense; one then suggests that the relevant feature of such situations is that they fail to satisfy some condition C (which may be negative in character); and one concludes that it is a characteristic of the concept expressed by α, a feature of the meaning or use of α, that $E(\alpha)$ is applicable only if C is satisfied. Such a conclusion may be associated with one or more of the following more specific claims: that the schema $E(\alpha)$ logically entails C, that it implies or presupposes C, or that C is an applicability/appropriateness-condition (in a specially explained sense) for α and that α is misused unless C obtains.

Before mentioning suspect examples of this type of maneuver, I would like to make two general remarks. First, if it is any part of one's philosophical concern, as it is of mine, to give an accurate general account of the actual meaning of this or that expression in nontechnical discourse, then one simply cannot afford to abandon this kind of maneuver altogether. So there is an obvious need for a method (which may not, of course, be such as to constitute a clear-cut decision procedure) for distinguishing its legitimate from its illegitimate applications. Second, various persons, including myself, have pointed to philosophical mistakes which allegedly have arisen from an uncritical application of the maneuver; indeed, the precept that one should be careful not to confuse meaning and use is perhaps on the way toward being as handy a philosophical vade-mecum as once was the precept that one should be careful to identify them. Though more sympathetic to the new precept than to the old, I am not concerned to campaign for or against either. My primary aim is rather to determine how any such distinction between meaning and use is to be drawn, and where lie the limits of its philosophical utility. Any serious attempt to achieve this aim will, I think, involve a search for a systematic philosophical theory of language, and I shall be forced to take some tottering steps in that direction. I shall also endeavor to interweave, in the guise of illustrations, some discussions of topics relevant to the question of the relation between the apparatus of formal logic and natural language.

Some of you may regard some of the examples of the maneuver which I am about to mention as being representative of an outdated style of philosophy. I do not think that one should be too quick to write off such a style. In my eyes the most promising line of answer lies in building up a theory which will enable one to distinguish between the case in which an utterance is inappropriate because it is false or fails to be true, or more generally fails to correspond with the world in some favored way, and the case in which it is inappropriate for reasons of a different kind. I see some hope of ordering the linguistic phenomena on these lines. But I do not regard it as certain that such a theory can be worked out, and I think that some of the philosophers in question were skeptical of just this outcome; I think also that sometimes they were unimpressed by the need to attach special importance to such notions as that of truth. So one might, in the end, be faced with the alternatives of either reverting to something like their theoretically unambitious style or giving up hope altogether of systematizing the linguistic phenomena of natural discourse. To me, neither alternative is very attractive.

Now for some suspect examples, many of which are likely to be familiar.

A. (1) An example has achieved some notoriety. Ryle maintained: "In their most ordinary employment 'voluntary' and 'involuntary' are used, with a few minor elasticities, as adjectives applying to actions which ought not to be done. We discuss whether someone's action was voluntary or not only when the action seems to have been his fault." From this he drew the conclusion that "in ordinary use, then, it is absurd to discuss whether satisfactory, correct or admirable performances are voluntary or involuntary"; and he characterized the application of these adjectives to such performances as an "unwitting extension of the ordinary sense of 'voluntary' and 'involuntary,' on the part of the philosophers." [1]

(2) Malcolm accused Moore of having misused the word "know" when he said that he knew that this was one human hand and that this was another human hand; Malcolm claimed, I think, that an essential part of the concept "know" is the implication that an inquiry is under way.[2] Wittgenstein made a similar protest against the philosopher's application of the word "know" to supposedly paradigmatic situations.

(3) Benjamin remarked: "One could generate a sense of the verb 'remember' such that from the demonstration that one has not forgotten p, i.e. that one has produced or performed p, it would follow that one remembers p . . . Thus one could speak of Englishmen conversing or writing in English as 'remembering' words in the English language; of accountants doing accounts as 'remembering how to add,' and one might murmur as one signs one's name 'I've remembered my name again.' The absurd inappropriateness of these examples, if 'remember' is understood in its usual sense, illustrates the opposition between the two senses." [3] (There is an analogy here with "know": compare the oddity of "The hotel clerk asked me what my name was, and fortunately I knew the answer.")

(4) Further examples are to be found in the area of the philosophy of perception. One is connected with the notion of "seeing . . . as." Wittgenstein observed that one does not see a knife and fork as a knife and fork.[4] The idea behind this remark was not developed in the passage in which it occurred, but presumably the thought was that, if a pair of objects plainly *are* a knife and fork, then while it *might* be correct to speak of someone as seeing them as something different (perhaps as a leaf and a flower), it would always (except possibly in very special circumstances) be incorrect (false, out of order, devoid of sense) to speak of seeing an x as an x, or at least of seeing what is plainly an x as an x. "Seeing . . . as," then, is seemingly

1. *Concept of Mind,* III, 69.
2. Malcolm, "Defending Common Sense," *Philosophical Review,* January 1949.
3. "Remembering," *Mind,* July 1956.
4. In *Philosophical Investigations.*

represented as involving at least some element of some kind of imaginative construction or supplementation.

Another example which occurred to me (as to others before me) is that the old idea that perceiving a material object involves having (sensing) a sense-datum (or sense-data) might be made viable by our rejecting the supposition that sense-datum statements report the properties of entities of a special class, whose existence needs to be demonstrated by some form of the Argument from Illusion, or the identification of which requires a special set of instructions to be provided by a philosopher; and by supposing, instead, that "sense-datum statement" is a class-name for statements of some such form as "x looks (feels, etc.) ϕ to A" or "it looks (feels, etc.) to A as if."[5] I hoped by this means to rehabilitate a form of the view that the notion of perceiving an object is to be analyzed in causal terms. But I had to try to meet an objection, which I found to be frequently raised by those sympathetic to Wittgenstein, to the effect that for many cases of perceiving the required sense-datum statements are not available; for when, for example, I see a plainly red object in ordinary daylight, to say "it looks red to me," far from being, as my theory required, the expression of a truth, would rather be an incorrect use of words. According to such an objection, a feature of the meaning of "x looks ϕ to A" is that such a form of words is correctly used only if *either* it is false that x is ϕ, *or* there is some doubt (or it has been thought or it might be thought that there is some doubt) whether x is ϕ.

(5) Another crop of examples is related in one way or another to action.

(a) *Trying.* Is it always correct, or only sometimes correct, to speak of a man who has done something as having *eo ipso* tried to do it? Wittgenstein and others adopt the second view. Their suggestion is that if, say, I now perform some totally unspectacular act, like scratching my head or putting my hand into my trouser pocket to get my handkerchief out, it would be inappropriate and incorrect to say that I tried to scratch my head or tried to put my hand into my pocket. It would be similarly inappropriate to speak of me as *not* having tried to do each of these things. From these considerations there emerges the idea that for "A tried to do x" to be correctly used, it is required either that A should not have done x (should have been

5. Grice, "Causal Theory of Perception," *Aristotle Society Supplementary Volume,* 1961.

prevented) or that the doing of x was something which presented A with some problems, was a matter of some difficulty. But a little reflection suggests that this condition is too strong. A doctor may tell a patient, whose leg has been damaged, to try to move his toes tomorrow, and the patient may agree to try; but neither is committed to holding that the patient will fail to move his toes or that it will be difficult for him to do so. Moreover, someone else who has not been connected in any way with, or even was not at the time aware of, the damage to the patient's leg may correctly say, at a later date, "On the third day after the injury the patient tried to move his toes (when the plaster was removed), though whether he succeeded I do not know." So to retain plausibility, the suggested condition must be weakened to allow for the appropriateness of "A tried to do x" when the *speaker,* or even someone connected in some way with the speaker, thinks or might think that A was or might have been prevented from doing x, or might have done x only with difficulty. (I am not, of course, maintaining that the meaning of "try" in fact includes such a condition.)

(b) *Carefully.* It seems a plausible suggestion that part of what is required in order that A may be correctly said to have performed some operation (a calculation, the cooking of a meal) carefully is that A should have been receptive to (on alert for) circumstances in which the venture might go astray (fail to reach the desired outcome), and that he should manifest, in such circumstances, a disposition to take steps to maintain the course towards such an outcome. I have heard it maintained by H. L. A. Hart that such a condition as I have sketched is insufficient; that there is a further requirement, namely that the steps taken by the performer should be *reasonable,* individually and collectively. The support for the addition of the supplementary condition lies in the fact (which I shall not dispute) that if, for example, a man driving down a normal road stops at every house entrance to make sure that no dog is about to issue from it at breakneck speed, we should not naturally describe him as "driving carefully," nor would we naturally ascribe carefulness to a bank clerk who counted up the notes he was about to hand to a customer fifteen times. The question is, of course, whether the natural reluctance to apply the adverb "carefully" in such circumstances is to be explained by the suggested meaning-restriction, or by something else, such as a feeling that, though "carefully" could be correctly applied, its application would fail to do justice to the mildly spectacular facts.

(c) Perhaps the most interesting and puzzling examples in this area are those provided by Austin, particularly as he propounded a general thesis in relation to them. The following quotations are extracts from the paragraph headed "No modification without aberration": "When it is stated that X did A, there is a temptation to suppose that given some, indeed, perhaps *any*, expression modifying the verb we shall be entitled to insert either it or its opposite or negation in our statement: that is, we shall be entitled to ask, typically, 'Did X do A Mly or not Mly?' (e.g., 'Did X murder Y voluntarily or involuntarily?'), and to answer one or the other. Or as a minimum it is supposed that if X did A there must be at least one modifying expression that we could, justifiably and informatively, insert with the verb. In the great majority of cases of the great majority of verbs ('murder' is perhaps not one of the majority) such suppositions are quite unjustified. The natural economy of language dictates that for the *standard* case covered by any normal verb . . . (e.g. 'eat,' 'kick,' or 'croquet') . . . no modifying expression is required or even permissible. Only if we do the action named in some *special* way or circumstances is a modifying expression called for, or even in order . . . It is bedtime, I am alone, I yawn; but I do not yawn involuntarily (or voluntarily!) nor yet deliberately. To yawn in any such peculiar way is just not to just yawn."[6] The suggested general thesis is then, roughly, that for most action-verbs the admissibility of a modifying expression rests on the action described being a nonstandard case of the kind of action which the verb designates or signifies.

B. Examples involve an area of special interest to me, namely that of expressions which are candidates for being natural analogues to logical constants and which may, or may not, "diverge" in meaning from the related constants (considered as elements in a classical logic, standardly interpreted). It has, for example, been suggested that because it would be incorrect or inappropriate to say "He got into bed and took off his trousers" of a man who first took off his trousers and then got into bed, it is part of the meaning, or part of *one* meaning, of "and" to convey temporal succession. The fact that it would be inappropriate to say "My wife is either in Oxford or in London" when I know perfectly well that she is in Oxford has led to the idea that it is part of the meaning of "or" (or of "either . . . or") to convey that the speaker is ignorant of the truth-values of the particular dis-

6. "A Plea for Excuses," *Philosophical Papers*, ed. Urmson and Warnock, p. 137.

juncts. Again, Strawson maintained that, while "if p then q" entails "p → q," the reverse entailment does not hold; and he characterized a primary or standard use of "if . . . then" as follows: "each hypothetical statement made by this use of 'if' is acceptable (true, reasonable) if the antecedent statement, if made or accepted, would in the circumstances be a good ground or reason for accepting the consequent statement; and the making of the hypothetical statement carries the implication either of uncertainty about, or of disbelief in, the fulfillment of both antecedent and consequent."[7]

C. My final group of suspect examples involves a latter-day philosophical taste for representing words, which have formerly, and in some cases naturally, been taken to have, primarily or even exclusively, a descriptive function, as being, rather, pseudo-descriptive devices for the performance of some speech-act, or some member of a range of speech-acts. Noticing that it would, for example, be unnatural to say "It is true that it is raining" when one merely wished to inform someone about the state of the weather or to answer a query on this matter, Strawson once advocated the view (later to be considerably modified) that the function (and therefore presumably the meaning) of the word "true" was to be explained by pointing out that to say "it is true that p" is not just to assert that p but also to endorse, confirm, concede, or agree to its being the case that p.[8] Somewhat analogous theses, though less obviously based on cases of linguistic inappropriateness, have been, at one time or another, advanced with regard to such words as "know" ("To say 'I know' is to give one's word, to give a guarantee") and "good" ("To say that something is 'good' is to recommend it").

So much for the suspect examples of the kind of maneuver which I initially outlined. All or nearly all of them have a particular feature in common, which helps to make them suspect. In nearly every case, the condition C, the presence of which is suggested as being required for the application of a particular word or phrase to be appropriate, is such that most people would, I think, on reflection have a more or less strong inclination to say that to apply the word or phrase in the absence of that condition would be to say something *true* (indeed usually trivially true), however *misleading* it would be to apply the word or phrase thus. This is connected with the point, noted by

---

7. *Introduction to Logical Theory*, III, pt. 2.
8. Strawson, "Truth," *Analysis*, June 1949.

Searle, that in a good many of these examples the suggested condition of applicability is one which would deny a word application to what are naturally regarded as paradigm cases, cases which would be obvious choices if one were explaining the meaning of the word or phrase by illustration.[9] What could be a clearer case of something which looks blue to me than the sky on a clear day? How could it be *more* certain that my wife is either in Oxford or in London than by its being certain that she is in Oxford? Such considerations as these, when they apply, prompt a desire to find some explanation of the relevant linguistic inappropriateness other than that offered in the examples.

It is not clear, however, with respect to most of the examples, just what explanation is being offered. Let us, for convenience, label a philosopher who takes up one or another of the positions mentioned in my list of suspect examples an "A-philosopher"; let us call the condition which he wishes to treat as involved in the meaning of a particular word (e.g., "remember," "voluntary") a "suspect condition"; and let us call the word in question a "crucial word," and a statement, the expression of which incorporates in an appropriate way a crucial word, a "crucial statement."

It seems to me that an A-philosopher might be occupying one of at least three positions:

(1) He might be holding that crucial statements entail the relevant suspect conditions (that, for example, to do something carefully entails that the doer's precautionary steps are reasonable, and that if the steps are unreasonable, then it is false that the deed was carefully executed).

(2) He might be holding that if the suspect condition fails to be true, then a related crucial statement is deprived of a truth-value.

(3) He might be holding that (a) if the suspect condition is false, the related crucial statement may be false or, alternatively, may lack a truth-value; and (b) if the suspect condition is true, then the related crucial statement will be either true or false.

The logical relationship, in this case, between the crucial statement and the suspect condition will be similar to that which, with some plausibility, may be supposed to hold between a pair of statements of

9. "Assertions and Aberrations," *Contemporary British Philosophy,* ed. Williams and Montefiore.

the form "A omitted to do x" and "A might have been expected to do x." Consider the relationship between:

(1) "A omitted to turn on the light."
(2) "A might have been expected to turn on the light."

The following account has some plausibility. If statement (2) is false, then statement (1) will be false if A turned on the light; if he turned on the light, then he certainly did not omit to turn it on, whether he should have turned it on or not. If, however, statement (2) being false, A did not turn on the light, then the truth or falsity of statement (1) is in doubt. Given, however, that statement (2) is true, that A might have been expected to turn on the light, then statement (1) is false or true according as A did, or did not, turn on the light.

A somewhat parallel account might be suggested for the relation between:

(1') "A tried to turn on the light."
(2') "It was, or might have been, a matter of some difficulty for A to turn on the light."

Suppose that statement (2') is false; then perhaps statement (1') is false if A just did not turn on the light; but if A did turn on the light, then perhaps statement (1') lacks a truth-value, or has an indefinite truth-value. But given that statement (2') is true, then statement (1') is true if A turned on the light or took (unsuccessful) steps toward that end, and statement (1') is false if A took no such steps. (I am not, of course, suggesting that such an account would be correct, only that it would have some plausibility.)

It is generally pretty difficult to pin an A-philosopher down to one rather than another of these three positions. One of the few cases in which this seems possible is that of Benjamin. Continuing the passage in which he contrasts the supposedly genuine (and certificatory) sense of "remember" with the invented sense, he says that the opposition between the two senses is not "one which permits the crude exposure of its existence by *denying* that in these examples one remembers one's name or one's language, for such a denial would in each case entail that one had forgotten them. The inappropriateness would lie in bringing up the notion of remembering in its usual sense at all in such connexions." This passage, though perhaps not absolutely con- clusive, strongly suggests that Benjamin thought of the genuine sense of the word "remember" as being such that, if the suspect condition was not fulfilled (if there is no chance that one should have forgotten), then the crucial statement (e.g., "I remember my name") cannot be assigned a truth-value. I think (though I am less sure) that Malcolm took the parallel position with regard to uses of "know" when the related suspect condition is unfulfilled.

But in other cases the situation is much less clear. In Strawson's characterization (in *Introduction to Logical Theory*) of "a primary or standard use of 'if . . . then,'" it is said that a hypothetical statement is acceptable (true, reasonable) if accepting the antecedent would be a good ground for accepting the consequent; but clearly he did not regard this connection between antecedent and consequent as a *sufficient* condition for the truth (acceptability) of the conditional, since he also held that the truth of the related material conditional was required (since the ordinary conditional was said to *entail* the material conditional). And the truth of the material conditional is not a consequence of the antecedent-consequent connection. So presumably he held that the ordinary conditional was false, given the falsity of the related material conditional; but it is difficult to determine whether he thought that such a conditional as "If I am now in Oxford, it is raining in Australia" (which, read materially, would be true, though the required connection between antecedent and consequent is presumably not present) is false, or is inappropriate (out of order, lacking an assignable truth-value).

Again, Searle attributes to Austin a position which is to be identified with a version of either the second or the third position of the A-philosopher, and there is perhaps some external evidence for interpreting Austin thus. But Austin himself is quite indecisive. He says "I sit in my chair, in the usual way—I am not in a daze or influenced by threats or the like: here it will not do to say either that I sat in it intentionally or that I did not sit in it intentionally, nor yet that I sat in it automatically or from habit or what you will." This sentence can perhaps be interpreted as saying, among other things, that in the described situation no truth-value is assignable to either of the statements "I sat in the chair intentionally" and "I did not sit in the chair intentionally." The quoted sentence is attended by a footnote: "Caveat or hedge: of course we can say 'I did *not* sit in it "intentionally"' as a way simply of repudiating the suggestion that I sat in it intentionally." The fact that Austin encloses in quotes the first occurrence of "intentionally" perhaps supports the view that he was thinking that the only *true* interpretation of "I did not sit in it intentionally" is one

which denies truth (without attributing falsity) to the result of applying the *word* "intentionally" to my sitting in the chair. But earlier in
the paper there is a plaintive footnote to the sentence "Only remember, it (ordinary language) is the *first* word" (he has just said that it is
not the last word). The footnote reads: "And forget, for once and for
a while, that other curious question 'Is it true?' May we?" Moreover,
in apparent pursuance of the plea in the footnote, he consistently
avoids the words "true" and "false," using instead such expressions
as "it will not do to say," "we could, justifiably and informatively,
insert with the verb (a modifying expression)," and "no modifying
expression is required or even permissible." I am very much afraid
that he was trying to have his cake and eat it; that he was arguing in
favor of using various inadmissibilities of application, in respect to
adverbs or adverbial phrases such as "voluntarily," "deliberately,"
and "under constraint," and so forth, as a basis for determining the
meaning of these expressions (the boundaries of the concepts which
they express), while at the same time endeavoring to put on one side
the question whether such applications would be inadmissible because they would be false, because they would lack a truth-value, or
for some other reason. It seems to me very doubtful, to say the least,
whether this combination of procedures is itself admissible.

Finally I turn to Searle's treatment of the topic with which we are
concerned. The following seem to be the salient points.

(1) He addresses himself to only a small part of the range of suspect
examples, specifically to the applicability restrictions which were supposed by Wittgenstein and Malcolm to attach to the word "know,"
by Benjamin to the word "remember," and by Austin to adverbial
expressions modifying action verbs. But Searle adds some specimens
which have not notably excited the interest of philosophers and
which in the end he uses as exemplary cases for the type of solution
which he favors for the philosophically interesting examples. One of
these is the sentence "The man at the next table is not lighting his
cigarette with a 20-dollar bill." The utterance of this sentence, Searle
suggests, would not be appropriate in a standard, nonaberrant situation, such as one in which a man in an ordinary restaurant is lighting
his cigarette with a match. But there would be no ground for regarding its utterance as inappropriate if it were uttered "in a Texas oil-
men's club, where it is a rule that cigarettes are lit with 20-dollar bills,
not 10 dollar or 5 dollar bills, much less matches, which are reserved
for igniting cash."

(2) He attributes to the A-philosophers whom he considers the view that the relevant crucial statements are, in certain circumstances, neither true nor false. That is, he represents them as holding either position (2), according to which the falsity of the suspect condition is supposed always to deprive a related crucial statement of a truth-value, or position (3), according to which the falsity of the suspect condition is supposed to prevent the crucial statement from being true, though whether it is false or lacks a truth-value depends on the facts.

(3) He supposes that the suspect condition attaching to the application of a crucial word consists (or perhaps would in the end have to be admitted by the A-philosopher to consist) in the real or supposed existence of a chance that the *negation* of the appropriate crucial sentence might be or might have been true, or might be supposed to be true. The A-philosopher will (or will have to) allow that the condition for, say, the applicability of the expression "of his own free will" to some action is that there should be (or there should be supposed to be) in the circumstances some chance of its being *false* to apply this expression to the action.

(4) He maintains that it is in fact a mistake, on the part of the A-philosophers whom he is considering, to have represented such suspect-conditions as being conditions for the applicability of particular words or phrases. The linguistic phenomena are better explained by the supposition that it is in general a condition of the assertibility of a proposition p (irrespective of the particular words contained in the expression of the proposition p) that there should be a real or supposed chance, in the circumstances, that p should be false. Austin's slogan "No modification without aberration" should be amended to "No assertion without assertibility" or "No remark without remark-ableness." To apply modifying adverbs in standard situations is to apply them when there is no real or supposed possibility of their application being false and so to apply them in circumstances which ensure that what their application expresses is unremarkable.

(5) Destructively (as regards the A-philosophers' theses) Searle relies on the claim that his own solution of the linguistic phenomena is simpler, more general, and perhaps more plausible than that of his opponents', and also on two arguments which he characterizes as being of a more "knock-down" nature. The first argument is that the negations of crucial statements are false (not neither true nor false) when the suspect conditions are unfulfilled—in which case, of course,

the crucial statements themselves will presumably have to be admitted as true. If I go to a philosophical meeting in the standard or normal way (whatever that is), my doing so would (according to Austin) disqualify my action from being properly a subject for the modifying phrase "of my own free will," and it would be (according to Searle) simply false to say "I didn't go to the meeting of my own free will; I was dragged there." Similarly, to say, in absolutely standard circumstances, "I didn't buy my car voluntarily; I was forced to," "I don't remember my own name," "I don't know whether the thing in front of me is a tree," or "He is now lighting his cigarette with a 20-dollar bill" would in every case be to say something false. Searle's second argument of a knock-down nature against the A-philosopher is that it is possible to find sentences of a somewhat more complex form than the simple sentences so far considered, which contain the crucial words, yet which are clearly appropriate independently of any assumption that a suspect condition obtains. Examples are: "The knowledge of and ability to remember such things as one's name and phone number is one of the foundation stones of modern organized society" and "It is more pleasant to do things of one's own free will than to be forced to do them."

I am, of course, in sympathy with the general character of Searle's method of dealing with the linguistic phenomena which have provided A-philosophers with their material. In particular, I, like Searle, would wish to make the explanation of the linguistic inappropriatenesses, which the A-philosophers have seized on, independent of any appeal to special semantic features of particular words. But I am not entirely happy about the details of his position.

In the first place, I do not find either of his knock-down arguments against the A-philosophers convincing. The first argument derives the truth of a crucial statement (when the suspect condition is unfulfilled) from the alleged falsity of that statement's negation, given the same circumstances. Now it is certainly the case that it would be false to say of the man using a match, "He is now lighting his cigarette with a 20-dollar bill," and so it is true that he is *not* lighting his cigarette with a 20-dollar bill. But so far as I know, no philosopher since the demise of the influence of Bradley has been in the least inclined to deny this. The matter is otherwise with the examples which are relevant to recent philosophy. If I go to a meeting in the normal way, it is certainly false that I was dragged there, and my being dragged there would certainly be incompatible with the *truth* of the statement that

I went of my own free will; if I had been dragged there, it would have been *false* that I went of my own free will. But there is no step from this to the conclusion that since I was *not* dragged there, it is *true* (rather than neither true nor false) that I went of my own free will. My own view is that it *is* true that I went of my own free will, but that Searle's argument does not prove this; it amounts to no more than a denial of his opponents' position. Again, once we put the statement "I don't remember my own name" into the third person (to avoid the possibly special features of the first person present tense of this verb), the situation seems to be the same; the A-philosopher has already declared himself reluctant to say either "He did remember his name" or "He did not remember his name."

As regards Searle's second argument, the attempt to find cases in which the crucial word is applicable, even though the suspect condition is unfulfilled, is a promising enterprise and can, I think, be carried through successfully. But I do not think that the generalities which I have quoted from Searle achieve this goal. Consider "It is more pleasant to do things of one's own free will than to be forced to do them." In fairness to the A-philosopher, we should perhaps replace this statement by a cumbrous paraphrase: "Acts to which the expression 'done of one's own free will' applies are more pleasant than acts to which 'done because one is forced to' applies." Once we redraft the statement thus, we can see that its appropriateness, and indeed its truth, carry no consequences at all with respect to the nature of the conditions in which the expression "done of one's own free will" *does* apply to an act (or can be correctly applied to an act). The A-philosopher can continue to take a more restrictive view on this matter than does Searle.

The other example, "The knowledge of and ability to remember such simple things as one's name and phone number," insofar as it relates to the concept of remembering, seems to me to suffer from a different defect. A reference to one's "ability to remember" can be interpreted as a reference to what one *can* remember, and this in turn may be understood as a reference to what is "in one's memory," what one has learned and not forgotten. It is by no means clear that it is remembering in this sense to which the A-philosopher wishes to attach the suspect condition. What Benjamin found inappropriate was a remark such as "I've remembered my name *again*," and the restriction he proposed seems to have been designed for the use of "remember" to refer to a datable occurrence. Insofar as this was so, his thesis seems unaffected by Searle's example.

Before turning to Searle's own thesis, I should like to mention a type of argument which, it seems to me, might be used with some effect against some A-philosophers, though it does not figure in Searle's paper. Imagine the following situation. I visit my bank, and as I am leaving, I see Mrs. Smith go to the counter, write a check, and present it to the clerk. At this point I leave. When I get home, my wife asks me whom I have seen, and I reply, "I saw Mrs. Smith cashing a check at the bank at noon today." Now it would have been, in these circumstances, inappropriate, for obvious reasons, for me to have said "I saw Mrs. Smith *trying* to cash a check at the bank at noon today." However, later in the day I meet Miss Jones, the local know-it-all, who also asks me whom I have seen. I again say "I saw Mrs. Smith cashing a check at the bank at noon today." Miss Jones replies "But she can't have been cashing a check; she knows that she is so overdrawn that the bank will not honor her checks." I do not believe Miss Jones, and we have an argument. In the end I say huffily "Well, I saw her trying to cash a check at the bank at noon today, and I have not the slightest doubt that she succeeded."

From this little narrative two lessons can be derived. (1) To account for the linguistic phenomena, the A-philosopher will have to weaken the suspect condition for the word "try" so that it demands only that the speaker of the sentence "A tried to do x" should think that someone thinks that A might have failed to do x, or found difficulty in x-ing. (2) Once the suspect condition becomes speaker-relative in this way, the A-philosopher runs into another difficulty. For it is very natural to suppose (and counterintuitive to deny) that if I had said to my wife "I saw Mrs. Smith trying to cash a check at noon," which would have been inappropriate and according to the A-philosopher would have lacked a truth-value, I should have made the *same* statement as the one which I later made to Miss Jones, appropriately and so (according to the A-philosopher as well as everyone else) *truly.* So the A-philosopher will either have to deny that the two uses of the sentence would have made the same statement, or will have to maintain that one and the same statement may have a truth-value at one time and lack a truth-value at another time. Neither alternative is attractive. This objection will apply to *any* suspect-condition which is speaker-relative in this kind of way.

As I have said, I am sympathetic with the general direction of Searle's positive thesis, but unhappy about some of its detail.

(1) Searle of course allows that his condition of assertibility (that there should be, or that it should be supposed that there is, some chance that the asserted proposition is false) is not strictly a necessary condition of assertibility; a necessary condition of assertibility would consist in a disjunction, of which his condition would be one disjunct. But he does not specify the other disjuncts and does not seem to regard them as having application to the current topic; so perhaps I am entitled to ignore them. His condition seems to me to fail to explain some cases which I think he would wish to explain. In particular, what seems to be required for the appropriateness of "x looks φ to A" concerns not the possibility that *x* might not *look* φ to A but the possibility that x might not *be* φ. And what makes "A tried to do x" appropriate is the real or supposed possibility, not that A might not have *tried* to do x, but that A might not have *succeeded* in doing x. Moreover, the fact that "look" and "try" are special in this respect is connected with the special character of the inappropriate use of these words. An inappropriate use of "it looks φ to me" is inadequate, says too little, whereas an inappropriate utterance of "He is not lighting his cigarette with a 20-dollar bill" is otiose.

(2) There seems to be considerable uncertainty about the status of a condition of assertibility. Sometimes Searle seems to hold that if the assertibility condition is unfulfilled in the case of a particular utterance, that utterance fails to *be* an assertion; sometimes he seems to hold that, in such a case, it is an assertion which is *out of order;* and sometimes that it is a *pointless* assertion (or remark).

(3) There also seems to be some uncertainty about the precise nature of the speech-act which Searle's condition is supposed to govern. This is said to be the act of assertion. Now, in the ordinary sense of the word, assertion is quite a specific speech-act. To assert is (approximately) to make a claim. If I say that "Heidegger is the greatest living philosopher," I have certainly made an assertion (on the assumption, at least, that I can expect you to take me seriously); but if I draw your attention to the presence of a robin by saying "There is a robin," or tell you that "I have a bad headache," or comment that "The weather is cold for the time of year," it is in the first two cases false and in the third case doubtful whether, properly speaking, I have made an assertion. In this ordinary sense of assertion, fairly clearly there are conditions the fulfillment of which is required if saying something is to

count as making an assertion. But since there are other perfectly reputable speech-acts which may be performed when one utters an indicative sentence, the failure of such an utterance to be an assertion is no ground for regarding the utterance as inappropriate or out of order. If, however, "assert" is to be understood in some more generous and more technical sense, then the question arises how far the introduction of such a sense, with a stipulation that assertion in this sense is to be subject to Searle's condition, would explain the inappropriateness of utterances which fail to satisfy the condition. This difficulty may perhaps be circumvented by taking "asserting" (in its new sense) as another name for remarking, which is a notion in current use; and maybe it would be a desideratum for a speaker that his saying what he says should achieve the status of a remark. But even inappropriate utterances achieve this status; a man who says (inappropriately) "He is not lighting his cigarette with a 20-dollar bill" has made an inappropriate remark.

It seems to me that the only tenable version of Searle's thesis (which is of course a version to which he subscribes) is that an utterance or remark to the effect that p will be inappropriate if it is pointless; that it will be pointless, in many situations, unless there is a real or supposed possibility that it is false that p; and that these facts can be used to account for some of the linguistic phenomena which have stimulated A-philosophers. Indeed, it would be difficult to disagree with this thesis, and much of what I have to say can be looked upon as a development and extension of the idea contained in it. I am nevertheless still somewhat apprehensive lest, in accepting this thesis, I be thought to be committing myself to more than I would want to commit myself to. My impression is that Searle (like Austin) thinks of speech-acts of the illocutionary sort as conventional acts, the nature of which is to be explained by a specification of the constitutive rules which govern each such act, and on which the possibility of performing the act at all depends. An infraction of one of these rules may mean (but need not mean) that an utterance fails to qualify as a specimen of the appropriate type of speech-act; it will at least mean that the utterance is deviant or infelicitous.

Now, while some speech-acts (like promising, swearing, accepting in marriage) may be conventional acts in some such sense as the one just outlined, and while remarking is no doubt a conventional act in some sense (since it involves the use of linguistic devices, which are in some sense conventional), I doubt whether so unpretentious an act as remarking is a conventional act in the above fairly strong sense. This issue cannot be settled in advance of an examination of the character of speech-acts and of the meaning of the phrase "conventional act." But even if remarking is a conventional act in the favored sense, I would regard as far from certain that any rule to the effect that a remark should not be made if to make it would be pointless, or that a remark should not be made unless (ceteris paribus) there is a real or supposed possibility that the proposition it expresses might be false, would be among the rules the exposition of which would be required to explain the nature of remarking. It seems to me more than likely that the nature of a remark could be explained without reference to such matters; the inappropriateness of remarks which failed to satisfy such putative rules might be consequential upon other features which remarks characteristically have, together perhaps with some more general principles governing communication or even rational behavior as such.

Let me gather together the main threads of this somewhat rambling introduction. I have tried to characterize a type of maneuver by which a conclusion is drawn about the meaning of a word or phrase from the inappropriateness of its application in certain sorts of situation, and to suggest that a method is needed for determining when such a maneuver is legitimate and when it is not. I have given various examples of this maneuver which are of some philosophical interest, and which are also suspect (and, in my own view, in most cases illegitimate). I have given an argument which I hope may show that, at least when a suspect condition is speaker-relative in a certain sort of way, it is a mistake to consider this condition to be a condition of applicability for a particular word or phrase, if by "condition of applicability" is meant a condition whose nonfulfillment deprives the application of the crucial word or phrase of a truth-value. I have suggested (in agreement with Searle's general attitude) that inappropriateness connected with the nonfulfillment of such speaker-relative conditions are best explained by reference to certain general principles of discourse or rational behavior. It is my view that most of the A-philosophical theses which I have been considering are best countered by an appeal to such general principles; but it has not been so far my objective to establish this contention. I shall, however, now turn to a direct consideration of such general principles, with a focus on their capacity for generating implications and suggestions rather than on their utility for explaining the specimens of inappropriateness which have interested A-philosophers; it will be my hope that their utility for this last purpose might emerge as a byproduct of their philosophical utility in other directions. From now on my primary interest will lie in the generation of an outline of a philosophical theory of language; so A-philosophers may be expected to reappear on the philosophical stage only intermittently.

2

Logic and Conversation

It is a commonplace of philosophical logic that there are, or appear to be, divergences in meaning between, on the one hand, at least some of what I shall call the formal devices—~, ∧, ∨, ⊃, (∀x), (∃x), (ιx) (when these are given a standard two-valued interpretation)—and, on the other, what are taken to be their analogues or counterparts in natural language—such expressions as *not, and, or, if, all, some* (or *at least one*), *the*. Some logicians may at some time have wanted to claim that there are in fact no such divergences; but such claims, if made at all, have been somewhat rashly made, and those suspected of making them have been subjected to some pretty rough handling.

Those who concede that such divergences exist adhere, in the main, to one or the other of two rival groups, which I shall call the formalist and the informalist groups. An outline of a not uncharacteristic formalist position may be given as follows: Insofar as logicians are concerned with the formulation of very general patterns of valid inference, the formal devices possess a decisive advantage over their natural counterparts. For it will be possible to construct in terms of the formal devices a system of very general formulas, a considerable number of which can be regarded as, or are closely related to, patterns of inferences the expression of which involves some or all of the devices: Such a system may consist of a certain set of simple formulas that must be acceptable if the devices have the meaning that has been assigned to them, and an indefinite number of further formulas, many of which are less obviously acceptable and each of which can be shown to be acceptable if the members of the original set are acceptable. We have, thus, a way of handling dubiously acceptable patterns of inference, and if, as is sometimes possible, we can apply a decision procedure, we have an even better way. Furthermore, from a philosophical point of view, the possession by the natural counterparts of those elements in their meaning, which they do not share with the corresponding formal devices, is to be regarded as an imperfection of natural languages; the elements in question are undesirable excrescences. For the presence of these elements has the result both that the concepts within which they appear cannot be precisely or clearly defined, and that at least some statements involving them cannot, in some circumstances, be assigned a definite truth value; and the indefiniteness of these concepts not only is objectionable in itself but also leaves open the way to metaphysics—we cannot be certain that none of these natural language expressions is metaphysically "loaded." For these reasons, the expressions, as used in natural speech, cannot be regarded as finally acceptable, and may turn out to be, finally, not fully intelligible. The proper course is to conceive and begin to construct an ideal language, incorporating the formal devices, the sentences of which will be clear, determinate in truth value, and certifiably free from metaphysical implications; the foundations of science will now be philosophically secure, since the statements of the scientist will be expressible (though not necessarily actually expressed) within this ideal language. (I do not wish to suggest that all formalists would accept the whole of this outline, but I think that all would accept at least some part of it.)

To this, an informalist might reply in the following vein. The philosophical demand for an ideal language rests on certain assumptions that should not be conceded; these are, that the primary yardstick by which to judge the adequacy of a language is its ability to serve the needs of science, that an expression cannot be guaranteed as fully intelligible unless an explication or analysis of its meaning has been provided, and that every explication or analysis must take the form of a precise definition that is the expression or assertion of a logical equivalence. Language serves many important purposes besides those of scientific inquiry; we can know perfectly well what an expression means (and so a fortiori that it is intelligible) without knowing its analysis, and the provision of an analysis may (and usually does) consist in the specification, as generalized as possible, of the conditions that count for or against the applicability of the expression being analyzed. Moreover, while it is no doubt true that the formal devices are especially amenable to systematic treatment by the logician, it remains the case that there are very many inferences and arguments, expressed in natural language and not in terms of these devices, which are nevertheless recognizably valid. So there must be a place for an unsimplified, and so more or less unsystematic, logic of the natural counterparts of these devices; this logic may be aided and guided by the simplified logic of the formal devices but cannot be supplanted by it. Indeed, not only do the two logics differ, but sometimes they come into conflict; rules that hold for a formal device may not hold for its natural counterpart.

On the general question of the place in philosophy of the reformation of natural language, I shall, in this essay, have nothing to say. I shall confine myself to the dispute in its relation to the alleged divergences. I have, moreover, no intention of entering the fray on behalf of either contestant. I wish, rather, to maintain that the common assumption of the contestants that the divergences do in fact exist is (broadly speaking) a common mistake, and that the mistake arises from inadequate attention to the nature and importance of the conditions governing conversation. I shall, therefore, inquire into the general conditions that, in one way or another, apply to conversation as such, irrespective of its subject matter. I begin with a characterization of the notion of "implicature."

Implicature

Suppose that A and B are talking about a mutual friend, C, who is now working in a bank. A asks B how C is getting on in his job, and B replies, *Oh quite well, I think; he likes his colleagues, and he hasn't been to prison yet.* At this point, A might well inquire what B was implying, what he was suggesting, or even what he meant by saying that C had not yet been to prison. The answer might be any one of such things as that C is the sort of person likely to yield to the temptation provided by his occupation, that C's colleagues are really very unpleasant and treacherous people, and so forth. It might, of course, be quite unnecessary for A to make such an inquiry of B, the answer to it being, in the context, clear in advance. It is clear that whatever B implied, suggested, meant in this example, is distinct from what B said, which was simply that C had not been to prison yet. I wish to introduce, as terms of art, the verb *implicate* and the related nouns *implicature* (cf. *implying*) and *implicatum* (cf. *what is implied*). The point of this maneuver is to avoid having, on each occasion, to choose between this or that member of the family of verbs for which *implicate* is to do general duty. I shall, for the time being at least, have to assume to a considerable extent an intuitive understanding of the meaning of *say* in such contexts, and an ability to recognize particular verbs as members of the family with which *implicate* is associated. I can, however, make one or two remarks that may help to clarify the more problematic of these assumptions, namely, that connected with the meaning of the word *say*.

In the sense in which I am using the word *say*, I intend what someone has said to be closely related to the conventional meaning of the words (the sentence) he has uttered. Suppose someone to have uttered the sentence *He is in the grip of a vice.* Given a knowledge of the English language, but no knowledge of the circumstances of the utterance, one would know something about what the speaker had said, on the assumption that he was speaking standard English, and speaking literally. One would know that he had said, about some particular male person or animal *x,* that at the time of the utterance (whatever that was), either (1) *x* was unable to rid himself of a certain kind of bad character trait or (2) some part of *x*'s person was caught in a certain kind of tool or instrument (approximate account, of course). But for a full identification of what the speaker had said, one would need to know (a) the identity of *x,* (b) the time of utterance, and (c) the meaning, on the particular occasion of utterance, of the phrase *in the grip of a vice* [a decision between (1) and (2)]. This brief indication of my use of *say* leaves it open whether a man who says (today) *Harold Wilson is a great man* and another who says (also today) *The British Prime Minister is a great man* would, if each knew that the two singular terms had the same reference, have said the same thing. But whatever decision is made about this question, the apparatus that I am about to provide will be capable of accounting for any implicatures that might depend on the presence of one rather than another of these singular terms in the sentence uttered. Such implicatures would merely be related to different maxims.

In some cases the conventional meaning of the words used will determine what is implicated, besides helping to determine what is said. If I say (smugly), *He is an Englishman; he is, therefore, brave,* I have certainly committed myself, by virtue of the meaning of my words, to its being the case that his being brave is a consequence of (follows from) his being an Englishman. But while I have said that he is an Englishman, and said that he is brave, I do not want to say that I have *said* (in the favored sense) that it follows from his being an Englishman that he is brave, though I have certainly indicated, and so implicated, that this is so. I do not want to say that my utterance of this sentence would be, *strictly speaking,* false should the consequence in question fail to hold. So *some* implicatures are conventional, unlike the one with which I introduced this discussion of implicature.

I wish to represent a certain subclass of nonconventional implicatures, which I shall call *conversational* implicatures, as being essentially connected with certain general features of discourse; so my next step is to try to say what these features are. The following may provide a first approximation to a general principle. Our talk exchanges do not normally consist of a succession of disconnected remarks, and would not be rational if they did. They are characteristically, to some degree at least, cooperative efforts; and each participant recognizes in them, to some extent, a common purpose or set of purposes, or at least a mutually accepted direction. This purpose or direction may be fixed from the start (e.g., by an initial proposal of a question for discussion), or it may evolve during the exchange; it may be fairly definite, or it may be so indefinite as to leave very considerable latitude to the participants (as in a casual conversation). But at each stage, *some* possible conversational moves would be excluded as conversationally unsuitable. We might then formulate a rough general principle which participants will be expected (ceteris paribus) to observe, namely: Make your conversational contribution such as is required, at the stage at which it occurs, by the accepted purpose or direction of the talk exchange in which you are engaged. One might label this the Cooperative Principle.

On the assumption that some such general principle as this is acceptable, one may perhaps distinguish four categories under one or another of which will fall certain more specific maxims and submaxims, the following of which will, in general, yield results in accordance with the Cooperative Principle. Echoing Kant, I call these categories Quantity, Quality, Relation, and Manner. The category of Quantity relates to the quantity of information to be provided, and under it fall the following maxims:

1. Make your contribution as informative as is required (for the current purposes of the exchange).
2. Do not make your contribution more informative than is required.

(The second maxim is disputable; it might be said that to be overinformative is not a transgression of the Cooperative Principle but merely a waste of time. However, it might be answered that such overinformativeness may be confusing in that it is liable to raise side issues; and there may also be an indirect effect, in that the hearers may be misled as a result of thinking that there is some particular *point* in the provision of the excess of information. However this may be, there is perhaps a different reason for doubt about the admission of this second maxim, namely, that its effect will be secured by a later maxim, which concerns relevance.)

Under the category of Quality falls a supermaxim—"Try to make your contribution one that is true"—and two more specific maxims:

1. Do not say what you believe to be false.
2. Do not say that for which you lack adequate evidence.

Under the category of Relation I place a single maxim, namely, "Be relevant." Though the maxim itself is terse, its formulation conceals a number of problems that exercise me a good deal: questions about what different kinds and focuses of relevance there may be, how these shift in the course of a talk exchange, how to allow for the fact that subjects of conversation are legitimately changed, and so on. I find the treatment of such questions exceedingly difficult, and I hope to revert to them in later work.

Finally, under the category of Manner, which I understand as relating not (like the previous categories) to what is said but, rather, to *how* what is said is to be said, I include the supermaxim—"Be perspicuous"—and various maxims such as:

1. Avoid obscurity of expression.
2. Avoid ambiguity.
3. Be brief (avoid unnecessary prolixity).
4. Be orderly.

And one might need others.

It is obvious that the observance of some of these maxims is a matter of less urgency than is the observance of others; a man who has expressed himself with undue prolixity would, in general, be open to milder comment than would a man who has said something he believes to be false. Indeed, it might be felt that the importance of at least the first maxim of Quality is such that it should not be included in a scheme of the kind I am constructing; other maxims come into operation only on the assumption that this maxim of Quality is satisfied. While this may be correct, so far as the generation of implicatures is concerned it seems to play a role not totally different from the other maxims, and it will be convenient, for the present at least, to treat it as a member of the list of maxims.

There are, of course, all sorts of other maxims (aesthetic, social, or moral in character), such as "Be polite," that are also normally observed by participants in talk exchanges, and these may also generate nonconventional implicatures. The conversational maxims, however, and the conversational implicatures connected with them, are specially connected (I hope) with the particular purposes that talk (and so, talk exchange) is adapted to serve and is primarily employed to serve. I have stated my maxims as if this purpose were a maximally effective exchange of information; this specification is, of course, too narrow, and the scheme needs to be generalized to allow for such general purposes as influencing or directing the actions of others.

As one of my avowed aims is to see talking as a special case or variety of purposive, indeed rational, behavior, it may be worth noting that the specific expectations or presumptions connected with at least some of the foregoing maxims have their analogues in the sphere of transactions that are not talk exchanges. I list briefly one such analogue for each conversational category.

1. *Quantity.* If you are assisting me to mend a car, I expect your contribution to be neither more nor less than is required. If, for example, at a particular stage I need four screws, I expect you to hand me four, rather than two or six.

2. *Quality.* I expect your contributions to be genuine and not spurious. If I need sugar as an ingredient in the cake you are assisting me to make, I do not expect you to hand me salt; if I need a spoon, I do not expect a trick spoon made of rubber.

3. *Relation.* I expect a partner's contribution to be appropriate to the immediate needs at each stage of the transaction. If I am mixing ingredients for a cake, I do not expect to be handed a good book, or even an oven cloth (though this might be an appropriate contribution at a later stage).

4. *Manner.* I expect a partner to make it clear what contribution he is making and to execute his performance with reasonable dispatch.

These analogies are relevant to what I regard as a fundamental question about the Cooperative Principle and its attendant maxims, namely, what the basis is for the assumption which we seem to make, and on which (I hope) it will appear that a great range of implicatures depends, that talkers will in general (ceteris paribus and in the absence of indications to the contrary) proceed in the manner that these principles prescribe. A dull but, no doubt at a certain level, adequate answer is that it is just a well-recognized empirical fact that people do behave in these ways; they learned to do so in childhood and have not lost the habit of doing so; and, indeed, it would involve a good deal of effort to make a radical departure from the habit. It is much easier, for example, to tell the truth than to invent lies.

I am, however, enough of a rationalist to want to find a basis that underlies these facts, undeniable though they may be; I would like to be able to think of the standard type of conversational practice not merely as something that all or most do *in fact* follow but as something that it is *reasonable* for us to follow, that we *should not* abandon. For a time, I was attracted by the idea that observance of the Cooperative Principle and the maxims, in a talk exchange, could be thought of as a quasi-contractual matter, with parallels outside the realm of discourse. If you pass by when I am struggling with my stranded car, I no doubt have some degree of expectation that you will offer help, but once you join me in tinkering under the hood, my expectations become stronger and take more specific forms (in the absence of indications that you are merely an incompetent meddler); and talk exchanges seemed to me to exhibit, characteristically, certain features that jointly distinguish cooperative transactions:

1. The participants have some common immediate aim, like getting a car mended; their ultimate aims may, of course, be independent and even in conflict—each may want to get the car mended in order to drive off, leaving the other stranded. In characteristic talk exchanges, there is a common aim even if, as in an over-the-wall chat, it is a second-order one, namely, that each party should, for the time being, identify himself with the transitory conversational interests of the other.

2. The contributions of the participants should be dovetailed, mutually dependent.

3. There is some sort of understanding (which may be explicit but which is often tacit) that, other things being equal, the transaction should continue in appropriate style unless both parties are agreeable that it should terminate. You do not just shove off or start doing something else.

But while some such quasi-contractual basis as this may apply to some cases, there are too many types of exchange, like quarreling and letter writing, that it fails to fit comfortably. In any case, one feels that the talker who is irrelevant or obscure has primarily let down not his audience but himself. So I would like to be able to show that observance of the Cooperative Principle and maxims is reasonable (rational) along the following lines: that anyone who cares about the goals that are central to conversation/communication (such as giving and receiving information, influencing and being influenced by others) must be expected to have an interest, given suitable circumstances, in participation in talk exchanges that will be profitable only on the assumption that they are conducted in general accordance with the Cooperative Principle and the maxims. Whether any such conclusion can be reached, I am uncertain; in any case, I am fairly sure that I cannot reach it until I am a good deal clearer about the nature of relevance and of the circumstances in which it is required.

It is now time to show the connection between the Cooperative Principle and maxims, on the one hand, and conversational implicature on the other.

A participant in a talk exchange may fail to fulfill a maxim in various ways, which include the following:

1. He may quietly and unostentatiously *violate* a maxim; if so, in some cases he will be liable to mislead.

2. He may *opt out* from the operation both of the maxim and of the Cooperative Principle; he may say, indicate, or allow it to become plain that he is unwilling to cooperate in the way the maxim requires. He may say, for example, *I cannot say more; my lips are sealed.*

3. He may be faced by a *clash:* He may be unable, for example, to fulfill the first maxim of Quantity (Be as informative as is required) without violating the second maxim of Quality (Have adequate evidence for what you say).

4. He may *flout* a maxim; that is, he may blatantly fail to fulfill it. On the assumption that the speaker is able to fulfill the maxim and to do so without violating another maxim (because of a clash), is not opting out, and is not, in view of the blatancy of his performance, trying to mislead, the hearer is faced with a minor problem: How can his saying what he did say be reconciled with the supposition that he is observing the overall Cooperative Principle? This situation is one that characteristically gives rise to a conversational implicature; and when a conversational implicature is generated in this way, I shall say that a maxim is being *exploited.*

I am now in a position to characterize the notion of conversational implicature. A man who, by (in, when) saying (or making as if to say) that p has implicated that q, may be said to have conversationally implicated that q, provided that (1) he is to be presumed to be observing the conversational maxims, or at least the Cooperative Principle;

(2) the supposition that he is aware that, or thinks that, q is required in order to make his saying or making as if to say p (or doing so in *those* terms) consistent with this presumption; and (3) the speaker thinks (and would expect the hearer to think that the speaker thinks) that it is within the competence of the hearer to work out, or grasp intuitively, that the supposition mentioned in (2) is required. Apply this to my initial example, to B's remark that C has not yet been to prison. In a suitable setting A might reason as follows: "(1) B has apparently violated the maxim 'Be relevant' and so may be regarded as having flouted one of the maxims conjoining perspicuity, yet I have no reason to suppose that he is opting out from the operation of the Cooperative Principle; (2) given the circumstances, I can regard his irrelevance as only apparent if, and only if, I suppose him to think that C is potentially dishonest; (3) B knows that I am capable of working out step (2). So B implicates that C is potentially dishonest."

The presence of a conversational implicature must be capable of being worked out; for even if it can in fact be intuitively grasped, unless the intuition is replaceable by an argument, the implicature (if present at all) will not count as a conversational implicature; it will be a conventional implicature. To work out that a particular conversational implicature is present, the hearer will rely on the following data: (1) the conventional meaning of the words used, together with the identity of any references that may be involved; (2) the Cooperative Principle and its maxims; (3) the context, linguistic or otherwise, of the utterance; (4) other items of background knowledge; and (5) the fact (or supposed fact) that all relevant items falling under the previous headings are available to both participants and both participants know or assume this to be the case. A general pattern for the working out of a conversational implicature might be given as follows: "He has said that p; there is no reason to suppose that he is not observing the maxims, or at least the Cooperative Principle; he could not be doing this unless he thought that q; he knows (and knows that I know that he knows) that I can see that the supposition that he thinks that q is required; he has done nothing to stop me thinking that q; he intends me to think, or is at least willing to allow me to think, that q; and so he has implicated that q."

Examples of Conversational Implicature

I shall now offer a number of examples, which I shall divide into three groups.

GROUP A: *Examples in which no maxim is violated, or at least in which it is not clear that any maxim is violated*

A is standing by an obviously immobilized car and is approached by B; the following exchange takes place:

(1)   A: *I am out of petrol.*
      B: *There is a garage round the corner.*

(Gloss: B would be infringing the maxim "Be relevant" unless he thinks, or thinks it possible, that the garage is open, and has petrol to sell; so he implicates that the garage is, or at least may be open, etc.)

In this example, unlike the case of the remark *He hasn't been to prison yet,* the unstated connection between B's remark and A's remark is so obvious that, even if one interprets the supermaxim of Manner, "Be perspicuous," as applying not only to the expression of what is said but also to the connection of what is said with adjacent remarks, there seems to be no case for regarding that supermaxim as infringed in this example. The next example is perhaps a little less clear in this respect:

(2)   A: *Smith doesn't seem to have a girlfriend these days.*
      B: *He has been paying a lot of visits to New York lately.*

B implicates that Smith has, or may have, a girlfriend in New York. (A gloss is unnecessary in view of that given for the previous example.)

In both examples, the speaker implicates that which he must be assumed to believe in order to preserve the assumption that he is observing the maxim of Relation.

GROUP B: *Examples in which a maxim is violated, but its violation is to be explained by the supposition of a clash with another maxim*

A is planning with B an itinerary for a holiday in France. Both know that A wants to see his friend C, if to do so would not involve too great a prolongation of his journey:

(3)   A: *Where does C live?*
      B: *Somewhere in the South of France.*

(Gloss: There is no reason to suppose that B is opting out; his answer is, as he well knows, less informative than is required to meet A's needs. This infringement of the first maxim of Quantity can be explained only by the supposition that B is aware that to be more informative would be to say something that infringed the second maxim of Quality. "Don't say what you lack adequate evidence for," so B implicates that he does not know in which town C lives.)

GROUP C: *Examples that involve exploitation, that is, a procedure by which a maxim is flouted for the purpose of getting in a conversational implicature by means of something of the nature of a figure of speech*

In these examples, though some maxim is violated at the level of what is said, the hearer is entitled to assume that that maxim, or at least the overall Cooperative Principle, is observed at the level of what is implicated.

(1a) *A flouting of the first maxim of Quantity*

A is writing a testimonial about a pupil who is a candidate for a philosophy job, and his letter reads as follows: "Dear Sir, Mr. X's command of English is excellent, and his attendance at tutorials has been regular. Yours, etc." (Gloss: A cannot be opting out, since if he wished to be uncooperative, why write at all? He cannot be unable, through ignorance, to say more, since the man is his pupil; moreover, he knows that more information than this is wanted. He must, therefore, be wishing to impart information that he is reluctant to write down. This supposition is tenable only if he thinks Mr. X is no good at philosophy. This, then, is what he is implicating.)

Extreme examples of a flouting of the first maxim of Quantity are provided by utterances of patent tautologies like *Women are women* and *War is war*. I would wish to maintain that at the level of what is said, in my favored sense, such remarks are totally noninformative and so, at that level, cannot but infringe the first maxim of Quantity in any conversational context. They are, of course, informative at the level of what is implicated, and the hearer's identification of their informative content at this level is dependent on his ability to explain the speaker's selection of this particular patent tautology.

(1b) *An infringement of the second maxim of Quantity, "Do not give more information than is required," on the assumption that the existence of such a maxim should be admitted*

A wants to know whether *p*, and B volunteers not only the information that *p*, but information to the effect that it is certain that *p*, and that the evidence for its being the case that *p* is so-and-so and such-and-such.

B's volubility may be undesigned, and if it is so regarded by A it may raise in A's mind a doubt as to whether B is as certain as he says he is ("Methinks the lady doth protest too much"). But if it is thought of as designed, it would be an oblique way of conveying that it is to some degree controversial whether or not *p*. It is, however, arguable that such an implicature could be explained by reference to the maxim of Relation without invoking an alleged second maxim of Quantity.

(2a) *Examples in which the first maxim of Quality is flouted*

Irony. X, with whom A has been on close terms until now, has betrayed a secret of A's to a business rival. A and his audience both know this. A says *X is a fine friend.* (Gloss: It is perfectly obvious to A and his audience that what A has said or has made as if to say is something he does not believe, and the audience knows that A knows that this is obvious to the audience. So, unless A's utterance is entirely pointless, A must be trying to get across some other proposition than the one he purports to be putting forward. This must be some obviously related proposition; the most obviously related proposition is the contradictory of the one he purports to be putting forward.)

Metaphor. Examples like *You are the cream in my coffee* characteristically involve categorial falsity, so the contradictory of what the speaker has made as if to say will, strictly speaking, be a truism; so it cannot be *that* that such a speaker is trying to get across. The most likely supposition is that the speaker is attributing to his audience some feature or features in respect of which the audience resembles (more or less fancifully) the mentioned substance.

It is possible to combine metaphor and irony by imposing on the hearer two stages of interpretation. I say *You are the cream in my coffee,* intending the hearer to reach first the metaphor interpretant "You are my pride and joy" and then the irony interpretant "You are my bane."

Meiosis. Of a man known to have broken up all the furniture, one says *He was a little intoxicated.*

Hyperbole. Every nice girl loves a sailor.

(2b) Examples in which the second maxim of Quality, "Do not say that for which you lack adequate evidence," is flouted are perhaps not easy to find, but the following seems to be a specimen. I say of X's wife, *She is probably deceiving him this evening.* In a suitable context, or with a suitable gesture or tone of voice, it may be clear that I have no adequate reason for supposing this to be the case. My partner, to preserve the assumption that the conversational game is still being played, assumes that I am getting at some related proposition for the acceptance of which I do have a reasonable basis. The related proposition might well be that she is given to deceiving her husband, or possibly that she is the sort of person who would not stop short of such conduct.

(3) *Examples in which an implicature is achieved by real, as distinct from apparent, violation of the maxim of Relation* are perhaps rare, but the following seems to be a good candidate. At a genteel tea party, A says *Mrs. X is an old bag.* There is a moment of appalled silence, and then B says *The weather has been quite delightful this summer, hasn't it?* B has blatantly refused to make what he says relevant to A's preceding remark. He thereby implicates that A's remark should not be discussed and, perhaps more specifically, that A has committed a social gaffe.

(4) *Examples in which various maxims falling under the super-maxim "Be perspicuous" are flouted*

Ambiguity. We must remember that we are concerned only with ambiguity that is deliberate, and that the speaker intends or expects to be recognized by his hearer. The problem the hearer has to solve is why a speaker should, when still playing the conversational game, go out of his way to choose an ambiguous utterance. There are two types of cases:

(a) Examples in which there is no difference, or no striking difference, between two interpretations of an utterance with respect to straightforwardness; neither interpretation is notably more sophisticated, less standard, more recondite or more far-fetched than the other. We might consider Blake's lines: "Never seek to tell thy love, Love that never told can be." To avoid the complications introduced by the presence of the imperative mood, I shall consider the related sentence, *I sought to tell my love, love that never told can be.* There may be a double ambiguity here. *My love* may refer to either a state of emotion or an object of emotion, and *love that never told can be* may mean either "Love that cannot be told" or "love that if told cannot continue to exist." Partly because of the sophistication of the poet and partly because of internal evidence (that the ambiguity is kept up), there seems to be no alternative to supposing that the ambiguities are deliberate and that the poet is conveying both what he would be saying if one interpretation were intended rather than the other, and vice versa; though no doubt the poet is not explicitly saying any one of these things but only conveying or suggesting them (cf. "Since she [nature] pricked thee out for women's pleasure, mine be thy love, and thy love's use their treasure").

(b) Examples in which one interpretation is notably less straightforward than another. Take the complex example of the British General who captured the province of Sind and sent back the message *Peccavi*. The ambiguity involved ("I have Sind"/"I have sinned") is phonemic, not morphemic; and the expression actually used is unambiguous, but since it is in a language foreign to speaker and hearer, translation is called for, and the ambiguity resides in the standard translation into native English.

Whether or not the straightforward interpretant ("I have sinned") is being conveyed, it seems that the nonstraightforward interpretant must be. There might be stylistic reasons for conveying by a sentence merely its nonstraightforward interpretant, but it would be pointless, and perhaps also stylistically objectionable, to go to the trouble of finding an expression that nonstraightforwardly conveys that *p*, thus imposing on an audience the effort involved in finding this interpretant, if this interpretant were otiose so far as communication was concerned. Whether the straightforward interpretant is also being conveyed seems to depend on whether such a supposition would conflict with other conversational requirements, for example, would it be relevant, would it be something the speaker could be supposed to accept, and so on. If such requirements are not satisfied, then the straightforward interpretant is not being conveyed. If they are, it is. If the author of *Peccavi* could naturally be supposed to think that he had committed some kind of transgression, for example, had disobeyed his orders in capturing Sind, and if reference to such a transgression would be relevant to the presumed interests of the audience, then he would have been conveying both interpretants: otherwise he would be conveying only the nonstraightforward one.

Obscurity. How do I exploit, for the purposes of communication, a deliberate and overt violation of the requirement that I should avoid obscurity? Obviously, if the Cooperative Principle is to operate, I must intend my partner to understand what I am saying despite the obscurity I import into my utterance. Suppose that A and B are having a conversation in the presence of a third party, for example, a child, then A might be deliberately obscure, though not too obscure, in the hope that B would understand and the third party not. Furthermore, if A expects B to see that A is being deliberately obscure, it seems reasonable to suppose that, in making his conversational contribution in this way, A is implicating that the contents of his communication should not be imparted to the third party.

Failure to be brief or succinct. Compare the remarks:

(a) *Miss X sang "Home Sweet Home."*
(b) *Miss X produced a series of sounds that corresponded closely with the score of "Home Sweet Home."*

Suppose that a reviewer has chosen to utter (b) rather than (a). (Gloss: Why has he selected that rigmarole in place of the concise and nearly synonymous *sang?* Presumably, to indicate some striking difference between Miss X's performance and those to which the word *singing* is usually applied. The most obvious supposition is that Miss X's performance suffered from some hideous defect. The reviewer knows that this supposition is what is likely to spring to mind, so that is what he is implicating.)

Generalized Conversational Implicature

I have so far considered only cases of what I might call "particularized conversational implicature"—that is to say, cases in which an implicature is carried by saying that *p* on a particular occasion in virtue of special features of the context, cases in which there is no room for the idea that an implicature of this sort is normally carried by saying that *p*. But there are cases of generalized conversational implicature. Sometimes one can say that the use of a certain form of words in an utterance would normally (in the absence of special circumstances) carry such-and-such an implicature or type of implicature. Noncontroversial examples are perhaps hard to find, since it is all too easy to treat a generalized conversational implicature as if it were a conventional implicature. I offer an example that I hope may be fairly noncontroversial.

Anyone who uses a sentence of the form *X is meeting a woman this evening* would normally implicate that the person to be met was someone other than X's wife, mother, sister, or perhaps even close platonic friend. Similarly, if I were to say *X went into a house yesterday and found a tortoise inside the front door,* my hearer would normally be surprised if some time later I revealed that the house was X's own. I could produce similar linguistic phenomena involving the expressions *a garden, a car, a college,* and so on. Sometimes, however, there would normally be no such implicature ("I have been sitting in a car all morning"), and sometimes a reverse implicature ("I broke a finger yesterday"). I am inclined to think that one would not lend a sympathetic ear to a philosopher who suggested that there are three senses of the form of expression *an X:* one in which it means roughly "something that satisfies the conditions defining the word *X*," another in which it means approximately "an X (in the first sense) that is only remotely related in a certain way to some person indicated by the context," and yet another in which it means "an X (in the first sense) that is closely related in a certain way to some person indicated by the context." Would we not much prefer an account on the following lines (which, of course, may be incorrect in detail): When someone, by using the form of expression *an X,* implicates that the X does not belong to or is not otherwise closely connected with some identifiable person, the implicature is present because the speaker has failed to be specific in a way in which he might have been expected to be specific, with the consequence that it is likely to be assumed that he is not in a position to be specific. This is a familiar implicature situation and is classifiable as a failure, for one reason or another, to fulfill the first maxim of Quantity. The only difficult question is why it should, in certain cases, be presumed, independently of information about particular contexts of utterance, that specification of the closeness or remoteness of the connection between a particular person or object and a further person who is mentioned or indicated by the utterance should be likely to be of interest. The answer must lie in the following region: Transactions between a person and other persons or things closely connected with him are liable to be very different as regards their concomitants and results from the same sort of transactions involving only remotely connected persons or things; the concomitants and results, for instance, of my finding a hole in my roof are likely to be very different from the concomitants and results of my finding a hole in someone else's roof. Information, like money, is often given without the giver's knowing to just what use the recipient will want to put it. If someone to whom a transaction is mentioned gives it further consideration, he is likely to find himself wanting the answers to further questions that the speaker may not be able to identify in advance; if the appropriate specification will be likely to enable the hearer to answer a considerable variety of such questions for himself, then there is a presumption that the speaker should include it in his remark; if not, then there is no such presumption.

Finally, we can now show that, conversational implicature being what it is, it must possess certain features:

1. Since, to assume the presence of a conversational implicature, we have to assume that at least the Cooperative Principle is being observed, and since it is possible to opt out of the observation of this principle, it follows that a generalized conversational implicature can be canceled in a particular case. It may be explicitly canceled, by the addition of a clause that states or implies that the speaker has opted out, or it may be contextually canceled, if the form of utterance that usually carries it is used in a context that makes it clear that the speaker is opting out.

2. Insofar as the calculation that a particular conversational implicature is present requires, besides contextual and background information, only a knowledge of what has been said (or of the conventional commitment of the utterance), and insofar as the manner of expression plays no role in the calculation, it will not be possible to find another way of saying the same thing, which simply lacks the implicature in question, except where some special feature of the substituted version is itself relevant to the determination of an implicature (in virtue of one of the maxims of Manner). If we call this feature nondetachability, one may expect a generalized conversational implicature that is carried by a familiar, nonspecial locution to have a high degree of nondetachability.

3. To speak approximately, since the calculation of the presence of a conversational implicature presupposes an initial knowledge of the conventional force of the expression the utterance of which carries the implicature, a conversational implicatum will be a condition that is not included in the original specification of the expression's conventional force. Though it may not be impossible for what starts life, so to speak, as a conversational implicature to become conventionalized, to suppose that this is so in a given case would require special justification. So, initially at least, conversational implicata are not part of the meaning of the expressions to the employment of which they attach.

4. Since the truth of a conversational implicatum is not required by the truth of what is said (what is said may be true—what is implicated may be false), the implicature is not carried by what is said, but only by the saying of what is said, or by "putting it that way."

5. Since, to calculate a conversational implicature is to calculate what has to be supposed in order to preserve the supposition that the

Cooperative Principle is being observed, and since there may be various possible specific explanations, a list of which may be open, the conversational implicatum in such cases will be disjunction of such specific explanations; and if the list of these is open, the implicatum will have just the kind of indeterminacy that many actual implicata do in fact seem to possess.

3

Further Notes on Logic and Conversation

I would like to begin by reformulating, in outline, the position which I took in Essay 2. I was operating, provisionally, with the idea that, for a large class of utterances, the total signification of an utterance may be regarded as divisible in two different ways. First, one may distinguish, within the total signification, between what is said (in a favored sense) and what is implicated; and second, one may distinguish between what is part of the conventional force (or meaning) of the utterance and what is not. This yields three possible elements—what is said, what is conventionally implicated, and what is nonconventionally implicated—though in a given case one or more of these elements may be lacking. For example, nothing may be said, though there is something which a speaker makes as if to say. Furthermore, what is nonconventionally implicated may be (or again may not be) conversationally implicated. I have suggested (1) that the Cooperative Principle and some subordinate maxims are standardly (though not invariably) observed by participants in a talk exchange and (2) that the assumptions required in order to maintain the supposition that they are being observed (or so far as is possible observed) either at the level of what is said—or failing that, at the level of what is implicated—are in systematic correspondence with nonconventional implicata of the conversational type.

Before proceeding further, I should like to make one supplementary remark. When I speak of the assumptions required in order to maintain the supposition that the Cooperative Principle and maxims are being observed on a given occasion, I am thinking of assumptions that are nontrivially required; I do not intend to include, for example, an assumption to the effect that some particular maxim is being observed, or is thought of by the speaker as being observed. This seemingly natural restriction has an interesting consequence with regard to Moore's "paradox." On my account, it will not be true that when I say that *p*, I conversationally implicate that I believe that *p*; for to suppose that I believe that *p* (or rather think of myself as believing that *p*) is just to suppose that I am observing the first maxim of Quality on this occasion. I think that this consequence is intuitively acceptable; it is not a natural use of language to describe one who has said that *p* as having, for example, "implied," "indicated," or "suggested" that he believes that *p*; the natural thing to say is that he has expressed (or at least purported to express) the belief that *p*. He has of course committed himself, in a certain way, to its being the case that he believes that *p*, and while this commitment is not a case of saying that he believes that *p*, it is bound up, in a special way, with saying that *p*. The nature of the connection will, I hope, become apparent when I say something about the function of the indicative mood.

In response to Essay 2, I was given in informal discussion an example which seemed to me, as far as it went, to provide a welcome kind of support for the picture I have been presenting, in that it appeared to exhibit a kind of interaction between the members of my list of maxims which I had not foreseen. Suppose that it is generally known that New York and Boston were blacked out last night, and A asks B whether C saw a particular TV program last night. It will be conversationally unobjectionable for B, who knows that C was in New York, to reply, *No, he was in a blacked-out city.* B could have said that C was in New York, thereby providing a further piece of just possibly useful or interesting information, but in preferring the phrase *a blacked-out city* he was implicating (by the maxim prescribing relevance) a more appropriate piece of information, namely, why C was prevented from seeing the program. He could have provided both pieces of information by saying, e.g. *He was in New York, which was blacked out,* but the gain would have been insufficient to justify the additional conversational effort.

In suggesting, at the end of Essay 2, five features which conversational implicatures must possess, or might be expected to possess, I was not going so far as to suggest that it is possible, in terms of some or all of these features, to devise a decisive test to settle the question whether a conversational implicature is present or not—a test, that is to say, to decide whether a given proposition p, which is normally part of the total signification of the utterance of a certain sentence, is on such occasions a conversational (or more generally a nonconventional) implicatum of that utterance, or is, rather, an element in the conventional meaning of the sentence in question. (I express myself loosely, but, I hope, intelligibly.) Indeed I very much doubt whether the features mentioned can be made to provide any such knock-down test, though I am sure that at least some of them are useful as providing a more or less strong prima facie case in favor of the presence of a conversational implicature. But I would say that any such case would at least have to be supported by a demonstration of the way in which what is putatively implicated could have come to be implicated (by a derivation of it from conversational principles and other data); and even this may not be sufficient to provide a decisive distinction between conversational implicature and a case in which what was originally a conversational implicature has become conventionalized.

Let us look at two features in turn. First, nondetachability. It may be remembered that I said that a conversational implicature might be expected to exhibit a fairly high degree of nondetachability insofar as the implicature was carried because of what is said, and not by virtue of the manner of expression. The implicature is nondetachable insofar as it is not possible to find another way of saying the same thing (or approximately the same thing) which simply lacks the implicature. The implicature which attaches to the word *try* exhibits this feature. One would normally implicate that there was a failure, or some chance of failure, or that someone thinks or thought there to be some chance of failure, if one said *A tried to do x;* this implicature would also be carried if one said *A attempted to do x, A endeavored to do x,* or *A set himself to do x.*

This feature is not a necessary condition of the presence of a conversational implicature, partly because, as stated, it does not appear if the implicature depends on the manner in which what is said has been said, and it is also subject to the limitation that there may be no alternative way of saying what is said, or no way other than one which will introduce peculiarities of manner, such as by being artificial or long-winded.

Neither is it a sufficient condition, since the implicatures of utterances which carry presuppositions (if there are such things) (*He has left off beating his wife*) will not be detachable; and should a question arise whether a proposition implied by an utterance is entailed or conversationally implicated, in either case the implication will be nondetachable. Reliance on this feature is effective primarily for distinguishing between certain conventional implicatures and nonconventional implicatures.

Second, cancelability. You will remember that a putative conversational implicature that *p* is explicitly cancelable if, to the form of words the utterance of which putatively implicates that *p*, it is admissible to add *but not p*, or *I do not mean to imply that p*, and it is contextually cancelable if one can find situations in which the utterance of the form of words would simply not carry the implicature. Now I think that all conversational implicatures are cancelable, but unfortunately one cannot regard the fulfillment of a cancelability test as decisively establishing the presence of a conversational implicature. One way in which the test may fail is connected with the possibility of using a word or form of words in a loose or relaxed way. Suppose that two people are considering the purchase of a tie which both of them know to be medium green; they look at it in different lights, and say such things as *It is a light green now*, or *It has a touch of blue in it in this light*. Strictly (perhaps) it would be correct for them to say *It looks light green now* or *It seems to have a touch of blue in it in this light*, but it would be unnecessary to put in such qualificatory words, since both know (and know that the other knows) that there is no question of a real change of color. A similar linguistic phenomenon attends such words as *see*: If we all know that Macbeth hallucinated, we can quite safely say that Macbeth saw Banquo, even though Banquo was not there to be seen, and we should not conclude from this that an implication of the existence of the object said to be seen is not part of the conventional meaning of the word *see*, nor even (as some have done) that there is one sense of the word *see* which lacks this implication.

Let us consider this point in relation to the word *or*. Suppose that someone were to suggest that the word *or* has a single "strong" sense, which is such that it is part of the meaning of *A or B* to say (or imply) not only (1) that A v B, but also (2) that there is some non-truth-functional reason for accepting that A v B, i.e. that there is some reasonable (though not necessarily conclusive) argument with A v B as conclusion which does not contain one of the disjuncts as a step (does not proceed via *A* or via *B*). Now it would be easy to show that the second of the two suggested conditions is cancelable: I can say to my children at some stage in a treasure hunt, *The prize is either in the garden or in the attic. I know that because I know where I put it, but I'm not going to tell you.* Or I could just say (in the same situation) *The prize is either in the garden or in the attic,* and the situation would be sufficient to apprise the children of the fact that my reason for accepting the disjunction is that I know a particular disjunct to be true. And in neither case would I be implying that there is a non-truth-functional ground, though I am not relying on it; very likely there would not be such a ground. To this objection, the "strong" theorist (about *or*) might try the move "Ah, but when you say *A v B,* without meaning to imply the existence of a non-truth-functional ground, you are using *A v B* loosely, in a relaxed way which the nature of the context of utterance makes permissible." At this point, we might either (1) produce further cancellation cases, which were less amenable to representation as "loose" uses, for example, to the appearance of disjunctions as the antecedents of conditionals (*If the prize is either in the garden or in the attic, Johnny will find it first*), or (2) point out that to characterize a use as "loose" carries certain consequences which are unwelcome in this case—if to say *Macbeth saw Banquo* is to speak loosely, then I speak "under license" from other participants; if someone objects, there is at least some onus on me to speak more strictly. But not even a stickler for correct speech could complain about the utterance (in the described circumstances) of *The prize is either in the garden or in the attic.*

But the strong theorist has another obvious resource. He may say that there are two senses of the word *or,* a strong one and a weak (truth-functional) one, and that all that is shown by the success of the cancelability test is that here the sense employed was the weak one. To counter this suggestion, we might proceed in one or more of the following ways.

1. We might argue that if *or* is to be supposed to possess a strong sense, then it should be possible to suppose it (*or*) to bear this sense in a reasonably wide range of linguistic settings; it ought to be possible, for example, to say *It is not the case that A or B* or *Suppose that A or B,* where what we are denying, or inviting someone to suppose, is that A or B (in the strong sense of *or*). But this, in the examples mentioned, does not seem to be possible; in anything but perhaps a very special case to say *It is not the case that A or B* seems to amount to saying that neither A nor B (that is, cannot be interpreted as based on a denial of the second condition), and to say *Suppose that A or B* seems to amount to inviting someone to suppose merely that

one of the two disjuncts is true. A putative second sense of *or* should not be so restricted in regard to linguistic setting as that, and in particular should not be restricted to "unenclosed" occurrences of *A or B*—for these an alternative account (in terms of implicature) is readily available. The strong theorist might meet a part of this attack by holding that the second condition is not to be thought of as part of what is said (or entailed) by saying *A or B*, and so not as something the denial of which would justify the denial of *A or B;* it should rather be thought of as something which is conventionally implicated. And to deny *A or B* might be to implicate that there was some ground for accepting *A or B*. But he is then open to the reply that, if a model case for a word which carries a conventional implicature is *but,* then the negative form *It is not the case that A or B,* if to be thought of as involving *or* in the strong sense, should be an uncomfortable thing to say, since *It is not the case that A but B* is uncomfortable. In any case the nature of conventional implicature needs to be examined before any free use of it, for explanatory purposes, can be indulged in.

2. We might try to convince the strong theorist that if *or* is to be regarded as possessing a strong sense as well as a weak one, the strong sense should be regarded as derivative from the weak one. The support for this contention would have to be a combination of two points: (a) that the most natural expression of the second condition involves a use of *or* in the "weak" sense; and even if the weak use of *or* is avoided the idea seems to be explicitly involved; it is difficult to suppose that people could use a word so as to include in its meaning that there is evidence of a certain sort for a proposition without having a distinct notion of that for which the evidence is evidence. (b) One who says that A or B, using *or* truth-functionally, could be shown in normal circumstances to implicate (conversationally) that there are non-truth-functional grounds for supposing that A v B. For to say that A or B (interpreted weakly) would be to make a weaker and so less informative statement than to say that A or to say that B, and (on the assumption, which I shall not here try to justify, that it would be of interest to an audience to know that one of the disjuncts is true) would therefore be to make a less informative statement than would be appropriate in the circumstances. So there is an implicature (provided the speaker is not opting out) that he is not in a position to make a stronger statement, and if, in conformity with the second maxim of Quality, the speaker is to be presumed to have evidence for what he says, then the speaker thinks that there are non-truth-

functional grounds for accepting A or B. We might next argue that if the strong sense of *or* is derivative from the weaker sense, then it ought to conform to whatever general principles there may be which govern the generation of derivative senses. This point is particularly strong in connection with a suggestion that *or* possesses a derivative sense; for we are not particularly at home with the application of notions such as "meaning" and "sense" to words so nondescriptive as *or;* the difficulties we encounter here are perhaps similar to, though not so severe as, the difficulties we should encounter if asked to specify the meaning or meanings of a preposition like *to* or *in.* So I suspect that we should need to rely fairly heavily on an application to the case of *or* of whatever general principles there may be which apply to more straightforward cases and which help to determine when a derivative sense should be supposed to exist, and when it should not.

It might be objected that whether one sense of a word is to be regarded as derivative from another sense of that word should be treated as a question about the history of the language to which the word belongs. This may be so in general (though in many cases it is obvious, without historical research, that one sense must be secondary to another), but if I am right in thinking that conversational principles would not allow the word *or* to be used in normal circumstances without at least an implicature of the existence of non-truth-functional grounds, then it is difficult to see that research could contribute any information about temporal priority in this case.

I offer three further reflections about the proliferation of senses.

1. I would like to propose for acceptance a principle which I might call Modified Occam's Razor, *Senses are not to be multiplied beyond necessity.* Like many regulative principles, it would be a near platitude, and all would depend on what was counted as "necessity." Still, like other regulative principles, it may guide. I can think of other possible precepts which would amount to much the same. One might think, for example, of not allowing the supposition that a word has a further (and derivative) sense unless the supposition that there is such a sense does some work, explains why our understanding of a particular range of applications of the word is so easy or so sure, or accounts for the fact that some application of the word outside that range, which would have some prima facie claim to legitimacy, is in fact uncomfortable. Again one might formulate essentially the same idea by recommending that one should not suppose what a speaker would mean when he used a word in a certain range of cases to count

as a special sense of the word, if it should be predictable, independently of any supposition that there is such a sense, that he would use the word (or the sentence containing it) with just that meaning. If one makes the further assumption that it is more generally feasible to strengthen one's meaning by achieving a superimposed implicature, than to make a relaxed use of an expression (and I don't know how this assumption would be justified), then Modified Occam's Razor would bring in its train the principle that one should suppose a word to have a less restrictive rather than a more restrictive meaning, where choice is possible.

What support would there be for Modified Occam's Razor? Perhaps we might look at two types of example of real or putative derivative senses. One type (unlike the case of *or*) would involve "transferred" senses; the other would involve derivative senses which are specificatory of the original senses (the proposed derivative sense of "or" would be a special case of this kind).

a. Consider such adjectives as *loose, unfettered,* and *unbridled* in relation to a possible application to the noun *life.* (I assume that such an application of each word would not be nonderivative or literal; that the ambiguous expression *a loose liver* would involve a nonderivative sense of *loose* if uttered for example by a nurse in a hospital who complained about the number of patients with loose livers, but not if uttered censoriously to describe a particular man.) It seems to me that (in the absence of any further sense for either word) one might expect to be able to mean more or less the same by *a loose life,* and *an unfettered life;* the fact that, as things are, *loose life* is tied to dissipation, whereas *unfettered life* seems quite general in meaning, suggests that perhaps *loose* does, and *unfettered* does not, have a derivative sense in this area. As for *unbridled life* (which one might perhaps have expected, prima facie, to mean much the same as *unfettered life*), the phrase is slightly uncomfortable (because *unbridled* seems to be tied to such words as *passion, temper, lust,* and so on).

b. As for words with specificatory derivative senses, there seems to be some tendency for one of two things to happen: Either the original general sense becomes obsolete (like *car,* meaning "wheeled vehicle"), or the specificatory condition takes over; we should perhaps continue to call gramophone records *discs* even if (say) they came to be made square (provided they remain not too unlike discs, in the original sense of the word), and perhaps the word *cylinder* exemplifies the same feature. But there are words of which neither is true: an obvious example is the word *animal* (meaning (i) "member of animal kingdom," (ii) "beast"). There is here some sort of a parallel, in relation to Modified Occam's Razor and its variants, between *animal* and the candidate word *or*. *Animal* perhaps infringes a weak principle to the effect that a further sense should not be recognized if, *on the assumption that* the word were to have a specificatory further sense, the identity of that sense would be predictable; for it could no doubt be predicted that *if* the word *animal* were to have such a sense, it would be one in which the word did not apply to human beings. But it would seem not to be predictable (history of language apart) that anyone would *in fact* use the word *animal* to mean "beast," whereas given a truth-functional *or* it is predictable (assuming conversational principles) that people would use *A or B* to imply the existence of non-truth-functional grounds. So, at least, so far as I can see (not far, I think), there is as yet no reason not to accept Modified Occam's Razor.

2. We must of course give due (but not undue) weight to intuitions about the existence or nonexistence of putative senses of a word (how could we do without them?). Indeed if the scheme which I have been proposing is even proceeding in the right direction, at least some reliance must be placed on such intuitions. For in order that a nonconventional implicature should be present in a given case, my account requires that a speaker shall be able to utilize the conventional meaning of a sentence. If nonconventional implicature is built on what is said, if what is said is closely related to the conventional force of the words used, and if the presence of the implicature depends on the intentions of the speaker, or at least on his assumptions, with regard to the possibility of the nature of the implicature being worked out, then it would appear that the speaker must (in some sense or other of the word *know*) know what is the conventional force of the words which he is using. This indeed seems to lead to a sort of paradox: If we, as speakers, have the requisite knowledge of the conventional meaning of sentences we employ to implicate, when uttering them, something the implication of which depends on the conventional meaning in question, how can we, as theorists, have difficulty with respect to just those cases in deciding where conventional meaning ends and implicature begins? If it is true, for example, that one who says *that A or B* implicates the existence of non-truth-functional grounds for A or B, how can there be any doubt whether the word "or" has a strong or weak sense? I hope that I can provide the answer to this question, but I am not certain that I can.

3. I have briefly mentioned a further consideration bearing on the

question of admissibility of a putative sense of a word, namely, whether on the supposition that the word has that sense, there would be an adequate range of linguistic environments in which the word could be supposed to bear that sense. Failure in this respect would indicate an implicature or an idiom.

There are, I am certain, other possible principles which ought to be considered with regard to the proliferation of senses. In particular I have said nothing explicitly about the adequacy of substitutability tests. But I propose to leave this particular topic at this point.

I have so far been considering two questions. (1) On the assumption that a word has only one conventional meaning (or only one relevant conventional meaning), how much are we to suppose to be included in that meaning? (2) On the assumption that a word has at least one conventional meaning (or relevant conventional meaning), are we to say that it has one, or more than one, such meaning? In particular, are we to ascribe to it a second sense or meaning, derivative from or dependent on a given first meaning or sense? We should consider also examples of elements in or aspects of utterances which, not being words, are candidates for conventional meaning (or significance). These include stress, irony, and truth.

Stress

Some cases of stress are clearly relevant to the possession of conventional meaning, such as (fixed) stress on particular syllables or a word, as in the contrast between "cóntent" with the stress on the "o" and contént with the stress on "tent"; we should not, of course, here assign meaning to the stress itself. I am concerned not with cases of that sort, but with cases in which we think of a word as being stressed, and variably so, stressed on some occasions but not on others.

We might start by trying to think of stress as a purely natural way of highlighting, or making prominent, a particular word; one might compare putting some object (such as a new hat) in an obvious place in a room so that someone coming into the room will notice or pay attention to it. But there are various suggestible ways of doing this with a word, such as intoning it or saying it in a squeaky voice. Such methods would not just be thought unusual, they would be frowned on. They would also very likely fail to achieve the effect of highlighting just because there is an approved way of doing this. So there is a good case for regarding stress as a conventional device for highlighting. But to say this much is not to assign to stress a conventional significance or meaning: it is only to treat it as a conventional way of fulfilling a certain purpose, which is not yet established as a purpose connected with communication. But stress clearly does in fact on many occasions make a difference to the speaker's meaning; indeed it is one of the elements which help to generate implicatures. Does this fact require us to attribute any conventional meaning to stress?

In accordance with the spirit of Modified Occam's Razor, we might attribute conventional meaning to stress only if it is unavoidable. Thus we might first introduce a slight extension to the maxim enjoining relevance, making it apply not only to what is said but also to features of the means used for saying what is said. This extension will perhaps entitle us to expect that an aspect of an utterance which it is within the power of the speaker to eliminate or vary, even if it is introduced unreflectively, will have a purpose connected with what is currently being communicated; unless, of course, its presence can be explained in some other way.

At least three types of context in which stress occurs seem to invite ordering:

(1) One such context includes replies to W-questions ("who," "what," "why," "when," and "where"):

A: *Who paid the bill?*　B: *Jónes did.*
A: *What did Jones do to the cat?*　B: *He kícked it.*

It also includes exchanges of such forms as:

A: $S(\alpha)$
B: $\bar{S}(\acute{\alpha})$: $S(\acute{\beta})$

For example:

A: *Jones paid the bill.*
B: *Jónes didn't pay the bill; Smíth paid it.*

In such examples, stress is automatic or a matter of habit (maybe difficult to avoid), and we are not inclined to say that anything is meant or implicated. However, the effect is to make perspicuous elements which complete open sentences for which questions (in effect) demand completion, or elements in respect of which what B is prepared to assert (or otherwise say) and what B has asserted differ.

(2) Another context in which stress occurs includes such cases as

incomplete versions of the conversational schema exemplified in the preceding example. Without a preceding statement to the effect that Jones paid the bill, B says *Jónes didn't pay the bill; Smith did.* Here, given that this sentence is to be uttered, the stress may be automatic, but the remark is not prompted by a previous remark (it is volunteered), and we are inclined to say that the implicature is that someone thinks or might think that Jones did pay the bill. The maxim of relation requires that B's remark should be relevant to something or other, and B, by speaking as he would speak in reply to a statement that Jones paid the bill, shows that he has such a statement in mind.

(3) In a third context B just says *Jónes didn't pay the bill.* B speaks as if he were about to continue as in the previous context. B therefore implicates that someone (other than Jones) paid the bill.

In general, $S(\alpha)$ is contrasted with the result of substituting some expression β for α, and commonly the speaker suggests that he would deny the substitute version, but there are other possibilities. For example, *I knéw that* may be contrasted with *I believed that,* and the speaker may implicate not that he would deny *I believed that p,* but that he would not confine himself to such a weaker statement (with the implicit completion *I didn't merely believe it*).

This last point has relevance to the theory of "knowledge." According to a certain "strong" account of knowledge:

A knows that p just in case   (1)   *p*
                                                 (2)   *A thinks that p*
                                                 (3)   *A has conclusive evidence that p*

This presents possible difficulties of a regressive nature:

(1) Does A have to know that the evidence for *p* is true?
(2) Does A have to know that the evidence is conclusive?

But in general the theory seems *too* strong. An examination candidate at an oral knows the date of the battle of Waterloo. He may know this without conclusive evidence; he may even answer after hesitation (showing in the end that he knows the answer). I suggest something more like the following:

A knows that p just in case   (1)   *p*
                                                 (2)   *A thinks that p*

(3) *Some conditions placing restriction on how he came to think p* (cf. causal theory)

If I say *I know that p,* then perhaps sometimes there is a nonconventional implicature of strong or conclusive evidence (not mere thinking that *p,* with *p* true)—cf. *He lóves her.* And this is not the only interpretation of stress; it can also mean, "You don't need to tell me."

Irony

The second example of an element in, or aspect of, some utterances, with regard to which there might be some doubt whether or not it has a conventional meaning, emerges from my (too) brief charaterization of irony in Essay 2. Discussion with Rogers Albritton showed me that something is missing in this account. It seems very dubious whether A's knowledge that B has been cheated by C, that B knows that A knows that this is so, that B's remark *He is a fine friend* is to be presumed to relate to this episode, and that the remark is seemingly false (even obviously false), is enough to ensure, with reasonable certainty, that A will suppose B to mean the negation of what he has made as if to say. A might just be baffled, or might suppose that, despite the apparent falsity of the remark, B was meaning something like *He is, usually, a fine friend: how could he have treated me like that?* It was suggested to me that what should have been mentioned in my account was, first, a familiarity with the practice of using a sentence, which would standardly mean that *p,* in order to convey that not-*p* (a familiarity which might be connected with a natural tendency in us to use sentences in this way), and, second, an ironical tone in which such utterances are made, and which (perhaps) conventionally signifies that they are to be taken in reverse.

This suggestion does not seem to me to remedy the difficulty. Consider the following example. A and B are walking down the street, and they both see a car with a shattered window. B says, *Look, that car has all its windows intact.* A is baffled. B says, *You didn't catch on; I was in an ironical way drawing your attention to the broken window.* The absurdity of this exchange is I think to be explained by the fact that irony is intimately connected with the expression of a feeling, attitude, or evaluation. I cannot say something ironically unless what I say is intended to reflect a hostile or derogatory judgment or a feeling such as indignation or contempt. I can for example say *What a scoundrel you are!* when I am well disposed toward you, but to say that will be playful, not ironical, and will be inappropriate unless there is some shadow of justification for a straightforward application—for example you have done something which some people (though not I) might frown upon. If when you have just performed some conspicuously disinterested action I say, *What an egotist you are, always giving yourself the satisfaction of doing things for other people!* I am expressing something like what might be the reaction of an extreme cynic. Whereas to say *He's a fine friend* is unlikely to involve any hint of anyone's approval.

I am also doubtful whether the suggested vehicle of signification, the ironical tone, exists as a specific tone; I suspect that an ironical tone is always a contemptuous tone, or an amused tone, or some other tone connected with one or more particular feelings or attitudes; what qualifies such a tone as ironical is that it appears, on this and other occasions, when an ironical remark is made. This question could no doubt be settled by experiment. Even if, however, there is no specifically ironical tone, it still might be suggested that a contemptuous or amused tone, when conjoined with a remark which is blatantly false, conventionally indicates that the remark is to be taken in reverse. But the suggestion does not seem to me to have much plausibility. While I may without any inappropriateness prefix the employment of a metaphor with *to speak metaphorically,* there would be something very strange about saying, *to speak ironically, he is a splendid fellow.* To be ironical is, among other things, to pretend (as the etymology suggests), and while one wants the pretense to be recognized as such, to announce it as a pretense would spoil the effect. What is possibly more important, it might well be essential to an element's having conventional significance that it could have been the case that some quite different element should have fulfilled the same semantic purpose; that if a contemptuous tone does conventionally signify in context that a remark is to be taken in reverse, then it might have been, for example, that a querulous tone should have been used (instead) for the same purpose. But the connection of irony with the expression of feeling seems to preclude this; if speaking ironically has to be, or at least appear to be, the expression of a certain feeling or attitude, then a tone suitable to such a feeling or attitude seems to be mandatory, at least for the unsophisticated examples.

Truth

Among the A-philosophical theses which I considered in Essay 1 was the original version of a "speech-act" account of truth, proposed by Strawson many years ago[1] though extensively modified by him since then. He was influenced, I think, by four main considerations: (1) that the word *true* is properly, or at least primarily, to be applied to statements (what is stated), in view of the difficulties which he thought he saw in the thesis that it should be understood as applying to utterances; (2) that given the correctness of the previous supposition, no theory which treats truth as consisting in a relation (or correlation) between statements and facts is satisfactory, since statements and facts cannot be allowed to be distinct items in the real world; (3) that Ramsey's account of truth[2]—namely, that to assert that a proposition is true is to assert that proposition—is correct so far as it goes; and (4) that it does not go far enough, since it omits to take seriously the fact that we should not always be willing to tolerate the substitution of, for example, *It is true that it is raining* for *It is raining*. So he propounded the thesis that to say of a statement that it is true is (1) insofar as it is to assert anything, to assert that statement and (2) not merely to assert it but to endorse, confirm, concede, or reassert it (the list is not, of course, intended to be complete).

Such a theory seems to me to have at least two unattractive features, on the assumption that it was intended to give an account of the meaning (conventional significance) of the word *true*. (1) (A familiar type of objection) it gives no account, or no satisfactory account, of the meaning of the word *true* when it occurs in unasserted subsentences (e.g. *He thinks that it is true that . . .* or *If it is true that . . .*). (2) It is open to an objection which I am inclined to think holds against Ramsey's view (of which the speech-act theory is an offshoot). A theory of truth has (as Tarski noted) to provide not only for occurrences of *true* in sentences in which what is being spoken of as true is specified, but also for occurrences in sentences in which no specification is given (e.g. *The policeman's statement was true*). According both to the speech-act theory, I presume, and to Ramsey's theory, at least part of what the utterer of such a sentence is doing is to assert whatever it was that the policeman stated. But the utterer may not

---

1. P. F. Strawson, "Truth," *Analysis* 9, no. 6 (1949).
2. *Foundations of Mathematics*, pp. 142–143.

know what that statement was; he may think that the policeman's statement was true because policemen always speak the truth, or that that policeman always speaks the truth, or that policeman in those circumstances could not but have spoken the truth. Now assertion presumably involves committing oneself, and while it is possible to commit oneself to a statement which one has not identified (I could commit myself to the contents of the Thirty-Nine Articles of the Church of England, without knowing what they say), I do not think I should be properly regarded as having committed myself to the content of the policeman's statement, merely in virtue of having said that it was true. When to my surprise I learn that the policeman actually said, *Monkeys can talk,* I say (perhaps), *Well, I was wrong,* not *I withdraw that,* or *I withdraw my commitment to that.* I never was committed to it.

My sympathies lie with theories of the correspondence family, which Strawson did (and I think still does) reject, but it is not to my present purpose (nor within my capacities) to develop adequately any such theory. What I wish to do is to show that, on the assumption that a certain sort of theory of this kind is correct, then, with the aid of the apparatus discussed in Essay 2 it is possible to accommodate the linguistic phenomena which led Strawson to formulate the original version of the speech-act theory. Let me assume (and hope) that it is possible to construct a theory which treats truth as (primarily) a property of utterances; to avoid confusion I shall use, to name such a property, not "true" but "factually satisfactory." Let me also assume that it will be a consequence of such a theory that there will be a class K of utterances (utterances of affirmative subject-predicate sentences) such that every member of K (1) *designates*[3] some item and *indicates*[3] some class (these verbs to be explained within the theory), and (2) is factually satisfactory if the item belongs to the class. Let me finally assume that there can be a method of introducing a form of expression *It is true that* . . . and linking it with the notion "factually satisfactory," a consequence of which will be that to say *It is true that Smith is happy* will be equivalent to saying that any utterance of class K which designates Smith and indicates the class of happy people is factually satisfactory (that is, any utterance which assigns Smith to the class of happy people is factually satisfactory).

If some such account of *It is true that* . . . is correct (or indeed any

---

3. These verbs to be explained within the theory.

account which represents saying *It is true that p* as equivalent to saying something about utterances) then it is possible to deal with the linguistic facts noted by Strawson. To say *Smith is happy* is not to make a (concealed) reference to utterances of a certain sort, whereas to say *It is true that Smith is happy* is to do just that, though of course if Smith is happy, it is true that Smith is happy. If I choose the form which does make a concealed reference to utterances, and which is also the more complex form, in preference to the simpler form, it is natural to suppose that I do so because an utterance to the effect that Smith is happy has been made by myself or someone else, or might be so made. Such speech acts as endorsing, agreeing, confirming, and conceding, which Strawson (presumably) supposed to be conventionally signaled by the use of the word *true* are just those which, in saying in response to some remark "That's true," one would be performing (without any special signal). And supposing no one actually to have said that Smith is happy, if I say "It is true that Smith is happy" (e.g. concessively) I shall implicate that someone might say so; and I do not select this form of words as, for example, a response to an inquiry whether Smith is happy when I do not wish this implicature to be present.

4

Indicative Conditionals

I am considering myself to have established, or at least put up a good case for supposing, that if any divergence exists between "if" and "⊃," it must be a divergence in sense (meaning, conventional force). I now aim to show, using the same material, that no such divergence exists. I shall start by considering a particular condition, which I shall call the Indirectness Condition, which has been much favored as being something the assertion or implication of which distinguishes "if p then q" (or some "use" or "uses" of "if p then q") from "p ⊃ q." This condition has been variously formulated: "that p would, in the circumstances, be a good reason for q," "that q is inferable from p," "that there are non-truth-functional grounds for accepting p ⊃ q," are all abbreviated versions of variants of it. As I think there are at most minor differences between these formulations, I shall select the last version, as being perhaps the most perspicuous. The thesis to be examined, then, is that in standard cases to say "if p then q" is to be conventionally committed to (to assert or imply in virtue of the meaning of "if") both the proposition that p ⊃ q and the Indirectness Condition.

Let us first examine this condition for detachability. Can we find a form of expression otherwise identical in meaning with "if p then q" which simply lacks the implication that the Indirectness Condition is fulfilled? The difficulty here is notorious. Consider the statement "If Smith is in London, he is attending the meeting." To say this would certainly be to imply the Indirectness Condition. What then of the following alternatives?

(1) "Either Smith is not in London, or he is attending the meeting."

(2) "It is not the case that Smith is both in London and not attending the meeting."

(3) "Not both of the following propositions are true: (*i*) Smith is in London and (*ii*) Smith is not attending the meeting."

(4) "I deny the conjunction of the statements that Smith is in London and that Smith is not attending the meeting."

The implication seems persistent. Let us try then to paraphrase the deliverance of the appropriate truth-table:

(5) "One of the combinations of truth-possibilities for the statements (*i*) that Smith is in London and (*ii*) that Smith is attending the meeting is realized, other than the one which consists in the first statement's being true and the second false."

After one has sorted this out, one still detects the implication. But if all these attempts to detach the implication (particularly the last) are failures, how does the "strong" theorist suppose that one can learn from the truth-table, that "p ⊃ q" has a meaning which diverges from that of "if p then q"? And is it not already beginning to look as if the Indirectness Condition is something which in general is *conversationally* implicated by saying that if p then q?

This impression may be confirmed by testing the condition for cancelability. The implication is explicitly cancelable. To say "If Smith is in the library, he is working" would normally carry the implication of the Indirectness Condition; but I might say (opting out) "I know just where Smith is and what he is doing, but all I will tell you is that if he is in the library he is working." No one would be surprised if it turned out that my basis for saying this was that I had just looked in the library and found him working. The implication is also contextually cancelable, that is, I can find contexts which, if known to participants in a talk-exchange, would make an explicit cancellation unnecessary. Here are two examples.

(a) You may know the kind of logical puzzle in which you are given the names of a number of persons in a room, their professions, and their current occupations, without being told directly which person belongs to which profession or is engaged in which occupation. You are then given a number of pieces of information, from which you have to assign each profession and each occupation to a named individual. Suppose that I am propounding such a puzzle, not about imaginary people but about real people whom I can see but my hearer cannot. I could perfectly properly say, at some point, "If Jones has black (pieces) then Mrs. Jones has black too." To say this would certainly not be to implicate the fulfillment of the Indirectness Condition; indeed, the total content of this utterance would be just what would be asserted (according to truth-table definition) by saying "Jones has black ⊃ Mrs. Jones has black." Thus one undertaking of the previous action has been fulfilled.

(b) There are now some very artificial bridge conventions. My system contains a bid of five no trumps, which is announced to one's opponents on inquiry as meaning "If I have a red king, I also have a black king." It seems clear to me that this conditional is unobjectionable and intelligible, carries no implicature of the Indirectness Condition, and is in fact truth-functional.

The generalized implicature of the Indirectness Condition has a high degree of nondetachability and is also explicitly cancelable and sometimes contextually cancelable. That it is always explicitly cancelable is indicated by the statement: "If you put that bit of sugar in water, it will dissolve, though so far as I know there can be no way of knowing in advance that this will happen." The cancellation clause in fact has the effect of labeling the initial statement as a pure guess or prophecy. The only oddity about this case is thus the empirical one, namely that someone could hardly fail to know the elementary facts about sugar and about chemistry and so think he had to guess, and that, having failed to know these facts, he could hardly be so fortunate as to make a guess as good as this one. These factors make a strong case for regarding the implication as a conversational implicature. This case must be completed by showing how such a conversational implicature is generated, and to this I shall address myself in a moment. But first I want to mention some cases in which the implicature either is canceled or is simply absent, which raise difficulties for a strong theorist and are also of philosophical importance.

(1) "If the Australians win the first Test, they will win the series, you mark my words."
(2) "Perhaps if he comes, he will be in a good mood."
(3) "See that, if he comes, he gets his money."

To say the last of these things, for example, would neither be to implicate that there are non-truth-functional grounds for rejecting the idea that he will come but not get his money, nor to instruct the hearer (inter alia) that there are. For some sub-modes of the indicative mode (e.g. guesses), and for some modes which are not indicative (e.g. imperatives), the suggestion that there is an implicature of the Indirectness Condition is nonplausible; and the strong theorist seems to be incorporating into the meaning of "if" a feature which, if it attaches by convention anywhere, belongs not there but to the conventional force of certain modal indicators (e.g. "I estimate" or "probably"), which may or may not be explicitly present. By so doing, however, the strong theorist debars himself from giving a unitary account of "if" which is mode-independent—a penalty which seems a heavy one.

A positive account of the presence of a generalized implicature of the Indirectness Condition is not difficult to devise, on the assumption that "if p then q" is identical in sense with "p ⊃ q." To say that p ⊃ q is to say something logically weaker than to deny that p or to assert that q, and is thus less informative; to make a less informative rather than a more informative statement is to offend against the first maxim of Quantity, provided that the more informative statement, if made, would be of interest. There is a general presumption that in the case of "p ⊃ q," a more informative statement would be of interest. No one would be interested in knowing that a particular relation (truth-functional or otherwise) holds between two propositions without being interested in the truth-value of at least one of the propositions concerned, unless his interest were of an academic or theoretical kind—an interest perhaps in the logical powers of the propositions concerned or in the nature or range of application of the relation in question. Either because we know, from a consideration of language as an institution, that the use of language for practical purposes is more fundamental than, and is in some way presupposed by, its use for theoretical purposes, or because it is simply a well-known fact about human nature that practical interests are commoner than theoretical interests, or for both reasons, we are justified in assuming, in the absence of any special contextual information, that an interest is practical rather than theoretical. An infringement of the first maxim of Quantity, given the assumption that the principle of conversational helpfulness is being observed, is most naturally explained by the supposition of a clash with the second maxim of Quality ("Have adequate evidence for what you say"), so it is natural to assume that the speaker regards himself as having evidence only for the less informative statement (that p ⊃ q)—that is, non-truth-functional evidence. So standardly he implicates that there is non-truth-functional evidence when he says that p ⊃ q; and there now seems to be no reason to reject the assumption that to say that p ⊃ q is the same as to say that if p then q, so far as concerns the presence of a generalized implicature of the Indirectness Condition (an implicature which, if conversational in character, need not be present in every special case, as in saying "If he was surprised, he didn't show it," provided that its absence in special cases can be satisfactorily explained).

I think that this account is satisfactory so far as it goes, but it clearly does not go far enough, and further inquiry will, I suggest, bring to light a deeper reason for the existence of the generalized implicature under consideration. Perhaps before we proceed further, we should recognize that the time has come for us to expose, and perhaps thereby to protect ourselves from, what might at some later point prove a source of serious error or confusion. The strong theorist about conditionals is not infrequently a traditionalist who is offended by the invasion of the tranquil Elysium of logic by not always wholly gentlemanly and perhaps even occasionally blue-collared practitioners of mathematics and the sciences. Perhaps for this reason or perhaps for some other reason many strong theorists seem to me to have been a little overanxious to differentiate the concepts of their logic from the concepts espoused by the interlopers. I am inclined to assign the main guilt in this matter to the traditionalists, though considerable provocation may have been provided by the other side. One effect of this situation has been an excessive eagerness to distinguish the "natural" conditionals of the ordinary citizen from the artificial concoctions which are given the name of "conditionals" by mathematical logicians, as if protection would be afforded by the existence of any kind of distinction between the "natural" conditional and the "artificial" Philonian or truth-functional conditional. This unseemly haste overlooks several different possibilities, none of which would be a source of comfort to the traditionalist. Each one of a number of different kinds of statement might properly be classified as a conditional, a classification which might nevertheless allow for semantic differences between one conditional form and another; and one, though only one, variety of conditionals might be a form which is semantically indistinguishable from the Philonian or Megarian conditional. Or again, even though no natural conditional might be identifiable with the Philonian conditional, it might be that every natural conditional possesses a sense which descends in a relatively simple way from that of the Philonian conditional. It seems to me that if either of these possibilities were realized, only a superficial observer could regard the strong theorist as having won his battle.

In fact, there seem to me to be quite a number of different forms of statement each of which has a good right to the title of conditional, and a number of which are quite ordinary or humdrum, such as "if p, q," "if p then q," "unless p, q," and "supposing p, (then) q," together with an indefinite multitude of further forms. The two forms which the strong theorist most signally fails to distinguish are "if p, q" and "if p then q"; and the strong theorist, therefore, also fails to differentiate between two distinct philosophical theses: (1) that the sense of "if p, q" is given by the material conditional, and (2) that the sense of "if p then q" is given by the material conditional. Thesis (1) seems to have a good chance of being correct, whereas thesis (2) seems to be plainly incorrect, since the meaning of "if p, then q" is little different from that of "if p, in that case q," a linguistic form which has a much closer connection with argument than would attach to the linguistic form in which the word "then" does not appear. We should be careful, therefore, not to allow ourselves to be convinced that the meaning of "if p, q" diverges from that of the corresponding material conditional by an argument which relies on a genuine but irrelevant difference between "if p then q" and the material conditional "p ⊃ q."

That the account so far given does not go far enough is shown by the objection that it could be applied not only to "if p then q" but also to "either p or q." The account would, if accepted, explain why someone who advances either a conditional or a disjunctive normally implicates that there are non-truth-functional grounds for saying what he has said. But an important difference between conditionals and disjunctives remains unaccounted for, namely that whereas there seems to be no general difficulty in the idea that a disjunctive statement which has been *advanced* on non-truth-functional grounds can be *confirmed* truth-functionally, by establishing one of the disjuncts, the parallel idea with regard to conditionals is not acceptable. Except perhaps in very special cases, we do not regard the mere discovery that it is not the case that p, or the mere discovery that q, as confirming a statement that if p then q. Such a statement is, of course, often regarded as being confirmable by the discovery that both p and q; but a *material* conditional would have to be confirmable by any of the combinations of truth-possibilities with which it is consistent. So "if p then q" is not normally used as a material conditional.

There are cases in which any combination of truth-possibilities except True-False would be regarded as confirming a statement that if p then q (or at least a statement that if p, q, since the presence or absence of the word "then" may be something not to be ignored). In my bridge example, my encoded claim that if I have a red king, I have a black king too, would be confirmed at a post mortem by establishing that I had one of the following:

(1) No red king and no black king
(2) No red king but a black king
(3) A red king and a black king

The same feature is exhibited by the statement that if Jones has black then Mrs. Jones has black, considered as being made in the "puzzle" context. So this objection does not refute my claim that there is *at least one* sense of "if" in which if p then q is a material conditional. But of course more than this is required.

Suppose you say "Either Wilson or Heath will be the next Prime Minister." I can disagree with you in one of two ways: (1) I can say "That's not so; it won't be either, it will be Thorpe." Here I am contradicting your statement, and I shall call this a case of "contradictory disagreement." (2) I can say "I disagree, it will be either Wilson or Thorpe." I am not now contradicting what you say (I am certainly not *denying* that Wilson will be Prime Minister). It is rather that I wish not to assert what you have asserted, but instead to substitute a different statement which I regard as preferable in the circumstances. I shall call this "substitutive disagreement." For either of us to be happily said to be right, it is (I think) a necessary condition that we should have had an initial list of mutually exclusive and genuine starters. If I had said "It will be either Wilson or Gerald Nabarro," this would be (by exploitation) a way of saying that it will be Wilson. Now if it turns out to be Heath you have won (have been shown to be right, what you said has been confirmed); if it turns out to be Thorpe, I have won. But suppose, drearily, it turns out to be Wilson. Certainly neither of us is right as against the other; and if it was perfectly obvious to one and all that Wilson was a likely candidate, though the same could not be definitely said of the others, then there would, I think, be some reluctance to say that either of us had been shown to be right, that what either of us had said had been confirmed (though of course there would be no inclination at all to say that we were wrong). This situation is one in which it is accepted as common ground that Wilson is a serious possibility, that the only reasonable disjunctive question to which one can address oneself is "Wilson or who?"

One point of some importance seems to me to be already emerging. It looks possible (I do not say that it is so, only that it might turn out to be so) that whether or not it is correct to say of a disjunctive statement that it is confirmed by a particular disjunct might depend on the particular circumstances in which the statement is made. Insofar as the meaning of "right" may well be tied to the meaning of "confirm," we might face the same possibility here; and we cannot rule out the possibility of the same thing applying to the word "true." Presumably we do not think (and I am precluded by my adherence to Modified Occam's Razor from thinking unless forced to) that the expression "either . . . or" changes its sense when the circumstances confer "common ground" status on one of the disjuncts. If we do not think there is a change of sense, and if we retain the assumption which gives the present discussion its point, namely that "either . . . or" is definable by truth-table, then we shall be well advised to consider the possibility of interpreting "T" and "F" in some way other than as "true" and "false" respectively. I do not see that the usual interpretation is sacrosanct, though it obviously should not be arbitrarily abandoned, and if abandoned should be replaced by a closely allied interpretation. But if it were to turn out that the applicability of "true" and "false" is situation-relative, then this would be a very good reason for abandoning the current interpretation, replacing "true" by such an expression as "factually satisfactory" (in conformity with the facts, involving no mistake), and replacing "confirmed" by "validated" (guaranteed as factually satisfactory). This course would leave open the possibility that, for example, "true" and "factually satisfactory" would turn out to signify the same concept.

To revert to the example under discussion, you might explicitly confer upon one disjunct a common-ground status. You might say "I think that either Wilson or Heath will be Prime Minister, but I wish discussion to be restricted to the question 'Wilson or who?'" I can either reject the proposed terms of discussion or fall in with them, then disagreement between us is limited to substitutive disagreement, and I shall be debarred from claiming, in the event of its turning out to be Wilson, that my statement has been confirmed. Or we might have a conventional device to indicate the assignation of common-ground status, such as enclosing (when writing) the appropriate clause in square brackets. Now if truth-functional, "if p then q" is exponible as "either not-p and not-q, or not-p and q, or p and q," and we might apply the conventional device here to the first two clauses: thus "[either -p and -q, or -p and q] or p and q," stipulating that discussion is to be related to the discussion of the third possibility as an alternative to the disjunction of the first two, and ruling out of order, so to speak, the truth-functional confirmation of "if p then q" by any disjunct but the last. We do in fact have a device which seems to work at least somewhat like this, namely "supposing p, then q," and it is notable that it would, for example, be very unnatural, in the formulation of my bridge convention, to substitute "supposing I have a red king, then I have a black king" for the conditional form which I employed.

If concern be felt that this is introducing an ad hoc device, specially designed to cope with problems about conditionals, I could reply that it could be employed in areas quite distinct from those closely connected with conditionals. The bracketing device could be applied to conjunctive statements [p]·q, indicating the fact (not of course merely the possibility) that p is, or is to be regarded as, common ground (cf. the difference between "The innings closed at 3:15, Smith not batting" and "The innings closed at 3:15, and Smith did not bat"). Whether a proposition is indicated as being allotted common-ground status as a fact or as a possibility would depend on whether the un-bracketed form of expression did or did not conventionally commit the speaker to the acceptance of that proposition.

But whether or not we actually have a conventional "subordinating" device, I certainly do not wish to attribute this function to "if" (in some uses) as part of its conventional force, for this would be to confess failure, by invoking a second meaning for "if." Yet to do so seems attractive. If instead of saying "Either Wilson or Heath will be Prime Minister," you were to say "If Wilson does not become Prime Minister, it will be Heath," the shift would seem to impose just such a restriction on discussion as the one assigned to the bracketing device. Can one explain the effect of the shift by indirect methods?

In an attempt to deal with this problem, let us first note a feature which distinguishes "if" ("⊃") from other familiar connectives. (From now on, I assume familiar ordinary language connectives to be truth-functional, at least given my weak interpretation of T and F.)

"If," unlike "and" and "or," is noncommutative: "if p, q" is not equivalent to "if q, p." This makes it possible to distinguish the components on grounds other than typography and other than their order of occurrence—indeed, to make a distinction on logical grounds. One component is F-sufficient; that is, its falsity (or factual unsatisfactoriness) is logically sufficient for the factual satisfactoriness of the molecular utterance of which it is a component. The other component is T-sufficient; that is, its truth (or factual satisfactoriness) is logically sufficient for the factual satisfactoriness of the molecular utterance of which it is a component.

I will now raise three questions:

(1) Why, granted the logical equivalence of "if p, q," "either not-p or q," and "not both p and not-q," should it be the case that there are many utterances employing "if," for which the substitution of one of the logically equivalent forms, while intelligible, would be extremely unnatural? Why, for example, is the transformation of "If he rings, the butler will let him in" into "Either he will not ring or the butler will let him in" one of which, at least for most contexts of utterance, we should be unhappy to avail ourselves?

(2) Why, given that the language contains expressions for negation and conjunction or that it contains expressions for negation and disjunction, should it also contain a unitary expression for the conditional form ("if")? Can we offer a rationale for having the connective "if" in the language, when it is possible, in more than one way, to express without "if" any facts that we can express by using it?

(3) Why, granted that we have the conditional form in the language, should it be thought appropriate to call the F-sufficient component "the antecedent" and the T-sufficient component "the consequent"?

Perhaps the attempt to answer these questions may help to solve our primary problem, namely, why it should be in general natural to "read in" to a conditional a subordinating device (in effect, to treat "if" *as if* it meant "supposing"), on the assumption that we have earlier provided grounds for assuming that there is no such element in the conventional meaning or force of "if."

It is possible, at least to some extent, to order the familiar connectives in respect of degree of primitiveness. There is at least some case for treating "not" and "and" as more primitive than "or" and "if." As regards "not": if our language did not contain a unitary negative device, there would be many things we can now say which we should be then unable to say, unless (1) the language contained some very artificial-seeming connective like one or other of the strokes or (2) we put ourselves to a good deal of trouble to find (more or less case by case) complicated forms of expression involving such expressions as "other than" or "incompatible with." As regards "and": in many cases the idea of conjunction might be regarded as present even without an explicit conjunctive device. To say "It is raining (*pause*). It will rain harder soon," seems to say no more and no less than would be said by saying "It is raining, and it will rain harder soon." In spite of this kind of emptiness in the notion of conjunction, we do, however, need explicit conjunctive devices in order to incorporate the expressions of conjunctive propositions into the expression of more complex molecular propositions. For example, we need to be able to deny a conjunctive utterance without committing ourselves with regard to the truth or falsity of the individual conjuncts, as in:

A: "It will rain tomorrow. It will be fine the day after."
B: "That's not so."
A: "What's not so?"
B: "That it will rain tomorrow *and* be fine the day after."

(B's final remark might rest on the idea (1) that the conjuncts cannot both be true, since it is never fine after only one day's rain, or (2) that one particular conjunct is false, or (3) that both conjuncts are false.) A standard (if not *the* standard) employment of "or" is in the specification of possibilities (one of which is supposed by the speaker to be realized, though he does not know which one), each of which is relevant in the same way to a given topic. "A or B" is characteristically employed to give a partial (or *pis aller*) answer to some "W"-question, to which each disjunct, if assertible, would give a fuller, more specific, more satisfactory answer. An ulterior conversational purpose may be either to provide a step on the way to an elimination of one disjunct (by modus tollendo ponens), leaving the other as assertible (there being no advance idea which is to be eliminated), or to have a limited number of alternatives for planning purposes (in which case the elimination of all disjuncts but one by modus tollendo ponens *may* be unnecessary). Obviously, to put a disjunction to such employment, the speaker must have non-truth-functional grounds for asserting the disjunction.

Support for this view of the natural employment of "or" is given by the following talk-exchange, which is perfectly natural:

A: "He didn't give notice of leaving and didn't pay his bill."
B: . . . . .

B (*after a conversational gap*): "It isn't true that he didn't give notice and didn't pay. He did both" (or did the first though not the second).

But the following would not be comfortable:

B: "He either did give notice or did pay his bill. Indeed, he did both things."

Here the specified conditions (such as addressing a "W"-question) are lacking, and the use of "or" is unnatural.

If the métier or raison d'être of "or" is its employment in answering explicit or background "W"-questions, why should this be so? Why is it suitable for this purpose? I can think of two possible explanations, the second more interesting than the first. The first explanation is linguistic (and perhaps conceptual) economy. On the assumption that "W"-questions usually, though not invariably, demand (as final answer) assertions of affirmative rather than negative propositions (utterance of affirmative rather than negative sentences), the expression of interim answers in terms of "or" is more economical than the expression in terms of "not" and "and." "A or B" is more economical typographically and perhaps in terms of concepts explicitly mentioned (if suitably interpreted) than "it is not the case that both not A and not B." If the disjuncts are negative in form, it is not clear that "not A or not B" is more economical than "it is not the case that both A and B." It does, however, seem to be the case that generally "W"-questions look for an affirmative final answer. We ask "Who killed Cock Robin?" not "Who didn't kill Cock Robin?" and similarly for "when," "where," and "what," though the matter is less clear for "why?" Since in general, though not necessarily invariably, the employment of "or" forms for interim answers to explicit or implicit "W"-questions will be more economical than the employment of the equivalent form involving "not" and "and," there exists a habit or practice of preferring the "or" form for this purpose. This being so (and being generally recognized as so) anyone who uses the "or" form implicates or suggests thereby (other things being equal) that he is addressing himself to some explicit or implicit "W"-question. We thus have an answer to a version of the question (asked of "or" instead of "if") why for certain cases (though not for others) the use of "or" forms rather than the use of logically equivalent forms should be specially natural or appropriate. Furthermore, given that the "or" form would, if it existed in the language, as against other equivalent forms, *in general* effect linguistic and conceptual economy if employed for certain purposes, we have a rationale for its existence in the language alongside the other equivalent forms.

The second possible explanation for the use of "or" to answer "W"-questions is that, at some stage, what I might call a "pointering" principle is involved. Let us develop this idea step by step.

(1) We start with the supposition that a certain segment of ordinary discourse is, at least to all appearances, free from logical connectives and other logical particles; whatever logical form it may possess is discreetly concealed. It might even be that actual languages not only in fact exhibit this feature but also must exhibit it.

(2) It then seems not implausible to suppose that, if rational beings are equipped to assert a certain range of statements, they must also be supposed to be equipped to deny just that range of statements. In that case the negations of the initial range of logically innocent statements may be supposed to lie within the compass of the speakers of the language; and these statements, by virtue of their character as denials, may not wear the same guise of logical innocence.

(3) We may also expect the language which we are sketching to contain words whose function is to express conjunction. This equipment might not be required in order to give speakers the capacity to make conjunctive assertions; this much they might achieve simply by piling up component assertions without giving them the luxury of a conjunctive garb, in the shape of linkage by the presence of such words as "and." Devices for expressing the conjunction are rather required because for reasons already given, speakers must be supposed to be capable of denying whatever it is they can assert. The presence in the language of words which signify conjunction will enable speakers to locate a plurality of conjunctive statements within the scope of a dominant negation-sign; and this in turn will equip them to withhold assent from a complex of subordinate statements without committing themselves to a precise identification of each rejected component.

(4) We may now inquire about the possibility, even the desirability, of augmenting the stock of simple and complex connectives by the addition of one or more further simple logical connectives. Is there a case, for instance, for the introduction of a special particle for the

expression of disjunction? It looks as if one standard reason for introducing such a new element into our vocabulary will not be available. We have already supposed ourselves to be equipped with negative and conjunctive propositional connectives, and the deployment of an exterior negation governing a conjunction of two interior negative clauses will provide us with the means to express precisely that content which the classical propositional calculus would ascribe to its disjunctive particle. If we accept Modified Occam's Razor, we had better go along with the propositional calculus in this matter, unless we can produce a good reason for not doing so.

(5) To support an attempt to find a different kind of reason for the expansion of the corpus of logical connectives by the addition of a unitary disjunctive particle, I shall suggest that it would be appropriate first to formulate, and then to try to justify, what I shall call a "pointering" principle. In the present context I shall confine myself to the formulation of this principle, leaving to another day any attempt to justify it. Suppose that a language contains an indefinite multitude of pairs of expressions, with each pair satisfying the following simple conditions. Each pair contains a "ϕ" member and a "ψ" member; both the ϕ-member and the ψ-member of each such pair tolerates completion by the addition of any one of an indefinite range of embedded sentences (propositional expressions); such completion is not merely legitimate but also mandatory in the generation of what are to be full sentences as distinct from sentence schemata. The completion of the ϕ-member of such a pair by a propositional expression α is to be supposed to possess exactly the same conventional meaning as the completion of the corresponding ψ-member of the pair by the negation of α. The pointering principle may be taken to prescribe that, should a speaker be envisaging the ultimate assertion, either by himself or by someone else, of the propositional expression represented by α rather than its ultimate denial, he should elect to use the ϕ-member of the pair with α as its completion; should he, however, be envisaging an ultimate denial of α rather than its ultimate assertion, he should select the ψ-member of the pair with the negation of α as its completion.

(6) If the foregoing principle could be justified, and if it were to be considered in relation to a language such as English, which contains the means both for issuing denials of conjunctions of negative statements and for what seems to be the exactly equivalent operation of issuing affirmations of disjunctions of affirmative statements, then the

pointering principle would equip speakers of the language with a comprehensive rational policy for handling φ-ψ pairs. Assume for the moment that the needed justification is available.

(7) If it be allowed that the foregoing pointering principle might be the foundation of a rational policy in the handling of φ-ψ pairs within a language in which such pairs already exist (a policy which would be based on the achievement of some prospective advantage), then it might also have to be allowed that in the case of a language in which φ-ψ pairs do not exist or are in limited supply, a justification could be found for the institution or augmentation of the availability of such φ-ψ pairs. So if a disjunctive particle does not already exist, there would be a case for inventing it.

(8) We have so far found reasons of one sort or another for supposing our language to be enriched by the addition of unitary particles (connectives) for the expression of the ideas of negation, of conjunction, and of disjunction. To complete this investigation, we should turn our attention to the possible justifiability of a further unitary particle, the business of which would be the construction of conditionals. I remarked at an earlier point that, of the familiar connectives, "if" seems to be the only one which is noncommutative; the order of the clauses of a conditional is not, from the semantic point of view, a matter of indifference. It would not perhaps be surprising if the justification for the addition to a language of a conditional particle bore some relation to this apparently special feature of "if."

Before embarking upon further speculation in this direction, we should have an adequate picture of the purposes and proprieties which govern the recently added disjunctive particles. I have already suggested that one function which is fulfilled by disjunctive statements is the provision of interim answers to certain "W"-questions. If, for example, it is asked "Who killed Cock Robin?" To reply "the sparrow or the hawk or the fox killed Cock Robin" might be to offer an interim solution to the problem of identifying the killer. The smaller the number of disjuncts which such a statement involves, the closer we may get, in favorable circumstances, to the provision of a final solution to this problem. Such a final solution might be achieved when we reach a form of statement in which no disjunctive particle appears—when, that is, we reach such a statement as "The sparrow killed Cock Robin." For this final stage to be reached, certain conditions have to be fulfilled:

(i) Some kind of guarantee is needed that, whatever the final solution turns out to be, it coincides with one member or another of the initial set of disjuncts.

(ii) As the inquiry proceeds, good grounds have to be found for eliminating disjuncts one by one.

(iii) The last surviving disjunct is, as consistency requires, unelimi-nated.

(iv) It should be obvious that disjunctive statements could not be put to work in the kind of way which I have been sketching unless initially they were accepted on non-truth-functional grounds. To suppose them to have been initially accepted on truth-functional grounds—that is, on the strength of the correctness of one particular disjunct, such as that which identifies the killer of Cock Robin as the sparrow—commits the gross absurdity of supposing that the problem which the initial disjunctive statement is invoked in order to solve has already been solved before the inquiry begins, and so is, after all, no problem.

(9) At least at first glance, it might perhaps appear that there is a further distinct mode of employment for which the newly introduced disjunctive particle might be suitable or even in some way useful. This mode of employment is one which I shall for the moment call "con-tingency planning." Suppose that my aunt has arranged to come to visit me but I do not yet know (if indeed a decision has yet been made in the matter) how, where, and when she will arrive. I might be rea-sonably confident that she will not be delivered by submarine at a neighboring naval base or by parachute to the Berkeley campus of the University of California. But with regard to the possibility and likeli-hood of arrival by commercial aircraft at the San Francisco airport, by passenger vessel at the San Francisco docks, or by train at the Oakland railroad station, I am quite in the dark, so I use an appro-priate disjunctive statement as the foundation for a process of reach-ing a decision about my projected response to each of these contin-gencies.

Despite initial appearances, however, I am inclined to think that further reflection will not confirm the suggestion that contingency planning will provide a distinct region of employment for the disjunc-tive particle. I am influenced in this matter primarily by two consid-erations. First, I have not yet mentioned what is in fact plainly the case, that progress from an initial interim solution to an ultimate final solution of problems involving disjunctives sometimes can and some-times cannot be completed through the unaided use of reason. Admittedly I may never learn in advance the precise character of my aunt's impending arrival; I may just have to wait and see. That creates no disanalogy with the inquiry about the killer of Cock Robin. There, too, I may be able to determine by reason alone just who killed Cock Robin; or alternatively, to reach a final solution, I may have to invoke the assistance of observation and empirical evidence. We must not be led astray by an illusion of disanalogy. Second, the two problems can, should we so desire, be characterized in structurally analogous ways. Just as I may debate which member of a set of individuals possesses the attribute of being the killer of Cock Robin or satisfies the predicate "killed Cock Robin," so I may debate which one of a number of transport facilities possesses or will possess the attribute of being my aunt's local destination, or satisfies (or will satisfy) the predicate "is where my aunt landed." The only immediately relevant consideration as regards the acceptance or rejection of a proposed style of characterization is whether such characterization would or would not bring the item or items characterized within the domain of fruitful general description and explanation. Whether the proposed characterization would furnish, for example, what might be thought of as "a good metaphysical portrait" of the item or items which are being characterized is, in the present context and possibly in any context, beside the point.

In the light of these reflections I am encouraged to reject the idea that contingency planning provides us with a distinct field for the deployment of the disjunctive particle, and I propose provisionally to take it as an adequate general characterization of the fundamental function of the disjunctive particle that it is an element in a procedure which:

(i) Seeks total or partial progress in the solution of "W"-questions.

(ii) Deploys a method which is of its nature eliminative.

(iii) And so involves a pattern of argument in which there are two premises, one essentially disjunctive, the other nondisjunctive (or if disjunctive only accidentally so).

(iv) Requires that the logical quality (affirmative, negative, doubly negative) of the nondisjunctive premise be contradictorily opposed to that of one of the components of the disjunctive premise.

(10) We may at last return to the question whether we can point to some purpose or function the fulfillment of which might call for the institution of a special unitary conditional connective, it being the case that, in the present context, when we speak of conditionals, we

are referring to material conditionals. The noncommutative character of "if," together with the formal structure of *modus ponendo ponens,* one of the forms of argument most intimately connected with the use of conditionals, seem to preclude the possibility that the function we are seeking consists in the operation of an eliminative procedure by which progress might be made toward the solution of "W"-questions, or for that matter toward a solution of some other kind of question. While the introduction of a special unitary conditional connective has some connection with questions, it has no particular connection with "W"-questions, and its connection with questions consists, in the first instance at least, in something other that the provision of a method for answering them.

I begin by taking up an idea suggested by Cook Wilson, who may, it seems to me, have been heavily though confusedly entangled in a not so distant relative of the question which is at the present moment exercising me. He noticed that when we turn our attention not to "W"-questions but to "Yes/No" questions, we find countless examples of pairs of such questions whose members are mutually independent, but we also find an indefinite multitude of such pairs in which the components are not mutually independent—pairs, that is, with respect to which one might say, as he put it, that "the question whether so and so is a case of the question whether such and such." By this characterization he fairly clearly meant that an affirmative answer to the first question would dictate an affirmative answer to the second question, while a negative answer to the second question would dictate a negative answer to the first. This relationship, which I call one of "interrogative subordination," holds, for example, between the components of the ordered pair of questions (1) "Does your aunt live in London?" and (2) "Does your aunt live in England?" In a more extended inquiry than this one it might become incumbent upon us to consider more finely grained applications of this initial idea, such as the possibility and desirability of distinguishing between examples of subordination which are and are not dependent upon particular circumstances.

(11) A preliminary account of the role to be expected as one to be fulfilled by a specially introduced unitary particle for the expression of conditionals might run along the following lines:

(i) Like the previously considered disjunctive particle, the conditional particle would have a function which is connected with questions. But unlike the disjunctive particle, the conditional particle would have no special association with some particular kind of question; the conditional particle would not be tied to any particular kind of question in a way analogous to that in which the disjunctive particle is being envisaged as specially related to "W"-questions. The link between the conditional particle and questions would be a link with questions in general.

(ii) Again unlike the disjunctive particle, the conditional particle would not be specially concerned with the institution or the operation of some recognized procedure for answering or solving questions, not even for answering or solving questions in general. Indeed, it might be better to regard the operation with the conditional particle as directed not toward the removal from the stage of thought—material which is not or, in the present context, is not likely to be of use—but rather toward the building up, on the basis of certain initial information, of a body of knowledge which can be brought to bear, when occasion arises, upon whatever questions call for solution. Operation with the conditional particle might be said to be not eliminative but rather accumulative.

(iii) The positive side of this account of the function of the conditional particle might be expressed by saying that it consists in an indefinitely prolonged process which involves the pursuit of chains of interrogative subordination. Beginning with certain starting points, one adds to these starting points, without discarding any of them, an indefinite multitude of further pieces of information which exhibit the feature of being affirmative answers to questions to which other questions lying earlier in the chain and already affirmatively answered are interrogatively subordinated. Thus, later questions in the chain have in effect already been answered through answering earlier questions which are subordinated to them. This representation of the role of the conditional particle would give it a predominant position in relation to argument and the extension of knowledge, a feature which might be expected to appeal to the strong theorist. The accumulation of knowledge which this account envisages would provide an informal analogue to the more regimented procedures on which professional mathematicians and scientists rely in building their theories. So the account just offered might fairly claim to do justice to the central place of the conditional in rational thought and research.

I shall now set out in a consecutive form a full account of my proposals for handling the conditional particle.

(a) In my view the strong theorist is right in seeing a special link between conditionals and relations of inferrability which may hold between one statement or proposition and another; I shall call inferrability connections of this sort "strong" connections. The existence of this link is attested both by intuition and by the practice of calling the first and second clauses of a conditional, respectively, the antecedent and the consequent.

(b) Though right about the existence of this link, the strong theorist is wrong about its nature. The conventional meaning of a conditional is given by a specification of the truth-conditions assigned by truth-tables to the material conditional. But even though a reference to strong connections may not be required in order to give the meaning of a conditional, there are two other kinds of link between conditionals and strong connections which may be of the utmost importance, and also be sources of nonconventional implicatures.

(c) First, it might be that either generally or at least in special contexts it is impossible for a rational speaker to employ the conditional form unless, at least in his view, not merely the truth-table requirements are satisfied but also some strong connection holds. In such a case a speaker will nonconventionally implicate, when he uses the conditional form in such a context, that a strong connection does hold.

(d) A different and more specialized source of nonconventional implicature might lie in the particular role or function which the conditional form is specially fitted to fulfill in rational discourse. If such a role or function can be assigned to the conditional form, this might justify both the existence of the conditional form in the language and an implicature, on the part of one who uses it, that he is using it to fulfill this role or function. Should the fulfillment of this function require that a strong connection holds between antecedent and consequent, that such a connection holds will also be nonconventionally implicated.

(e) The fact that, among the familiar binary propositional connectives, "if" alone is noncommutative is taken by me as an indication of the existence of such a special role for the conditional form. I take the noncommutative character of the conditional form as an indication that its special role lies in the presentation of cases in which a passage of thought, or inferential passage, is envisaged from antecedent to consequent, and possibly to a further consequent with respect to which the first consequent occupies the position of antecedent. Any such chain of passages of thought or inference may be thought of, in line with Cook Wilson's insight, as involving a chain of interrogatively subordinated questions, in which an affirmative answer to an earlier question determines affirmative answers to later questions, and equally a negative answer to a later question determines negative answers to earlier questions.

(f) The conditional form can fulfill this role only insofar as the truth-value of the conditional itself can be recognized independently of knowledge of the truth-values of the components of the conditional, that is to say, by virtue of strong connections between antecedents and consequents. A speaker, therefore, who nonconventionally implicates that he is using a conditional to fulfill its special function will thereby implicate that a strong connection holds between antecedent and consequent.

(g) The building up of a storehouse of interrogatively subordinated sequences of question-schemata or question-patterns, where each such sequence may be specifically diversified into a multiplicity of interrogatively subordinated sequences of questions, is a vital element in our equipping ourselves to handle the world in which we live.

(h) There will thus be both an important link and an important contrast between the special function of the disjunctive particle and the special function of the conditional particle. Both may be thought of as connected with questions; but unlike the disjunctive particle, the conditional particle is not specially associated with an eliminative procedure, or indeed with any kind of procedure, for the solution of questions. Its special function is not eliminative but accumulative.

Grice's Paradox

Yog and Zog play chess according to normal rules, but with two special conditions:

(1) Yog has white 9 out of 10 times.
(2) there are no draws.

To date there have been 100 games:

(1) Yog when white won 80 out of 90.
(2) Yog when black lost 10 out of 10.

They played one of the 100 games last night.

The Law of Contraposition states that "if A, B" is equivalent to "if not B, not A." So, seemingly, the probabilities are:

(1) ⁸⁄₉ that if Yog had white, Yog won.
(2) ½ that if Yog lost, Yog had black.
(3) ⁹⁄₁₀ that either Yog didn't have white or he won.

What is to be done? Abandon the Law of Contraposition?

Dummett and Kripke suggest that we distinguish between: (1) the notion of the probability of a conditional relative to certain evidence h, a notion which is not altered if, for that conditional, we substitute its standard contrapositive, or (for that matter) its standard disjunctive counterpart; for (if p, q)/h is equivalent to (if not q, not p)/h, and also to (either not p or q)/h; and (2) the notion of conditional probability as it is exemplified in the probability of p, relative to both q and h, a notion which cannot be treated as identical with the probability of the negation of q, relative to the conjunction of the negation of p and h. They further suggest that the puzzle about Yog and Zog should be taken to relate to conditional probabilities and not to the probability of conditionals.

Perhaps we might deal with the "belief" version of the paradox by distinguishing:

(1) The belief that if p, q, which is identical with the belief that if not-q, not-p, and also with the belief that either not-p or q.
(2) The belief that (on the supposition that p) q, which is not identical with the belief that (on the supposition that not-q) not-p.

I do not propose to quarrel with this solution to the paradoxical aspect of my example. My problem is: "Assuming that the proposed distinction is acceptable, and assuming, as I do, that 'if p, q' does not *mean,* for example, 'on the supposition that p, q,' why should it in this example be read or interpreted as if it did? Why should it be naturally assumed that a speaker would here mean 'on the supposition that p, q,' if this is not part of the conventional force of 'if'?"

The problem is solved if we assume that "if p, q" is (as I have suggested) naturally adapted for (looks toward) a possible employment in *modus ponendo ponens.* We then think what background information we would use if given the second premise "Yog had white" (when we would not, of course, consider what happened when Yog had black). Similarly, if we are asked the probability that if Yog did not win, he did not have white, and if we take this question to "look toward" the possession of information that Yog did not win, we consider only what was the case when Yog did not win (as regards his having white or black) and ignore cases in which Yog won. If we are asked the probability that he either did not have white or won, there is no direction (pointering) to *modus ponendo ponens,* so we consider the whole series of games which were either ones in which Yog had black or ones in which Yog won.

Now a serious difficulty has to be faced. If, as the thesis under consideration maintains, the conventional meaning of "if p, q" is the same as that of "p ⊃ q," then the conventional meaning of the negation of "if p, q" might be the same as the conventional meaning of the negation of "p ⊃ q," namely "both p and not-q." But it seems implausible to suppose that this *is* the conventional meaning of "it is not the case that, if p, q." To employ a striking example of Bromberger's: suppose that A says "If God exists, we are free to do whatever we like," and B replies "That's not the case" (which he would be prepared to expand into "It is not the case that if God exists, we are free to do whatever we like"). B could not, it seems, in any circumstances be supposed to have committed himself to the conjunctive thesis that (1) God does exist and (2) we are not free to do whatever we like. So ordinary conditionals cannot, in general, be material. Thus the objection; is there a reply to it?

As a preliminary, one might observe that it is by no means always clear just what a speaker who says (or says in effect) "it is not the case that if p, q" is committing himself to, or intending to convey. There seem to be three kinds of cases:

(1) Cases in which the unnegated conditional has (would have) no implicatures, and in which the total signification of its utterance is representable by the content of the material conditional. For example, suppose partner A is using my special bridge convention ("five no trumps" = "If I have a red king, I have a black king") and has bid five no trumps. If his partner B, during the post-mortem, were to say "What you told me by bidding five no trumps was not correct (not true)," it seems to me that he would have to have meant that A had a red king but no black king; that is, here the denial of "if p, q" has the force of "p and not-q." Such examples cause the thesis no trouble.

(2) Sometimes a denial of a conditional is naturally taken as a way of propounding a counterconditional, the consequent of which is the negation of the consequent of the original conditional. If A says "If he proposes to her, she will refuse him" and B says "That's not the case," B would quite naturally be taken to mean "If he proposes to her, she will not refuse him" (in context meaning, perhaps, "If he proposes, she will accept him").

(3) Sometimes a denial of a conditional has the effect of a refusal to assert the conditional in question, characteristically because the denier does not think that there are adequate non-truth-functional grounds for such an assertion. In such a case, he denies, in effect, what the thesis represents as an implicature of the utterance of the un-negated conditional. For example, to say "It is not the case that if X is given penicillin, he will get better" might be a way of suggesting that the drug might have no effect on X at all.

To cope with cases of kind (2), we might redefine the bracketing device as a device the function of which is to give a certain sort of precedence (closely allied to precedence in respect of scope) to the enclosed expression. At the same time we might point out that such a device might have an application in areas quite unconnected with conditionals. The general pattern for the definition of this device is as follows. Suppose I have a sentence $\beta \smile \gamma$ (β and γ being subexpressions, the linkage sign $\smile$ indicating typographical sequence). Suppose β is an expression of a type for which enclosure has been licensed. Then, provided that no further subexpression precedes $[\beta]$, the sentence $[\beta] \smile \gamma$ will be true in all those and only those circumstances in which $\beta \smile \gamma$ (without enclosure) is true. But suppose an expression α (of a specified type or range of types, such as a negation sign) precedes $[\beta] \smile \gamma$ yielding $\alpha \smile [\beta] \smile \gamma$. Then the result thus achieved is to have the same conventional force as $\beta \alpha \gamma$ (without enclosure).

I may remark at this point that in Essay 17 I present a slightly more elaborate version of the foregoing bracketing device and suggest the possibility of using it to deal with problems about presupposition and Russell's Theory of Descriptions. There are indeed two possible ways in which this might be done. One of these ways will involve the introduction and use of the bracketing device in the philosophical treatment of definite descriptions. The other way would avoid the suggestion that the bracketing device would specify a feature of the conventional meaning of definite descriptions but would give reasons for treating definite descriptions *as if* their conventional meaning is in part represented by means of the bracketing device. In effect, both possibilities are considered in Essay 17.

Two somewhat similar positions might be taken up with respect to the relation between the bracketing device and the conditional. The first position invokes a sense for "if p, q" which diverges from that of the material conditional, and so cannot be adopted by one who supports the thesis that "if" and "⊃" are identical in meaning. According to this position, sometimes "if p, q" is identical in meaning with

"[either not-p or]q," the bracketing device being (as before) understood as giving "precedence" (over at least a prefixed negation sign)
to the bracketed expression. Given that "if p, q" is used in this sense,
"it is not the case that if p, q" means the same as "it is not the case
that [either not-p or]q," which in turn means the same as "either not-
p or not-q" (the "if" here being material). This yields a result which
squares with what I suggested as being a natural interpretation of "It
is not the case that if he proposes to her, she will refuse him," namely,
"If he proposes, she will not refuse him." To utter the bracket-
including disjunctive "[either A or] B" is to utter something the denial
of which means "either A or not B." Both the bracketed disjunctive
and its denial allow (at least by implication) the possibility that A is
true. So one would presumably only use the bracketed form (or some
form equivalent to it) if one wished to indicate both that one was
treating it as an admitted possibility that A is true and that one
wished to address oneself to the question "A or what?" ("Supposing
not-A, what?"). And this is what was previously suggested as being
the conventional force of "[A or] B."

The second position that might be taken with respect to "if p, q"
(required if the identity thesis as regards "if" and "⊃" is to be maintained) consists in holding that, though "if p, q" does not mean
"[either not-p or] q," its utterance is often to be interpreted as implicating just that. The argument for this contention proceeds on the
following lines. Insofar as "if p, q" is geared toward possible employment in *modus ponendo ponens* argument and so toward the possible
assertion of "p," an utterance of "if p, q" will tend to have the effect
of an utterance of "supposing p, q" (though "supposing p, q" and "if
p, q" are not identical in meaning). But "supposing p, q" would be a
fair reading of the bracket-including disjunction "[either not-p or] q."
So, given that "if p, q" is to be understood as implicating "[either
not-p or] q," its denial should be interpreted as having the effect of
"if p, not q."

In cases of type (3), saying "it is not the case that if p, q" is to be
interpreted as a refusal to assert "if p, q," and is in consequence an
implicit denial that there are adequate grounds for such an assertion.
This type of case raises no particular difficulty. A denial of a disjunctive statement can be made with parallel intentions. If you say "X or
Y will be elected," I may reply "That's not so; X or Y *or* Z will be
elected." Here, too, I am rejecting "X or Y will be elected" not as
false but as *unassertable*. But the possibility of speaking in this way

gives no ground for supposing that "or" is not truth-functional.

We now, however, have to face a radical objection to the kind of defense which I have been attempting to provide for the thesis that "if" and "⊃" are identical in meaning. The suggested treatment of the negation of conditionals proceeds on the following principle: if the affirmation of "if p, q" does not (would not) carry any implicature (as in the bridge example), then its denial has to be interpreted as equivalent to the assertion "that p and not-q." But if the affirmation of "if p, q" carries an implicature, its denial has to be interpreted as the denial of the implicature. This principle does not appear to be acceptable. Certainly there are cases in which a denial has to be interpreted as the denial of an implicature. "She is not the cream in my coffee" must be understood as denying, for example, that she is my pride and joy, not as denying that she is *literally* the cream in my coffee. If an utterance is not absurd when taken literally, a denial of it is standardly a denial of its literal meaning. If you say ironically "He is a splendid fellow" and I reply "He is not a splendid fellow," I must be saying, directly (and feebly), just what you have implicated; I cannot be meaning "He *is* a splendid fellow." Again, if I say "He has been visiting New York a lot lately," implicating that he has a girlfriend in New York, it is simply not possible to mean by "No, he hasn't" merely that he has not got a girlfriend in New York. I am afraid I do not yet see what defense (if any) can be put up against this objection.

It might help to clarify the somewhat tortuous course of my treatment of indicative conditionals if I specify, in a summary form, the sequence of ideas which have been canvassed in that treatment.

(1) My main initial effort has been to develop the idea that the conventional (lexical) meaning of "if" is that which is provided by a truth-table for material implication.

(2) Though a stronger condition than that provided by the truth-table is often implied, it is a mistake to regard this implication as lexical in origin, rather than as a conversational implicature.

(3) Two ways in which an implicature of such a stronger condition might be generated are discussed. One is as a generalized implicature founded on the Cooperative Principle and the conversational maxims, particularly the first maxim of Quantity.

(4) The second way in which such an implicature might arise is dependent on the supposed role or function in the language of a conditional particle. Other logical particles may be supposed to have

their own special roles or functions, but these will be distinct from that of the conditional particle, which relates to the setting up of chains of interrogatively subordinated questions.

(5) Alongside and connected with this second source of implicature will be a suggestion or implication that the negation of the antecedent of a conditional is to be thought of as common ground, as a possibility though not necessarily as a fact, between those who debate the pros and cons of a particular conditional.

(6) The attribution of such common-ground status might be thought of either as something which has to be "read in" as a non-conventional implicatum, or as an element in the lexical meaning of certain conditionals, such as those the expression of which involves words or phrases such as "supposing," "suppose that," "if . . . then," and perhaps even "if" itself.

(7) It is further open to question, should it be necessary to attribute common-ground status, just what constitutes being common ground. There are two possibilities.

(8) One is that it lies in an understanding by speakers that they are debating the nature of the acceptable alternative to that which is taken as being common ground as a possibility. ("If not so-and-so, then what?")

(9) The other possibility would be one which involves the specification of a syntactical rule which would dictate the allocation of scope within a rewritten formulation of the original conditional.

(10) If the second version is preferred, it will be difficult to avoid the supposition that it is a feature of the lexical meaning of the conditional, even though possibly a feature which rests upon prelexical considerations, and which introduces no new concepts.

In conclusion, I present a Kant-type antinomy which, I think, reinforces one of my suggestions for the treatment of Indicative Conditionals.

I. *Thesis.* "Proof" that "if A, B" is a material conditional.
Assume:

(1) $A \supset B$ is true.

By definition of $\supset$, we derive:

(2) At least one of the pair of statements (not-A,B) is true.

From (2) we derive:

(3) If not-A is false, then B is true.

Provided that not-A is false iff A is true, then we derive:

(4) If A is true, then B is true.

This surely would yield:

(5) The conditional "if A,B" is true.

So an ordinary conditional is derivable from the corresponding material conditional.

II. *Antithesis.* "Proof" that "if A, B" is not a material conditional.

If the thesis is valid, that is, if (1) yields (2) yields (3) yields (4) yields (5), there must be a valid series of steps starting with the assumption that (5) is false, which derives that (1) is false. That is to say, assuming the negation of (5) (that it is false that if A, B) we must be able to derive the negation of (1) (that it is false that A ⊃ B), but "it is false that A ⊃ B" is by definition equivalent to "the conjunction of A with the negation of B is true." So, since "it is not the case that if A, B" does not entail "A and the negation of B are both true," it is false that the negation of (5) yields the negation of (1).

So the "proof" given in the Thesis is invalid.

III. It may be possible to reach a solution of this puzzle by invoking my bracketing device. If it should be true that "if A, B" means, or at least has the effect of, "[either not-A or]B," then "A ⊃ B" will yield "if A, B," but the negation of "if A, B" will not yield the negation of "A ⊃ B"; in which case the paradox disappears.

5

Utterer's Meaning and Intentions

1. Saying and Meaning

Let us take stock. My main efforts so far have been directed as follows:

(1) I have suggested a provisional account of a kind of nonconventional implicature, namely a conversational implicature; what is implicated is what it is required that one assume a speaker to think in order to preserve the assumption that he is observing the Cooperative Principle (and perhaps some conversational maxims as well), if not at the level of what is said, at least at the level of what is implicated.

(2) I have attempted to see to what extent the explanation of implicature is useful for deciding about the connection of some of the A-philosophical theses, listed in Essay 1.

A lot of unanswered questions remain:

(1) The reliance (without much exposition) on a favored notion of "saying" needs to be further elucidated.

(2) The notion of conventional force (conventional meaning) deserves more attention, and the notion itself needs to be characterized.

(3) The notion of conventional implicature requires attention, and the relation between what is conventionally implicated and what is said needs characterization.

(4) "Implicature" is a blanket word to avoid having to make choices between words like "imply," "suggest," "indicate," and "mean." These words are worth analyzing.

(5) Also needed are a clarification of the notion of relevance, a more precise specification of when relevance is expected (filling out

the maxim of relevance), and a further consideration of why there is a general expectation that this maxim (and indeed all maxims) be observed.

I doubt if I shall be able here to address myself to all of these questions. I shall, in the first instance, try to pursue question (1) further, which will carry with it some attention to questions (2) and (3).

What follows is a sketch of direction, rather than a formulation of a thesis, with regard to the notion of saying that *p* (in the favored sense of *say*).

I want to say that (1) "*U* (utterer) said that *p*" entails (2) "*U* did something *x* by which *U* meant that *p*." But of course many things are examples of the condition specified in statement (2) which are not cases of saying. For example, a man in a car, by refraining from turning on his lights, means that I should go first, and he will wait for me.

Let us try substituting, for (2), (2'):

"*U* did something *x* (1) by which *U* meant that *p*

(2) which is of a type which means '*p*.'" (that is, has for some person or other an established standard or conventional meaning).

There is a convenient laxity of formulation here: quite apart from troubles about the quoted variable, "*p*" will be in direct speech and so cannot be a quotation of a clause following "*U* meant that". Again many things satisfy the condition mentioned in this example which are not cases of saying, such as hand-signaling a left turn.

We want doing *x* to be a linguistic act; with hideous oversimplification we might try the formulation:

"*U* did something *x* (1) by which *U* meant that *p*

(2) which is an occurrence of an utterance type *S* (sentence) such that

(3) *S* means '*p*'

(4) *S* consists of a sequence of elements (such as words) ordered in a way licensed by a system of rules (syntactical rules)

(5) *S* means '*p*' in virtue of the particular meanings of the elements of *S*, their order, and their syntactical character."

I abbreviate this to:

"*U* did something *x*   (1)   by which *U* meant that *p*
                        (2)   which is an occurrence of a type *S* which
                              means '*p*' in some linguistic system."

This is still too wide. *U*'s doing *x* might be his uttering the sentence "She was poor but she was honest." What *U* meant, and what the sentence means, will both contain something contributed by the word "but," and I do not want this contribution to appear in an account of what (in my favored sense) *U* said (but rather as a conventional implicature).

I want here to introduce some such idea as that of "central meaning." I want to be able to explain or talk about what (within what *U* meant) *U* centrally meant, to give a sense to "In meaning that *p*, *U* centrally meant that *q*."

So "*U* said that *p*" may finally come out as meaning:

"*U* did something *x*   (1)   by which *U* centrally meant that *p*
                        (2)   which is an occurrence of a type *S* part of
                              the meaning of which is '*p*'."

This leaves various questions to be pursued:

(1) How is "U meant that *p*" to be explicated?

(2) How is "W (word or phrase) means '. . .'" to be explicated, and how is this locution related to "*U* meant that *p*"?

(3) How is "*S* means (would mean) '*p*'" (also "*S* meant '*p*' here, on this occasion" and "*U* meant by *S* '*p*'") to be explicated, and how does this relate to the locutions mentioned in questions (1) and (2)?

(4) How is "*U* centrally meant that *p*" to be explicated?

2. Varieties of Nonnatural Meaning

Within the range of uses of the word "mean" which are specially connected with communication (uses, that is, of the word "mean" in one or another of what I have called "nonnatural" senses), there are distinctions to be made. Consider the following sentence (*S*):

"If I shall then be helping the grass to grow, I shall have no time for reading."

(1*a*) It would be approximately true to say that *S* means (has as one of its meanings) "If I shall then be assisting the kind of thing of which lawns are composed to mature, I shall have no time for reading." It would also perhaps be approximately true to say that *S* means (has as another of its meanings, in at least one version of English) "If I shall then be assisting the marijuana to mature, I shall have no time for reading." Such meaning-specification I shall call the specifications of the *timeless meaning(s)* of a "complete" utterance-type (which may be a sentence or may be a "sentence-like" nonlinguistic utterance-type, such as a hand-signal).

(1*b*) It would be true to say that the word "grass" means (loosely speaking) "lawn-material," and also true to say that the word "grass" means "marijuana." Such meaning-specifications I shall call the specifications of the *timeless meaning(s)* of an "incomplete" utterance-type (which may be a nonsentential word or phrase, or may be a nonlinguistic utterance-type which is analogous to a word or phrase).

(2*a*) Since a complete utterance-type *x* may have more than one timeless meaning, we need to be able to connect with a particular utterance of *x* just one of the timeless meanings of *x* to the exclusion of the others. We need to be able to say, with regard to a particular utterance of *S*, that *S* meant *here* (on this occasion) "If I shall be assisting the kind of thing of which lawns are composed to mature, I shall have no time for reading," and that "I shall then be assisting the grass to grow" meant *here* "I shall be assisting the kind of thing of which lawns are composed to mature." Such meaning-specifications I shall call specifications of the *applied timeless meaning* of a complete utterance-type (on a particular occasion of utterance). Such specifications aim to give one the correct reading of a complete utterance-type on a particular occasion of utterance.

(2*b*) Similarly, we need to be able to specify what I shall call the *applied timeless meaning* of an incomplete utterance-type; we need to be able to say, with respect to the occurrence of the word "grass" in a particular utterance of *S*, that *here,* on this occasion, the word "grass" meant (roughly) "lawn-material" and not "marijuana."

(3) It might be true to say that when a particular utterer *U* uttered *S, he* meant *by S* (by the words of *S*):

(*i*) "If I am then dead, I shall not know what is going on in the world," and possibly, in addition, (*ii*) "One advantage of being dead will be that I shall be protected from the horrors of the world."

If it were true to say of U that, when uttering S, he meant by S (*i*), it would also be true to say of U that *he* meant *by the words,* "I shall be helping the grass to grow" (which occur within S), "I shall then be dead."

On the assumption (which I make) that the phrase "helping the grass to grow," unlike the phrase "pushing up the daisies," is *not* a recognized idiom, none of the specifications just given of what U meant by S (or by the words "I shall be helping the grass to grow") would be admissible as specifications of a timeless meaning or of the applied timeless meaning of S (or of the words constituting the antecedent in S). The words "I shall be helping the grass to grow" neither mean nor mean *here* "I shall be dead."

The kind of meaning-specification just cited I shall call the specification of the *occasion-meaning of an utterance-type.*

(4) The varieties of meaning-specification so far considered all make use of quotation marks (or, perhaps better, italics) for the specification of what is meant. The fourth and last type to be considered involves, instead, the use of indirect speech. If it were true to say of U that *he* meant by S (*i*) (and[*ii*]), it would also be true to say of him that when he uttered S (by uttering S) *he meant that* if he would then be dead he would not know what was going on in the world, and that when he uttered S *he meant that* (or *part of what he meant was that*) one advantage of being dead would be that he would be protected from the horrors of the world. Even if, however, when he uttered S, he meant, by the words "I shall then be helping the grass to grow," "I shall then be dead," it would not be true to say that he meant by these words *that* he would then be dead. To have meant that he would then be dead, U would have had to commit himself to its being the case that he would then be dead; and this, when uttering S, he has not done. This type of meaning-specifications I shall call specifications of *an utterer's occasion-meaning.*

We can, then, distinguish four main forms of meaning-specification:

(1) "*x* (utterance-type) means '. . .'" (Specification of *timeless meaning* for an utterance-type which is either [1*a*] complete or [1*b*] incomplete)

(2) "*x* (utterance-type) meant here '. . .'" (Specification of *applied timeless meaning* for an utterance-type which is either [2*a*] complete or [2*b*] incomplete)

(3) "*U* meant by *x* (utterance-type) '. . .'" (Specification of *utterance-type occasion-meaning*)

(4) "*U* meant by uttering *x* that . . ." (Specification of *utterer's occasion-meaning*)

There is, of course, an element of legislation in the distinction between the four cited linguistic forms; these are not quite so regimented as I am, for convenience, pretending.

In Essay 6 I consider in some detail the relations between timeless meaning, applied timeless meaning, and what I am now calling utterer's occasion-meaning. Starting with the assumption that the notion of an utterer's occasion-meaning can be explicated, in a certain way, in terms of an utterer's intentions, I argue in support of the thesis that timeless meaning and applied timeless meaning can be explicated in terms of the notion of utterer's occasion-meaning (together with other notions), and so ultimately in terms of the notion of intention. In that essay I do not distinguish utterance-type occasion-meaning from utterer's occasion-meaning; but once the distinction is made, it should not prove too difficult to explicate utterance-type occasion-meaning in terms of utterer's occasion-meaning. The following provisional definition, though inadequate, seems to provide a promising start in this direction.

Let "$\sigma(x)$" denote a complete utterance-type (σ) which contains an utterance-type *x*; *x* may be complete or incomplete, and may indeed be identical with σ. Let "ϕ" denote an utterance-type. Let "$\sigma(\phi/x)$" denote the result of substituting ϕ for *x* in σ. Then I propose for consideration the following loosely framed definition:

"By *x*, *U* meant ϕ iff ($\exists\sigma$) {*U* uttered σ (*x*), and by uttering σ (*x*) *U* meant that . . .[the lacuna to be completed by writing $\sigma(\phi/x)$]}."

My task is, however, to consider further the assumption made in the essay to which I have been referring, that the notion of utterer's occasion-meaning is explicable, in a certain way, in terms of the notion of utterer's intention, and I shall now turn to that topic.

I shall take as a starting-point the account of nonnatural meaning which appears in Essay 14 in this volume, treating this as an attempt to define the notion of utterer's occasion-meaning. To begin with, I shall take as my definiendum not the form of expression which is of primary interest, namely (1) "By uttering x, U meant that p," but rather another form of expression, discussed in my 1957 article, namely (2) "By uttering x, U meant *something*." My 1957 account, of course, embodied the idea that an adequate definiens for (2) would involve a reference to an intended effect of, or response to, the utterance of x, and that a specification of this intended effect or response would provide the material for answering the question *what U* meant by uttering x. Later, I shall revert to definiendum (1), and shall attempt to clarify the supposed link between the nature of the intended response and the specification of what U meant by uttering x.

I start, then, by considering the following proposed definition:

"U meant something by uttering x" is true iff, for some audience A,
U uttered x intending:
(1) A to produce a particular response r
(2) A to think (recognize) that U intends (1)
(3) A to fulfill (1) on the basis of his fulfillment of (2).

Two explanatory remarks may be useful. I use the terms "uttering" and "utterance" in an artificially extended way, to apply to any act or performance which is or might be a candidate for nonnatural meaning. And to suppose A to produce r "*on the basis of*" his thinking that U intends him to produce r is to suppose that his thinking that U intends him to produce r is at least part of his reason for producing r, and not merely the *cause* of his producing r. The third subclause of the definiens is formulated in this way in order to eliminate what would otherwise be a counterexample. If, for subclause (3), we were to substitute:

(3a) A to fulfill (1) as a result of his fulfillment of (2)

we should have counterintuitively to allow that U meant something by doing x if (as might be the case) U did x intending:

(1) A to be amused
(2) A to think that U intended him to be amused
(3a) A to be amused (at least partly) as a result of his thinking that U intended him to be amused.

But though A's thought that U intended him to be amused might be a part-cause of his being amused, it could not be a part of his reason for being amused (one does not, indeed, have reasons for being amused). So the adoption of (3) rather than of (3a) excludes this case.

I shall consider objections to this account of utterer's occasion-meaning under two main heads: first, those which purport to show that the definiens is too weak, that it lets in too much; and second, those which purport to show that the definiens is too strong, that it excludes clear cases of utterer's occasion-meaning. To meet some of these objections, I shall at various stages offer redefinitions of the notion of utterer's occasion-meaning; each such redefinition is to be regarded as being superseded by its successor.

3. Alleged Counterexamples Directed against the Sufficiency of the Suggested Analysans

(*i*) (J. O. Urmson in conversation) There is a range of examples connected with the provision by *U* (the utterer) of an inducement, or supposed inducement, so that *A* (the recipient or audience) shall perform some action. Suppose a prisoner of war is thought by his captors to possess some information which they want him to reveal; he knows that they want him to give this information. They subject him to torture by applying thumbscrews. The appropriate analysans for "They meant something by applying the thumbscrews (that he should tell them what they wanted to know)" are fulfilled:

(1) They applied the thumbscrews with the intention of producing a certain response on the part of the victim.

(2) They intended that he should recognize (know, think) that they applied the thumbscrews with the intention of producing this response.

(3) They intended that the prisoner's recognition (thought) that they had the intention mentioned in (2) should be at least part of his reason for producing the response mentioned.

If in general to specify in (1) the nature of an intended response is to specify what was meant, it *should* be correct not only to say that the torturers meant something by applying the thumbscrews, but also to say that they meant that he should (was to) tell them what they wished to know. But in fact one would not wish to say either of these things; only that they meant him *to* tell. A similar apparent counterexample can be constructed out of a case of bribery.

A restriction seems to be required, and one which might serve to eliminate this range of counterexamples can be identified from a comparison of the two following examples:

(1) I go into a tobacconist's shop, ask for a pack of my favorite cigarettes, and when the unusually suspicious tobacconist shows that he wants to see the color of my money before he hands over the goods, I put down the price of the cigarettes on the counter. Here nothing has been meant.

(2) I go to my regular tobacconist (from whom I also purchase other goods) for a pack of my regular brand X, the price of which is distinctive (say 43 cents). I say nothing, but put down 43 cents. The tobacconist recognizes my need and hands over the pack. Here, I think, by putting down 43 cents, I meant something—namely, that I wanted a pack of brand X. I have at the same time provided an inducement.

The distinguishing feature of the second example seems to be that here the tobacconist recognized, and was intended to recognize, what he was intended to do from my "utterance" (my putting down the money), whereas in the first example this was not the case. Nor is it the case with respect to the torture example. So the analysis of meaning might be amended accordingly, in the first redefinition:

"U meant something by uttering x" is true iff:

(1) U intended, by uttering x, to induce a certain response in A

(2) U intended A to recognize, *at least in part from the utterance of x,* that U intended to produce that response

(3) U intended the fulfillment of the intention mentioned in (2) to be at least in part A's reason for fulfilling the intention mentioned in (1).

While this might cope with this range of counterexamples, there are others for which it is insufficient.

(*ii*) (Stampe, Strawson, Schiffer)

(*a*) (D. W. Stampe in conversation) A man is playing bridge against his boss. He wants to earn his boss's favor, and for this reason he wants his boss to win, and furthermore he wants his boss to *know* that he wants him to win (his boss likes that kind of self-effacement). He does not want to do anything too blatant, however, like telling his boss by word of mouth, or in effect telling him by some action amounting to a signal, for fear the boss might be offended by his crudity. So he puts into operation the following plan: when he gets a good hand, he smiles in a certain way; the smile is *very* like, but not *quite* like, a spontaneous smile of pleasure. He intends his boss to detect the difference and to argue as follows: "That was not a genuine giveaway smile, but the simulation of such a smile. That sort of simulation might be a bluff (on a weak hand), but this is bridge, not poker, and he would not want to get the better of me, his boss, by such an impropriety. So probably he has a good hand, and, wanting me to win, he hoped I would learn that he has a good hand by taking his smile as a spontaneous giveaway. That being so, I shall not raise my partner's bid."

In such a case, I do not think one would want to say that the employee had *meant,* by his smile (or by smiling), that he had a good hand, nor indeed that he had meant anything at all. Yet the conditions so far listed are fulfilled. When producing the smile:

(1) The employee intended that the boss should think that the employee had a good hand.

(2) The employee intended that the boss should think, at least in part because of the smile, that the employee intended the boss to think that the hand was a good one.

(3) The employee intended that at least part of the boss's reason for thinking that the hand was a good one should be that the employee wanted him to think just that.

(*b*) To deal with an example similar to that just cited, Strawson[1] proposed that the analysans might be restricted by the addition of a further condition, namely that the utterer *U* should utter *x* not only, as already provided, with the intention that *A* should think that *U* intends to obtain a certain response from *A*, but also with the intention that *A* should think (recognize) that *U* has the intention just mentioned. In the current example, the boss is intended to think that the employee wants him to think that the hand is a good one, but he is *not* intended to think that he is *intended* to think that the employee wants him to think that the hand is a good one. He is intended to think that it is only as a result of being too clever for the employee that he has learned that the employee wants him to think that the hand is a good one; he is to think that he was supposed to take the smile as a spontaneous giveaway.

(*c*) (S. Schiffer in conversation) A more or less parallel example, where the intended response is a practical one, can be constructed,

1. P. F. Strawson, "Intention and Convention in Speech Acts," *Philosophical Review* 73 (1964): 439–460.

which seems to show the need for the addition of a fifth condition. *U* is in a room with a man *A* who is notoriously avaricious, but who also has a certain pride. *U* wants to get rid of *A*. So *U*, in full view of *A*, tosses a five-pound note out of the window. He intends that *A* should think as follows: "*U* wants to get me to leave the room, thinking that I shall run after the money. He also wants me to know that he wants me to go (so contemptuous was his performance). But I am not going to demean myself by going after the banknote; I shall go, but I shall go because he wants me to go. I do not care to be where I am not wanted." In this example, counterparts of all four of the conditions so far suggested for the analysans are fulfilled; yet here again I do not think that one would want to say that *U* had meant something by throwing the banknote out of the window—that he had meant, for example, that *A* was to (should) go away. The four conditions which are fulfilled are:

U uttered *x* (threw the banknote) with the intention
    (1) that *A* should leave the room
    (2) that *A* should think (at least partly on the basis of *x*) that *U* had intention (1)
    (3) that *A* should think that *U* had intention (2)
    (4) that in the fulfillment of intention (1), at least part of *A*'s reason for acting should be that he thought that *U* had intention (1)—(that is, that intention (2) is fulfilled).

So unless this utterance is to qualify as having meant something, yet a further restriction is required. A feature of this example seems to be that though *A*'s leaving the room was intended by *U* to be based on *A*'s thought that *U* wanted him to leave the room, *U* did not intend *A* to *recognize* that *U* intended *A*'s departure to be so based. *A* was intended to think that *U*'s purpose was to get him to leave in pursuit of the five-pound note. So the needed restriction is suggested as being that *U* should intend:

    (5) that *A* should think (recognize) that *U* intended that (4).

We can now formulate the general form of these suggested conditions, the second redefinition, version A:

"*U* meant something by *x*" is true iff *U* uttered *x* intending thereby:
    (1) that *A* should produce response *r*
    (2) that *A* should, at least partly on the basis of *x*, think that *U* intended (1)

(3) that A should think that U intended (2)

(4) that A's production of r should be based (at least in part) on A's thought that U intended that (1) (that is, on A's fulfillment of [2])

(5) that A should think that U intended (4).

A notable fact about this analysans is that at several points it exhibits the following feature: U's nth "sub-intention" is specified as an intention that A should think that U has his $(n-1)$th "sub-intention." The presence of this feature has led to the suggestion that the analysis of meaning (on these lines) is infinitely or indefinitely regressive, that further counterexamples could always be found, however complex the suggested analysans, to force the incorporation of further clauses which exhibit this feature; but that such a regress might be virtuous, not vicious; it might be as harmless as a regress proceeding from "Z knows that p" to "Z knows that Z knows that p" to "Z knows that Z knows that Z knows that p."

I am not sure just how innocent such a regress in the analysans would be. It certainly would not exhibit the kind of circularity, at least prima facie strongly objectionable, which would be involved in giving, for example, a definiens for "U meant that p" which at some point reintroduced the expression "U meant that p," or introduced the expression "U meant that q." On the other hand, it would not be so obviously harmless as it would be to suppose that whenever it is correct to say "it is true that p," it is also correct to say "it is true that it is true that p," and so on; or as harmless as it would be to suppose that if Z satisfies the conditions for knowing that p, he also satisfies the condition for knowing that he knows that p. In such cases, no extra conditions would be required for the truth of an iteration of, for example, "he knows that" over and above those required for the truth of the sentence with respect to which the iteration is made. But the regressive character of the analysans for "U meant something by x" is designed to meet possible counterexamples at each stage, so each additional clause imposes a restriction, requires that a further condition be fulfilled. One might ask whether, for example, on the assumption that it is always possible to know that p without knowing that one knows that p, it would be legitimate to define "Z super-knows that p" by the open set of conditions:

(1) Z knows that p.

(2) Z knows that (1).

(3) Z knows that (2), and so forth.

There is, however, the possibility that no decision is required on this question, since it might be that the threatened regress cannot arise.

It does not seem easy to construct examples which will force the addition of clauses involving further iterations of "*U* intended *A* to think that . . ." The following is an attempt by Schiffer. *U* sings "Tipperary" in a raucous voice with the intention of getting *A* to leave the room; *A* is supposed to recognize (and to know that he is intended to recognize) that *U* wants to get rid of *A*. *U*, moreover, intends that *A* shall, in the event, leave because he recognizes *U*'s intention that he shall go. *U*'s scheme is that *A* should (*wrongly*) think that *U* intends *A* to *think* that *U* intends to get rid of *A* by means of the recognition of *U*'s intention that *A* should go. In other words *A* is supposed to argue: "*U* intends me to *think* that he intends to get rid of me by the raucous singing, but he really wants to get rid of me by means of the recognition of his intention to get rid of me. I am really intended to go because he wants me to go, not because I cannot stand the singing." The fact that *A*, while thinking he is seeing through *U*'s plans, is really conforming to them, is suggested as precluding one from saying, here, that *U* meant by the singing that *A* should go.

But once one tries to fill in the detail of this description, the example becomes baffling. How is *A* supposed to reach the idea that *U* wants him to *think* that *U* intends to get rid of him by the singing? One might suppose that *U* sings in a particular nasal tone which he knows not to be displeasing to *A*, though it is to most people. *A* knows that *U* knows this tone not to be displeasing to *A*, but thinks (wrongly) that *U* does not know that *A* knows this. *A* might then be supposed to argue: "He cannot want to drive me out by his singing, since he knows that this nasal tone is not displeasing to me. He does not know, however, that I know he knows this, so maybe he wants me to think that he intends to drive me out by his singing." At this point one would expect *A* to be completely at a loss to explain *U*'s performance; I see no reason at all why *A* should then suppose that *U* really wants to get rid of him in some other way.

Whether or not this example could be made to work, its complexity is enormous, and any attempt to introduce yet further restrictions would involve greater complexities still. It is in general true that one cannot have intentions to achieve results which one sees no chance of achieving; and the success of intentions of the kind involved in communication requires those to whom communications or near communications are addressed to be capable in the circumstances of having certain thoughts and drawing certain conclusions. At some early stage in the attempted regression the calculations required of A by U will be impracticably difficult; and I suspect the limit was reached (if not exceeded) in the examples which prompted the addition of a fourth and fifth condition. So U could not have the intentions required of him in order to force the addition of further restrictions. Not only are the calculations he would be requiring of A too difficult, but it would be impossible for U to find cues to indicate to A that the calculations should be made, even if they were within A's compass. So one is tempted to conclude that no regress is involved.

But even should this conclusion be correct, we seem to be left with an uncomfortable situation. For though we may know that we do not need an infinite series of "backward-looking" subclauses, we cannot say just how many such subclauses are required. Indeed, it looks as if the definitional expansion of "By uttering x U meant something" might have to vary from case to case, depending on such things as the nature of the intended response, the circumstances in which the attempt to elicit the response is made, and the intelligence of the utterer and of the audience. It is dubious whether such variation can be acceptable.

This difficulty would be avoided if we could eliminate potential counterexamples, not by requiring U to have certain additional ("backward-looking") intentions, but rather by requiring U *not* to have a certain sort of intention or complex of intentions. Potential counterexamples of the kind with which we are at present concerned all involve the construction of a situation in which U intends A, in the reflection process by which A is supposed to reach his response, *both* to rely on some "inference-element" (some premise or some inferential step) E *and* also to think that U intends A *not* to rely on E. Why not, then, eliminate such potential counterexamples by a single clause which prohibits U from having this kind of complex intention?

So we reach the second redefinition, version B:

"U meant something by uttering x" is true iff (for some A and for some r):
  (a) U uttered x intending
    (1) A to produce r
    (2) A to think U to intend (1)
    (3) A's fulfillment of (1) to be based on A's fulfillment of (2)
  (b) there is no inference-element E such that U uttered x intending

both (1') that *A*'s determination of *r* should rely on *E* and (2')
that *A* should think *U* to intend that (1') be false.

(*iii*) (Searle)[2] An American soldier in the Second World War is captured by Italian troops. He wishes to get the troops to believe that he
is a German officer, in order to get them to release him. What he
would like to do is to tell them in German or Italian that he is a
German officer, but he does not know enough German or Italian to
do that. So he "as it were, attempts to put on a show of telling them
that he is a German officer" by reciting the only line of German that
he knows, a line he learned at school: "*Kennst du das Land, wo die
Zitronen blühen.*" He intends to produce a certain response in his
captors, namely that they should believe him to be a German officer,
and he intends to produce this response by means of their recognition
of his intention to produce it. Nevertheless, Searle maintained, it is
false that when the soldier says "*Kennst du das Land,*" what he
means is "I am a German officer" (or even the German version of "I
am a German officer"), because what the words mean is "Knowest
thou the land where the lemon trees bloom." Searle used this example
to support a claim that something is missing from my account of
meaning; this would (I think he thought) be improved if it were supplemented as follows (my conjecture): "*U* meant something by *x*"
means "*U* intended to produce in *A* a certain effect by means of the
recognition of *U*'s intention to produce that effect, and (if the utterance of *x* is the utterance of a sentence) *U* intends *A*'s recognition of
U's intention (to produce the effect) to be achieved by means of the
recognition that the sentence uttered is conventionally used to produce such an effect."

Now even if I should be here faced with a genuine counterexample,
I should be very reluctant to take the way out which I suspect was
being offered me. (It is difficult to tell whether this is what was being
offered, since Searle was primarily concerned with the characterization of a particular speech-act [promising], not with a general discussion of the nature of meaning; and he was mainly concerned to adapt
my account of meaning to his current purpose, not to amend it so as
to be better suited to its avowed end.) Of course, I would not want to
deny that when the vehicle of meaning is a sentence (or the utterance

2. John R. Searle, "What Is a Speech Act?" in *Philosophy in America,* ed. Max Black
(Ithaca, N.Y., 1965), pp. 221–239.

of a sentence), the speaker's intentions are to be recognized, in the normal case, by virtue of a knowledge of the conventional use of the sentence (indeed my account of nonconventional implicature depends on this idea). But as I indicated earlier, I would like, if I can, to treat meaning something by the utterance of a sentence as being only a special case of meaning something by an utterance (in my extended sense of utterance), and to treat a conventional correlation between a sentence and a specific response as providing only one of the ways in which an utterance may be correlated with a response.

Is Searle's example, however, a genuine counterexample? It seems to me that the imaginary situation is underdescribed, and that there are perhaps three different cases to be considered:

(1) The situation might be such that the only real chance that the Italian soldiers would, on hearing the American soldier speak his German line, suppose him to be a German officer, would be if they were to argue as follows: "He has just spoken in German (perhaps in an authoritative tone); we don't know any German, and we have no idea what he has been trying to tell us, but if he speaks German, then the most likely possibility is that he is a German officer—what other Germans would be in this part of the world?" If the situation was such that the Italians were likely to argue like that, and the American knew that to be so, then it would be difficult to avoid attributing to him the intention, when he spoke, that they *should* argue like that. As I recently remarked, one cannot in general intend that some result should be achieved, if one knows that there is no likelihood that it will be achieved. But if the American's intention was as just described, then he certainly would not, by my account, be meaning that he is a German officer; for though he would intend the Italians to believe him to be a German officer, he would not be intending them to believe this on the basis of their recognition of his intention. And it seems to me that though this is not how Searle wished the example to be taken, it would be much the most likely situation to have obtained.

(2) I think Searle wanted us to suppose that the American hoped that the Italians would reach a belief that he was a German officer via a belief that the words which he uttered were the German for "I am a German officer" (though it is not easy to see how to build up the context of utterance so as to give him any basis for this hope). Now it becomes doubtful whether, after all, it is right to say that the American did not mean "I am a German officer." Consider the following example. The proprietor of a shop full of knickknacks for tourists is

standing in his doorway in Port Said, sees a British visitor, and in dulcet tones and with an alluring smile says to him the Arabic for "You pig of an Englishman." I should be quite inclined to say that he had meant that the visitor was to come in, or something of the sort. I would not, of course, be in the least inclined to say that he had meant by the *words which he uttered* that the visitor was to come in; and to point out that the German *line* means not "I am a German officer" but "Knowest thou the land" is not relevant. If the American could be said to have meant that he was a German officer, he would have meant that by saying the line, or by saying the line in a particular way; just as the Port Said merchant would have meant that the visitor was to come in by *saying* what he said, or by speaking to the visitor in the way he did.

(3) It has been suggested, however, that it makes a difference whether U merely intends A to think that a particular sentence has a certain meaning which it does not in fact have, or whether he also intends him to think of himself as supposed to make use of his (mistaken) thought that it has this meaning in reaching a belief about U's intentions. The Port Said merchant is perhaps thought of as not intending the visitor to think of himself in this way; the visitor is not to suppose that the merchant thinks he can speak Arabic. But if A is intended to think that U expects A to understand the sentence spoken and is intended to attribute to it a meaning which U knows it does not have, then the utterer should not be described as meaning something by his utterance. I do not see the force of this contention, nor indeed do I find it easy to apply the distinction which it makes. Consider just one example. I was listening to a French lesson being given to the small daughter of a friend. I noticed that she thinks that a certain sentence in French means "Help yourself to a piece of cake," though in fact it means something quite different. When there is some cake in the vicinity, I address to her this French sentence, and as I intended, she helps herself. I intended her to think (and to think that I intended her to think) that the sentence uttered by me meant "Help yourself to some cake"; and I would say that the fact that the sentence meant and was known by me to mean something quite different is no obstacle to *my* having meant something by my utterance (namely, that she was to have some cake). Put in a more general form, the point seems to be as follows. Characteristically, an utterer intends an audience to recognize (and to think himself intended to recognize) some

"crucial" feature *F*, and to think of *F* (and to think himself intended to think of *F*) as correlated in a certain way with some response which the utterer intends the audience to produce. It does not matter, so far as the attribution of the speaker's meaning is concerned, whether *F* is thought by *U* to be *really* correlated in that way with the response or not; though of course in the normal case *U* will think *F* to be so correlated.

Suppose, however, we fill in the detail of the "American soldier" case, so as to suppose he accompanies "*Kennst du das Land*" with gesticulations, chest-thumping, and so forth. He might then hope to succeed in conveying to his listeners that he intends them to understand the German sentence, to learn from the particular German sentence that the American intends them to think that he is a German officer (whereas really, of course, the American does not expect them to learn *that* way, but only by assuming, on the basis of the situation and the character of the American's performance, that he must be trying to tell them that he is a German officer). Perhaps in this case we should be disinclined to say that the American meant that he was a German officer and ready to say only that he meant them to think that he was a German officer.

How can this example be differentiated from the "little girl" example? I would like to suggest a revised set of conditions for "*U* meant something by *x*," the third redefinition, version A:

Ranges of variables: *A:*   audiences
                         f: features of utterance
                         r: responses
                         c: modes of correlation (such as iconic, associative, conventional)

$(\exists A)\,(\exists f)\,(\exists r)\,(\exists c)$:

U uttered *x* intending   (1)   *A* to think *x* possesses *f*
                                  (2)   *A* to think *U* intends (1)
                                  (3)   *A* to think of *f* as correlated in way *c* with the type to which *r* belongs
                                  (4)   *A* to think *U* intends (3)
                                  (5)   *A* to think on the basis of the fulfillment of (1) and (3) that *U* intends *A* to produce *r*

(6)   *A*, on the basis of fulfillment of (5), to produce *r*

(7)   *A* to think *U* intends (6).

In the case of the "little girl" there is a single feature *f* (that of being an utterance of a particular French sentence) with respect to which *A* has all the first four intentions. (The only thing wrong is that this feature is not *in fact* correlated conventionally with the intended responses, and this does not disqualify the utterance from being one by which *U* means something.)

In the "American soldier" case there is no such single feature *f*. The captors are intended (1) to recognize, and go by, feature f_1 (*x*'s being a bit of German and being uttered with certain gesticulations, and so forth) but (2) to think that they are intended to recognize *x* as having f_2 (as being a *particular* German sentence).

The revised set of conditions also takes care of the earlier bridge example. The boss is intended to recognize *x* as having *f* (being a fake smile) but not to think that he is so intended. So intention (2) on our revised list is absent. And so we do not need the condition previously added to eliminate this example. I think, however, that condition (7)—(the old condition (5) is still needed to eliminate the "banknote" example, unless it can be replaced by a general "antideception" clause. Such replacement may be possible; it may be that the "backward-looking" subclauses (2), (4), and (7) can be omitted and replaced by the prohibitive clause which figures in the second redefinition, version B. We have then to consider the merits of the third redefinition, version B, the definiens of which runs as follows:

$(\exists A)\ (\exists f)\ (\exists r)\ (\exists c)$: (a)   *U* uttered *x* intending

(1)   *A* to think *x* possesses *f*

(2)   *A* to think *f* correlated in way *c* with the type to which *r* belongs

(3)   *A* to think, on the basis of the fulfillment of (1) and (3) that *U* intends *A* to produce *r*

(4)   *A*, on the basis of the fulfillment of (3) to produce *r*,

and (b)   there is no inference-element *E* such that *U* intends both

(1')   *A* in his determination of *r* to rely on *E*

(2') *A* to think *U* to intend (1') to be false.

4. Examples Directed toward Showing the Three-Prong Analysans Too Strong

Let us (for simplicity) revert to the original analysans of "*U* means something by uttering *x*":

"*U* utters *x* intending *A* (1) to produce *r*
(2) to think *U* intends *A* to produce *r*
(3) to think *U* intends the fulfillment of (1) to be based on the fulfillment of (2)."

Now abbreviate this to "*U* utters *x* M-intending that *A* produce *r*."

I originally supposed that the identification of *what U* meant by *x* would turn on the identification of the M-intended response or effect. In particular, I supposed that generic differences in type of response would be connected with generic differences within what is meant. To take two central examples, I supposed that "*U* meant by *x* that so-and-so is the case" would (roughly speaking) be explicated by "*U* uttered *x* M-intending to produce in *A* the belief that so-and-so," and that "*U* meant by *x* that *A* should do such-and-such" would be explicated by "*U* uttered *x* M-intending to produce in *A* the doing of such-and-such." Indicative or quasi-indicative utterances are connected with the generation of beliefs, imperative or quasi-imperative utterances are connected with the generation of actions.

I wish to direct our consideration to the emendation of this idea: to substitute in the account of imperative or quasi-imperative utterances, as the direct, M-intended response, "intention on the part of *A* to do such-and-such" (vice "*A*'s doing such-and-such"). This has the advantages (1) that symmetry is achieved, in that the M-intended response will be a propositional attitude in both cases (indicative and imperative), and (2) that it accommodates the fact that agreement ("yes," "all right") in the case of "The engine has stopped" signifies belief, and in the case of "Stop the engine" signifies *intention*. Of course action is the *ultimate* objective of the speaker. Cases of immediate response by acting are treatable, however, as special cases of forming an intention—namely, the intention with which the agent acts. Imperatives always call for *intentional* action.

Alleged counterexamples are best seen as attempts to raise trouble, not for the suggested analysis for "*U* means *something* by uttering *x*," but for this analysis when supplemented by the kind of detail just mentioned, so as to offer an outline of an account of "By uttering *x*, *U* means (meant) that . . ." In particular, it is suggested that to explicate "By uttering *x*, *U* meant that so-and-so is the case" by "*U* uttered *x* *M*-intending to produce in *A* the belief that so-and-so" is to select as explicans a condition that is too strong. We need to be able to say on occasion that *U* meant that so-and-so, without committing ourselves to the proposition that *U* *M*-intended to produce a belief that so-and-so.

The following examples seem to present difficulties:

Examinee: Q: "When was the Battle of Waterloo?"
              A: "1815."

Here the examinee meant that the Battle of Waterloo was fought in 1815 but hardly *M*-intended to induce a belief to that effect in his examiner. The examiner's beliefs (whatever they may be) are naturally to be thought of by the examinee as independent of candidates' answers. The *M*-intended effect is (perhaps) that the examiner knows or thinks that the examinee thinks the Battle of Waterloo was fought in 1815, *or* (perhaps) that the examiner knows whether the examinee knows the correct answer to the question (perhaps the former is the direct, and the latter the indirect, intended effect).

Confession (some cases):

    Mother: "It's no good denying it: you broke the window, didn't
              you?"
    Child: "Yes, I did."

Here the child knows his mother already thinks he broke the window; what she wants is that he should say that he did. Perhaps the *M*-intended effect, then, is that the mother should think the child willing to say that he did (what does "say" mean here—how should it be explicated?) or that the mother should think the child willing not to pretend that he did not break the window (not to say things or perform acts intended to induce the belief that the child *did not* break the window). Confession is perhaps a sophisticated and ritual case.

Reminding: Q: "Let me see, what was that girl's name?"
               A: "Rose" (or produces a rose).

The questioner is here presumed already to believe that the girl's name is Rose (at least in a dispositional sense); it has just slipped his mind. The intended effect seems to be that A should have it in mind that her name is Rose.

Review of facts: Both speaker and hearer are supposed already to believe that p (q, and so forth). The intended effect again seems to be that A (and perhaps U also) should have "the facts" in mind (altogether).

Conclusion of argument: p, q, therefore r (from already stated premises).

While U intends that A should think that r, he does not expect (and so intend) A to reach a belief that r on the basis of U's intention that he should reach it. The premises, not trust in U, are supposed to do the work.

The countersuggestible man: A regards U as being, in certain areas, almost invariably mistaken, or as being someone with whom he cannot bear to be in agreement. U knows this. U says "My mother thinks very highly of you" with the intention that A should (on the strength of what U says) think that U's mother has a low opinion of him. Here there is some inclination to say that, despite U's intention that A should think U's mother thinks ill of him, what U *meant* was that U's mother thinks well of A.

These examples raise two related difficulties.

(1) There is some difficulty in supposing that the indicative form is *conventionally tied* to indicating that the speaker is M-intending to induce a certain belief in his audience, if there are quite normal occurrences of the indicative mood for which the speaker's intentions are different, in which he is not M-intending (nor would be taken to be M-intending) to induce a belief (for example, in reminding). Yet it seems difficult to suppose that the function of the indicative mood has *nothing to do* with the inducement of belief. The indication of the speaker's intention that his audience should act (or form an intention to act) is plausibly, if not unavoidably, to be regarded as by convention the function of the imperative mood; surely the function of the indicative ought to be analogous. What is the alternative to the suggested connection with an intention to induce a belief?

The difficulty here might be met by distinguishing questions about what an indicative sentence means and questions about what a *speaker* means. One might suggest that a full specification of sentence meaning (for indicative sentences) involves reference to the fact that the indicative form conventionally signifies an intention on the part of the utterer to induce a belief; but that it may well be the case that the speaker's meaning does not coincide with the meaning of the sentence he utters. It may be clear that, though he uses a device which conventionally indicates an intention on his part to induce a belief, *in this case* he has not this but some other intention. This is perhaps reinforceable by pointing out that *any* device, the primary (standard) function of which is to indicate the speaker's intention to induce a belief that *p, could* in appropriate circumstances be easily and intelligibly employed for related purposes—for example (as in the "examinee" example), to indicate that the *speaker* believes that *p*. The problem then would be to exhibit the alleged counterexamples as natural adaptations of a device or form primarily connected with the indication of an intention to induce a belief.

I think we want, if possible, to avoid treating the counterexamples as extended uses of the indicative form and to find a more generally applicable function for that form. In any case, the second difficulty is more serious.

(2) Even if we can preserve the idea that the indicative form is tied by convention to the indication of a speaker's intention to induce a belief, we should have to allow that the speaker's meaning will be different for different occurrences of the same indicative sentence— indeed, this is required by the suggested solution for difficulty (1). We shall have to allow this if differences in intended response involve differences in speaker's meaning. But it is not very plausible to say that if *U* says, "The Battle of Waterloo was fought in 1815"

(1) as a schoolmaster (intending to induce a belief)
(2) as an examinee
(3) as a schoolmaster in *revision class,*

U would mean something different by uttering this sentence on each of the three occasions. Even if the examinee *M*-intends to induce a belief that he (the examinee) thinks the Battle of Waterloo was fought in 1815, it does not seem attractive to say that when *he* said "Waterloo was fought in 1815," he meant that *he thought* that Waterloo was fought in 1815 (unlike the schoolmaster teaching the period for the first time).

We might attempt to deal with some of the examples (such as reminding and fact-reviewing) by supposing the standard M-intended effect to be not just a belief but an "activated belief" (that A should be in a state of believing that p and having it in mind that p). One may fall short of this in three ways: one may

(1) neither believe that p nor have it in mind that p
(2) believe that p but not have it in mind that p
(3) not believe that p, but have it in mind that p.

So one who reminds intends the same final response as one who informs, but is intending to remedy a different deficiency.

This (even for the examples for which it seems promising) runs into a new difficulty. If U says (remindingly) "Waterloo was fought in 1815," two of my conditions are fulfilled:

(1) U intends to induce in A the *activated* belief that Waterloo was fought in 1815.
(2) U intends A to recognize that (1).

But if the date of Waterloo was "on the tip of A's tongue" (as it might be), U cannot expect (and so cannot intend) that A's activated belief will be produced via A's recognition that U intends to produce it. If A already believes (though has momentarily forgotten) that Waterloo was fought in 1815, then the mention of this date will induce the activated belief, regardless of U's intention to produce it.

This suggests dropping the requirement (for speaker's meaning) that U should intend A's production of response to be *based* on A's recognition of U's intention that A should produce the response; it suggests the retention merely of conditions (1) and (2). But this will not do: there are examples which require this condition:

(a) Herod, showing Salome the head of St. John the Baptist, cannot, I think, be said to have meant that St. John the Baptist was dead.
(b) Displaying a bandaged leg (in response to a squash invitation).

In (b) the displayer could mean   (1)   that he cannot play squash
or (dubiously)   (2)   that he has a bad leg (the bandages might be fake)

but not   (3)   that his leg is bandaged.

The third condition seems to be required in order to protect us from counterintuitive results in these cases.

Possible Remedies

(*i*) We might retain the idea that the intended effect or response (for cases of meaning that it is the case that *p*—indicative type) is activated belief, retaining in view the distinction between reaching this state (1) from assurance-deficiency and (2) from attention-deficiency, and stipulate that the third condition (that *U* intends the response to be elicited on the basis of a recognition of his intention to elicit that response) is operative *only* when *U* intends to elicit activated belief by eliminating *assurance-deficiency, not* when he intends to do so by eliminating attention-deficiency. This idea might be extended to apply to imperative types of cases, too, provided that we can find cases of reminding someone to do something (restoring him to *activated* intention) in which *U*'s intention that *A* should reach the state is similarly otiose, in which it is not to be expected that *A*'s reaching the activated intention will be dependent on his recognition that *U* intends him to reach it. So the definition might read roughly as follows ($*_\psi$ is a mood marker, an auxiliary correlated with the propositional attitude ψ from a given range of propositional attitudes):

"*U* means by uttering *x* that $*_\psi p$" = "*U* utters *x* intending

(1) that *A* should actively ψ that *p*

(2) that *A* should recognize that *U* intends (1) and (unless *U* intends the utterance of *x* merely to remedy attention-deficiency)

(3) that the fulfillment of (1) should be based on the fulfillment of (2)."

This remedy does not, however, cope with (1) the "examinee" example, (2) the "confession" examples, or (3) the countersuggestible man.

(*ii*) Since, when *U* does intend, by uttering *x,* to promote in *A* the belief that *p*, it is standardly requisite that *A* should (and should be intended to) think that *U* thinks that *p* (otherwise *A* will not think that *p*), why not make the *direct* intended effect not that *A* should think that *p*, but that *A* should think that *U thinks* that *p*? In many but not all cases, *U* will intend *A* to pass, from thinking that *U* thinks that *p*, to thinking that *p* himself ("informing" cases). But such an effect is to be thought of as indirect (even though often of prime interest).

We can now retain the third condition, since even in reminding cases *A* may be expected to think *U*'s intention that *A* should think that *U* thinks that *p* to be relevant to the question whether *A* is to think that U thinks that p. We have coped, not only with the "reminding" example, but also with the "examinee" example and with the "countersuggestible man" (who is intended to think that U thinks that p, though not to think that p himself). And though the fact-review example is not yet provided for (since A may be thought of as already knowing that U thinks that p), if we are understanding "U believes that p" as "U has the activated belief that p," this example can be accommodated, too. A, though he is to be supposed to know that U believes that p, does not, until U speaks, know that U has it in mind that p.

But while a solution along these lines may be acceptable for indicative-type cases, it cannot be generalized to all non-indicative cases. Contrast:

(*a*) "You shall not cross the barrier."
(*b*) "Do not cross the barrier."

When uttering (*a*), U would characteristically intend A to think that U intends that A shall not cross the barrier; but it seems that a specification of U's meaning, for a normal utterance of (*b*), would be incompletely explicated unless it is stated that U intends A not merely to think that U intends that A shall not cross the barrier, but also himself to form the intention not to cross.

Let us then draw a distinction between what I might call "purely exhibitive" utterances (utterances by which the utterer U intends to impart a belief that he [U] has a certain propositional attitude), and utterances which are not only exhibitive but also what I might call "protreptic" (that is, utterances by which U intends, via imparting the belief that he [U] has a certain propositional attitude, to induce a corresponding attitude in the hearer).

We reach, then, the fourth redefinition, version A:

"By uttering x U meant that $*_\psi p$" is true iff
$(\exists A)\ (\exists f)\ (\exists c)$:

U uttered x intending (1) ⎫
                        (2) ⎪
                        (3) ⎪
                        (4) ⎬ [as in the third redefinition, version A,
                                         with "ψ-ing that p"
                        (5) ⎪   substituted for "r"]
                        (6) ⎪
                        (7) ⎭

and (for some cases)

(8)⌡   *A*, on the basis of the fulfillment of (6),
       himself to ψ that *p*.

Whether a substitution-instance of subclause (8) is to appear in the expansion of a statement of the form represented in the definiendum will depend on the nature of the substitution for "$*_ψ$" which that statement incorporates.

We can also reach the fourth redefinition, version B, by adding what appears above as subclause (8) to the definiens of the third redefinition, version B, as subclause (*a*) (5), together with a modification of clause (*b*) of the third redefinition, version B, to take into account that the intended response *r* is now specified in terms of the idea of ψ-ing that *p*.

Whether either version of the fourth redefinition is correct as it stands depends crucially on the view to be taken of an imperatival version of the "countersuggestible man" example. Mr. A, wishing to be relieved of the immediate presence of Mrs. A, but regarding her as being, so far as he is concerned, countersuggestible, says to her, "Now, dear, keep me company for a little." Would it be correct to say that Mr. A, who clearly did not mean Mrs. A to keep him company, meant by his remark that she was to (should) keep him company? If the answer is "yes," the fourth redefinition is inadequate since, according to it, to have meant that Mrs. A was to keep him company, Mr. A would have had to intend that she form the intention to keep him company, an intention which he certainly did not have. Emendation, however, would not be difficult; we alter the new subclause from "*A*, on the basis of the fulfillment of (6), himself to ψ to that *p*" to "*A*, on the basis of the fulfillment of (6), *to think U to intend A* to ψ that *p*." If, however, the answer is "no," then the fourth redefinition is left intact.

5. Utterer's Occasion-Meaning in the Absence of an Audience

There are various examples of utterances by which the utterer could correctly be said to have meant something (to have meant that so-and-so), such that there is no actual person or set of persons whom the utterer is addressing and in whom he intends to induce a response. The range of these examples includes, or might be thought to include, such items as the posting of notices, like "Keep out" or "This bridge is dangerous," entries in diaries, the writing of notes to clarify one's thoughts when working on some problem, soliloquizing, rehearsing a part in a projected conversation, and silent thinking. At least some of these examples are unprovided for in the definitions so far proposed.

The examples which my account should cover fall into three groups:

(a) Utterances for which the utterer thinks there may (now or later) be an audience. *U* may think that some particular person, for example, himself at a future date in the case of a diary entry, may (but also may not) encounter *U*'s utterance; or *U* may think that there may or may not be some person or other who is or will be an auditor of his utterance.

(b) Utterances which the utterer knows not to be addressed to any actual audience, but which the utterer pretends to address to some particular person or type of person, or which he thinks of as being addressed to some imagined audience or type of audience (as in the rehearsal of a speech or of his part in a projected conversation).

(c) Utterances (including "internal" utterances) with respect to which the utterer neither thinks it possible that there may be an actual audience nor imagines himself as addressing an audience, but nevertheless intends his utterance to be such that it would induce a certain sort of response in a certain perhaps fairly indefinite kind of audience were it the case that such an audience was present. In the case of silent thinking the idea of the presence of an audience will have to be interpreted liberally, as being the idea of there being an audience for a public counterpart of the utterer's internal speech. In this connection it is perhaps worth noting that some cases of verbal thinking fall outside the scope of my account. When verbal thoughts merely pass through my head as distinct from being "framed" by me, it is inappropriate to talk of me as having meant something by them; I am, perhaps, in such cases more like a listener than a speaker.

I shall propose a final redefinition which, I hope, will account for the examples which need to be accounted for, and which will allow as special cases the range of examples in which there is, and it is known by the utterer that there is, an actual audience. This redefinition will be relatively informal; I could present a more formal version which would gain in precision at the cost of ease of comprehension.

Let "ϕ" (and "ϕ'") range over properties of persons (possible audiences); appropriate substituends for "ϕ" (and "ϕ'") will include such diverse expressions as "is a passerby," "is a passerby who sees this notice," "is a native English speaker," and "is identical with Jones." As will be seen, for U to mean something it will have to be possible to identify the value of "ϕ" (which may be fairly indeterminate) which U has in mind; but *we* do not have to determine the range from which U makes a selection.

The fifth redefinition is as follows:

"U meant by uttering x that $*_\psi p$" is true iff
($\exists\phi$) ($\exists f$) ($\exists c$):

I. U uttered x intending x *to be such that* anyone who has ϕ would think that
   (1) x has f
   (2) f is correlated in way c with ψ-ing that p
   (3) ($\exists\phi'$): U intends x to be such that anyone who has ϕ' would think, via thinking (1) and (2), that U ψ's that p
   (4) in view of (3), U ψ's that p;

and

II. (operative only for certain substituends for "$*_\psi$")
   U uttered x intending that, *should there actually be* anyone who has ϕ, he would via thinking (4), himself ψ that p;

and

III. It is not the case that, for some inference-element E, U intends x to be such that anyone who has ϕ will both
   (1') rely on E in coming to ψ^+ that p
   (2') think that ($\exists\phi'$): U intends x to be such that anyone who has ϕ' will come to ψ^+ that p *without* relying on E.

Notes: (1) "ψ^+" is to be read as "ψ" if clause (II) is operative, and as "think that U ψ's" if clause (II) is nonoperative.
         (2) We need to use both "ϕ" and "ϕ'," since we do not wish to require that U should intend his possible audi-

ence to think of *U*'s possible audience under the same
description as *U* does himself.

Explanatory Comments

(1) It is essential that the intention which is specified in clause (II)
should be specified as *U*'s intention "that should there be anyone who
has φ, he would (will) . . ." rather than, analogously with clauses (I)
and (II), as *U*'s intention "that *x should be such that,* should anyone
be φ, he would . . ." If we adopt the latter specification, we shall be
open to an objection raised by Schiffer, as can be shown with the aid
of an example of the same kind as his. Suppose that, infuriated by an
afternoon with my mother-in-law, when I am alone after her departure I relieve my feelings by saying, aloud and passionately, "Don't
you ever come near me again." It will no doubt be essential to my
momentary well-being that I should speak with the intention that my
remark be such that were my mother-in-law present, she would form
the intention not to come near me again. It would, however, be unacceptable if it were represented as following from my having this
intention that I *meant that* she was never to come near me again, for
it is false that, in the circumstances, I meant this by my remark. The
redefinition as formulated avoids this difficulty.

(2) Suppose that in accordance with the definiens of the latest redefinition, (∃φ): *U* intends *x* to be such that anyone who is φ will
think . . . , and suppose that the value of "φ" which *U* has in mind is
the property of being identical with a particular person *A*. Then it
will follow that *U* intends *A* to think . . . ; and given the further condition, fulfilled in any normal case, that *U* intends *A* to think that he
(*A*) is the intended audience, we are assured of the truth of a statement from which the definiens of the fourth redefinition, version B, is
inferrable by the rule of existential generalization (assuming the legitimacy of this application of E. G. to a statement the expression of
which contains such "intensional" verbs as "intend" and "think"). I
think it can also be shown that, for any case in which there is an
actual audience who knows that he is the intended audience, if the
definiens of the fourth redefinition, version B, is true then the definiens of the fifth redefinition will be true. If that is so, given that the
fifth redefinition is correct, for any normal case in which there is an
actual audience the fulfillment of the definiens of the fourth redefini-

tion, version B, will constitute a necessary and sufficient condition for
U's having meant that $*_\psi p$.

6. Conclusion

I see some grounds for hoping that, by paying serious attention to
the relation between nonnatural and natural meaning, one might be
able not only to reach a simplified account of utterer's occasion-
meaning but also to show that any human institution, the function of
which is to provide artificial substitutes for natural signs, must embody, as its key-concept, a concept possessing approximately the features which I ascribe to the concept of utterer's occasion-meaning.
But such an endeavor lies beyond the scope of this essay.

6

Utterer's Meaning,
Sentence-Meaning,
and Word-Meaning

This essay analyzes in greater detail members of the quartet of specific conceptions of meaning which were distinguished in the preceding essay, with the exception of Utterer's Occasion-Meaning which I have just been subjecting to exhaustive examination. The present essay will, however, provide indications of how the meaning of words may be connected with the meaning of speakers.

A. Introductory Remarks

My aim in this essay is to throw light on the connection between (a) a notion of meaning which I want to regard as basic, namely the notion which is involved in saying of someone that by (when) doing such-and-such he meant that so-and-so (in what I have called a non-natural sense of the word "meant"), and (b) the notions of meaning involved in saying (i) that a given sentence means "so-and-so" (ii) that a given word or phrase means "so-and-so." What I have to say on these topics should be looked upon as an attempt to provide a sketch of what might, I hope, prove to be a viable theory, rather than as an attempt to provide any part of a finally acceptable theory. The account which I shall offer of the (for me) basic notion of meaning is one which I shall not here seek to defend; I should like its approximate correctness to be assumed, so that attention may be focused on its utility, if correct, in the explication of other and (I hope) derivative notions of meaning. This enterprise forms part of a wider program which I shall in a moment delineate, though its later stages lie beyond the limits which I have set for this essay.

The wider program arises out of a distinction which, for purposes which I need not here specify, I wish to make within the total signification of a remark: a distinction between what the speaker has *said* (in a certain favored, and maybe in some degree artificial, sense of "said"), and what he has *implicated* (e.g. implied, indicated, suggested), taking into account the fact that what he has implicated may be either conventionally implicated (implicated by virtue of the meaning of some word or phrase which he has used) or nonconventionally implicated (in which case the specification of the implicature falls outside the specification of the conventional meaning of the words used). The program is directed toward an explication of the favored sense of "say" and a clarification of its relation to the notion of conventional meaning.

There are six stages in the program.

(I) To distinguish between locutions of the form "U (utterer) meant *that* ..." (locutions which specify what might be called "occasion-meaning") and locutions of the form "X (utterance-type) means '...'" In locutions of the first type, meaning is specified without the use of quotation marks, whereas in locutions of the second type the meaning of a sentence, word, or phrase is specified with the aid of quotation marks. This difference is semantically important.

(II) To attempt to provide a definiens for statements of occasion-meaning, or more precisely, to provide a definiens for "By (when) uttering x, U meant that *p." Some explanatory comments are needed here.

(a) I use the term "utter" (together with "utterance") in an artificially wide sense, to cover any case of doing x or producing x by the performance of which U meant that so-and-so. The performance in question need not be a linguistic or even a conventionalized performance. A specificatory replacement of the dummy "x" will in some cases be a characterization of a deed, in others a characterization of a product (e.g. a sound).

(b) "*" is a *dummy* mood-indicator, distinct from specific mood-indicators like "⊢" (indicative or assertive) or "!" (imperative). More precisely, one may think of the schema "Jones meant that *p" as yielding a full English sentence after two transformational steps:

(i) Replace "*" by a specific mood-indicator and replace "p" by an indicative sentence. One might thus get to

"Jones meant that ⊢ Smith will go home" or
"Jones meant that ! Smith will go home."

(ii) Replace the sequence following the word "that" by an appropriate clause in indirect speech (in accordance with rules specified in a linguistic theory). One might thus get to

"Jones meant that Smith will go home."
"Jones meant that Smith is to go home."

(III) To attempt to elucidate the notion of the conventional meaning of an utterance-type, or more precisely, to explicate sentences which make claims of the form "X (utterance-type) means '*p,'" or, in case X is a nonsentential utterance-type, claims of the form "X means '...,'" where the locution is completed by a nonsentential expression. Again, some explanatory comments are required.

(a) It will be convenient to recognize that what I shall call statements of *timeless meaning* (statements of the type "X means '...,'" in which the specification of meaning involves quotation marks) may be subdivided into (i) statements of timeless "idiolect-meaning," such as "For U (in U's idiolect) X means '...'" and (ii) statements of timeless "language meaning," such as "In L (language) X means '...'" It will be convenient to handle these separately, and in the order just given.

(b) The truth of a statement to the effect that "X means '...'" is of course not incompatible with the truth of a further statement to the effect that "X means '__,'" when the two lacunae are quite differently completed. An utterance-type may have more than one conventional meaning, and any definiens which we offer must allow for this fact. "X means '...'" should be understood as "One of the meanings of X is '...'"

(IV) In view of the possibility of multiplicity in the timeless meaning of an utterance-type, we shall need to notice, and to provide an explication of, what I shall call the *applied timeless meaning* of an utterance-type. That is, we need a definiens for the schema "X (utterance-type) meant *here* '...,'" a schema the specifications of which announce the correct reading of X for a given occasion of utterance.

Comments. (a) We must be careful to distinguish the applied timeless meaning of X (type) with respect to a particular token x (belonging to X) from the occasion-meaning of U's utterance of x. The following are not equivalent:

(i) "When U uttered it, the sentence 'Palmer gave Nicklaus quite a beating' meant 'Palmer vanquished Nicklaus with some ease' (rather than, say, 'Palmer administered vigorous corporal punishment to Nicklaus')."

(ii) "When U uttered the sentence 'Palmer gave Nicklaus quite a beating,' U meant that Palmer vanquished Nicklaus with some ease." U might have been speaking ironically, in which case he would likely have meant that *Nicklaus* vanquished *Palmer* with some ease. In that case (ii) would clearly be false; but nevertheless (i) would still have been true.

(b) There is some temptation to take the view that the conjunction of

(i) "By uttering X, U meant that *p" and
(ii) "When uttered by U, X meant '*p'"

provides a definiens for "In uttering X, U said that *p." Indeed, if we give consideration only to utterance-types for which there are available adequate statements of timeless meaning that take the exemplary form "X meant '*p'" (or, in the case of applied timeless meaning, the form "X meant here '*p'"), it may even be possible to uphold the thesis that such a coincidence of occasion-meaning and applied timeless meaning is a necessary and sufficient condition for saying that *p. But a little reflection should convince us of the need to recognize the existence of statements of timeless meaning which instantiate forms other than the cited exemplary form; there are, I think, at least some sentences whose timeless meaning is not adequately specifiable by a statement of the exemplary form. Consider the sentence "Bill is a philosopher and he is, therefore, brave" (S_1). It would be appropriate, I think, to make a partial specification of the timeless meaning of S_1 by saying "Part of one meaning of S_1 is 'Bill is occupationally engaged in philosophical studies.'" One might, indeed, give a full specification of timeless meaning for S_1 by saying "One meaning of S_1 includes 'Bill is occupationally engaged in philosophical studies' and 'Bill is courageous' and 'That Bill is courageous follows from his being occupationally engaged in philosophical studies,' and that is all that is included." We might re-express this as "One meaning of S_1 *comprises* 'Bill is occupationally engaged (etc.),' 'Bill is courageous,' and 'That Bill is courageous follows (etc.).'" It is preferable to specify the timeless meaning of S_1 in this way than to do so as follows: "One meaning of S_1 is 'Bill is occupationally engaged (etc.) and Bill is courageous and that Bill is courageous follows (etc.),'" for the latter formulation at least suggests that S_1 is synonymous with the conjunctive sentence quoted in the formulation, which does not seem to be the case.

Since it is true that *another* meaning of S₁ includes "Bill is addicted to general reflections about life" (in place of "Bill is occupationally engaged [etc.]"), one could have occasion to say (truly), with respect to a given utterance by U of S₁, "The meaning of S₁ *here* comprised 'Bill is occupationally engaged (etc.),' 'Bill is courageous,' and 'That Bill is courageous follows (etc.),'" or to say "The meaning of S₁ *here* included 'That Bill is courageous follows (etc.).'" It could also be true that when U uttered S₁ he meant (part of what he meant was) *that* that Bill is courageous follows (etc.).

Now I do not wish to allow that, in my favored sense of "say," one who utters S₁ will have *said* that Bill's being courageous follows from his being a philosopher, though he may well have said that Bill is a philosopher and that Bill is courageous. I would wish to maintain that the semantic function of the word 'therefore' is to enable a speaker to *indicate,* though not to *say,* that a certain consequence holds. *Mutatis mutandis,* I would adopt the same position with regard to words like "but" and "moreover." My primary reason for opting for this particular sense of "say" is that I expect it to be of greater theoretical utility than some other sense of "say" would be. So I shall be committed to the view that applied timeless meaning and occasion-meaning may coincide, that is to say, it may be true both (i) that when U uttered X, the meaning of X included "*p" and (ii) that part of what U meant when he uttered X was that *p, and yet it may be false that U has said, among other things, that *p. I would like to use the expression "conventionally meant that" in such a way that the fulfillment of the two conditions just mentioned, while insufficient for the truth of "U said that *p" will be sufficient (and necessary) for the truth of "U conventionally meant that *p."

(V) This distinction between what is said and what is conventionally meant creates the task of specifying the conditions in which what U conventionally meant by an utterance is also part of what U said. I have hopes of being able to discharge this task by trying:

(1) To specify conditions which will be satisfied only by a limited range of speech-acts, the members of which will thereby be stamped as specially central or fundamental.

(2) To stipulate that in uttering X, U will have said that *p, if both (i) U has Y-ed that *p, where Y-ing is a central speech-act, and (ii) X embodies some conventional device the meaning of which is such that its presence in X indicates that its utterer is Y-ing that *p.

(3) To define, for each member Y of the range of central speech-acts, "U has Y-ed that *p" in terms of occasion-meaning (meaning

that . . .) or in terms of some important elements involved in the already provided definition of occasion-meaning.

(VI) The fulfillment of the task just outlined will need to be supplemented by an account of the elements in the conventional meaning of an utterance which are *not* part of what has been said. This account, at least for an important subclass of such elements, might take the following shape:

(1) The problematic elements are linked with certain speech-acts which are exhibited as posterior to, and such that their performance is dependent upon, some member or disjunction of members of the central range; for example, the meaning of "moreover" would be linked with the speech-act of adding, the performance of which would require the performance of one or another of the central speech-acts.

(2) If Z-ing is such a noncentral speech-act, the dependence of Z-ing that *p upon the performance of some central speech-act would have to be shown to be of a nature which justifies a reluctance to treat Z-ing that *p as a case not merely of saying that *p but also of saying that #p, or of saying that #*p, where "#p" or "#*p" is a representation of one or more sentential forms specifically associated with Z-ing (as "moreover" is specifically associated with the speech-act of adding).

(3) The notion of Z-ing that *p (where Z-ing is noncentral) would be explicated in terms of the notion of *meaning that* (or in terms of some important elements in the definition of that notion).

B. Treatment of Some of the Problems Raised

The problems which I shall consider in the remainder of this essay are those which are presented by Stages II–IV of the program.

Stage II. I shall offer, without arguing for it, a somewhat oversimplified account of the notion of occasion-meaning, which (as I said at the outset) I should like to be treated as if it were correct.

In my 1957 article on Meaning (Essay 14) I suggested, for the schema "U meant (nonnaturally) something by uttering x," a three-clause definiens which may be compendiously reformulated as "For some audience A, U intended his utterance of x to produce in A some effect (response) E, by means of A's recognition of that intention." As I wish to continue to use the central idea of this definition, I shall introduce an abbreviation: "U intends to produce in A effect E by means of A's recognition of that intention" is abbreviated to "U *M-intends* to produce in A effect E" ("M" is for "meaning").

The point of divergence between my current and my earlier accounts lies in the characterization of the M-intended effect (response). In the earlier account I took the view that the M-intended effect is, in the case of indicative-type utterances, that the hearer should *believe* something, and, in the case of imperative-type utterances, that the hearer should *do* something. I wish for present purposes to make two changes here.

(1) I wish to represent the M-intended effect of imperative-type utterances as being that the hearer should *intend* to do something (with of course the ulterior intention on the part of the utterer that the hearer should go on to do the act in question).

(2) I wish to regard the M-intended effect common to indicative-type utterances as being, not that the hearer should believe something (though there is frequently an ulterior intention to that effect), but that the hearer should *think that the utterer believes* something.

The effect of the first change will be that the way is opened to a simplified treatment of the M-intended effect, as being always the generation of some propositional attitude. The effect of the second change (made in order to unify the treatment of indicative-type utterances, some of which are, and some of which are not, cases of informing or telling) will be to introduce a distinction between what I might call *exhibitive* utterances (utterances by which the utterer U M-intends to impart a belief that he (U) has a certain propositional attitude) and utterances which are not only exhibitive but also what I might call *protreptic* (utterances by which U M-intends, *via* imparting a belief that he (U) has a certain propositional attitude, to induce a corresponding attitude in the hearer).

I shall now try to reformulate the account in a generalized form. Let "A" range over audiences or hearers. Let the device "$*_\psi$" (read "asterisk-sub-ψ") be a dummy, which represents a specific mood-indicator which corresponds to the propositional attitude ψ-ing (whichever that may be), as, for example, "⊢" corresponds to believing (thinking) and "!" corresponds to intending. I can, using this device, offer the following rough definition:

D1: "By (when) uttering x U meant that $*_\psi$ p" = df. "($\exists$A) (U uttered x M-intending [i] that A should think U to ψ that p and [in some cases only, depending on the identification of $*_\psi$ p] (ii) that A should, via the fulfillment of [i], himself ψ that p)."

It is convenient to have an abbreviated version of this definiens. Let the device "$\psi^\dagger$" (read "ψ-dagger) be a dummy which operates as follows: in some cases the phrase "that A should $\psi^\dagger$ that p" is to be interpreted as "that A should think U to ψ that p"; in other cases this phrase is to be interpreted as "that A should ψ that p (via thinking U to ψ that p)." Which interpretation is to be selected is determined by the specification of "$*_\psi$p." We may now reformulate D1 as follows:

D1′: "By (when) uttering x, U meant that $*_\psi$ p" = df. "($\exists$A) (U uttered x M-intending that A should $\psi^\dagger$ that p)."

To meet all the difficulties to which my earlier account (which was only intended as a model) is exposed, a very much more complicated definition is required. But as the examples which force the introduction of this complexity involve relatively sophisticated kinds of communication or linguistic performance, I hope that, for working purposes, the proffered definition will be adequate.

Stage III. Step (1): timeless meaning for unstructured utterance-types.

It is, I think, extremely important to distinguish two problems:

(1) What is the relation between timeless meaning (for complete utterance-types) and occasion-meaning?

(2) In the case of syntactically structured (linguistic) utterance-types, how is the timeless meaning of a complete (sentential) utterance-type related to the timeless meanings of its noncomplete structured and unstructured elements (approximately, phrases and words), and what account is to be given of timeless meaning for noncomplete utterance-types?

If we do not treat these problems separately, we shall have only ourselves to blame for the confusion in which we shall find ourselves. So initially I shall restrict myself to examining the notion of timeless meaning in its application to unstructured utterance-types. My main example will be a gesture (a signal), and it will be convenient first to consider the idea of its timeless meaning for an individual (within a signaling idiolect, so to speak), and only afterward to consider the extension of this idea to groups of individuals. We shall thus preserve for the time being the possibility of keeping distinct the ideas of having an *established* meaning and of having a *conventional* meaning.

Suppose that a particular sort of hand wave (to be referred to as

"HW") for a particular individual U (within U's idiolect) means "I know the route." We are to look for an explication of the sentence "For U, HW means 'I know the route'" which will relate timeless meaning to occasion-meaning. As a first shot, one might suggest something like "It is U's policy (practice, habit) to utter HW in order to *mean that* U knows the route" (where "mean that" is to be analyzed in accordance with D1); or more perspicuously, "It is U's policy (practice, habit) to utter HW if U is making an utterance by which U *means that* U knows the route."

If we apply D1 to this suggested definiens, we shall get the following expanded definiens: "It is U's policy (practice, habit) to utter HW if U is making an utterance by means of which (for some A) U M-intends to effect that A thinks U to think that U knows the route." Now, whether or not this definiens is otherwise acceptable, I wish to argue that the notion of M-intention is otiose here, and that only the notion of simple intention need be invoked; if U's policy (practice, habit) is such that his use of HW is tied to the presence of a *simple* intention to affect an audience in the way described, it will follow that when, on a given occasion, he utters HW, he will do so, on that occasion, M-intending to affect his audience in that way.

Suppose that, using only the notion of simple intention, we specify U's policy as follows: "I (that is, utterer U) shall utter HW if I intend (want) some A to think that I think I know the route." Now, if U is ever to have the particular intentions which will be involved in every implementation of this policy, he must (logically) be in a position, when uttering HW, to suppose that there is at least some chance that these intentions will be realized; for such a supposition to be justified, as U well knows, a given audience A must be aware of U's policy and must suppose it to apply to the utterance of HW with which U has presented him. U, then, when uttering HW on a particular occasion, must expect A to think (or at least to be in a position to think) as follows: "U's policy for HW is such that he utters HW now with the intention that I should think that he thinks that he knows the route; in that case, I take it that he does think that he knows the route." But to utter HW expecting A to respond in such a way *is* to utter HW M-intending that A should think that U thinks that U knows the route. So a formulation of U's policy of HW in terms of the notion of simple intention is adequate to ensure that, by a particular utterance of HW, U will *mean that* he knows the route.

We may, then, suggest a simplified definition: "For U, HW means

'I know the route'" = df. "It is U's policy (practice, habit) to utter HW if, for some A, U intends (wants) A to think that U thinks U knows the route." This definition, however, is doubly unacceptable. (1) For U, HW may have a second meaning; it may also mean "I am about to leave you." If that is so, U's policy (etc.) cannot be to utter HW *only if* U wants some A to think that U thinks U knows the route; sometimes he will be ready to utter HW wanting some A to think that U thinks that U is about to leave A. (2) U may have other ways of getting an A to think that U thinks that U knows the route (such as saying "I know the route") and may be ready, on occasion, to employ them. That being so, U's policy (etc.) cannot be to utter HW *if* (i.e. whenever) U wants A to think that U thinks U knows the route.

To cope with these difficulties, I think I need some such idea as that of "having a certain procedure in one's repertoire." This idea seems to me to be intuitively fairly intelligible and to have application outside the realm of linguistic, or otherwise communicative, performances, though it could hardly be denied that it requires further explication. A faintly eccentric lecturer might have in his repertoire the following procedure: if he sees an attractive girl in his audience, to pause for half a minute and then take a sedative. His having in his repertoire this procedure would not be incompatible with his also having two further procedures: (a) if he sees an attractive girl, to put on a pair of dark spectacles (instead of pausing and taking a sedative); (b) to pause and take a sedative when he sees in his audience not an attractive girl, but a particularly distinguished colleague. Somewhat similarly, if U has in his repertoire the procedure of uttering HW if he wants an audience A to think U thinks U knows the route, this fact would not be incompatible with his having at least two further procedures; (1) to say "I know the route" if he wants some A to think U thinks U knows the route, and (2) to utter HW if U wants some A to think U thinks he is about to leave A. So I propose the definition:

D2: "For U utterance-type X means (has as one of its meanings) '$*_\psi p$'" = df. "U has in his repertoire the following procedure: to utter a token of X if U intends (wants) A to $\psi^\dagger$ that p."

We may now turn from the idea of timeless meaning within an idiolect to that of timeless meaning for a group or class of individuals. If U utters HW, his measure of expectation of success as regards effecting the intended response obviously depends (as has already been remarked) on A's knowledge of U's procedure; and normally, unless the signal is to be explained to each A, on A's repertoire containing the same procedure. So obviously each member of some group G (within which HW is to be a tool of communication) will want his procedure with respect to HW to conform to the general practice of the group. So I suggest the following rough definition:

D3: "For group G, utterance-type X means '*$_\psi$p'" = df. "At least some (many) members of group G have in their repertoires the procedure of uttering a token of X if, for some A, they want A to ψ† that p, the retention of this procedure being for them conditional on the assumption that at least some (other) members of G have, or have had, this procedure in their repertoires."

D3 gets in the idea of aiming at conformity and so perhaps (derivatively) also that of *correct* and *incorrect* use of X, as distinct from the idea merely of usual or unusual use of X.

The explication of the notion of "having a procedure in one's repertoire" is, to my mind, a task of considerable difficulty. I have felt inclined to propose, as a makeshift definition, the following:

"U has in his repertoire the procedure of ..." = df. "U has a standing readiness (willingness, preparedness), in some degree, to ...," a readiness (etc.) to do something being a member of the same family (a weaker brother, so to speak) as an intention to do that thing.

But this definition would clearly be inadequate as it stands. It may well be true that, for my exceedingly prim Aunt Matilda, the expression "he is a runt" means "he is an undersized person," and yet quite false that she has *any* degree of readiness to utter the expression in any circumstances whatsoever. What one seems to need is the idea of her being *equipped* to use the expression, and the analysis of *this* idea is also problematic.

So for the present I shall abandon the attempt to provide a definition, and content myself with a few informal remarks. There seem to me to be three main types of case in which one may legitimately speak of an established procedure in respect of utterance-type X:

(1) That in which X is current for some group G; that is to say, to utter X in such-and-such circumstances is part of the practice of many members of G. In that case my Aunt Matilda (a member of G) may be said to have a procedure for X, even though she herself would rather be seen dead than utter X, for she knows that some other mem-

bers of G *do* have a readiness to utter X in such-and-such circumstances.

(2) That in which X is current only for U; it is only *U's* practice to utter X in such-and-such circumstances. In this case U *will* have a readiness to utter X in such-and-such circumstances.

(3) That in which X is not current at all, but the utterance of X in such-and-such circumstances is part of some system of communication which U has devised but which has never been put into operation (like the new highway code which I invent one day while lying in my bath). In that case U has a procedure for X in the attenuated sense that he has envisaged a possible system of practices which *would* involve a readiness to utter X in such-and-such circumstances.

Stage IV. Step (1): applied timeless meaning for unstructured utterance-types.

We are now in a position to define a notion of applied timeless meaning which will apply to HW:

D4: "When U uttered X (type), X meant '∗p'" = df. "(∃A) (U intended A to recognize [? and to recognize that U intended A to recognize] what U meant [occasion-meaning] by his uttering X, on the basis of A's knowledge [assumption] that, for U, X means [has as one of its meanings] '∗p' [as defined by D2]."

Or it can be more fully defined (let "∗" and "∗'" both be dummy mood-indicators):

D4': "When U uttered X, X meant '∗$_\psi$p'" = df. "(∃A) (∃q) (U meant by uttering X that ∗'q; and U intended A to recognize [? and to recognize that he was intended to recognize] that, by uttering X, U meant that ∗'q *via* A's knowledge [assumption] that in U's repertoire is the procedure of uttering X if, for some A', U wants A' to ψ^t that p)" ["p" may, or may not, represent that propositional content to which indefinite reference is made in the existential quantification of "q"].

D4 and of course D4' allow both for the case in which U meant by HW *that* he knew the route (coincidence of meaning "..." and meaning *that* ...), and also for the case in which, for example, U (a criminal) has lured a victim into his car and signals (non-literally, so to speak) to his accomplice that he knows how to handle the victim. In both cases it is expected by U that the audience's understanding of the utterance of HW will be based on its knowledge that U has a certain procedure (to utter HW if U wants an audience to think that U thinks U knows the route).

Stages III and IV. Step (2): timeless and applied timeless meaning for structured utterance-types, complete and noncomplete.

To deal with structured utterance-types and their elements, I think I need the following apparatus.

(1) Let "$S_1(S_2)$" (read "S_1-with-S_2") denote a sentence of which S_2 is a subsentence. Allow that a sentence is a subsentence of itself, so that S_2 may $= S_1$.

(2) Let $v[S_1(S_2)]$ (read "v-of-S_1-with-S_2") be a particular utterance (token) of $S_1(S_2)$ uttered by U. $v[S_1(S_2)]$ is to be a *complete* utterance; that is, it is not to be part of $v[S_3(S_1(S_2))]$ (not, for example, to be the utterance of a disjunct within the utterance of a disjunction).

(3) It is a characteristic of sentences (a characteristic shared with phrases) that their standard meaning is consequential upon the meaning of the elements (words, lexical items) which enter into them. So I need the notion of a "resultant procedure": as a first approximation, one might say that a procedure for an utterance-type X is a resultant procedure if it is determined by (its existence is inferrable from) a knowledge of procedures (1) for particular utterance-types which are elements in X, and (2) for any sequence of utterance-types which exemplifies a particular ordering of syntactical categories (a particular syntactical form).

Now let us deal with the notion of timeless meaning in U's idiolect:

D5: "For U, S means '$*_\psi$p'" = df. "U has a resultant procedure for S, namely to utter S if, for some A, U wants A to $\psi^\dagger$ that p" (D5 parallels D2).

An explication of timeless meaning in a language can, perhaps, be provided by adapting D3, but I shall not attempt this task now.

For applied timeless meaning I offer:

D6: "S_2 in $v[S_1(S_2)]$ meant '$*_\psi$p'" = df. "($\exists$A) ($\exists$q) (U meant by $v[S_1(S_2)]$ that $*$'q, and U intended A to recognize that U meant by $v[S_1(S_2)]$ that $*$'q at least partly on the basis of A's thought that U has a resultant procedure for S_2, namely (for suitable A') to utter S_2 if U wants A' to $\psi^\dagger$ that p)" (D6 parallels D4').

So far (maybe) so good. But the notion of "resultant procedure" has been left pretty unilluminated, and if we are to shed any light on the notion of word meaning, and its connection with "meaning that," we ought to look at the nature of the more fundamental procedures from which a resultant procedure descends. It would be nice to give a general schema, to show the role of word meanings (covering every type of word) in determining (in combination) sentence meanings (covering sentences of any syntactical structure). But this looks like a Herculean task (in our present state of knowledge). The best we can hope for is a sketch, for a very restricted (but central) range of word types and syntactical forms, of a fragment of what might be the kind of theory we need. Let us take as our range all or part of the range of affirmative categorical (not necessarily indicative) sentences involving a noun (or definite description) and an adjective (or adjectival phrase).

The apparatus needed (for one such attempt) would be:

(1) Suppose σ to be an indicative sentence. Then we need to be able to apply the ideas of an indicative version of σ (σ itself), an imperative version of σ, an optative version of σ, etc. (mood variations). It would be the business of some linguistic theory to equip us to apply such characterizations (so as philosophers of language we can assume this as given).

(2) We need to be able to apply some such notion as a predication of β (adjectival) on α (nominal). "Smith is tactful," "Smith, be tactful," "Let Smith be tactful," and "Oh, that Smith may be tactful" would be required to count, all of them, as predications of "tactful" on "Smith." It would again be the business of some linguistic theory to set up such a sentential characterization.

(3) Suppose we, for a moment, take for granted two species of correlation, R-correlation (referential) and D-correlation (denotational). We want to be able to speak of some particular object as an R-correlate of α (nominal), and of each member of some class as being a D-correlate of β (adjectival).

Now suppose that U has the following two procedures (P):

P1: To utter the indicative version of σ if (for some A) U wants/intends A to think that U thinks ... (the blank being filled by the infinitive version of σ, e.g. "Smith to be tactful"). Also, P1': obtained from P1 by substituting "imperative"/"indicative" and "intend"/"think that U thinks." (Such procedures set up correlations between moods and specifications of "$\psi^\dagger$.")

P2: To utter a $\psi^\dagger$-correlated (cf. P1 and P1′ predication of β on α if (for some A) U wants A to $\psi^\dagger$ a particular R-correlate of α to be one of a particular set of D-correlates of β.

Further suppose that, for U, the following two correlations hold:

C1: Jones's dog is an R-correlate of "Fido."
C2: Any hairy-coated thing is a D-correlate of "shaggy."

Given that U has the initial procedures P1 and P2, we can infer that U has the resultant procedure (determined by P1 and P2):

RP1: to utter the indicative version of a predication of β on α if U wants A to think U to think a particular R-correlate of α to be one of a particular set of D-correlates of β.

Given RP1 and C1, we can infer that U has:

RP2: To utter the indicative version of a predication of β on "Fido" if U wants A to think U to think Jones's dog to be one of a particular set of D-correlates of β.

Given RP2 and C2, we can infer that U has:

RP3: To utter the indicative version of a predication of "shaggy" on "Fido" if U wants A to think U to think Jones's dog is one of the set of hairy-coated things (i.e. is hairy-coated).

And given the information from the linguist that "Fido is shaggy" is the indicative version of a predication of "shaggy" on "Fido" (assumed), we can infer U to have:

RP4: To utter "Fido is shaggy" if U wants A to think U to think that Jones's dog is hairy-coated. And RP4 is an interpretant of "For U, 'Fido is shaggy' means 'Jones's dog is hairy-coated.'"

I have not yet provided an explication for statements of timeless meaning relating to noncomplete utterance-types. I am not in a position to provide a definiens for "X (noncomplete) means '...'" Indeed, I am not certain that a general form of definition *can* be provided for this schema; it may remain impossible to provide a definiens until the syntactical category of X has been given. I can, however, provide a definiens which may be adequate for *adjectival* X (e.g. "shaggy"):

D7: "For U, X (adjectival) means '...'" = df. "U has this procedure: to utter a $\psi^\dagger$-correlated predication of X on α if (for some A) U wants A to $\psi^\dagger$ a particular R-correlate of α to be ..." (where the two lacunae represented by dots are identically completed).

Any specific procedure of the form mentioned in the definiens of D7 can be shown to be a *resultant* procedure. For example, if U has P2 and also C2, it is inferable that he has the procedure of uttering a $\psi^\dagger$-correlated predication of "shaggy" on α if (for some A) U wants A to $\psi^\dagger$ a particular R-correlate of α to be one of the set of hairy-coated things, that is, that for U "shaggy" means "hairy-coated."

I can now offer a definition of the notion of a *complete* utterance-type which has so far been taken for granted:

D8: "X is complete" = df. "A fully expanded definiens for "X means '...'" contains no explicit reference to correlation, other than that involved in speaking of an R-correlate of some referring expression occurring within X." (The expanded definiens for the complete utterance-type "He is shaggy" may be expected to contain the phrase "a particular R-correlate of 'he.'")

Correlation. We must now stop taking for granted the notion of correlation. What does it mean to say that, for example, Jones's dog is the/an R-correlate of "Fido"? One idea (building in as little as possible) would be to think of "Fido" and Jones's dog as paired, in some system of pairing in which names and objects form ordered pairs. But in *one* sense of "pair," any one name and any one object form a pair (an ordered pair, the first member of which is the name, the second the object). We want a sense of "paired" in which "Fido" is paired with Jones's dog but not with Smith's cat. "Selected pair"? But what does "selected" mean? Not "selected" in the sense in which an apple and an orange may be selected from a dish: perhaps in the sense in which a dog may be selected (as something with which [to which] the selector intends to do something). But in the case of the word-thing pair, do what? And what is the process of selecting?

I suggest we consider initially the special case in which linguistic and nonlinguistic items are *explicitly* correlated. Let us take this to consist in performing some act as a result of which a linguistic item and a nonlinguistic item (or items) come to stand in a relation in which they did not previously stand, and in which neither stands to noncorrelates in the other realm. Since the act of correlation *may* be a verbal act, how can this set up a relation between items?

Suppose U produces a particular utterance (token) V, which belongs to the utterance-type "shaggy: hairy-coated things." To be able to say that U had by V correlated "shaggy" with each member of the set of hairy-coated things, we should need to be able to say that there is some relation R such that: (a) by uttering V, U effected that "shaggy" stood in R to each hairy-coated thing, and only to hairy-coated things; (b) uttered V *in order that,* by uttering V he should effect this. It is clear that condition (b), on which some will look askance because it introduces a reference to U's *intention* in performing his act of correlation, is required, and that condition (a) alone would be inadequate. Certainly by uttering V, regardless of his intentions, U has set up a situation in which a relation R holds exclusively between "shaggy" and each hairy-coated thing Z, namely the relation which consists in being an expression uttered by U on a particular occasion O in conversational juxtaposition with the name of a class to which Z belongs. But by the same act, U has also set up a situation in which another relation R' holds exclusively between "shaggy" and each *non*-hairy-coated thing Z', namely the relation which consists in being an expression uttered by U on occasion O in conversational juxtaposition with the name of the *complement* of a class to which Z' belongs. We do not, however, for our purposes, wish to think of U as having correlated "shaggy" with each non-hairy-coated thing. The only way to ensure that R' is eliminated is to add condition (b), which confines attention to a relationship which U *intends* to set up. It looks as if intensionality is embedded in the very foundations of the theory of language.

Let us, then, express more formally the proposed account of correlation. Suppose that V = utterance-token of type "'Shaggy': hairy-coated things" (written). Then, by uttering V, U has correlated "shaggy" with (and only with) each hairy-coated thing $\equiv (\exists R)$ {(U effected by V that $[\forall x]$ [R "shaggy" $x \equiv x \in y$ (y is a hairy-coated thing)]) and (U uttered V in order that U effect by V that $[\forall x]$ . . .)}.[1]

If so understood, U will have correlated "shaggy" with hairy-

1. The definiens suggested for explicit correlation is, I think, insufficient as it stands. I would not wish to say that if A deliberately detaches B from a party, he has thereby correlated himself with B, nor that a lecturer who ensures that just one blackboard is visible to each member of his audience (and to no one else) has thereby explicitly correlated the blackboard with each member of the audience, even though in each case the analogue of the suggested definiens is satisfied. To have explicitly correlated X with each member of a set K, not only must I have intentionally effected that a *particular* relation R holds between X and all those (and only those) items which belong to K, but also my purpose or end in setting up this relationship must have been to perform an act as a result of which *there will be some relation or other* which holds between X and all those (and only those) things which belong to K. To the definiens, then, we should add, within the scope of the initial quantifier, the following clause: "& U's purpose in effecting that $\forall x$ (......) is that $(\exists R')$ $(\forall z)$ (R' 'shaggy'$z \equiv z \in y$ (y is hairy-coated))."

coated things only if there is an identifiable R' for which the condition specified in the definiens holds. What is such an R'? I suggest $R'xy \equiv x$ is a (word) type such that V is a sequence consisting of a token of x followed by a colon followed by an expression ("hairy-coated things") the R-correlate of which is a set of which y is a member. $R'xy$ holds between "shaggy" and each hairy-coated thing given U's utterance of V. Any utterance V' of the form exemplified by V could be uttered to set up $R''xy$ (involving V' instead of V) between any expression and each member of any set of nonlinguistic items.

There are other ways of achieving the same effect. The purpose of making the utterance can be specified in the utterance: V = utterance of "To effect that, for some R, 'shaggy' has R only to each hairy-coated thing, 'shaggy': hairy-coated things." The expression of the specified R will now have "V is a sequence *containing*" instead of "V is a sequence *consisting of . . .* " Or U can use the performative form: "I correlate 'shaggy' with each hairy-coated thing." Utterance of this form will at the same time set up the required relation and label itself as being uttered with the purpose of setting up such a relation.

But by whichever form an act of explicit correlation is effected, to say of it that it is (or is intended to be) an act of correlation is always to make an indefinite reference to a relationship which the act is intended to set up, and the specification of the relation involved in turn always involves a further use of the notion of correlation (e.g. as above in speaking of a set which is the correlate [R-correlate] of a particular expression [e.g. "Hairy-coated things"]). This seems to involve a regress which might well be objectionable; though "correlation" is not used in definition of correlation, it is used in specification of an indefinite reference occurring in the definition of correlation. It might be considered desirable (even necessary) to find a way of stopping this regress at some stage. (Is this a characteristically *empiricist* demand?) If we don't stop it, can correlation even get started (if prior correlation is presupposed)? Let us try "ostensive" correlation. In an attempted ostensive correlation of the word "shaggy" with the property of hairy-coatedness:

(1) U will perform a number of acts in each of which he ostends an object (a_1, a_2, a_3, etc.).

(2) Simultaneously with each ostension he utters a token of the word "shaggy."

(3) It is his intention to ostend, and to be recognized as ostending,

only objects which are either, in his view, plainly hairy-coated or are, in his view, plainly not hairy-coated.

(4) In a model sequence these intentions are fulfilled. For a model sequence to succeed in correlating the word "shaggy" with the property of being hairy-coated, it seems necessary (and perhaps also sufficient) that there should be some relation R which holds between the word "shaggy" and each hairy-coated thing, y, just in case y is hairy-coated. Can such a relation R be specified? Perhaps at least in a sequence of model cases, in which U's linguistic intentions are rewarded by success, it can; the relation between the word "shaggy" and each hairy-coated object y would be the relation which holds between each plainly hairy-coated object y and the word "shaggy" and which consists in the fact that y is a thing to which U does and would apply, rather than refuse to apply, the word "shaggy." In other words in a limited universe consisting of things which in U's view are either plainly hairy-coated or plainly not hairy-coated, the relation R holds only between the word "shaggy" and each object which is for U plainly hairy-coated.

This suggestion seems not without its difficulties:

(1) It looks as if we should want to distinguish between two relations R and R'; we want U to set up a relation R which holds between the word "shaggy" and each hairy-coated object; but the preceding account seems not to distinguish between this relation and a relation R' which holds between the word "shaggy" and each object which is in U's view unmistakably hairy-coated. To put it another way, how is U to distinguish between "shaggy" (which means hairy-coated) and the word "shaggy"* (which means "in U's view unmistakably hairy-coated")?

(2) If in an attempt to evade these troubles we suppose the relation R to be one which holds between the word "shaggy" and each object to which U would in certain circumstances apply the word "shaggy," how do we specify the circumstances in question? If we suggest that the circumstances are those in which U is concerned to set up an explicit correlation between the word "shaggy" and each member of an appropriate set of objects, our proposal becomes at once unrealistic and problematic. Normally correlations seem to grow rather than to be created, and attempts to connect such growth with potentialities of creation may give rise to further threats of circularity.

The situation seems to be as follows:

(1) We need to be able to invoke such a resultant procedure as the following, which we will call RP12, namely to predicate β on "Fido," when U wants A to $\psi^\dagger$ that Jones's dog is a D-correlate of β; and we want to be able to say that at least sometimes such a resultant procedure may result from among other things, a *nonexplicit* R-correlation of "Fido" and Jones's dog.

(2) It is tempting to suggest that a nonexplicit R-correlation of "Fido" and Jones's dog *consists* in the fact that U *would,* explicitly, correlate "Fido" and Jones's dog.

(3) But to say that U would explicitly correlate "Fido" and Jones's dog must be understood as an elliptical way of saying something of the form "U would explicitly correlate 'Fido' and Jones's dog, *if p.*" How is "if p" to be specified?

(4) Perhaps as "If U were asked to give an explicit correlation for 'Fido.'" But if U were actually faced with a request, he might well take it that he is being asked to make a stipulation, in the making of which he would have an entirely free hand. If he is not being asked for a stipulation, then it must be imparted to him that his explicit correlation is to satisfy some nonarbitrary condition. But what condition can this be? Again it is tempting to suggest that he is to make his explicit correlation such as to match or fit existing procedures.

(5) In application to RP12, this seems to amount to imposing on U the demand that he should make his explicit correlation such as to yield RP12.

(6) In that case, RP12 results from a nonexplicit correlation which consists in the fact that U *would* explicitly correlate "Fido" and Jones's dog if he wanted to make an explicit correlation which would generate relevant existing procedures, namely RP12 itself. There is an apparent circularity here. Is this tolerable?

(7) It may be tolerable inasmuch as it may be a special case of a general phenomenon which arises in connection with the explanation of linguistic practice. We can, if we are lucky, identify "linguistic rules," so called, which are such that our linguistic practice is *as if* we accepted these rules and consciously followed them. But we want to say that this is not just an interesting fact about our linguistic practice but also an explanation of it; and this leads us on to suppose that "in some sense," "implicitly," we *do* accept these rules. Now the proper interpretation of the idea that we *do* accept these rules becomes something of a mystery, if the "acceptance" of the rules is to be distinguished from the existence of the related practices—but it seems like

a mystery which, for the time being at least, we have to swallow, while recognizing that it involves us in an as yet unsolved problem.

C. Concluding Note

It will hardly have escaped notice that my account of the cluster of notions connected with the term "meaning" has been studded with expressions for such intensional concepts as those of intending and believing, and my partial excursions into symbolic notation have been made partly with the idea of revealing my commitment to the legitimacy of quantifying over such items as propositions. I shall make two highly general remarks about this aspect of my procedure. First, I am not sympathetic toward any methodological policy which would restrict one from the start to an attempt to formulate a theory of meaning in extensional terms. It seems to me that one should at least *start* by giving oneself a free hand to make use of any intensional notions or devices which seem to be required in order to solve one's conceptual problems, at least at a certain level, in ways which (metaphysical bias apart) reason and intuition commend. If one denies oneself this freedom, one runs a serious risk of underestimating the richness and complexity of the conceptual field which one is investigating.

Second, I said at one point that intensionality seems to be embedded in the very foundations of the theory of language. Even if this appearance corresponds with reality, one is not, I suspect, precluded from being, in at least one important sense, an extensionalist. The psychological concepts which, in my view, are needed for the formulation of an adequate theory of language may not be among the most primitive or fundamental psychological concepts (like those which apply not only to human beings but also to quite lowly animals), and it may be possible to derive (in *some* relevant sense of "derive") the intensional concepts which I have been using from more primitive extensional concepts. Any extensionalist has to deal with the problem of allowing for a transition from an extensional to a nonextensional language; and it is by no means obvious to me that intensionality can be explained only via the idea of concealed references to language and so presupposes the concepts in terms of which the use of language has to be understood.

7

Some Models for Implicature

1. A Possible Charge of Circularity

Some have worried about circularity problems that might arise in an attempt to define timeless meaning ("mean$_t$") in terms of occasion meaning (here referred to as "mean$_s$").

(a) There is certainly no definitional circle. I have at least hinted at the possibility of defining "mean$_t$" in terms of "mean$_s$," but I have never regarded "mean$_s$" as potentially definable in terms of "mean$_t$"; indeed, in nonconventional communications, utterers mean$_s$ without any dependence on the meaning$_t$ of their utterances (which usually have no meaning$_t$).

(b) There is a possibility of "epistemic regress" (or circle). Suppose C to be a conventional ad hoc device (which will mean$_t$ something). Then the identification of what U means$_s$ by uttering C will require the identification of what C means$_t$. But if "C means$_t$ 'p'" = "people normally mean$_s$ by C that p," then to discover what C means$_t$ requires discovery of what individual utterers mean$_s$ on this or that occasion. But this in turn presupposes a knowledge of what C means$_t$. And so on.

This objection seems to hold *only* if it is supposed that "C means$_t$ 'p'" (if this = "people normally mean$_s$ by C that p") has to be established *inductively* from data consisting of facts to the effect that U meant$_s$ by C on occasion O that p (etc.), that is, data about the meaning$_s$ of particular utterances of C. But this supposition need not be made. One might even allow (without discussion) that "people normally mean$_s$ by C that p" is an inductive conclusion from data such as "U normally means$_s$ by C that p"; but what U normally means$_s$ by C need not (should not) be regarded as itself an inductive conclusion from the meaning$_s$ of individual utterances of C by U. What U normally means$_s$ by C could be (should be) a matter of U's disposition with regard to the employment of C, and this could be (should be) thought of as consisting of a *general intention* (readiness) on the part of U; U has the general intention to use C on particular occasions, to mean$_s$ that p. The existence of such a general intention is not (necessarily) inductively derived from its manifestations.

Nevertheless, I am not sure that it is desirable or correct to try to define "meaning$_t$" in terms of meaning$_s$ (understood in terms of M-intending), though I hope that it is correct to explicate "meaning$_t$" in terms of intending or intention (though not M-intention). My reason for rejecting the account of "means$_t$" in terms of "means$_s$" (M-intends) is that the special qualifications involved in the notion of M-intending seem to be otiose and do not seem to be required in the account of "means$_t$."

2. Two Models for Conversational Implicature

Let us, for a start, consider the language of perception, in which there will appear three different kinds of locution: (1) subperceptual locutions, like "it seems to X that the flowers are red"; (2) perceptual locutions, like "X perceives the flowers to be red"; and (3) factual locutions, like "the flowers are red." Of subperceptual locutions I wish to distinguish two versions, which I will call "unaccented" versions and "accented" versions. It is at least plausible to suggest (and I think that in Essay 15, "The Causal Theory of Perception," I did in fact suggest something very like it) that unaccented subperceptual locutions express one, but only one, of the truth conditions governing the corresponding perceptual locutions. The remainder of the list of truth conditions might be thought of as specified by the factual locution, together perhaps with the suggestion that it is the truth of the factual locution which accounts for the truth of the subperceptual locution. The truth of the statement that X perceives the flowers to be red would be derived from the truth of the statement that it seems to X that the flowers are red, that the flowers are red, and that the second fact explains the first. As thus conceived, the truth of the subperceptual locution in no way conflicts with any of the truth conditions for the related perceptual locution.

The situation is altered when we come to accented versions of a subperceptual locution. A subperceptual locution may be said to be accented when the verb "seem" which it contains displays any kind of highlighting or low-lighting, which distinguishes it from the general run of words in its environment. This would include, but would not be restricted to, such features as increased or decreased sound volume. The only constraint will be that the feature in question should be a natural feature, not a product of a communication of some kind to the effect that the occurrence of the word "seem" is distinctively marked. The presence of the distinctive feature is to be thought of as generating, not as being generated by, communication. Standardly the generated communication will be an informal one to the effect that the use of the word "seem" is well chosen in relation to that of some identifiable contrasting expression to which it is preferred. In the example on hand the identifiable contrasting expression is likely to be either the phrase "is perceived to be," which appears in the perceptual locution, or the word "are," which appears in the factual locution. The appearance of accent will introduce an implicature that the perceptual locution, or one of its other truth conditions—perhaps the factual condition—is false or is at least doubtful. An accented version will therefore undermine the noncommittal character of the corresponding unaccented version.

A structurally parallel situation arises when we turn from perceptual to cognitive examples. The unaccented "It seemed to X that the actor had forgotten his lines" is perhaps noncommittal on the question whether the actor had forgotten his lines and whether X did or did not know him to have done so.

First, distinguishing three cases of contrasting terms:

(1) Low subjective contrasters
(2) High subjective contrasters
(3) Objective contrasters

Examples of (1) could be "It seems to X that p," "X thinks that p," or "It looks to X as if p." Examples of (2) could be "X knows that p," "X sees that p," possibly "It is clear to X that p," or "It is apparent to X that p." In (3), whatever condition is expressed by "p," the objective contraster would be the sentence saying what p is.

Second, there is a standard, though possibly not universal, mode of connection between the three contrasters. Standardly the truth conditions for a High Subjective contraster lie in the truth of the related

Low Subjective contraster because of, or on account of, the fulfillment of the Objective contraster. Thus, the truth conditions for the statement that it is apparent to X that the actor had forgotten his lines would lie in its appearing to X that the actor had forgotten his lines because of, or on account of, the fact that the actor had indeed forgotten his lines.

Third, we may now consider the effect of the introduction of accenting. Accenting a Low Subjective contraster will informally claim justification for the speaker's restraint in not deploying the corresponding High Subjective contraster. So, saying with accent "I *know* that p" informally claims justification for not stopping short at "I think that p," and saying with accent "I *think* that p" claims justification for not going on to claim knowledge of p.

Fourth, the attribution of certainty will not tolerate inclusion in a context which withholds certainty from whatever it is that occurs in that context. If it is to be certain for X that p, then it must be the case that it is certain for X that it is certain for X that p, or at least that it should not be uncertain for X that it is certain for X that p.

If X has High Subjective contraster doubt feelings about the color of the flowers, then X cannot have an anterior presence of doubt about whether he has the aforementioned doubt feelings about the color of the flowers. The aforementioned doubt feelings will be unmistakably present or absent, but though the presence or absence of the feelings may be unmistakable the nature of the explanation of their presence or absence need not, it seems, be similarly unmistakable; there may be room for doubt whether the presence of doubt feelings does or does not depend on the color of the flowers. If that is so, then the admissibility of the presence or absence of High Subjective doubts about the flower color seems after all to go beyond the question of the actual presence or absence of such doubt feelings, and this goes against our supposition about the semantic relations between High Subjective and Low Subjective states. It looks as if the idea of a High Subjective state as consisting in a Low Subjective state which is explained in a certain kind of way may not, after all, be tenable.

The foregoing picture of the importation of implications or suggestions over and above the strictly asserted content of sentences used by a speaker—suggestions, that is, which would be generated by the introduction of accenting—will not, I fear, prove adequate for handling any supernumerary suggestions involved in claims about what words or word users mean, and, I suspect, a different model is needed. In the direction in which I have started, it will be desirable to distinguish two forms of paraphrase, the explicit introduction of which might be the source of misleading suggestions. The first form of paraphrase will be the supplementation of elliptical omissions. At this stage we shall encounter the expansion by paraphrase of statements about the meaning of words into statements about what words mean to word users or what word users mean by their words. At this stage it is notable that the word "mean" recurs in a supplemental setting. The second form of paraphrase involves a reductive analysis of the appearances of the verb "mean"; according to my theoretical suggestion, these appearances will be replaced by references to psychological states or attitudes. The primary difficulty for me about the second form of paraphrase is to decide how to handle specifications of thoughts on the assumption that thinking essentially involves the intelligible use of language and that the intelligibility of language in turn involves reference to underlying psychological attitudes on the part of those whose language it is. The presence of attitudes is supposed to involve the possibility of related thought episodes, the thought episodes will essentially involve the use of language; the language used will have to be intelligible; and its intelligibility will in turn involve a reference or related original stock of psychological attitudes. So thinking looks back to the intelligible use of language, which in turn rests on its connection with thinking, and this is a fairly short circle.

The solution to this seemingly knotty problem may perhaps lie in the idea that the psychological attitudes which, in line with my theory of meaning, attend the word flows of thought do so as causes and effects of the word flows in question, but not as *natural* causes and effects and so not as states that are manifested in psychological episodes or thoughts which are numerically distinct from word flows which set them off or arise from them; they are due or proper antecedents or consequences of the word flows in question and as such are legitimately deemed to be present in those roles; this is part of one's authority as a rational thinker to assign acceptable interpretations to one's own internal word flows. What they may be deemed to generate or arise from is ipso facto something which they do generate or arise from. The interpretation, therefore, of one's own verbally formulated thoughts is part of the privilege of a thinking being. The association of our word flows and our psychological attitudes is fixed by us as an outflow from our having learned to use our language for descriptive purposes to describe the world, so the attitudes which, when speaking spontaneously and yet nonarbitrarily, we assign as causes or effects of our word flows have to be accepted as properly occupying that position.

Part II

Explorations in Semantics and Metaphysics

8

Common Sense and Skepticism

In the earlier part of this essay, which is here omitted, I directed my attention to a number of issues raised by Moore's famous paper *A Defense of Common Sense*. First, I recapitulated a list of things which Moore claims to know with certainty with regard to himself, together with a further list of corresponding things which Moore claims to know that very many other people know with regard to themselves. Second, I noted various claims which Moore makes with respect to the propositions which figure in this alleged body of knowledge: that the acceptance of their truth does not have to await a determination of the meaning of the expressions which are used to report them; that the kind of knowledge he is claiming requires no mysterious faculties, but rests on the possibility of knowing things the evidence for which one no longer remembers; and that while Moore is defending Common Sense against the philosophers his claim is only that (the "Common Sense" view of the world is in *certain fundamental features* wholly true), it is not claimed that no Common Sense beliefs are vulnerable to philosophical attack. Third, I suggested that in Moore's view the prime sin committed by those who improperly question Common Sense would be that of questioning or denying things which they both in fact and, according to Moore, know with certainty to be true, a sin the authenticity of which depends crucially on Moore's claims to knowledge with certainty. Fourth, I distinguished two different varieties of skepticism concerning empirical propositions about material objects or about other minds, which for brevity I referred to merely as "empirical propositions." The first, which at the time of writing I was inclined to regard (I now suspect wrongly) as the less interesting and important variety of skepticism, holds that not merely is no empirical proposition ever known with certainty to be true, but no such proposition is ever known to be more probably true than false. I connected this version of skepticism with two different interpretations of Descartes's discussion in the First Meditation of the "Malignant Demon"; and I suggested (I now think overoptimistically), that on either interpretation Descartes's argument failed to establish this kind of skepticism even as an initial stumbling block clamoring to be removed by further metaphysical reflection. The second (and I thought then), the more interesting, variety of skepticism denies merely that any empirical proposition is ever known with certainty to be true but allows that the truth of such propositions may be a matter of the highest possible degree of probability. To this form of skepticism I considered a number of objections, some of them fairly well known. To six of these objections I sketched replies which I thought might leave the skeptics' position intact. My primary interest, however, was declared to lie in the final objection, to my mind the most serious and radical objection, which forms the topic of the segment of the essay which follows.

Final Objection. This objection is most clearly propounded by Malcolm.[1] The Skeptic, when he claims that neither he nor anyone else knows, for example, that there is cheese on the table, is in a very odd position. He is not suggesting that what appears to be cheese might just possibly turn out to be soap, nor that we have not looked to see whether the appearance might not be the effect of a conjuring trick performed with mirrors, nor even that though we have been quite careful to eliminate the possibility of error, we have not been quite careful enough, and if we went on a bit (or a lot) longer with our tests we should be better off and should be able finally to say "Now I know." The Skeptic will still refuse to admit that we can say correctly "I know" *however* long we continue with our test (and this goes not only for *there is cheese on the table* but for every other empirical proposition as well). Since, therefore, the accumulation of further evidence is irrelevant to the dispute between the Skeptic and his opponent, the Skeptic's thesis must be an *a priori* one, namely that to say that, for example "I know that there is cheese on the table" is to

---

1. In *The Philosophy of G. E. Moore*, ed. Schilpp; cf. also "Certainty and Empirical Statements," *Mind*, 1942.

assert (or try to assert) something self-contradictory or logically absurd.

But this contention on the part of the Skeptic, says Malcolm, itself involves a self-contradiction or logical absurdity (when taken in conjunction with something else which the Skeptic will have to admit). For the Skeptic will have to admit that "I know there is cheese on the table" is an *ordinary* expression, where by "ordinary expression" Malcolm means "an expression that has an ordinary use, i.e. an expression that is ordinarily used to describe a certain sort of situation" (an "ordinary expression" need not *in fact* ever be used—"there is a mermaid on the table" is an ordinary expression—but it must be such that it *would* be used to describe a certain sort of situation if that situation existed or were believed to exist). The Skeptic then will have to admit that "I know that there is cheese on the table" is in this sense an ordinary expression, and so, to remain a Skeptic, he will have to maintain that some ordinary expressions are self-contradictory or absurd. But this is itself an absurdity, since a self-contradictory expression is by definition one which would *never* be used to describe any situation whatever. If that is so, it is absurd to suggest that any expression is *both* self-contradictory *and* an ordinary expression. But this is just what the Skeptic is maintaining as regards "I know that there is cheese on the table."

(Some philosophers, paying a charitable tribute to the perspicacity of their Skeptical colleagues, have suggested that in view of the argument just stated, the latter cannot have been intending to deny the correctness of the "ordinary" use of the word "know," but must (very misleadingly) have been either (a) insisting on using the word "know" in a way of their own, or (b) suggesting a change in the existing usage. I do not think Skeptics would be very happy about either of these interpretations of their intentions.)

I shall now turn my attention to an attempt to construct a line of defense for the Skeptic against this very serious objection. I may at this point say, in order to forestall the possibility of snorts of disapproval from my audience that I am not myself a Skeptic; but I do think that the Skeptical position is liable to be somewhat cavalierly treated as hopeless.

The Skeptic might admit that in his view it is always an incorrect use of language to say "I know that there is cheese on the table," and he might also admit that it was the kind of incorrect use of language which is self-contradictory (plainly not all incorrect use of language involves a self-contradiction). He might also admit that in *some* sense of "ordinary use" no self-contradictory expression has an ordinary use and that in *some* sense of ordinary use such expressions as "I know that there is cheese on the table" do have an ordinary use. But he might go on to pose the question whether the senses of "ordinary use" just mentioned are the *same* sense.

Consider what I take to be Malcolm's definition of a self-contradictory expression, namely "an expression which would *never* be used to describe any situation" (he does not actually say that this is a complete definition of "self-contradictory expression," but equally he does not say that it is not, and I strongly suspect that he intends it as such, as indeed his manner of expression suggests). Is it really satisfactory as it stands? Take the expression "I'm not copperbottoming 'em, ma'am, I'm aluminiuming 'em, ma'am." I doubt very much if this expression would ever be used to describe any situation; it is too difficult to enunciate, and certainly no one would think of using it as a written symbol with a descriptive use (I of course am not using it descriptively). It would no doubt be possible to fill in the gaps in "The———archbishop fell down the———stairs and bumped——— ———like———," with such a combination of indecencies and blasphemies that no one would ever use such an expression. But in neither of these cases would we be tempted to describe the expressions as self-contradictory. Indeed, the number of possible reasons why an expression would in fact never be used might be, as far as I can see, in principle unlimited. Should we not then have to amend Malcolm's definition by adding a specification of the particular reason which would preclude the use of a self-contradictory expression? But if we did that should we not have to say "because to use it would be to say something self-contradictory"? But we are now defining "self-contradictory" in terms of itself.

But is it even true that self-contradictory expressions *are* never in fact used to describe any situation? No doubt if they are used to describe a situation, they do not *succeed* in describing that situation, but that is another matter. Might I not, as a result of miscalculation, say "there are eight lots here, each containing eight eggs; so there are sixty-two eggs." Malcolm perhaps would say that I would be, *in this case,* employing the expression "sixty-two" to mean what is normally meant by "sixty-four"; but such a suggestion would surely be most counterintuitive, and a well-constructed "catch-question," such as a vocal utterance of the words "can you write down 'there are two

ways of spelling————'?'" where the actual utterer substitutes for
————a sound represented by "throo," may elicit from a large number of persons the absurd answer "Yes."

If, then, the Skeptic is admitting that expressions such as "I know
that there is cheese on the table" have *in a sense* an ordinary use (in
that they are sometimes used descriptively), he might claim to be admitting nothing inconsistent with their being self-contradictory (i.e.
having no ordinary use in *some other* sense of "ordinary use"). But
he would have to admit not merely that such expressions are sometimes used to describe certain kinds of situations but that they are
very frequently indeed used to describe such situations. The question
remains then "Is it logically possible for it to be true that most people
would usually, or more often than not, use an expression 'p' to describe a certain kind of situation, and yet be false that 'p' is a correct
description of that situation (or perhaps of *any* situation, in which
case it would be self-contradictory)?" The Skeptic would have to
maintain that it is. An imaginary illustration may illuminate the path
we might take.

Suppose a state of society in which our linguistic behavior were
such that all of us, on most occasions when we wished to describe a
situation involving a rose, used expressions such as "that is a cauliflower" (or other suitable expressions containing the word "cauliflower"); and all of us on all occasions also used expressions containing the word "cauliflower" to describe cauliflower situations.
Suppose, however, also that on all those occasions when we had before our minds the thought *both* of a rose *and* a cauliflower (for example, when our attention was drawn to our practice of using the
word "cauliflower" in descriptions both of rose situations and cauliflower situations), we then called a rose "a rose" and refused to call
it "a cauliflower" and insisted that on all the occasions when we had
called "a rose" "a cauliflower" we had been wrong. In such a state of
society would the word "cauliflower" be a correct expression to use
to refer to a rose? Should we say, confronted with such linguistic behavior, (1) that "cauliflower" would be a correct expression to use to
refer to a rose (that is, that "cauliflower" would be ambiguous and
would in one sense apply to roses and in another apply to cauliflowers; or (2) that the question is undecidable, that we would not know
whether to say that it would be correct or to say that it would be
incorrect to apply the expression "cauliflower" to roses (that is, that
the situation would fall within the margin of vagueness between

"being correct" and "being incorrect"); or (3) that we are uncertain about this question, but are somewhat inclined to alternative (2)?

Now the Skeptic, I think, may be maintaining that something like this is the case with regard to the common use of the word "know." We all frequently do apply the word "know" to empirical propositions (just as in the imaginary example we in fact call roses "cauliflowers"); but the Skeptic would claim that for every situation to describe which we are inclined to use the expression "I know p" (where p is an empirical proposition) he could produce some proposition q (in his notorious arguments for example, q might be *I may be dreaming*) such that (1) we should admit that q is logically incompatible with *I know p*, and (2) we should deny *I know p* rather than deny q. In other words he could produce arguments to show that if we reflected adequately, we should always correct our application of the word "know" to empirical propositions.

Assume for the moment that the Skeptic is right in his ability to produce arguments to show that we should so correct our use of the word "know." How in that case do we stand? (1) If answer (1) to the "cauliflower" problem is right (namely that "cauliflower" would be a correct expression to use to refer to a rose), then, presumably, however good the Skeptic's arguments to show that on reflection we should abandon our application of the word "know" to empirical propositions, the Skeptic will be entirely wrong and his opponent entirely right. (2) If answer (2) to the "cauliflower" problem is right (namely the question is undecidable), then presumably the Skeptic will be right insofar as he denies his opponent's thesis that it is *definitely* correct to apply the word "know" to empirical propositions, and will be wrong insofar as he himself asserts that it is *definitely* incorrect to do so. (3) If answer (3) to the "cauliflower" problem is right (namely that "cauliflower" would not be a correct expression to apply to roses), then presumably the Skeptic would be entirely right and his opponent entirely wrong.

I shall conclude by just listing some possible arguments which the Skeptic might use in defense of this thesis (which I have put into his mouth) that we should on reflection abandon our use of expressions such as "I know p" (where p is an empirical proposition). I am doubtful if any of them will work (and we should of course remember that the traditional Skeptical arguments turning on the use of the phrase "it is always possible that" have already been exploded); but I do not have time to consider them in detail.

(a) The Skeptic might argue as follows: If it is to be true that I know an empirical proposition p to be true, it must also be true that I have conclusive evidence for p. But we cannot say without self-contradiction "I had conclusive evidence for p but p was false," whereas if p is an empirical proposition, we can always say without self-contradiction "the evidential propositions which support p are true, but p is false." Since therefore (the Skeptic might say) we shall have to admit that the evidence for an empirical proposition is never conclusive, we shall have to correct our use of the word "know."

(b) He might argue: "If it is proper for me to say 'I know that there is cheese on the table,' I shall have to claim (if I am asked) to know that future observations on the part of myself and of others will not render the proposition *there is cheese on the table* doubtful." But we are reluctant under pressure to make such claims to knowledge of propositions about the future.

(c) He might note that it seems very odd to say "I know p but I might have had better evidence for p than I do in fact have," but if p is an empirical proposition (the Skeptic would say), I shall have to admit this odd statement as being true.

(d) For it to be true (the Skeptic might say) that I know that s is p (where *s is p* is an empirical proposition), it would have to be true that I know that no one has ever had as good evidence for some other proposition, say s_1 *is p* as I have for *s is p,* and yet have been wrong in asserting s_1 *is p*. If I cannot claim this, someone may say "What is the difference between your evidence for *s is p* and some other person's evidence for s_1 *is p* which entitles you to claim that you know that s is p and yet admit that *he* may not have known that s_1 is p?" I think this would be a difficult question to answer (or rather avoid answering). Now take the proposition *I have a body* (not obviously amenable to Skeptical treatment). Do I know that no disembodied spirit has ever had as good evidence for the proposition that it (or he) has a body as I now have for the proposition that I have a body? To know this, either I must claim to know that there are no disembodied spirits, or I must claim that even if there are disembodied spirits, none of them has ever been systematically deceived in such a way as to have all the sensations (etc.) which provide evidence for the existence of one's own body, though he (it) in fact has no body. Am I prepared to say that I know one or the other of these things?"

9

G. E. Moore and
Philosopher's Paradoxes

I shall begin by discussing two linked parts of Moore's philosophy, one of which is his method of dealing with certain philosophical paradoxes, the other his attitude toward Common Sense. These are particularly characteristic elements in Moore's thought and have exerted great influence upon, and yet at the same time perplexed other British philosophers. Later in this paper I shall pass from explicit discussion of Moore's views to a consideration of ways of treating philosophical paradoxes which might properly be deemed to be either interpretations or developments of Moore's own position.

First, Moore's way of dealing with philosopher's paradoxes. By "philosopher's paradoxes" I mean (roughly) the kind of philosophical utterances which a layman might be expected to find at first absurd, shocking, and repugnant. Malcolm[1] gives a number of examples of such paradoxes and in each case specifies the kind of reason or proof which he thinks Moore would offer to justify his rejection of these paradoxical statements; Moore, moreover, in his "Reply to my Critics" in the same volume, gives his approval, with one qualification, to Malcolm's procedure. I quote three of Malcolm's examples, together with Moore's supposed replies:

Example 1
Philosopher: "There are no material things."
Moore: "You are certainly wrong, for here's one hand and here's another; and so there are at least two material things."

1. Malcolm, "Moore and Ordinary Language," in *The Philosophy of G. E. Moore*, ed. Schlipp.

Example 2
Philosopher: "Time is unreal."
Moore: "If you mean that no event can follow or precede another event, you are certainly wrong: for after lunch I went for a walk, and after that I took a bath, and after that I had tea."

Example 3
Philosopher: "We do not know for certain the truth of any statement about material things."
Moore: "Both of us know for certain that there are several chairs in this room, and how absurd it would be to suggest that we do not know it, but only believe it, and that perhaps it is not the case!"

Example 1 is an abbreviated version of perhaps the most famous application of Moore's technique (for dealing with paradoxes), that contained in his British Academy lecture "Proof of an External World." There he makes what amounts to the claim that the reply in Example 1 contains a rigorous proof of the existence of material things; for it fulfills the three conditions he lays down as being required of a rigorous proof: (a) its premise ("here's one hand and here's another") is different from the conclusion ("there are at least two material things"); (b) the speaker (Moore), at the time of speaking, knows for certain that the premise is true; and (c) the conclusion follows from the premise. Moore of course would have admitted that condition (c) is fulfilled only if "there are material things" is given one particular possible interpretation; he is aware that some philosophers, in denying the existence of material things, have not meant to deny, for example, that Moore has two hands; but he claims (quite rightly, I think) that the sentence "material things do not exist" has sometimes been used by philosophers to say something incompatible with its being true to say that Moore has two hands.

Now the technique embodied in the examples I have just quoted is sometimes regarded as being an appeal to Common Sense. Though it may, no doubt, be correctly so regarded in some sense of "Common Sense," I am quite sure that it is not an appeal to Common Sense as *Moore* uses the expression "Common Sense." In "A Defense of Common Sense"[2] Moore claims to know for certain the truth of a range of propositions about himself, similar in character to those asserted in the replies contained in my three examples, except that the propo-

2. *Contemporary British Philosophy,* vol. 2.

sitions mentioned in the article are less specific than those asserted in the replies; and he further claims to know for certain that very many other persons have known for certain propositions about themselves corresponding to these propositions about himself. It is true that Moore rejects certain philosopher's paradoxes because they conflict with some of the propositions which Moore claims to know with certainty, and it is further true that Moore describes his position, in general terms, as being "that the 'Common Sense view of the world' is, in certain fundamental features, wholly true." But it is also clear that when Moore talks about Common Sense, he is thinking of a set of very generally accepted beliefs, and, for him, to "go against Common Sense" would be to contradict one or more of the members of this set of beliefs. Two points are here relevant. (1) Most of the propositions which serve as the premises of Moore's disproofs of paradoxical views are not themselves propositions of Common Sense (objects of Common Sense belief), for they are, standardly, propositions about individual people and things (e.g. Moore and hands), and obviously too few people have heard of Moore for there to be any *very* generally accepted beliefs about him. Of course, Moore's premises may justify some Common Sense beliefs, but that is not the point here. (2) In any case, it is quite clear that for Moore there is nothing sacrosanct about Common Sense beliefs as such; in the Defense he says (p. 207), "for all I know, there may be many propositions which may be properly called features in 'the Common Sense view of the world' or 'Common Sense belief' which are not true, and which deserve to be mentioned with the contempt with which some philosophers speak of 'Common Sense beliefs.'" And in *Some Main Problems* he cites propositions which were once, but have since ceased to be, Common Sense beliefs, and are now rejected altogether. So, if to describe Moore's technique as an appeal to Common Sense is to imply that in his view philosopher's paradoxes are to be rejected *because* they violate Common Sense (in Moore's sense of the term), then such a description is quite incorrect (it is, I think, fair to maintain that Moore's use of the term "Common Sense" is not the ordinary one, in which a person who lacks Common Sense is someone who is silly or absurd; and this suggests a sense in which Moore does "appeal to Common Sense" in dealing with paradoxes, for he does often say or imply that the adoption of a paradoxical view commits one to some absurdity).

Now it is time to turn to the perplexity which Moore's technique has engendered. A quite common reaction to Moore's way with paradoxes has, I think, been to feel that it really can't be as easy as that, that Moore counters philosophical theses with what amounts to just a blunt denial, and that his "disproofs" fail therefore to carry conviction. As Malcolm observes, we tend to feel that the question has been begged, that a philosopher who denies that there are material objects is well aware that he is committed to denying the truth of such propositions as that Moore has two hands and so cannot be expected to accept the premise of Moore's proof of an external world. For Moore's technique to convince a philosophical rival, something more would have to be said about the *point* of Moore's characteristic maneuver; some account will have to be given of the nature of the absurdity to which a philosophical paradox allegedly commits its propounder. Malcolm himself (loc. cit.) argues that such an account can be given; he represents Moore's technique as being a (concealed) way of showing that philosophical paradoxes "go against ordinary language" (say or imply that such ordinary expressions are absurd or meaningless), and argues that to do this is to commit an absurdity, indeed to involve oneself in contradiction. I shall enter into the details of this thesis later; at the moment I am only concerned with the question how far Moore's own work can properly be understood on the general lines which Malcolm suggests. I must confess it seems very doubtful to me whether it can. (1) Moore in his "Reply to My Critics" neither accepts nor rejects Malcolm's suggestion; indeed he does not mention it, and it very much looks as if Malcolm's idea was quite new to him, and one which he needed time to consider. (2) Moore (loc. cit.) makes a distinction (in effect) between my Example 1 and my Example 3 (this is the qualification I mentioned earlier). He allows that one can *prove* that material objects exist by holding up one's hands and saying "Here is one hand and here is another"; but he does not allow that one can *prove* that one sometimes knows for certain the truth of statements about material things from such a premise as "Both of us know for certain that there are chairs in this room." In his view, to say "We know for certain that there are chairs in this room, so sometimes one knows for certain the truth of propositions about material things" is to give not a "proof" but a "good argument" in favor of knowledge about material things; it is a good argument but (he says) some further argument is called for, and in this case the need for further argument is said to be connected with the fact that many more philosophers have asserted that *nobody knows* that there are material things than have said that there are no material things. Now I find it very difficult to see how Moore can successfully maintain that Example 1 gives a proof of the existence of material things and yet that Example 3 does not give a proof of our knowledge of material things. (Can he deny that his three requirements for a rigorous proof are satisfied in this case?) But this is not the point I am concerned with here. What I wish to suggest is that for Moore's technique to be properly represented as being in all cases a concealed appeal to ordinary language, he would surely have had to have treated Example 1 and Example 3 alike, for the denial of knowledge about material things does not go against ordinary language any less than the denial of the existence of material things. It might well be, of course, that no satisfactory and comprehensive account can be given of Moore's procedure, and that an account in terms of the appeal to ordinary language fits what he is doing most of the time, and so perhaps shows what he was (more or less unconsciously) getting at or feeling after. But to say this is different from saying outright that the applications of his technique are appeals to ordinary language.

One or two passages in *Some Main Problems in Philosophy* indicate a different (or at any rate apparently different) procedure. I shall try to present, in connection with a particular example, a somewhat free version of the position suggested by the passages I have in mind. Some philosophers have advanced the (paradoxical) thesis that we never know for certain that any inductive generalization is true, that inductive generalizations can at best be only probably true. Their acceptance of this thesis will be found to rest on a principle, in this case maybe some such principle as that for a proposition to be known with certainty to be true, it must either be a necessary truth or a matter of "direct experience" (in some sense) or be logically derivable from propositions of one or the other of the first two kinds. But inductive generalizations do not fall under any of these heads, so they cannot be known with certainty to be true. The sort of maneuver Moore would make in response to such a thesis (e.g. "But of course we know for certain that the offspring of two human beings is always another human being") might be represented as having the following force: "The principle on which your thesis depends is not self-evident, that is, it requires some justification; and since it is *general* in form, its acceptability will have to depend on consideration of the particular cases to which it applies; that is, the principle that all knowledge is of certain specified kinds will be refuted if there can be found a case of knowledge which is *not* of any of the specified kinds, and will be confirmed if after suitably careful consideration, no such counter-example is forthcoming. But I have just produced a counterexample, a case of knowledge which is not of any of the specified kinds, and which, furthermore, is an inductive generalization. You cannot, without cheating, *use* the principle to discredit my counterexample, i.e. to argue that my specimen is not really a case of knowledge; if the principle depends on consideration of the character of the particular cases of knowledge, then it cannot be invoked to ensure that apparent counterexamples are not after all to be counted as cases of knowledge. If you are to discredit my counterexample it must be by some other method, and there is no other method." This line of attack could, of course, be applied mutatis mutandis, to other paradoxical philosophical theses.

I have a good deal of sympathy with the idea I have just outlined; in particular, it seems to me to bring out the way in which, primarily at least, I think philosophical theses should be tested, namely by the search for counterexamples. Moreover, I think it might prove effective, in some cases, against the upholders of paradoxes. But I doubt whether a really determined paradox-propounder would be satisfied. He might reply: "I agree that my principle that all knowledge is of one or another specified kind is not self-evident, but I do not have to justify it by the method you suggest, that of looking for possible counterexamples. I can justify it by a careful consideration of the nature of knowledge, and of the relation between knowledge and other linked concepts. Since I can do this, I can, without begging the question, use my principle to discredit your supposed counterexamples." The paradox-propounder might seek also to turn the tables on his opponent by adding, "You, too, are operating with a philosophical principle, namely a principle about how philosophical theses are to be tested; but the acceptability of your principle, too, will (in your view) have to depend on whether or not my own thesis about knowledge constitutes a counterexample; and to determine this question, you will have to investigate independently of your principle the legitimacy of the grounds upon which I rely." To meet this reply, I would have to anticipate the latter part of my paper; and in any case I suspect that in meeting it, I should exhibit the rationale of Moore's procedure as being after all only a particular version of the "appeal to ordinary language." So I shall pass on to discuss the efficacy of this way of dealing with paradoxes, without explicit reference to Moore's work.

I can distinguish two different types of procedure in the face of a philosopher's paradox, each of which might count as being, in some sense, an appeal to ordinary language. Procedure 1 would seek to refute or dispose of paradoxes without taking into account what the paradox-propounders would say in elaboration or defense of their theses; these theses would simply be rebutted by the charge that they went against ordinary language, and this would be held sufficient to show the theses to be untenable, though of course a philosopher might well be required to do more than merely show the theses to be untenable. Procedure 2, on the other hand, would take into account what the paradox-propounder would say, or could be forced to say, in support of his thesis, and would aim at finding some common and at the same time objectionable feature in the positions of those who advance such paradoxes. Procedure 2, unlike Procedure 1, would not involve the claim that the fact that a thesis "went against" ordinary language was, by itself, sufficient to condemn it; I propose now to consider two versions of Procedure 1, to argue that at least as they stand, they are not adequate to silence a wide-awake opponent, or even to extract from him the reaction, "I see that you must be right, and yet . . . ," and finally to consider Procedure 2.

My first version is drawn from Malcolm. In the form in which I state it, this procedure applies only against nonempirically based paradoxes; indeed, Malcolm does not make any distinction between different types of paradox and in effect seems to treat all philosophical paradoxes as if they were of the nonempirically based kind. The kernel of Malcolm's position seems to be as follows. The propounder of a paradox is committed to holding that the ordinary use of certain expressions (e.g. "Decapitation was the cause of Charles I's death") is (a) incorrect and (b) self-contradictory or absurd. But this contention is itself self-contradictory or absurd. For if an expression is an ordinary expression, that is, "has an ordinary (or accepted) use"— that is to say, if it is an expression which "would be used to describe situations of a certain sort if such situations existed or were believed to exist"—then it cannot be self-contradictory (or absurd). For a self-contradictory expression is one which would never be used to describe any situation, and so has *no* descriptive use. Moreover, if an expression which *would* be used to describe situations of a certain sort (etc.) is in fact on a given occasion used to describe that sort of situation, then it is on that occasion correctly used, for correct use is just standard use. It will be seen that Malcolm's charge against the paradoxes is, that they go against ordinary language not by misdescribing its use (to do that would be merely to utter falsehoods, not absurdities) nor by misusing it (that would be merely eccentric or misleading) nor by ill-advisedly proposing to change it (that would be merely giving bad advice), but by *flouting* it, that is, admitting a use of language to be ordinary and yet calling it incorrect or absurd. Furthermore, it will be seen that he attempts to substantiate his charge by consideration of what he takes to be the interrelation between the concepts of (a) ordinary use, (b) self-contradiction, and (c) correctness.

This version of Procedure 1 has three difficulties:

(1) The word "would," as it occurs in the phrase "expression which would be used to describe situations of a certain sort, if such situations existed or were believed to exist," seems to me to give rise to some trouble. The phrase I have just quoted might be taken as roughly equivalent to "expression which, given that a certain sort of situation had to be described, would be used." But this cannot be what Malcolm means; it is just not true that always or usually, when called upon to describe such a situation as a man's having lost his money, one would say "he has become a pauper." There are all sorts of things one would be more likely to say; yet presumably "he has become a pauper" is to be counted as an ordinary expression. It would be clearer perhaps to substitute, for the quoted phrase, the phrase "expression of which it would not be true to say that it would not be used to describe . . ." or more shortly "expression which *might be* used to describe . . ." Let us then take the original phrase in this sense. Now what about the sentence "Sometimes the ordinary use of language is incorrect" (which Malcolm says is self-contradictory)? This sentence (or some other sentence to the same effect) no doubt has been uttered seriously by paradox-propounders, and it might well seem that they *have* used it to describe the situation they believed to obtain with regard to the use of ordinary language. Does it not then follow that this sentence is one of which it is untrue to say that it would *not* be used to describe a certain sort of situation, or more simply, that this sentence is one which might be used to describe a certain sort of situation; that is, the sentence is *not* self-contradictory? If we can combine "has been used to describe" with "would not be used to describe" (and perhaps we can), then, at least, the sense of "would not be used" seems to demand scrutiny. I suspect, however, that Malcolm himself would not admit the legitimacy of the combi-

nation. He would rather say that the sentence in question has been uttered seriously, even perhaps has been "used," but has not been used to describe a certain sort of situation (just because it commits an absurdity); and so there is no difficulty in going on to say that it would not be used to describe any sort of situation, that is, is self-contradictory (and so nonordinary). This points the way to what seems to me a fundamental difficulty.

(2) I think Malcolm's opponent might legitimately complain that the question has been begged against him. For he might well admit that the expressions of which he complains are ordinary expressions, and even that they would be used to describe certain sorts of situation which the speaker believed to exist, but go on to say that the situations in question are (logically) impossible. This being so, the expressions are both ordinary *and* absurd. If he is ready in the first place to claim that an ordinary expression may be absurd, why should he jib at saying that an ordinary expression may be used to describe an *impossible* situation which the speaker mistakenly believes to exist? Malcolm's argument can be made to work only if we assume that no situation which a sentence would ordinarily be used to describe would be an impossible situation, and to assume this is to assume the falsity of the paradox-propounder's position.

Alternatively, the paradox-propounder might agree that an ordinary expression of the kind which he is assailing (e.g. "Decapitation was the cause of Charles I's death") would be used to describe such a situation as that actually obtaining at Charles I's death (i.e., it would be used to describe an *actual* situation and not merely an *impossible* situation); but then he might add that the user of such an expression would not *merely* be describing this situation but also be committing himself to an absurd gloss on the situation (e.g. that Charles's decapitation willed his death), or again (much the same thing) that the user would indeed be merely describing this situation, but would be doing so in terms which committed him to an absurdity. And to meet this rejoinder by redefinition would again be to beg the question in Malcolm's favor.

The paradox-propounder might even concede that an expression which would be used to describe a certain sort of situation would be correctly used to describe a situation of that sort, provided that all that is implied is that it is common form to use this expression in this sort of situation; but nevertheless maintaining that the correctness of use (in this sense) would not guarantee freedom from contradiction or absurdity.

Put summarily, my main point is that *either* Malcolm must allow that, in order to satisfy ourselves that an expression is "ordinary," we must first satisfy ourselves that it is free from absurdity (in which case it is not yet established that such an expression as "Decapitation caused Charles I's death" *is* an ordinary one), or he must use the word "ordinary" in such a way that the sentence I have just mentioned is undoubtedly an ordinary expression, in which case the link between being ordinary and being free from absurdity is open to question.

(3) Is it in fact true that an ordinary use of language cannot be self-contradictory, unless the "ordinary use of language" is *defined* by stipulation as non-self-contradictory, in which case, of course, Malcolm's version of the appeal to ordinary language becomes useless against the philosopher's paradox? The following examples would seem to involve nothing but an ordinary use of language by any standard but that of freedom from absurdity. They are not, so far as I can see, technical, philosophical, poetic, figurative, or strained; they are examples of the sorts of things which have been said and meant by numbers of actual persons. Yet each is open, I think, at least to the suspicion of self-contradictoriness, absurdity, or some other kind of meaninglessness. And in this context suspicion is perhaps all one needs.

(a) "He is a lucky person" ("lucky" being understood as dispositional). This might on occasion turn out to be a way of saying "He is a person to whom what is unlikely to happen is likely to happen."

(b) "Departed spirits walk along this road on their way to Paradise" (it being understood that departed spirits are supposed to be bodiless and imperceptible).

(c) "I wish that I had been Napoleon" (which does not mean the same as "I wish I were like Napoleon"). "I wish that I had lived not in the XXth century but in the XVIIIth century."

(d) "As far as I know, there are infinitely many stars."

Of course, I do not wish to suggest that these examples are likely in the end to prove of much assistance to the propounder of paradoxes. All I wish to suggest is that the principle "The ordinary use of language cannot be absurd" is either trivial or needs justification.

Another, possibly less ambitious version of Procedure 1 might be represented as being roughly as follows. Every paradox comes down to the claim that a certain word or phrase (or type of word or phrase) cannot without linguistic impropriety or absurdity be incorporated (in a specified way) in a certain sort of sentence T. For example, bearing in mind Berkeley, one might object to the appearance of the word "cause" as the main verb in an affirmative sentence the subject of which refers to some entity other than a spirit. The paradox-propounder will however have to admit that, if we were called on to explain the use of W to someone who was ignorant of it, we should not in fact hesitate to select certain exemplary sentences of type T which incorporated W, and indicate ostensively or by description typical sorts of circumstances in which such sentences would express truths. Now if it be admitted that such a mode of explanation of W's use is one we should naturally adopt, then it must also be admitted that it is a proper mode of explanation; and if it is a proper mode of explanation, how can a speaker who uses such an exemplary sentence, believing the prevailing circumstances to be of the typical kind, be guilty of linguistic impropriety or absurdity? You cannot obey the rules, and yet not obey them.

The paradox-propounder's reply might run on some such lines as these. If it were true that we always supposed the typical sorts of circumstances, to which reference is made in such an explanation of the meaning of a word, to be as they really are, and as observation or experience would entitle us to suppose, then the paradox would fall. But it may be that in the case of some words (such as possibly "cause") for some reason (perhaps because of a Hume-like natural disposition) we have a tendency to read more into the indicated typical situation than is really there, or than observation would entitle us to suppose to be there. Furthermore, the addition we make may be an absurdity. For instance, we might have a tendency to read into what the common sense philosopher would regard as typical causal transactions between natural objects or events the mistaken and absurd idea that something is *willing* something else to happen. If we do do this (and how is it shown that we do not?), then even though we use the word "cause" in just the kinds of situations indicated by model explanations of the word's meaning, we shall still have imported into our use of the word "cause" an implication which will make objectionable the application of the word to natural events. Whenever we so apply the word "cause," what we say will imply an absurdity.

Let us ask how a philosophical paradox is standardly supported. One standard procedure (and this is the only one I shall consider, though there may be other quite different methods) is to produce one or more alleged entailments or equivalences which, if accepted, would commit one to the paradox. For example, the philosopher who maintains that only spirits can be causes might try to persuade us as follows: if there is a cause, then there is action; if there is action, then there is an agent; if there is an agent, then there is a spirit at work; and there we are. This particular string of alleged entailments is not perhaps very appetizing, but obviously in other cases something more alluring can be provided. Now if we ask how the propounder of the paradox supposes it to be determined whether or not his entailments or equivalences hold, we obviously cannot reply that the question is to be decided in the light of the circumstances in which we apply the terms involved, for it is obvious that we do not restrict our application of the word "cause" to spirits, and if we did, then all suspicion of paradox would disappear. The paradox-propounder seemingly must attach special weight to what we say, or what we can be got to say, about the meaning or implication of such a word as "cause." In effect he asks us what we mean by "cause" or "know" (giving us some help) and then insists that our answers show what we *do* mean.

Leaving on one side for the moment the question why he does this and with what justification, let us consider the fact that the interpretation which he gives of such a word as "mean" seems to differ from the interpretation of that word which would be given by his opponent. To differentiate between the two interpretations, let us use "mean$_1$," as a label for the sense that the paradox-propounder attributes to the word "mean" (in which what a man says he means by a word is paramount in determining what he in fact does mean), and let us use "mean$_2$," as a label for the sense which the opponent of the paradox-propounder would attribute to the word "mean" (in which what a man means is, roughly speaking, determined by the way in which he applies the word). The paradox-propounder would say "'Cause' means (that is, means$_1$) so and so," and his opponent would say "'Cause' means (that is, means$_2$) such and such." Now it seems that the dispute between them cannot be settled without settling the divergence between them with regard to the word "mean." Can this divergence be settled? It seems to be difficult, for if the paradox-propounder claims that "mean" means (that is, "mean$_1$") and his opponent claims that "mean" means (that is, "mean$_2$"), then we seem to have reached an impasse. And it is likely that this would in fact be the situation between them.

But then we might reflect that the dispute between them, in becoming unsettlable, has evaporated. For the paradox-propounder is going to say "Certain ordinary utterances are absurd because what (in certain circumstances) we say that we mean by them is absurd, but these can be replaced by harmless utterances which eradicate this absurdity, and the job of philosophical analysis is to find these replacements," while his opponent is going to say "No ordinary utterances are absurd, though sometimes what we say we mean by them is absurd, and the job of philosophical analysis is to explain what we really do mean by them." Does it matter which way we talk? The facts are the same.

I do not feel inclined to rest with this situation, and fortunately there seem to be two ways out of it, in spite of the apparent deadlock:

(1) I suspect that some philosophers have assumed or believed that "mean" means "mean" (that what a man says he means is paramount in determining what he does mean) because they have thought of "meaning so and so" as being the name of an introspectible experience. They have thought a person's statements about what he means have just the same kind of incorrigible status as a person's statements about his current sensations, or about the color that something seems to him to have at the moment. It seems to me that there are certainly some occasions when what a speaker says he means is treated as specially authoritative. Consider the following possible conversations between myself and a pupil:

Myself: "I want you to bring me a paper tomorrow."
Pupil: "Do you mean that you want a newspaper or that you want a piece of written work?"
Myself: "I mean 'a piece of written work.'"

It would be absurd at this point for the pupil to say "Perhaps you only think, mistakenly, that you mean 'a piece of written work,'" whereas really you mean 'a newspaper.'" And this absurdity seems like the absurdity of suggesting to someone who says he has a pain in his arm that perhaps he is mistaken (unless the suggestion is to be taken as saying that perhaps there is nothing physically wrong with him, however his arm feels). It is important to notice that although there is this point of analogy between meaning something and having a pain, there are striking differences. A pain may start and stop at specifiable times; equally something may begin to look red to one at 2:00 P.M. and cease to look red to one at 2:05 P.M. But it would be absurd for my pupil (in the preceding example) to say to me "When did you begin to mean that?" or "Have you stopped meaning it yet?" Again there is no *logical* objection to a pain arising in any set of concomitant sentences; but it is surely absurd to suppose that I might find myself meaning that it is raining when I say "I want a paper"; indeed, it is odd to speak at all of "my finding myself meaning so and so," though it is not odd to speak of my finding myself suffering from a pain. At best, only *very* special circumstances (if any) could enable me to say "I want a paper," meaning thereby that it is raining. In view of these differences, we may perhaps prefer to label such statements as "I mean a piece of written work" (in the conversation with my pupil) as "declarations" rather than as "introspection reports." Such statements as these are perhaps like declarations of intention, which also have an authoritative status in some ways like and in some ways unlike that of a statement about one's own current pains.

But the immediately relevant point with regard to such statements about meaning as the one I have just been discussing is that, insofar as they have the authoritative status which they seem to have, they are not statements which the speaker could have come to accept as the result of an investigation or of a train of argumentation. To revert to the conversation with my pupil, when I say "I mean a piece of written work," it would be quite inappropriate for my pupil to say "How did you discover that you meant that?" or "Who or what convinced you that you meant that?" And I think we can see why a "meaning" statement cannot be both specially authoritative and also the conclusion of an argument or an investigation. If a statement is accepted on the strength of an argument or an investigation, it always makes sense (though it may be foolish) to suggest that the argument is unsound or that the investigation has been improperly conducted; and if this is conceivable, then the statement maker *may* be mistaken, in which case, of course, his statement has not got the authoritative character which I have mentioned. But the paradox-propounder who relies on the type of argumentation I have been considering requires *both* that a speaker's statement about what he means should be specially authoritative *and* that it should be established by argumentation. But this combination is impossible.

(2) A further difficulty for the paradox-propounder is one which is linked with the previous point. There is, I hope, a fairly obvious distinction (though also a connection) between (a) what a given expression means (in general), or what a particular person means *in general* by a given expression, and (b) what a particular speaker means, or meant, by that expression on a particular occasion; (a) and (b) may clearly diverge. I shall give examples of the ways in which such divergence may occur. (1) The sentence "I have run out of fuel" means in

general (roughly) that the speaker has no material left with which to propel some vehicle which is in his charge; but a particular speaker on a particular occasion (given a suitable context) may be speaking figuratively and may mean by this sentence that he can think of nothing more to say. (2) "Jones is a fine fellow" means in general that Jones has a number of excellences (either without qualification or perhaps with respect to some contextually indicated region of conduct or performance); but a particular speaker, speaking ironically, may mean by this sentence that Jones is a scoundrel. In neither of these examples would the particular speaker be giving any unusual sense to any of the words in the sentences; he would rather be using each sentence in a special way, and a proper understanding of what he says involves knowing the *standard* use of the sentence in question. (3) A speaker might mean, on a particular occasion, by the sentence "It is hailing" what would standardly be expressed by the sentence "It is snowing" *either* if he had mislearned the use of the word "hailing" *or* if he thought (rightly or wrongly) that his addressee (perhaps because of some family joke) was accustomed to giving a private significance to the word "hailing." In either of these cases, of course, the speaker will be using some particular word in a special nonstandard sense.

These trivial examples are enough, I hope, to indicate the possibility of divergence between (a) and (b). But (a) and (b) are also connected. It is, I think, approximately true to say that what a particular speaker means by a particular utterance (of a statement-making character) on a particular occasion is to be identified with what he intends by means of the utterance to get his audience to believe (a full treatment would require a number of qualifications which I do not propose to go into now). It is also, I think, approximately true to say that what a sentence means in general is to be identified with what would *standardly* be meant by the sentence by particular speakers on particular occasions; and what renders a particular way of using a sentence *standard* may be different for different sentences. For example, in the case of sentences which do not contain technical terms it is, I think, roughly speaking, a matter of general practice on nonspecial occasions; such sentences mean in *general* what people of some particular group would normally mean by using them on particular occasions (this is, of course, oversimplified). If this outline of an elucidation of the distinction is on the right lines, then two links may be found between (a) and (b). First, if I am to mean something by a statement-making utterance on a particular occasion—that is, if I intend by means of my utterance to get my audience to believe something—I must think that there is some chance that my audience will recognize from my utterance what it is they are supposed to believe; and it seems fairly clear that the audience will not be able to do this unless it knows what the general practice, or what my practice, is as regards the use of this type of utterance (or unless I give it a supplementary explanation of my meaning on this occasion). Second (and obviously), for a sentence of a nontechnical character to have a certain meaning in general, it must be the case that a certain group of people do (or would) use it with that meaning on particular occasions.

I think we can confront my paradox-propounder with a further difficulty (which I hope will in the end prove fatal). When he suggests that to say "x (a natural event) caused y" means (wholly or in part) "x willed y," does he intend to suggest that particular speakers use the sentence "x caused y" on particular occasions to mean (wholly or in part) "x willed y" (that this is what they are telling their audience, that this is what they intend their audience to think)? If he is suggesting this, he is suggesting something that he must admit to be false. For part of his purpose in getting his victim to admit "x caused y" means (in part at least) "x willed y" to get his victim to admit that he should not (strictly) go on saying such things as that "x caused y" just because of the obvious falsity or absurdity of part of what it is supposed to mean; and he is relying on his victim's *not* intending to induce beliefs in obvious falsehoods or absurdities. However, if he is suggesting that "x caused y" means *in general* (at least in part) "x willed y," even though no particular speaker ever means this by it (or would mean this by it) on a particular occasion, then he is accepting just such a divorce between the *general* meaning of a sentence and its *particular* meaning on particular occasions as that which I have been maintaining to be inadmissible.

In conclusion, I should like to remind you very briefly what in this paper I have been trying to do. I have tried to indicate a particular class of statements which have been not unknown in the history of philosophy, and which may be described as being (in a particular sense) paradoxes. I have considered a number of attempts to find a general principle which would serve to eliminate all such statements, independently of consideration of the type of method by which they would be supported by their propounders. I have suggested that it is difficult to find any principle which will satisfactorily perform this task, though I would not care to insist that no such principle can be found, nor to deny that further elaboration might render satisfactory one or another of the principles which have been mentioned. I have considered a specimen of what I suspect is one characteristic method in which a paradox-propounder may support his thesis (though this may not be the *only* method which paradox-propounders have used); and finally I have tried to show that the use of this method involves its user in serious (indeed I hope fatal) difficulties.

10

Postwar Oxford Philosophy

The other day a philosopher of science in a university quite a long way from Oxford asked me whether I thought that "The Ordinary Language Approach to Philosophy" had anything to contribute to the Philosophy of Science. Finding this question difficult to handle for more than one reason, I eventually asked him what he meant by "The Ordinary Language Approach to Philosophy." He replied that he had been hoping that I would not ask that question, as he did not know much about the matter. Perhaps he thought that the reference of this phrase ought to have been immediately clear to me, since it was intended merely to pick out the sort of philosophizing in which I myself (and others at Oxford) habitually engage. Unfortunately I do not find it by any means easy to give a general characterization of the philosophizing in which I engage; indeed I am not sure that it is all of one sort; moreover, I am sure that one could find numerous methodological divergences among Oxford philosophers, though there does, no doubt, also exist a noticeable family resemblance. Again, difficult as it may be to characterize one's own philosophical performance, I was faced with a further difficulty, for I strongly suspected that his *idea* of my variety of philosophizing might not coincide with the reality. So I shall devote myself here to an attempt (necessarily schematic and fragmentary) to get clearer about my conception of the relation between my own philosophical practice and ordinary language. You must understand that I am speaking on behalf of no one but myself, even though it may well be the case that some philosophers, both in and out of Oxford, might be ready to agree in greater or lesser degree with what I have to say.

First of all, it is certainly true that I am not alone in thinking that ordinary discourse, what we ordinarily say, is worthy of the philosopher's special attention. But to say this is not to say very much. To be more specific, I will subscribe to two propositions. (1) It is, in my view, an important part, though by no means the whole, of the philosopher's task to analyze, describe, or characterize (in as general terms as possible) the ordinary use or uses of certain expressions or classes of expressions. If I philosophize about the notion of cause, or about perception, or about knowledge and belief, I expect to find myself considering, among other things, in what sort of situations we should, in our ordinary talk, be willing to speak (or again be unwilling to speak) of something as causing something else to happen; or again of someone as seeing a tree; or again of someone as knowing rather than merely believing that something is the case. Particular mention should perhaps be made of the cases in which one tries to find things that would not ordinarily be said at all; for example, in discussing knowledge and belief, one may find it helpful or indeed essential to take note of such linguistic facts as that one may without linguistic impropriety, speak of someone as "firmly believing" something, but not of someone as "firmly knowing" something. Such linguistic facts, or at least the answers to the question why these *are* linguistic facts, may be of philosophical importance. (2) It is in my view the case that a philosophical thesis which involves the rejection as false, or absurd, or linguistically incorrect, of some class of statements which would ordinarily be made, and accepted as true, in specifiable types of situation is itself almost certain (perhaps quite certain) to be false; though to say that such a thesis is false is not quite to deny that it may have other virtues, for the philosopher who propounds it may be "getting at" some important truth which could be more properly expressed in another way. To reformulate my second proposition in another way: it is almost certainly (perhaps quite certainly) wrong to reject as false, absurd, or linguistically incorrect some class of ordinary statements if this rejection is based merely on philosophical grounds. If, for example, a philosopher advances a philosophical argument to show that we do not in fact ever see trees and books and human bodies, despite the fact that in a variety of familiar situations we would ordinarily say that we do, then our philosopher is almost (perhaps quite) certainly wrong.

Before proceeding, I must briefly protect myself against a crude misconception (of which I am sure that none of you will be guilty).

Neither of my two propositions commits me to holding that non-ordinary uses of language are to be prohibited, or even to be disregarded by the philosopher. I do not for one moment suppose that either a nonphilosopher or a philosopher should confine himself to using only expressions with an ordinary use and to using these only in that ordinary way. The only restriction is that a philosopher who uses a technical term should recognize that it is a technical term and therefore stands in need of a special explanation. When one philosopher objects to another philosopher's argument (as sometimes happens) by saying "But that is not an ordinary use of the expression so-and-so" or "But that expression is being used as a technical term," his objection is not to the nonordinary or technical use of the expression but to the use of an expression in a nonordinary way *without* the necessary explanation, indeed (usually) to the speaker's failing to recognize that he has substituted a nonordinary for an ordinary use. It is usually a way of making a charge of equivocation.

I will now mention one or two objections that may be raised to my first proposition, that is, to the proposition that it is an important part of the philosopher's task to characterize the ordinary use of language.

Objection A

"Can your sort of philosophizing be distinguished from a sociological study of people's language habits, which (moreover) you conduct without collecting the empirical evidence on which such a study should be based, without making the polls which would be required? Alternatively, can what you do be distinguished from lexicography? Surely philosophy is not either head-counting or dictionary-making."

To deal with this double-headed objection, I shall introduce the notion of "conceptual analysis." I am using this expression in such a way that a piece of conceptual analysis is not necessarily a piece of philosophizing, though it is necessarily in certain respects *like* philosophizing. It is a very old idea in philosophy that you cannot ask, in a philosophical way, what something is unless (in a sense) you already know what it is. Plato (I think) recognized that you are not in a position to ask such a philosophical question as "What is justice?" unless, *in a sense,* you already know what justice is. This idea reappears in new dress when Moore draws a distinction between knowing what an expression means and knowing its analysis. People who ask philosophically what justice is already are able to *apply* the word "justice" and its congener "just" in particular cases; they will be confronted with many sorts of actions, be ready to apply or withhold the word "just" without hesitation, though there will of course be further sorts of actions with regard to which they would be uncertain whether to apply or withhold this adjective. But people who are in this position of being more or less adequately equipped to decide, with regard to particular actions of different kinds, whether they are to be called "just" or not may very well be at a loss if one asks them (or they ask themselves) to give a *general* account of the distinction between the sorts of actions which they would, and the sorts of actions which they would not, call "just."

I hope it will now be fairly clear what sort of thing I mean by "conceptual analysis." To be looking for a conceptual analysis of a given expression E is to be in a position to apply or withhold E in particular cases, but to be looking for a general characterization of the types of case in which one would apply E rather than withhold it. And we may notice that in reaching one's conceptual analysis of E, one makes use of one's ability to apply and withhold E, for the characteristic procedure is to think up a possible general characterization of one's use of E and then to test it by trying to find or imagine a particular situation which fits the suggested characterization and yet would *not* be a situation in which one would apply E. If one fails, after careful consideration on these lines, to find any such situation, then one is more or less confident that the suggested characterization of the use of E is satisfactory. But one could not test a suggested characterization in this way, unless one relied on one's ability to apply or withhold E in *particular* cases.

It may further be remarked that expressions for which one may wish to find a conceptual analysis are not necessarily expressions which are directly of concern to philosophy. One might (wanting a conceptual analysis) ask such a question as "What is a battle?" "What is a game?" "What is reading?"—for it may be by no means clear how one would distinguish battles from skirmishes, campaigns, and wars, or how one would distinguish games from, for example, recreations or sports, or how one would distinguish reading from all of a range of such things as reciting by heart with the pages open before one's eyes. But the nature of battles, games, and reading would not be regarded either by myself or by most people as falling within the subject matter of philosophy. So to practice conceptual analysis is not necessarily to practice philosophy; some further condition or conditions must be satisfied for a piece of conceptual analysis to count as a piece of philosophy.

We are now in a position to deal directly with this objection. You may regard me, when I engage in a piece of conceptual analysis (whether of a philosophical or nonphilosophical nature), as primarily concerned to provide a conceptual analysis *of my own* use of a given expression (of course, I may enlist the aid of others in this enterprise). To reach a conceptual analysis of one's own use of an expression is often extremely difficult, and you must expect most of my discussion about the conceptual analysis of an expression to relate to this difficulty. But if I think that I have reached a satisfactory conceptual analysis of my own use, I do not then go on to conduct a poll to see if this analysis fits other people's use of the expression. For one thing, I assume (justifiably, I think) that it does in general fit other people's use, for the expressions with which (as a philosopher) I am normally concerned are pretty commonly used ones; and if a particular expression E was given by some of the people with whom I talk in my daily life a substantially different use from the one which I gave to it, then I should almost certainly have discovered this; one does discover people's linguistic idiosyncrasies. But more important, even if my assumption that what goes for me goes for others is mistaken, it does not matter; my philosophical puzzles have arisen in connection with my use of E, and my conceptual analysis will be of value to me (and to any others who may find that their use of E coincides with mine). It may also be of value to those whose use of E is different, though different only in minor respects, from mine; but if this is not so, then we have a different use of E, to be dealt with separately, to be subjected to separate conceptual analysis. This we can do *if the need arises* (since cooperation in conceptual analysis does not demand identity as regards the use of the analyzed expression; I can, with you, attempt the conceptual analysis of your use of an expression, even if your use is different from mine). So conceptual analysis is not a sociological inquiry; the analyst is not interested in percentages.

Nor is conceptual analysis to be identified with lexicography (as I suspect the objector is conceiving of lexicography). I suspect the objector is thinking of dictionaries as providing a particular sort of definition, of which an example would be the definition of a father as a male parent. In fact, examination of dictionaries will very soon show that what they contain is very rarely capable of being represented as a definition of this kind, but I will not press this point. Let us now compare the following two written definitions:

(1) father————male parent
(2) awe————mixture of fear and admiration

(1) could be regarded as indicating to us that the expression "father" is correctly applied to a person if and only if he is a male parent; equally, correlation (2) could be regarded as indicating to us that the expression "awe" is applied to a state of feeling if and only if it is a mixture of fear and admiration. So far the correlations are alike. But there is an important difference between them. Roughly, anyone who knows the meaning of the expression "male parent," who did not assent at once to the suggestion that someone is correctly called a father if and only if he is a male parent, would be taken not to know the meaning of the expression "father" (as this expression is standardly used) (unless, of course, his refusal is taken as a sign of noncooperation, of refusal to play). But a person might be unwilling at once to assent to the suggestion that a state of feeling is correctly called "awe" if and only if it is a mixture of fear and admiration, *without* thereby showing that he just did not know the meaning of "awe" (did not know how to use it correctly), for he might legitimately wish to see, for example, whether he could think of a situation in which he would be willing to apply the word "awe" even though what he would be applying it to would not be a mixture of fear and admiration. So what the objector conceives of as dictionary definitions give the meaning of the expressions defined in a sense in which conceptual analyses—of which (2) would be an example—do not give the meaning of the expressions analyzed (though no doubt in another sense of "give the meaning," conceptual analyses do give the meaning of the expressions analyzed). This difference is connected closely with the idea that dictionaries are designed for people who wish to learn to use an expression correctly, whereas conceptual analyses (as already pointed out) are not.

I will deal more shortly with one or two other objections.

Objection B

"Ordinary language suffers from various defects which unfit it for conceptual analysis, or at least prevent conceptual analysis, or at least prevent conceptual analysis from achieving any results which are worth the effort involved in reaching them. Such defects are ambiguity, misleadingness, vagueness, and the incorporation of mistakes or absurd assumptions."

Let us take the suggested defects one by one. (a) That ordinary expressions are ambiguous (or better, have more than one meaning) is no reason for not subjecting them to conceptual analysis. This duplicity of meaning will either be obvious, in which case the conceptual analysis will be directed to one or more particular senses of an expression, or it will not be obvious, in which case part of the function of the conceptual analysis will be to bring out into the open what is (or might be) regarded as a duplicity of meaning. (b) That an expression is misleading if it means that it is *philosophically* misleading, namely that one may be tempted to fail to distinguish the character of its use from that of other expressions which are grammatically similar (e.g. fail to distinguish the character of the use of "exist" from that of such expressions as "growl"), is obviously a reason *for* rather than *against* engaging in the conceptual analysis of the expression, for conceptual analysis counteracts the tendency to be misled. (c) To say that an expression is vague (in a broad sense of vague) is presumably, roughly speaking, to say that there are cases (actual or possible) in which one just does not know whether to apply the expression or to withhold it, and one's not knowing is not due to ignorance of the facts. For instance one may not know whether or not to describe a particular man as "bald"; and it may be of no help at all to be told exactly how many hairs he has on his head. The fact that there are cases (even lots of cases) where the applicability of an expression E is undecidable in this kind of way may prevent one from providing a *neat and tidy* conceptual analysis of E; it may prevent one from specifying a set of conditions the fulfillment of which is both necessary and *sufficient* for correct application of E. But it does not prevent one from giving *any* sort of conceptual analysis of E; one can *include* in one's general characterization of the use of E not only the specification of the types of situation to which E would definitely apply or definitely not apply but also the specification of the types of situation with regard to which the applicability of E would be undecidable (without linguistic legislation). Moreover, these undecidable cases may yield one information about one's use of E in the decidable cases. To mention an example given by Locke, if Locke's contemporaries had found that Locke could tell them all kinds of intimate details of the life of Nestor (some at least of which could be independently checked), and if they were satisfied that Locke had not acquired this information by historical research, they might then have hesitated whether or not to say that Locke was the same person as Nestor. If so, they would have been pulled in two directions; consideration of the continuity of memory would have inclined them to say "same person," consideration of the absence of bodily identity would have inclined them to say "different person." But this example identifies for us two conditions which are standardly fulfilled in the case in which we say "same person" and neither of which is standardly fulfilled in the case in which we say "different person."

Of course, if any expression were *impossibly* vague, this might make it unfit for conceptual analysis; indeed, "impossibly vague" might mean "so vague as to be incapable of conceptual analysis." But this seems to me no reason to suppose that the expressions which, as a philosopher, I would wish to subject to conceptual analysis are, in general, impossibly vague. Moreover, one could only discover that they are impossibly vague by attempting to subject them to conceptual analysis and failing to reach any satisfactory result; it is odd, therefore, that the people who complain that ordinary language is too vague to be the subject of satisfactory conceptual analysis are usually also people who have never seriously tried to find satisfactory conceptual analyses, who have never philosophized in this way.

Objection C

"The sort of thing you say is an important part of philosophy is not worthy of the name 'philosophy.' Philosophy is not just a matter of talking about words."

I cannot here discuss at length this particular objection, which is, I am sure, quite widely subscribed to; I can only indicate very briefly some lines which might be developed in reply.

(i) Why should "words" be mentioned with such contempt in this objection? Would the objector say to the grammarian, or to the philologist, or to the linguist, in the same contemptuous tone, "You are merely concerned with talking about words"? I think not. Why then do "words" suddenly become contemptible if the philosopher talks about them?

(ii) There is a fairly close connection between some of the conceptual analyses proffered by contemporary philosophers and the discussion which forms a central part of the writings of those who are generally recognized as great philosophers. Many of the great philosophers' questions can be interpreted as requests for a conceptual analysis (not necessarily in full with the greatest precision). No doubt the great philosophers themselves did not recognize the possibility of this kind of interpretation (how could they have?), but the link between contemporary discussion and their work is sufficiently close to provide some justification for the continued use of the term "philosophy." Moreover, it seems to me that many of the questions and puzzles raised by the great philosophers are capable of really clear and detailed and rigorous treatment after reinterpretation of this kind. If I have to choose between reinterpretation and continued mystification, I choose reinterpretation.

(iii) I carefully did not say that I thought that conceptual analysis of ordinary expressions was the whole of what I regard as the task of the philosopher. To begin with, I do not think it is necessary that, to be suitable for philosophical analysis, the use of an expression has to be "ordinary." The professional apparatus of the literary critic and the physicist (for example) may not consist of expressions in their ordinary use; nevertheless it may well be a philosopher's business to subject them to conceptual analysis, provided that they are expressions which their users can be in a position to use in particular cases, without being in a position to say (in general terms) everything there is to be said about *how* they are used. Furthermore, I think philosophers should be concerned with other questions besides questions of conceptual analysis. To mention only one example, a philosopher who has reached a decision about how an expression, or family of expressions, is used may well want (and often *should* want) to go on to ask such questions as "Why do we use these expressions this way, rather than some other way?" or "Could we have had a language in which there were no expressions which were used in this way" (e.g. "Could we have had a language in which there were no singular terms?).

But I doubt if any of the other tasks which I would like to see the philosophers fulfill will be enough to satisfy some people who raise this objection. They want philosophy to be grand, to yield one important, nonempirical information which will help one to solve either the world's problems or one's personal problems, or both. To them I feel inclined to reply *in the end:* "You are crying for the moon; philosophy has never really fulfilled this task, though it may sometimes have appeared to do so (and the practical consequences of its appearing to do so have not always been very agreeable). It is no more sensible to complain that philosophy is no longer capable of solving practical problems than it is to complain that the study of the stars no longer enables one to predict the course of world events."

11

Conceptual Analysis and the Province of Philosophy

As I look back, over a distance of twenty-nine years, at the discussion of postwar Oxford philosophy which appears here as Essay 10, I find myself not wholly dissatisfied. That essay received its only other airing at Wellesley College, Massachusetts, in 1958; and though the points made in it were by no means fully or properly pursued, at least in some respects it seems to me that my nose was pointed in the right direction. The ambivalence about the relation between the kind of conceptual analysis which I was discussing and the prosecution of philosophy was not just the product of my hazy mind; it was discernible in the practice of some of the leading figures of the Oxford scene, particularly Austin himself. When in the late nineteen-forties the Playgroup was instituted, its official (even if perhaps slightly tongue-in-cheek) rationale, as given by Austin, was that all of us were local philosophical hacks, spending our weekdays wrestling with the philosophical inabilities of our pupils, and that we deserved to be able to spend our Saturday mornings in restorative *non*philosophical activities, which would nonetheless be both enjoyable and possibly even, in the long run, philosophically beneficial. And so we started on such paraphilosophical topics as maps and diagrams and (in another term) rules of games. At this point, evidently, paraphilosophy was conceived of as not being philosophy, though in some ways akin to philosophy. However, when some of us raised questions about this relationship and showed signs of impatience for a distinguishing criterion, we were met with a not uncharacteristic shift of position. When we asked for a distinction between what is important and what is not important (by which, of course, we meant a distinction between linguistic data which are, and again which are not, *philosophically* important), we were liable to be met by the statement (also made at the end of Austin's paper *Pretending*) that he, Austin, was not very good at distinguishing between what is important and what is not. I now take this to have been a way of withdrawing, or at least weakening, his own earlier differentiation of philosophy from what I am calling "paraphilosophy." And if the Master wobbles thus, what should we expect from his friends, or for that matter, from his enemies?

It seems to me that this issue should be faced and not fudged; and I intend to conclude my contribution with an endeavor to get the question or questions involved clear, even if shortage of time and intellectual equipment compel me to leave it, or them, unanswered. The "enemies" of midcentury Oxford philosophy may be misguided, but at least they have a right to a rational, rather than a merely dismissive, response.

Type A Cases

Let us suppose that we are seriously interested in investigating the insubstantiation of a certain concept K within a certain range of material r. In such a case it would seem natural for us to look for a science or discipline which would offer us a system of ways of determining, with respect to that range of material, the presence or absence of K. We might, however, be disappointed in more than one way. We might not be able to locate any discipline which even professed to be able to provide us with such a systematic method; or, though we could locate such a discipline, we might believe or suspect that the discipline was spurious and that it was no better qualified to cater to our needs than astrology would be to assure us of our complete safety during our next visit to Beirut. We might, however, be fortunate; we might be able to satisfy ourselves that the available discipline was authentic. In such a case, however, we might have to recognize that the discipline in question would be powerless to provide for our needs unless the propositions which we wished it to certify for us were first re-expressed in a pattern congenial to demonstration by that discipline; what we wish to know has to be re-expressed in a theory-relevant form; and the procedure for achieving this kind of "rational reconstruction" might vary according to the *kind* of theory which we need to call into play.

In a certain limited range of further cases, what we have just said might be insufficient to satisfy us. For we might want to take seriously, and so scientifically, not merely questions about whether K is realized in r (for which we need discipline θ_1) but also questions about whether it is (in an appropriate way) *incumbent* on θ_1 to determine for us whether and when K is realized in r; and to settle these further questions, we may require a further theory θ_2 which, when provided with suitable (θ_2-relevant) rational reconstructions of statements which (informally) saddle θ_1 with such obligations or incumbencies, will decide for us concerning their truth or falsehood. We thus have a prospect of an indefinite sequence of disciplines, each pronouncing upon the adequacy, in a certain respect, of its predecessor in the sequence.

Type B Cases

In this range of examples, perhaps in order to avoid the real or supposed viciousness of such an unending sequence, this feature does not appear. In these cases, to be called type B cases, the adequacy of discipline D in a desired respect is certified by appeal not to a further discipline D but to discipline D itself, which is, in an appropriate sense, self-justifying. It might (for example) be possible to prove in discipline D a general thesis or law (θ_1), one particular instance or specification of which (θ_{11}) would in effect assert the adequacy of D to prove its own adequacy in a desired respect; and, maybe, yet a further instance or specification of θ_{11}, namely θ_{111}, would be provable which in effect asserts the adequacy of D to prove the adequacy of D to prove the adequacy of D in the desired respect. We should thus, in a type B case, have substituted for the unending sequence of justifying disciplines typical of type A cases, each feeding on its predecessor, an unending sequence of laws or theorems within a *single* discipline; and the logical gain from this alteration might be appreciable.

Type B Cases and Philosophy

We should, finally, turn briefly to the impact of the preceding discussion on matters at issue between Oxonians and a certain group of their foes—foes who might accept as their battle cry the once famous slogan "Clarity is not enough." These foes will hold that one part of the business of philosophy is to decide about, even perhaps to enact, the competence and authority of philosophy to determine the answers to certain nonlinguistic questions about Reality. Some might even go so far as to say that philosophy is a supremely sovereign science, perhaps even the *only* supremely sovereign science, in that among sciences it alone has authority to determine its own competence in *every* area in which a demand for the justification of competence is legitimate. But whether one accepts a more or a less extreme version of this position, one will hold that the material characterization of the work of philosophy must be such as to allow for the fulfillment of this role, and that in either case it cannot be a full characterization of the work of philosophy to describe it as the achievement of conceptual clarity. Indeed, this activity may not even be a *part* of philosophy, though it will no doubt represent a capacity for which philosophers will have a need.

It is, I think, quite uncertain whether such demands on the part of anti-Oxonians are justified, or even whether they are coherent, but it is no part of my purpose here to decide upon the outcome of battles between Oxonians and their foes, only to make a little progress in deciding the location of the battleground or the battlegrounds, though I will confess to a hope that a knowledge of where the fighting is taking place might have a beneficial effect on the upshot of that fighting.

But perhaps someone will say: "You have not yet done enough to help us much, and so we are not yet ready to exhibit any trace of excitement. For it might be that there is no even faintly plausible candidate for a description of the material content of philosophizing which would give the anti-Oxonian any chance of making good his claim that the work of philosophy extends beyond conceptual clarification and reaches as far as self-vindication as a rational discipline. So say more, lest the battle you locate turn out to be over before it begins."

At this point I reply: "If you insist on twisting my arm, I am not compelled to remain silent. For philosophy to achieve any end at all, or to fulfill any function, indeed for there to *be* such a thing as philosophy, there have to be (or to have been) philosophers. Just as the poet said that the proper study of mankind is Man, the anti-Oxonian can say that (in the first instance) the proper study of philosopher-kind is Philosophers. To be less cryptic, he will say that there will be a possibly not well-defined set of attributes or capacities, the possession of the totality of which (each in this or that degree) will fully determine the philosophical capability of the possessor. For example, everyone will probably allow that this step will include reasoning-power, most would perhaps allow that it would contain a certain kind of theoretical imagination, but few would suppose it to contain a good digestion. For though a failure to reach a minimal digestive standard would probably terminate a philosophical career, once the minimum had been reached further digestive improvement would (probably) be irrelevant to philosophical merit, whereas reasoning-power is (probably) not subject to this limitation. The anti-Oxonian, then, might suggest that the province of philosophy is the identification and vindication of that totality of capacities on which the varying degrees of philosophical capability ultimately rest. How good his prospects might be I would not presume to guess."

12

Descartes on Clear and Distinct Perception

I. How to Interpret the Notion of Clear and Distinct Perception

The main references to this notion, outside the Meditations, are contained in Discourse on Method II (first rule), Regulae III and XII, Principles of Philosophy I 45–46 Replies to Objections II ('Thirdly,' 'Fourthly,' and Appendix: Proposition IV). In Principles I, 45, perception is said to be clear when it is "present and apparent to an attentive mind." We may compare Regulae III, where intuition is described as an "indubitable conception formed by an unclouded and attentive mind" ("unclouded" connects with "distinct"). In Principles 45 a perception is said to be distinct "if it is so precise and different from all other objects that it contains within itself nothing but what is clear." In the case of severe pain, perception is said to be very clear but may not be distinct if it is confused with an obscure judgment about the cause of the pain (physical damage). So a perception may be clear without being distinct, but cannot be distinct without being clear.

Descartes's account is obscured by (1) predominance of visual analogy in exposition, (2) failure to distinguish between perception (conception) of objects or concepts and perception (knowledge, assurance) of propositions. Propositions might be his primary concern, and it is not too difficult to give a more or less precise interpretation to clear and distinct perception of a proposition. A proposition is clearly and distinctly perceived by me if I have no doubt at all that it is true after having adequately (and perhaps *successfully*) satisfied myself just what it entails and does not entail (it is clear to me what it contains, and so what it contains is clear to me [clearly true], since I cannot *both* have no doubt that p *and* have no doubt that p − > q, unless I have no doubt that q).

Descartes's failure to distinguish between objects or concepts, on the one hand, and propositions, on the other, comes out particularly clearly in Regulae XII. His account there of the knowledge of "simple natures" and "their blending or conjunction" is fairly clearly an account of the supposed objects of clear and distinct perception (or at least of a very important subclass of such objects). "Simple natures" are, rightly, unanalyzable concepts of a high, but not too high, level of generality. Figure is a simple nature (entailing no more general concept); but limit (i.e. terminus) is not, though more general than figure, applying not only to regions of space but also to stretches of time, for according to Descartes, the expression "limit" does not apply unambiguously to spaces and to times (presumably because of the categorical difference between spaces and times). Knowledge of simple natures is said to be incapable of error (according to Descartes because of their simplicity), but surely the cash value of this immunity is that simple natures are not propositions and so not the sort of things to be false (or true). And Descartes in this section speaks in one breath of knowledge of simple natures (concepts) and knowledge of their blending or combination (perhaps propositions) and of "axioms" (certainly propositions).

At the time of Regulae, an early work, Descartes's position seems to have been: (1) Certain knowledge is confined to intuition and deduction; intuition is infallible; and deduction, which is a concatenation of intuitions, is fallible only insofar as memory-mistake may be involved (no account is taken of fallacies). (2) Intuition, qua understanding/apprehension of simple concepts, is infallible, since I cannot misapprehend or fail completely to apprehend what has no internal complexity. (3) Intuition of propositions is recognition of *necessary* connection between simple concepts; this consists in recognition of one concept as implicitly contained in another (cf. Kant on "analytic").

So Descartes is in a position to hold that certain knowledge of propositions is really only a matter of *articulated* understanding of concepts. This is not at all absurd; it resembles the more or less contemporary view of an analytic proposition as one that cannot be denied by anyone who understands it (denial [conflicts with], counts against understanding). All the same, for Descartes it is incoherent; necessary connection between *simple* concepts cannot consist in one concept's being implicitly contained in another, for the containing concept would have to be complex. It is not clear how far this line of thinking survives in Descartes's later thought; "simple natures" is a technical term which does not appear in later work.

However, possible confusion between knowledge of propositions and understanding of concepts is detectable in the Meditations. Descartes's main use of clear and distinct perception is to provide a criterion of truth and certainty for *propositions*. But in the proof of the distinctness of mind and body, he relies on the principle that if A can be clearly and distinctly conceived or understood apart from B, then A and B are logically distinct and can exist separately. This can, of course, be represented as the clear and distinct perception (knowledge) of the modal proposition that it is possible that A should exist (be exemplified) when B does not exist, but I suggest that Descartes thought of this proposition as grounded on the distinct conception of A (a conception not involving the conception of B).

Finally it is important to remember that though for Descartes the primary cases of clear and distinct perception are *necessary* truths, not all cases of clear and distinct perception are necessary truths. "I exist" and "I have a pain" are not expressions of necessary truths, though Descartes may have failed to see clearly that the first is not.

II. How to Understand This Criterion

Discourse IV (cf. Meditations III) specifies the question at issue as being "what is requisite to the truth and certainty of a proposition?" and lays down the general rule that "whatever we conceive (Meditations III "perceive") very clearly and very distinctly is true," and adds that there is some difficulty in discerning what conceptions really are distinct.

One may wonder just why truth and certainty are spoken of so indifferently, since they are not identical notions (though there may be some inclination to suppose them to coincide in the area of necessary truth; it is attractive [though because of Gödel, wrong] to equate mathematical proof with provability). "Certain" occurs in at least two distinguishable contexts: (i) "it is certain that p" (label this "objective" certainty), (ii) "x is certain that p" (label this "subjective" certainty). Perhaps, then, Descartes is subscribing to two rules (conflated): (1) whatever is clearly and distinctly perceived is objectively certain, (2) whatever is objectively certain is true.

It is fairly clear that Descartes wants to hold not only that if something is clearly and distinctly perceived, it is certain, but also that *only if* something is clearly and distinctly perceived is it certain (or at least that only if we are satisfied that we clearly and distinctly perceive that p are we *entitled* to say that it is certain that p).

What status did Descartes attribute to his general rule? The natural supposition is that he thought of it as itself a *necessary* truth. If it is a necessary truth, then it might be *either* an implicit definition of "certain" *or* the specification of a sure sign or mark of the presence or certainty. But there are indications of a different interpretation. Discourse II (first rule) speaks of accepting only "what presented itself to my mind so clearly and so distinctly that I had no occasion to doubt it." And in Replies II ("Fourthly") Descartes says "to begin with, directly we think that we rightly perceive something, we spontaneously persuade ourselves that it is true!" He goes on: "Further, if this conviction is so strong that we have no reason to doubt concerning that of the truth of which we have persuaded ourselves, there is nothing more to inquire about, we have here all the certainty that can reasonably be desired." This suggests two further possibilities of interpretation; (i) that the rule specifies a psychological fact about us that we cannot but assent to what we clearly and distinctly perceive (or think we clearly and distinctly perceive), (ii) that our only *reasonable policy* is to assent to what we (think we) clearly and distinctly perceive. There are altogether, then, four possible ways of viewing the rule; it might specify:

(1) Necessary truth defining certainty
(2) Necessary truth specifying sure sign of certainty
(3) Psychological fact about when we have to give our assent
(4) Only reasonable procedure for attribution of certainty

We shall revert to at least some of these.

III. Difficulties Arising with Regard to Criterion

(1) Descartes regards the establishment of his general rule as consequential upon or derivative from his arrival at the certitude of his own existence. But in what way? The step is obviously not supposed

to be a deductive one, so of what kind is it? It may be that Descartes thought of it as an example of so-called "intuitive induction," being led to recognition of the general necessity of an A being a B by detecting the coinstantiation of A and B in a particular case. But whether or not Descartes believed this, the nature of such a step is extremely obscure; it is not clear what function the individual case can have other than to draw attention to the possibility of a general connection between A and B, to put the idea of a general truth into one's head. But the Cogito does not seem especially qualified for this purpose, since the certainty of my existence seems to depend not notably on clear and distinct perception, but rather on (i) the fact that it is immune to the hypothesis of a malignant demon and (ii) the fact that "I exist" is one of a special class of propositions (statements) (cf. "I am awake") whose truth is required in order that their expression should count as the making of an assertion; an utterance of "I exist" is either true or not a statement-making utterance at all. Descartes might just as well have had his attention drawn to the general rule by, for example, the simple arithmetical propositions which initially he seems to have regarded as open to doubt; indeed, if such examples were no good to him to begin with (as being questionable), then they will remain questionable even after the general rule is accepted; and this Descartes does not want.

One may, of course, diagnose a condition A on which a particular feature B (e.g. certainty) depends by considering what is common to clear cases of B and seeing what we seem to go by in ascribing B; but for this we need consideration of a range of examples, not just a single one (e.g. the Cogito). And the existence of such a range (cf. mathematical examples) is just what Descartes seems initially to put in question.

(2) The well-known Cartesian circle presents another difficulty. Descartes seems to say that the acceptability of the general rule is dependent on the acceptability of the existence of a beneficent God—a malignant demon might deceive us even about what we clearly and distinctly perceive. But the existence of God needs proof, and the premises and conclusion of such a proof must be accepted on the grounds that they are clearly and distinctly perceived. But this involves a reliance on the criterion in advance of its guarantee from God.

In Replies II Descartes answers that he never intended the beneficence of God to guarantee the general rule; what he intended it to guarantee was the reliance, in the conduct of a proof, on one's memory that certain propositions have been successfully proved, the proofs of which are not any longer before one's mind.[1] He is being somewhat disingenuous in this answer. Admittedly in Meditations V he does put forward just the position he outlines in Replies II, but at the beginning of Meditations III he does explicitly say that the use of the general rule to reestablish simple arithmetical propositions questioned in Meditations I has to wait upon the proof of the existence of God. Descartes has in fact spoken with two voices, and will not admit it.

In any case, the favored position is not without its own difficulties:

(i) Two of Descartes's proofs of the existence of God are extremely elaborate and could not be conducted without an (unguaranteed) reliance on memory. However, the Ontological Proof is very short, and maybe Descartes could say that here reliance on memory is not involved.

(ii) It looks as if the beneficence of God will guarantee too much, for if it guarantees *every* reliance on memory, then we should not be able to make the memory-mistakes we all know that we do make. And if it guarantees only *some* memory, how do we characterize and identify the kind of memory that is guaranteed?

Descartes, it seems to me, has a perfectly good line at his disposal here with regard to memory, analogous to the one he takes in Meditations VI about the material world. Very baldly put, his position there is that there are all sorts of ordinary nonphilosophical doubts and beliefs about the material world, which we are in a perfectly good position to resolve or correct, provided that we can rely on the general assumption that our sensory ideas are generated by material objects (and perhaps, it should be added, on the assumption of the legitimacy of certain checking procedures). That our sensory ideas are so generated (and perhaps that these procedures are legitimate) is "lesson of nature"; something we are naturally disposed to believe; but if skeptical philosophical doubts are raised about them, we have no way of meeting these doubts; if our natural beliefs are incorrect, we have no way of discovering that they are. We need to know that God is no deceiver in order to be sure that we have not been constituted with a

---

1. I am informed that Cartesian scholars no longer take seriously the suggestion that the function of Descartes's criterion was to justify a reliance on memory in the conduct of demonstration. This idea was, however, discernibly alive at the time when this essay was written.

built-in set of erroneous natural beliefs. (For all this cf. Hume on natural dispositions.)

Similarly, Descartes could say we are in a position to correct or confirm erroneous or dubious memory claims (ideas of memory), provided we can assure that memory claims are in general generated by past events and situations, and provided that certain checking procedures (considerations of recency, distinctness, and coherence) are legitimate. But if the skeptic attacks these, we have no recourse, save to the beneficence of God, which would preclude our having been created with natural tendencies to assume that memory ideas in general correspond with the past, when in fact there is no such general correspondence. The proof of God's existence is required solely to defend us from the Skeptic and does not provide for the infallibility of memory.

(3) It has been argued by Prichard in "Knowledge and Perception" that Descartes is attempting to fulfill an impossible task, namely to provide a universally applicable mark or criterion of certainty (or, what comes to the same thing) of knowledge. He is trying to specify a mark (being a state of clear and distinct perception) such that, if and only if we can recognize our state of mind as regards some proposition p as exemplifying M can we call it a state of knowledge that p. Any such attempt fails on account of two different vicious circles/ regresses. (i) To know that a state S is a state of knowledge that p, we need to know that it exemplifies M; but to know this, we need to know that our state S_1 with regard to the proposition that S exemplifies M itself exemplifies M and so on. (ii) To know that the general rule is true, we have to know that our state of mind with respect to the general rule exemplifies M, but this information is no use to us unless we can already use the rule (i.e., already know it to be true). We have to use the rule to certify itself.

These objections may well be fatal to any attempt to provide an absolutely general sure sign of certainty (interpretation 2). But Descartes may not be making such an attempt. The objections would not, I think, apply against interpretation (1) (the definitional variant); but if we take Descartes in this way, there are other objections. For while it might be legitimate to define "x is certain that p" as "x clearly and distinctly perceives that p," it would not be so attractive to attempt to define "it is certain that p" (objective certainty) in terms of clear and distinct perception. Indeed, the problem about certainty might be posed as the question when and how a step from "I am certain" to "it is certain" is justified.

I am inclined to think that Descartes was, not very clear-headedly, espousing interpretation (4), insofar as this is distinct from interpretation (3). To amplify this, I will mark some distinctions which may be of general philosophical interest. For any proposition or range of propositions three different kinds of conditions may be specifiable, which I shall call:

(1) Truth-conditions
(2) Establishment-conditions
(3) Reassurance-conditions

Let me consider these in relation to a class of propositions in which Descartes was specially interested, namely mathematical propositions.

(1) Truth-conditions will be explicit or implicit definitions. For any given proposition or propositions a wide variety of alternative specifications may be available; which one selects will depend on one's interests, on what the concepts are to which one is concerned to link the concepts involved in the original proposition or range of propositions. One might, for certain purposes, wish to specify the truth-conditions for $\frac{x}{y} = z$: $\frac{x}{y} = z$ is true iff the result of adding z to itself y − 1 times is identical with x.

(2) Establishment-conditions. These would be specifiable for a given system of mathematical propositions. A proposition p would be established if there has been found a proof of it within the system; if (that is) starting from such-and-such axioms, it has been possible to reach, in a finite number of steps constructed in accordance with such-and-such inferential rules, an expression of p.

(3) Reassurance-conditions. The establishment-conditions will specify a procedure or achievement, which, if successfully realized, guarantees that p. But the question might arise whether the achievement or procedure has after all been successfully realized, whether something may not have gone wrong, and if such a question is not disposed of, we are not in a position to say "it is certain that p," even though *in fact* nothing may have gone wrong. So we need directions like "Go over the proof again (and if necessary again), looking out for misapplications of inferential rules, etc." Such specifications of reassurance-conditions have two notable features: (1) They are exceedingly unexciting, though supplementary directions, about what sort of mistakes to look out for, may be of general interest. And just because the specifications are liable to be general in character and

unexciting, to put this into execution may require considerable skill and intelligence; it is not a mechanical operation. (2) Reassurance-conditions are open-ended: there is no point at which carrying them out is *finally* completed. One can always check again, though at some point (usually quite soon) it will become unreasonable to insist on further checking. But there is no general way of specifying precisely when that point is reached.

A partial application of these ideas to propositions about physical objects may have some philosophical point. What would be an appropriate method of specifying truth-conditions in a general form for material object propositions is not clear to me, and I shall not attempt the task. But it is fairly clear how establishment-conditions should be specified, at least for the optimal or favored method of establishing a central class of material object propositions, those about "medium-size" objects. To establish p in such cases is perceptually to observe that p. Since the achievement of perceptual observations may fail to be successfully realized (something may go wrong, not usually as the fault of the observer but rather as the fault of nature), we have re-assurance-directives such as "Make further observations, bring different senses into play, compare your observational findings with those of others etc." It seems to me that the phenomenalist may have made the mistake of taking what is a perfectly sound reassurance-directive and dressing it up so as to serve as a specification of truth-conditions for material object propositions in general. The stock objection to the phenomenalist, that his analyses are not completable and have to be supposed to be of infinite length, is worth bearing in mind here, for it may be a way of making the point that the open-endedness which is characteristic of reassurance-directives becomes objectionable if the attempt is made to convert reassurance-directives into specifications of truth-conditions.

The bearing of this discussion of Descartes is that I am suggesting that his general rule should be looked upon as an attempt to provide a reassurance-directive of maximal generality, one that will apply to all propositions which can ever be said to be certain, regardless of what their truth-conditions are, what their specific establishment-conditions are, and what more specific reassurance-directives are applicable once the establishment-conditions are identified. The directive is in effect "Take all steps to satisfy yourself just what a given proposition entails and does not entail, and that having done this, you can find no ground for doubting the proposition in question."

Whether the provision of a maximally generalized reassurance-directive is a proper philosophical undertaking and whether, if it is, Descartes has adequately discharged it, are larger questions than it is the purpose of this essay to decide. I wish to argue only (1) that it is not obvious and has not been proved that it is an improper philosophical undertaking and (2) that if it is a proper undertaking, then it is not easy to see how to improve upon Descartes's attempt to fulfill it. Our primary concern should, I think, be to ask, not whether Descartes's criterion is acceptable, but how and with what justification he has managed, by the application of what is apparently so unexceptionable a principle, to make at least plausible a skeptical position which is an affront to common sense.

13

In Defense of a Dogma
With P. F. Strawson

In his article "Two Dogmas of Empiricism,"[1] Professor Quine advances a number of criticisms of the supposed distinction between analytic and synthetic statements, and of other associated notions. It is, he says, a distinction which he rejects.[2] We wish to show that his criticisms of the distinction do not justify his rejection of it.

There are many ways in which a distinction can be criticized, and more than one in which it can be rejected. It can be criticized for not being a sharp distinction (for admitting of cases which do not fall clearly on either side of it); or on the ground that the terms in which it is customarily drawn are ambiguous (have more than one meaning); or on the ground that it is confused (the different meanings being habitually conflated). Such criticisms alone would scarcely amount to a rejection of the distinction. They would, rather, be a prelude to clarification. It is not this sort of criticism which Quine makes.

Again, a distinction can be criticized on the ground that it is not useful. It can be said to be useless for certain purposes, or useless altogether, and, perhaps, pedantic. One who criticizes in this way may indeed be said to reject a distinction, but in a sense which also requires him to acknowledge its existence. He simply declares he can get on without it. But Quine's rejection of the analytic-synthetic distinction appears to be more radical than this. He would certainly say he could get on without the distinction, but not in a sense which would commit him to acknowledging its existence.

1. W. V. O. Quine, *From a Logical Point of View* (Cambridge, Mass., 1953), pp. 20–46. All references are to page numbers in this book.
2. Page 46.

Or again, one could criticize the way or ways in which a distinction is customarily expounded or explained on the ground that these explanations did not make it really clear. And Quine certainly makes such criticisms in the case of the analytic-synthetic distinction.

But he does, or seems to do, a great deal more. He declares, or seems to declare, not merely that the distinction is useless or inadequately clarified, but also that it is altogether illusory, that the belief in its existence is a philosophical mistake. "That there is such a distinction to be drawn at all," he says, "is an unempirical dogma of empiricists, a metaphysical article of faith."[3] It is the existence of the distinction that he here calls in question; so his rejection of it would seem to amount to a denial of its existence.

Evidently such a position of extreme skepticism about a distinction is not in general justified merely by criticisms, however just in themselves, of philosophical attempts to clarify it. There are doubtless plenty of distinctions, drawn in philosophy and outside it, which still await adequate philosophical elucidation, but which few would want on this account to declare illusory. Quine's article, however, does not consist wholly, though it does consist largely, in criticizing attempts at elucidation. He does try also to diagnose the causes of the belief in the distinction, and he offers some positive doctrine, acceptance of which he represents as incompatible with this belief. If there is any general prior presumption in favor of the existence of the distinction, it seems that Quine's radical rejection of it must rest quite heavily on this part of his article, since the force of any such presumption is not even impaired by philosophical failures to clarify a distinction so supported.

Is there such a presumption in favor of the distinction's existence? Prima facie, it must be admitted that there is. An appeal to philosophical tradition is perhaps unimpressive and is certainly unnecessary. But it is worth pointing out that Quine's objection is not simply to the words "analytic" and "synthetic," but to a distinction which they are supposed to express, and which at different times philosophers have supposed themselves to be expressing by means of such pairs of words or phrases as "necessary" and "contingent," "a priori" and "empirical," "truth of reason" and "truth of fact"; so Quine is certainly at odds with a philosophical tradition which is long and not wholly disreputable. But there is no need to appeal only to tradition;

3. Page 37.

for there is also present practice. We can appeal, that is, to the fact that those who use the terms "analytic" and "synthetic" do to a very considerable extent agree in the applications they make of them. They apply the term "analytic" to more or less the same cases, withhold it from more or less the same cases, and hesitate over more or less the same cases. This agreement extends not only to cases which they have been *taught* so to characterize, but to new cases. In short, "analytic" and "synthetic" have a more or less established philosophical *use;* and this seems to suggest that it is absurd, even senseless, to say that there is no such distinction. For, in general, if a pair of contrasting expressions are habitually and generally used in application to the same cases, *where these cases do not form a closed list,* this is a suffi-cient condition for saying that there are *kinds* of cases to which the expressions apply; and nothing more is needed for them to mark a distinction.

In view of the possibility of this kind of argument, one may begin to doubt whether Quine really holds the extreme thesis which his words encourage one to attribute to him. It is for this reason that we made the attribution tentative. For on at least one natural interpreta-tion of this extreme thesis, when we say of something true that it is analytic and of another true thing that it is synthetic, it simply never is the case that we thereby mark a distinction between them. And this view seems terribly difficult to reconcile with the fact of an established philosophical usage (i.e., of general agreement in application in an open class). For this reason, Quine's thesis might be better represented not as the thesis that there is *no difference at all* marked by the use of these expressions, but as the thesis that the nature of, and reasons for, the difference or differences are totally misunderstood by those who use the expressions, that the stories they tell themselves *about* the difference are full of illusion.

We think Quine might be prepared to accept this amendment. If so, it could, in the following way, be made the basis of something like an answer to the argument which prompted it. Philosophers are noto-riously subject to illusion, and to mistaken theories. Suppose there were a particular mistaken theory about language or knowledge, such that, seen in the light of this theory, some statements (or propositions or sentences) appeared to have a characteristic which no statements really have, or even, perhaps, which it does not make sense to suppose that any statement has, and which no one who was not consciously or subconsciously influenced by this theory would ascribe to any statement. And suppose that there were other statements which, seen in this light, did not appear to have this characteristic, and others again which presented an uncertain appearance. Then philosophers who were under the influence of this theory would tend to mark the supposed presence or absence of this characteristic by a pair of contrasting expressions, say "analytic" and "synthetic." Now in these circumstances it still could not be said that there was no distinction at all being marked by the use of these expressions, for there would be at least the distinction we have just described (the distinction, namely, between those statements which appeared to have and those which appeared to lack a certain characteristic), and there might well be other assignable differences too, which would account for the difference in appearance; but it certainly could be said that *the* difference these philosophers supposed themselves to be marking by the use of the expressions simply did not exist, and perhaps also (supposing the characteristic in question to be one which it was absurd to ascribe to any statement) that these expressions, as so used, were senseless or without meaning. We should only have to suppose that such a mistaken theory was very plausible and attractive, in order to reconcile the fact of an established philosophical usage for a pair of contrasting terms with the claim that *the* distinction which the terms purported to mark did not exist at all, though not with the claim that there simply did not exist a difference of any kind between the classes of statements so characterized. We think that the former claim would probably be sufficient for Quine's purposes. But to establish such a claim on the sort of grounds we have indicated evidently requires a great deal more argument than is involved in showing that certain explanations of a term do not measure up to certain requirements of adequacy in philosophical clarification—and not only more argument, but argument of a very different kind. For it would surely be too harsh to maintain that the *general* presumption is that philosophical distinctions embody the kind of illusion we have described. On the whole, it seems that philosophers are prone to make too few distinctions rather than too many. It is their assimilations, rather than their distinctions, which tend to be spurious.

So far we have argued as if the prior presumption in favor of the existence of the distinction which Quine questions rested solely on the fact of an agreed *philosophical* usage for the terms "analytic" and "synthetic." A presumption with only this basis could no doubt be countered by a strategy such as we have just outlined. But, in fact, if we are to accept Quine's account of the matter, the presumption in question is not only so based. For among the notions which belong to the analyticity group is one which Quine calls "cognitive synonymy," and in terms of which he allows that the notion of analyticity could at any rate be formally explained. Unfortunately, he adds, the notion of cognitive synonymy is just as unclarified as that of analyticity. To say that two expressions *x* and *y* are cognitively synonymous seems to correspond, at any rate roughly, to what we should ordinarily express by saying that *x* and *y* have the same meaning or that *x* means the same as *y*. If Quine is to be consistent in his adherence to the extreme thesis, then it appears that he must maintain not only that the distinction we suppose ourselves to be marking by the use of the terms "analytic" and "synthetic" does not exist, but also that the distinction we suppose ourselves to be marking by the use of the expressions "means the same as," "does not mean the same as" does not exist either. At least, he must maintain this insofar as the notion of *meaning the same as,* in its application to predicate-expressions, is supposed to differ from and go beyond the notion of *being true of just the same objects as.* (This latter notion—which we might call that of "coextensionality"—he is prepared to allow to be intelligible, though, as he rightly says, it is not sufficient for the explanation of analyticity.) Now since he cannot claim this time that the pair of expressions in question (namely "means the same," "does not mean the same") is the special property of philosophers, the strategy outlined above of countering the presumption in favor of their marking a genuine distinction is not available here (or is at least enormously less plausible). Yet the denial that the distinction (taken as different from the distinction between the coextensional and the non-coextensional) really exists, is extremely paradoxical. It involves saying, for example, that anyone who seriously remarks that "bachelor" means the same as "unmarried man" but that "creature with kidneys" does not mean the same as "creature with a heart"—supposing the last two expressions to be coextensional—*either* is not in fact drawing attention to any distinction at all between the relations between the members of each pair of expressions *or* is making a philosophical mistake about the nature of the distinction between them. In either case, what he says, taken as he intends it to be taken, is senseless or absurd. More generally, it involves saying that it is always senseless or absurd to make a statement of the form "Predicates *x* and *y* in fact apply to the same objects, but do not have the same meaning." But the paradox is more violent than this. For we frequently talk of the presence or absence of relations of synonymy between kinds of expressions—e.g., conjunctions, particles of many kinds, whole sentences—where there does not appear to be any obvious substitute for the ordinary notion of synonymy, in the way in which coextensionality is said to be a substitute for synonymy of predicates. Is all such talk meaningless? Is all talk of correct or incorrect *translation* of sentences of one language into sentences of another meaningless? It is hard to believe that it is. But if we do successfully make the effort to believe it, we have still harder renunciations before us. If talk of sentence-synonymy is meaningless, then it seems that talk of sentences having a meaning at all must be meaningless too. For if it made sense to talk of a sentence having a meaning, or meaning something, then presumably it would make sense to ask "What does it mean?" And if it made sense to ask "What does it mean?" of a sentence, then sentence-synonymy could be roughly defined as follows: Two sentences are synonymous if and only if any true answer to the question "What does it mean?" asked of one of them, is a true answer to the same question, asked of the other. We do not, of course, claim any clarifying power for this definition. We want only to point out that if we are to give up the notion of sentence-synonymy as senseless, we must give up the notion of sentence-significance (of a sentence having meaning) as senseless too. But then perhaps we might as well give up the notion of sense. It seems clear that we have here a typical example of a philosopher's paradox. Instead of examining the actual use that we make of the notion of *meaning the same,* the philosopher measures it by some perhaps inappropriate standard (in this case some standard of clarifiability), and because it falls short of this standard, or seems to do so, denies its reality, declares it illusory.

We have argued so far that there is a strong presumption in favor of the existence of the distinction, or distinctions, which Quine challenges—a presumption resting both on philosophical and on ordinary usage—and that this presumption is not in the least shaken by the fact, if it is a fact, that the distinctions in question have not been, in some sense, adequately clarified. It is perhaps time to look at what Quine's notion of adequate clarification is.

The main theme of his article can be roughly summarized as follows. There is a certain circle or family of expressions, of which "analytic" is one, such that if any one member of the circle could be taken to be satisfactorily understood or explained, then other members of the circle could be verbally, and hence satisfactorily, explained in terms of it. Other members of the family are: "self-contradictory" (in a broad sense), "necessary," "synonymous," "semantical rule," and perhaps (but again in a broad sense) "definition." The list could be added to. Unfortunately each member of the family is in as great need of explanation as any other. We give some sample quotations: "The notion of self-contradictoriness (in the required broad sense of inconsistency) stands in exactly the same need of clarification as does the notion of analyticity itself."[4] Again, Quine speaks of "a notion of synonymy which is in no less need of clarification than analyticity itself."[5] Again, of the adverb "necessarily," as a candidate for use in the explanation of synonymy, he says, "Does the adverb *really make sense?* To suppose that it does is to suppose that we have already *made satisfactory sense* of 'analytic.'"[6] To make "satisfactory sense" of one of these expressions would seem to involve two things. (1) It would seem to involve providing an explanation which does not incorporate any expression belonging to the family-circle. (2) It would seem that the explanation provided must be of the same general character as those rejected explanations which do incorporate members of the family-circle (i.e., it must specify some feature common and peculiar to all cases to which, for example, the word "analytic" is to be applied; it must have the same general form as an explanation beginning, "a statement is analytic if and only if . . ."). It is true that Quine does not explicitly state the second requirement; but since he does not even consider the question whether any other kind of explanation would be relevant, it seems reasonable to attribute it to him. If we take these two conditions together, and generalize the result, it would seem that Quine requires of a satisfactory explanation of an expression that it should take the form of a pretty strict definition but should not make use of any member of a group of interdefinable terms to which the expression belongs. We may well begin to feel that a satisfactory explanation is hard to come by. The other element in Quine's position is one we have already commented on in general, before enquiring what (according to him) is to count as a satisfactory explanation. It is the step from "We have not made satisfactory sense (provided a satisfactory explanation) of *x*" to "*x* does not make sense."

4. Page 20.
5. Page 23.
6. Page 30, our italics.

It would seem fairly clearly unreasonable to insist *in general* that the availability of a satisfactory explanation in the sense sketched above is a necessary condition of an expression's making sense. It is perhaps dubious whether *any* such explanations can *ever* be given. (The hope that they can be is, or was, the hope of reductive analysis in general.) Even if such explanations can be given in some cases, it would be pretty generally agreed that there are other cases in which they cannot. One might think, for example, of the group of expressions which includes "morally wrong," "blameworthy," "breach of moral rules," etc.; or of the group which includes the propositional connectives and the words "true" and "false," "statement," "fact," "denial," "assertion." Few people would want to say that the expressions belonging to either of these groups were senseless on the ground that they have not been formally defined (or even on the ground that it was impossible formally to define them) except in terms of members of the same group. It might, however, be said that while the unavailability of a satisfactory explanation in the special sense described was not a *generally* sufficient reason for declaring that a given expression was senseless, it was a sufficient reason in the case of the expressions of the analyticity group. But anyone who said this would have to advance a reason for discriminating in this way against the expressions of this group. The only plausible reason for being harder on these expressions than on others is a refinement on a consideration which we have already had before us. It starts from the point that "analytic" and "synthetic" themselves are technical philosophical expressions. To the rejoinder that other expressions of the family concerned, such as "means the same as" or "is inconsistent with," or "self-contradictory," are not at all technical expressions, but are common property, the reply would doubtless be that, to qualify for inclusion in the family circle, these expressions have to be used in specially adjusted and precise senses (or pseudo-senses) which they do not ordinarily possess. It is the fact, then, that all the terms belonging to the circle are *either* technical terms *or* ordinary terms used in specially adjusted senses, that might be held to justify us in being particularly suspicious of the claims of members of the circle to have any sense at all, and hence to justify us in requiring them to pass a test for significance which would admittedly be too stringent if generally applied. This point has some force, though we doubt if the special adjustments spoken of are in every case as considerable as it suggests. (This seems particularly doubtful in the case of the word "inconsistent"—a per-

fectly good member of the nontechnician's meta-logical vocabulary.)
But though the point has some force, it does not have whatever force
would be required to justify us in insisting that the expressions concerned should pass exactly that test for significance which is in question. The fact, if it is a fact, that the expressions cannot be explained
in precisely the way which Quine seems to require, does not mean
that they cannot be explained at all. There is no need to try to pass
them off as expressing innate ideas. They can be and are explained,
though in other and less formal ways than that which Quine considers. (And the fact that they are so explained fits with the facts, first,
that there is a generally agreed philosophical use for them, and second, that this use is technical or specially adjusted.) To illustrate the
point briefly for one member of the analyticity family. Let us suppose
we are trying to explain to someone the notion of *logical impossibility*
(a member of the family which Quine presumably regards as no
clearer than any of the others) and we decide to do it by bringing out
the contrast between logical and natural (or causal) impossibility. We
might take as our examples the logical impossibility of a child of
three's being an adult, and the natural impossibility of a child of
three's understanding Russell's Theory of Types. We might instruct
our pupil to imagine two conversations one of which begins by someone (X) making the claim:

(1) "My neighbor's three-year-old child understands Russell's
Theory of Types,"

and the other of which begins by someone (Y) making the claim:

(1') "My neighbor's three-year-old child is an adult."

It would not be inappropriate to reply to X, taking the remark as a
hyperbole:

(2) "You mean the child is a particularly bright lad."

If X were to say:

(3) "No, I mean what I say—he really does understand it,"

one might be inclined to reply:

(4) "I don't believe you—the thing's impossible."

But if the child were then produced, and did (as one knows he would
not) expound the theory correctly, answer questions on it, criticize it,

and so on, one would in the end be forced to acknowledge that the claim was literally true and that the child was a prodigy. Now consider one's reaction to Y's claim. To begin with, it might be somewhat similar to the previous case. One might say:

(2') "You mean he's uncommonly sensible or very advanced for his age."

If Y replies:

(3') "No, I mean what I say,"

we might reply:

(4') "Perhaps you mean that he won't grow any more, or that he's a sort of freak, that he's already fully developed."

Y replies:

(5') "No, he's not a freak, he's just an adult."

At this stage—or possibly if we are patient, a little later—we shall be inclined to say that we just don't understand what Y is saying, and to suspect that he just does not know the meaning of some of the words he is using. For unless he is prepared to admit that he is using words in a figurative or unusual sense, we shall say, not that we don't believe him, but that his words have *no* sense. And whatever kind of creature is ultimately produced for our inspection, it will not lead us to say that what Y said was literally true, but at most to say that we now see what he meant. As a summary of the difference between the two imaginary conversations, we might say that in both cases we would tend to begin by supposing that the other speaker was using words in a figurative or unusual or restricted way; but in the face of his repeated claim to be speaking literally, it would be appropriate in the first case to say that we did not believe him and in the second case to say that we did not understand him. If, like Pascal, we thought it prudent to prepare against very long chances, we should in the first case know what to prepare for; in the second, we should have no idea.

We give this as an example of just one type of informal explanation which we might have recourse to in the case of one notion of the analyticity group. (We do not wish to suggest it is the only type.) Further examples, with different though connected types of treatment, might be necessary to teach our pupil the use of the notion of logical impossibility in its application to more complicated cases—if indeed he did not pick it up from the one case. Now of course this type of explanation does not yield a formal statement of necessary and sufficient conditions for the application of the notion concerned. So it does not fulfill one of the conditions which Quine seems to require of a satisfactory explanation. On the other hand, it does appear to fulfill the other. It breaks out of the family circle. The distinction in which we ultimately come to rest is that between not believing something and not understanding something; or between incredulity yielding to conviction, and incomprehension yielding to comprehension. It would be rash to maintain that *this* distinction does not need clarification; but it would be absurd to maintain that it does not exist. In the face of the availability of this informal type of explanation for the notions of the analyticity group, the fact that they have not received another type of explanation (which it is dubious whether *any* expressions *ever* receive) seems a wholly inadequate ground for the conclusion that the notions are pseudo-notions, that the expressions which purport to express them have no sense. To say this is not to deny that it would be philosophically desirable, and a proper object of philosophical endeavor, to find a more illuminating general characterization of the notions of this group than any that has been so far given. But the question of how, if at all, this can be done is quite irrelevant to the question of whether or not the expressions which belong to the circle have an intelligible use and mark genuine distinctions.

So far we have tried to show that sections 1 to 4 of Quine's article—the burden of which is that the notions of the analyticity group have not been satisfactorily explained—do not establish the extreme thesis for which he appears to be arguing. It remains to be seen whether sections 5 and 6, in which diagnosis and positive theory are offered, are any more successful. But before we turn to them, there are two further points worth making which arise out of the first two sections.

(1) One concerns what Quine says about *definition* and *synonymy.* He remarks that definition does not, as some have supposed, "hold the key to synonymy and analyticity," since "definition—except in the extreme case of the explicitly conventional introduction of new notations—hinges on prior relations of synonymy."[7] But now con-

7. Page 27.

sider what he says of these extreme cases. He says: "Here the defin-iendum becomes synonymous with the definiens simply because it has been expressly created for the purpose of being synonymous with the definiens. Here we have a really transparent case of synonymy created by definition; would that all species of synonymy were as intelligible." Now if we are to take these words of Quine seriously, then his posi-tion *as a whole* is incoherent. It is like the position of a man to whom we are trying to explain, say, the idea of one thing fitting into another thing, or two things fitting together, and who says: "I can understand what it means to say that one thing fits into another, or that two things fit together, in the case where one was specially made to fit the other; but I cannot understand what it means to say this in any other case." Perhaps we should not take Quine's words here too seriously. But if not, then we have the right to ask him exactly what state of affairs he thinks *is* brought about by explicit definition, what relation between expressions *is* established by this procedure, and why he thinks it unintelligible to suggest that the same (or a closely analo-gous) state of affairs, or relation, should exist in the absence of this procedure. For our part, we should be inclined to take Quine's words (or some of them) seriously, and reverse his conclusions; and maintain that the notion of synonymy by explicit convention would be unintel-ligible if the notion of synonymy by usage were not presupposed. There cannot be law where there is no custom, or rules where there are not practices (though perhaps we can understand better what a practice is by looking at a rule).

(2) The second point arises out of a paragraph on page 32 of Quine's book. We quote:

I do not know whether the statement "Everything green is ex-tended" is analytic. Now does my indecision over this example really betray an incomplete understanding, an incomplete grasp, of the "meanings" of "green" and "extended"? I think not. The trouble is not with "green" or "extended," but with "analytic."

If, as Quine says, the trouble is with "analytic," then the trouble should doubtless disappear when "analytic" is removed. So let us re-move it, and replace it with a word Quine himself has contrasted favorably with "analytic" in respect of perspicuity—the word "true." Does the indecision at once disappear? We think not. The indecision over "analytic" (and equally, in this case, the indecision over "true") arises, of course, from a further indecision: namely, that which we feel when confronted with such questions as "Should we count a *point* of green light as *extended* or not?" As is frequent enough in such cases, the hesitation arises from the fact that the boundaries of application of words are not determined by usage in all possible directions. But the example Quine has chosen is particularly unfortunate for his thesis, in that it is only too evident that our hesitations are not *here* attributable to obscurities in "analytic." It would be possible to choose other examples in which we should hesitate between "analytic" and "synthetic" and have few qualms about "true." But no more in these cases than in the sample case does the hesitation necessarily imply any obscurity in the notion of analyticity; since the hesitation would be sufficiently accounted for by the same or a similar kind of indeterminacy in the relations between the words occurring within the statement about which the question, whether it is analytic or synthetic, is raised.

Let us now consider briefly Quine's positive theory of the relations between the statements we accept as true or reject as false on the one hand and the "experiences" in the light of which we do this accepting and rejecting on the other. This theory is boldly sketched rather than precisely stated.[8] We shall merely extract from it two assertions, one of which Quine clearly takes to be incompatible with acceptance of the distinction between analytic and synthetic statements, and the other of which he regards as barring one way to an explanation of that distinction. We shall seek to show that the first assertion is not incompatible with acceptance of the distinction, but is, on the contrary, most intelligibly interpreted in a way quite consistent with it, and that the second assertion leaves the way open to just the kind of explanation which Quine thinks it precludes. The two assertions are the following:

(1) It is an illusion to suppose that there is any class of accepted statements the members of which are in principle "immune from revision" in the light of experience, i.e., any that we accept as true and must continue to accept as true whatever happens.

(2) It is an illusion to suppose that an individual statement, taken in isolation from its fellows, can admit of confirmation or disconfirmation at all. There is no particular statement such that a particular experience or set of experiences decides once for all whether that statement is true or false, independently of our attitudes to all other statements.

8. Cf. pp. 37–46.

The apparent connection between these two doctrines may be summed up as follows. Whatever our experience may be, it is in principle possible to hold on to, or reject, any particular statement we like, so long as we are prepared to make extensive enough revisions elsewhere in our system of beliefs. In practice our choices are governed largely by considerations of convenience: we wish our system to be as simple as possible, but we also wish disturbances to it, as it exists, to be as small as possible.

The apparent relevance of these doctrines to the analytic-synthetic distinction is obvious in the first case, less so in the second.

(1) Since it is an illusion to suppose that the characteristic of immunity in principle from revision, come what may, belongs, or could belong, to any statement, it is an illusion to suppose that there is a distinction to be drawn between statements which possess this characteristic and statements which lack it. Yet, Quine suggests, this is precisely the distinction which those who use the terms "analytic" and "synthetic" suppose themselves to be drawing. Quine's view would perhaps also be (though he does not explicitly say this in the article under consideration) that those who believe in the distinction are inclined at least sometimes to mistake the characteristic of strongly resisting revision (which belongs to beliefs very centrally situated in the system) for the mythical characteristic of total immunity from revision.

(2) The connection between the second doctrine and the analytic-synthetic distinction runs, according to Quine, through the verification theory of meaning. He says: "If the verification theory can be accepted as an adequate account of statement synonymy, the notion of analyticity is saved after all."[9] For, in the first place, two statements might be said to be synonymous if and only if any experiences which contribute to, or detract from, the confirmation of one contribute to, or detract from, the confirmation of the other, to the same degree; and, in the second place, synonymy could be used to explain analyticity. But, Quine seems to argue, acceptance of any such account of synonymy can only rest on the mistaken belief that individual statements, taken in isolation from their fellows, can admit of confirmation or disconfirmation at all. As soon as we give up the idea of a set of experiential truth-conditions for each statement taken separately, we must give up the idea of explaining synonymy in terms of identity of such sets.

9. Page 38.

Now to show that the relations between these doctrines and the analytic-synthetic distinction are not as Quine supposes. Let us take the second doctrine first. It is easy to see that acceptance of the second doctrine would not compel one to abandon, but only to revise, the suggested explanation of synonymy. Quine does not deny that individual statements are regarded as confirmed or disconfirmed, are in fact rejected or accepted, in the light of experience. He denies only that these relations between single statements and experience hold independently of our attitudes to *other* statements. He means that experience can confirm or disconfirm an individual statement, only given certain assumptions about the truth or falsity of other statements. When we are faced with a "recalcitrant experience," he says, we always have a choice of what statements to amend. What we have to renounce is determined by what we are anxious to keep. This view, however, requires only a slight modification of the definition of statement-synonymy in terms of confirmation and disconfirmation. All we have to say now is that two statements are synonymous if and only if any experiences which, *on certain assumptions about the truth-values of other statements,* confirm or disconfirm one of the pair, also, *on the same assumptions,* confirm or disconfirm the other to the same degree. More generally, Quine wishes to substitute for what he conceives to be an oversimple picture of the confirmation-relations between particular statements and particular experiences, the idea of a looser relation which he calls "germaneness" (p. 43). But however loosely "germaneness" is to be understood, it would apparently continue to make sense to speak of two statements as standing in the same germaneness-relation to the same particular experiences. So Quine's views are not only consistent with, but even suggest, an amended account of statement-synonymy along these lines. We are not, of course, concerned to defend such an account, or even to state it with any precision. We are only concerned to show that acceptance of Quine's doctrine of empirical confirmation does not, as he says it does, entail giving up the attempt to define statement-synonymy in terms of confirmation.

Now for the doctrine that there is no statement which is in principle immune from revision, no statement which might not be given up in the face of experience. Acceptance of this doctrine is quite consistent with adherence to the distinction between analytic and synthetic statements. Only, the adherent of *this* distinction must also insist on another; on the distinction between that kind of giving up which consists in merely admitting falsity, and that kind of giving up which involves changing or dropping a concept or set of concepts. Any form of words at one time held to express something true may, no doubt, at another time, come to be held to express something false. But it is not only philosophers who would distinguish between the case where this happens as the result of a change of opinion solely as to matters of fact, and the case where this happens at least partly as a result of a shift in the sense of the words. Where such a shift in the sense of the words is a necessary condition of the change in truth-value, then the adherent of the distinction will say that the form of words in question changes from expressing an analytic statement to expressing a synthetic statement. We are not now concerned, or called upon, to elaborate an adequate theory of conceptual revision, any more than we were called upon, just now, to elaborate an adequate theory of synonymy. If we can make sense of the idea that the same form of words, taken in one way (or bearing one sense), may express something true, and taken in another way (or bearing another sense), may express something false, then we can make sense of the idea of conceptual revision. And if we can make sense of this idea, then we can perfectly well preserve the distinction between the analytic and the synthetic, while conceding to Quine the revisability-in-principle of everything we say. As for the idea that the same form of words, taken in different ways, may bear different senses and perhaps be used to say things with different truth-values, the onus of showing that this is somehow a mistaken or confused idea rests squarely on Quine. The point of substance (or one of them) that Quine is making, by this emphasis on revisability, is that there is no absolute necessity about the adoption or use of any conceptual scheme whatever, or, more narrowly and in terms that he would reject, that there is no analytic proposition such that we *must* have linguistic forms bearing just the sense required to express that proposition. But it is one thing to admit this, and quite another thing to say that there are no necessities within any conceptual scheme we adopt or use, or, more narrowly again, that there are no linguistic forms which do express analytic propositions.

The adherent of the analytic-synthetic distinction may go further and admit that there may be cases (particularly perhaps in the field of science) where it would be pointless to press the question whether a change in the attributed truth-value of a statement represented a conceptual revision or not, and correspondingly pointless to press the analytic-synthetic distinction. We cannot quote such cases, but this inability may well be the result of ignorance of the sciences. In any case, the existence, if they do exist, of statements about which it is pointless to press the question whether they are analytic or synthetic, does not entail the nonexistence of statements which are clearly classifiable in one or other of these ways and of statements our hesitation over which has different sources, such as the possibility of alternative interpretations of the linguistic forms in which they are expressed.

This concludes our examination of Quine's article. It will be evident that our purpose has been wholly negative. We have aimed to show merely that Quine's case against the existence of the analytic-synthetic distinction is not made out. His article has two parts. In one of them, the notions of the analyticity group are criticized on the ground that they have not been adequately explained. In the other, a positive theory of truth is outlined, purporting to be incompatible with views to which believers in the analytic-synthetic distinction either must be, or are likely to be, committed. In fact, we have contended, no single point is established which those who accept the notions of the analyticity group would feel any strain in accommodating in their own system of beliefs. This is not to deny that many of the points raised are of the first importance in connection with the problem of giving a satisfactory general account of analyticity and related concepts. We are here only criticizing the contention that these points justify the rejection, as illusory, of the analytic-synthetic distinction and the notions which belong to the same family.

14

Meaning

Consider the following sentences:

"Those spots mean (meant) measles."
"Those spots didn't mean anything to me, but to the doctor they meant measles."
"The recent budget means that we shall have a hard year."

(1) I cannot say, "Those spots meant measles, but he hadn't got measles," and I cannot say, "The recent budget means that we shall have a hard year, but we shan't have." That is to say, in cases like the above, *x meant that p* and *x means that p* entail *p*.

(2) I cannot argue from "Those spots mean (meant) measles" to any conclusion about "what is (was) meant by those spots"; for example, I am not entitled to say, "What was meant by those spots was that he had measles." Equally I cannot draw from the statement about the recent budget the conclusion "What is meant by the recent budget is that we shall have a hard year."

(3) I cannot argue from "Those spots meant measles" to any conclusion to the effect that somebody or other meant by those spots so-and-so. *Mutatis mutandis*, the same is true of the sentence about the recent budget.

(4) For none of the above examples can a restatement be found in which the verb "mean" is followed by a sentence or phrase in quotation marks. Thus "Those spots meant measles" cannot be reformulated as "Those spots meant 'measles'" or as "Those spots meant 'he has measles.'"

(5) On the other hand, for all these examples an approximate re-

statement can be found beginning with the phrase "The fact that
...."; for example, "The fact that he had those spots meant that he
had measles" and "The fact that the recent budget was as it was
means that we shall have a hard year."

Now contrast the specimen sentences with the following:

"Those three rings on the bell (of the bus) mean that the bus is
full."

"That remark, 'Smith couldn't get on without his trouble and
strife,' meant that Smith found his wife indispensable."

(1) I can use the first of these and go on to say, "But it isn't in fact
full—the conductor has made a mistake"; and I can use the second
and go on, "But in fact Smith deserted her seven years ago." That is
to say, here *x means that p* and *x meant that p* do not entail *p*.

(2) I can argue from the first to some statement about "what is
(was) meant" by the rings on the bell and from the second to some
statement about "what is (was) meant" by the quoted remark.

(3) I can argue from the first sentence to the conclusion that somebody (namely the conductor) meant, or at any rate should have
meant, by the rings that the bus is full, and I can argue analogously
for the second sentence.

(4) The first sentence can be restated in a form in which the verb
"mean" is followed by a phrase in quotation marks, that is, "Those
three rings on the bell mean 'the bus is full.'" So also can the second
sentence.

(5) Such a sentence as "The fact that the bell has been rung three
times means that the bus is full" is not a restatement of the meaning
of the first sentence. Both may be true, but they do not have, even
approximately, the same meaning.

When the expressions "means," "means something," "means that"
are used in the kind of way in which they are used in the first set of
sentences, I shall speak of the sense, or senses, in which they are used,
as the *natural* sense, or senses, of the expressions in question. When
the expressions are used in the kind of way in which they are used in
the second set of sentences, I shall speak of the sense, or senses, in
which they are used, as the *nonnatural* sense, or senses, of the expressions in question. I shall use the abbreviation "means$_{NN}$" to distinguish the nonnatural sense or senses.

I propose, for convenience, also to include under the head of natural senses of "mean" such senses of "mean" as may be exemplified in

sentences of the pattern "*A* means (meant) *to do* so-and-so (by *x*)," where *A* is a human agent. By contrast, as the previous examples show, I include under the head of nonnatural senses of "mean" any senses of "mean" found in sentences of the patterns "*A* means (meant) something by *x*" or "*A* means (meant) by *x* that . . ." (This is overrigid; but it will serve as an indication.)

I do not want to maintain that *all* our uses of "mean" fall easily, obviously, and tidily into one of the two groups I have distinguished; but I think that in most cases we should be at least fairly strongly inclined to assimilate a use of "mean" to one group rather than to the other. The question which now arises is this: "What more can be said about the distinction between the cases where we should say that the word is applied in a natural sense and the cases where we should say that the word is applied in a nonnatural sense?" Asking this question will not of course prohibit us from trying to give an explanation of "meaning$_{NN}$" in terms of one or another natural sense of "mean."

This question about the distinction between natural and non-natural meaning is, I think, what people are getting at when they display an interest in a distinction between "natural" and "conventional" signs. But I think my formulation is better. For some things which can mean$_{NN}$ something are not signs (e.g. words are not), and some are not conventional in any ordinary sense (e.g. certain gestures); while some things which mean naturally are not signs of what they mean (cf. the recent budget example).

I want first to consider briefly, and reject, what I might term a causal type of answer to the question, "What is meaning$_{NN}$?" We might try to say, for instance, more or less with C. L. Stevenson,[1] that for *x* to mean$_{NN}$ something, *x* must have (roughly) a tendency to produce in an audience some attitude (cognitive or otherwise) and a tendency, in the case of a speaker, to *be* produced *by* that attitude, these tendencies being dependent on "an elaborate process of conditioning attending the use of the sign in communication."[2] This clearly will not do.

(1) Let us consider a case where an utterance, if it qualifies at all as meaning$_{NN}$ something, will be of a descriptive or informative kind and the relevant attitude, therefore, will be a cognitive one, for example,

1. *Ethics and Language* (New Haven, 1944), ch. 3.
2. Ibid., p. 57.

a belief. (I use "utterance" as a neutral word to apply to any candidate for meaning$_{NN}$; it has a convenient act-object ambiguity.) It is no doubt the case that many people have a tendency to put on a tailcoat when they think they are about to go to a dance, and it is no doubt also the case that many people, on seeing someone put on a tailcoat, would conclude that the person in question was about to go to a dance. Does this satisfy us that putting on a tailcoat means$_{NN}$ that one is about to go to a dance (or indeed means$_{NN}$ anything at all)? Obviously not. It is no help to refer to the qualifying phrase "dependent on an elaborate process of conditioning." For if all this means is that the response to the sight of a tailcoat being put on is in some way learned or acquired, it will not exclude the present case from being one of meaning$_{NN}$. But if we have to take seriously the second part of the qualifying phrase ("attending the use of the sign in communication"), then the account of meaning$_{NN}$ is obviously circular. We might just as well say, "X has meaning$_{NN}$ if it is used in communication," which, though true, is not helpful.

(2) If this is not enough, there is a difficulty—really the same difficulty, I think—which Stevenson recognizes: how we are to avoid saying, for example, that "Jones is tall" is part of what is meant by "Jones is an athlete," since to tell someone that Jones is an athlete would tend to make him believe that Jones is tall. Stevenson here resorts to invoking linguistic rules, namely, a permissive rule of language that "athletes may be nontall." This amounts to saying that we are not prohibited by rule from speaking of "nontall athletes." But why are we not prohibited? Not because it is not bad grammar, or is not impolite, and so on, but presumably because it is not meaningless (or, if this is too strong, does not in any way violate the rules of meaning for the expressions concerned). But this seems to involve us in another circle. Moreover, one wants to ask why, if it is legitimate to appeal here to rules to distinguish what is meant from what is suggested, this appeal was not made earlier, in the case of groans, for example, to deal with which Stevenson originally introduced the qualifying phrase about dependence on conditioning.

A further deficiency in a causal theory of the type just expounded seems to be that, even if we accept it as it stands, we are furnished with an analysis only of statements about the *standard* meaning, or the meaning in general, of a "sign." No provision is made for dealing with statements about what a particular speaker or writer means by a sign on a particular occasion (which may well diverge from the standard meaning of the sign); nor is it obvious how the theory could be adapted to make such provision. One might even go further in criticism and maintain that the causal theory ignores the fact that the meaning (in general) of a sign needs to be explained in terms of what users of the sign do (or should) mean by it on particular occasions; and so the latter notion, which is unexplained by the causal theory, is in fact the fundamental one. I am sympathetic to this more radical criticism, though I am aware that the point is controversial.

I do not propose to consider any further theories of the "causal-tendency" type. I suspect no such theory could avoid difficulties analogous to those I have outlined without utterly losing its claim to rank as a theory of this type.

I will now try a different and, I hope, more promising line. If we can elucidate the meaning of

"x meant$_{NN}$ something (on a particular occasion)" and
"x meant$_{NN}$ that so-and-so (on a particular occasion)"

and of

"A meant$_{NN}$ something by x (on a particular occasion)" and
"A meant$_{NN}$ by x that so-and-so (on a particular occasion),"

this might reasonably be expected to help us with

"x means$_{NN}$ (timeless) something (that so-and-so)"
"A means$_{NN}$ (timeless) by x something (that so-and-so),"

and with the explication of "means the same as," "understands," "entails," and so on. Let us for the moment pretend that we have to deal only with utterances which might be informative or descriptive.

A first shot would be to suggest that "x meant$_{NN}$ something" would be true if x was intended by its utterer to induce a belief in some "audience" and that to say what the belief was would be to say what x meant$_{NN}$. This will not do. I might leave B's handkerchief near the scene of a murder in order to induce the detective to believe that B was the murderer; but we should not want to say that the handkerchief (or my leaving it there) meant$_{NN}$ anything or that I had meant$_{NN}$ by leaving it that B was the murderer. Clearly we must at least add that, for x to have meant$_{NN}$ anything, not merely must it have been "uttered" with the intention of inducing a certain belief but also the utterer must have intended an "audience" to recognize the intention behind the utterance.

This, though perhaps better, is not good enough. Consider the following cases:

(1) Herod presents Salome with the head of St. John the Baptist on a charger.

(2) Feeling faint, a child lets its mother see how pale it is (hoping that she may draw her own conclusions and help).

(3) I leave the china my daughter has broken lying around for my wife to see.

Here we seem to have cases which satisfy the conditions so far given for meaning$_{NN}$. For example, Herod intended to make Salome believe that St. John the Baptist was dead and no doubt also intended Salome to recognize that he intended her to believe that St. John the Baptist was dead. Similarly for the other cases. Yet I certainly do not think that we should want to say that we have here cases of meaning$_{NN}$.

What we want to find is the difference between, for example, "deliberately and openly letting someone know" and "telling" and between "getting someone to think" and "telling."

The way out is perhaps as follows. Compare the following two cases:

(1) I show Mr. X a photograph of Mr. Y displaying undue familiarity to Mrs. X.

(2) I draw a picture of Mr. Y behaving in this manner and show it to Mr. X.

I find that I want to deny that in (1) the photograph (or my showing it to Mr. X) meant$_{NN}$ anything at all; while I want to assert that in (2) the picture (or my drawing and showing it) meant$_{NN}$ something (that Mr. Y had been unduly familiar), or at least that I had meant$_{NN}$ by it that Mr. Y had been unduly familiar. What is the difference between the two cases? Surely that in case (1) Mr. X's recognition of my intention to make him believe that there is something between Mr. Y and Mrs. X is (more or less) irrelevant to the production of this effect by the photograph. Mr. X would be led by the photograph at least to suspect Mrs. X even if, instead of showing it to him, I had left it in his room by accident; and I (the photograph shower) would not be unaware of this. But it will make a difference to the effect of my picture on Mr. X whether or not he takes me to be intending to inform him (make him believe something) about Mrs. X, and not to be just doodling or trying to produce a work of art.

But now we seem to be landed in a further difficulty if we accept this account. For consider now, say, frowning. If I frown spontaneously, in the ordinary course of events, someone looking at me may well treat the frown as a natural sign of displeasure. But if I frown deliberately (to convey my displeasure), an onlooker may be expected, provided he recognizes my intention, *still* to conclude that I am displeased. Ought we not then to say, since it could not be expected to make any difference to the onlooker's reaction whether he regards my frown as spontaneous or as intended to be informative, that my frown (deliberate) does *not* mean$_{NN}$ anything? I think this difficulty can be met; for though in general a deliberate frown may have the same effect (with respect to inducing belief in my displeasure) as a spontaneous frown, it can be expected to have the same effect only *provided* the audience takes it as intended to convey displeasure. That is, if we take away the recognition of intention, leaving the other circumstances (including the recognition of the frown as deliberate), the belief-producing tendency of the frown must be regarded as being impaired or destroyed.

Perhaps we may sum up what is necessary for A to mean something by x as follows. A must intend to induce by x a belief in an audience, and he must also intend his utterance to be recognized as so intended. But these intentions are not independent; the recognition is intended by A to play its part in inducing the belief, and if it does not do so something will have gone wrong with the fulfillment of A's intentions. Moreover, A's intending that the recognition should play this part implies, I think, that he assumes that there is some chance that it will in fact play this part, that he does not regard it as a foregone conclusion that the belief will be induced in the audience whether or not the intention behind the utterance is recognized. Shortly, perhaps, we may say that "A meant$_{NN}$ something by x" is roughly equivalent to "A uttered x with the intention of inducing a belief by means of the recognition of this intention." (This seems to involve a reflexive paradox, but it does not really do so.)

Now perhaps it is time to drop the pretense that we have to deal only with "informative" cases. Let us start with some examples of imperatives or quasi-imperatives. I have a very avaricious man in my room, and I want him to go; so I throw a pound note out of the window. Is there here any utterance with a meaning$_{NN}$? No, because in behaving as I did, I did not intend his recognition of my purpose to be in any way effective in getting him to go. This is parallel to the photograph case. If, on the other hand, I had pointed to the door or given him a little push, then my behavior might well be held to constitute a meaningful$_{NN}$ utterance, just because the recognition of my intention would be intended by me to be effective in speeding his departure. Another pair of cases would be (1) a policeman who stops a car by standing in its way and (2) a policeman who stops a car by waving.

Or, to turn briefly to another type of case, if, as an examiner, I fail a man, I may well cause him distress or indignation or humiliation; and if I am vindictive, I may intend this effect and even intend him to recognize my intention. But I should not be inclined to say that my failing him meant$_{NN}$ anything. On the other hand, if I cut someone in the street, I do feel inclined to assimilate this to the cases of meaning$_{NN}$, and this inclination seems to me dependent on the fact that I could not reasonably expect him to be distressed (indignant, humiliated) unless he recognized my intention to affect him in this way. If my college stopped my salary altogether, I should accuse them of ruining me; if they cut it by one pound, I might accuse them of insulting me; with some larger cuts I might not know quite what to say.

Perhaps then we may make the following generalizations.

(1) "A meant$_{NN}$ something by x" is (roughly) equivalent to "A intended the utterance of x to produce some effect in an audience by means of the recognition of this intention"; and we may add that to ask what A meant is to ask for a specification of the intended effect (though, of course, it may not always be possible to get a straight answer involving a "that" clause, for example, "a belief that . . .").

(2) "x meant something" is (roughly) equivalent to "Somebody meant$_{NN}$ something by x." Here again there will be cases where this will not quite work. I feel inclined to say that (as regards traffic lights) the change to red meant$_{NN}$ that the traffic was to stop; but it would be very unnatural to say, "Somebody (e.g. the Corporation) meant$_{NN}$ by the red-light change that the traffic was to stop." Nevertheless, there seems to be *some* sort of reference to somebody's intentions.

(3) "x means$_{NN}$ (timeless) that so-and-so" might as a first shot be equated with some statement or disjunction of statements about what "people" (vague) intend (with qualifications about "recognition") to effect by x. I shall have a word to say about this.

Will any kind of intended effect do, or may there be cases where an effect is intended (with the required qualifications) and yet we should not want to talk of meaning$_{NN}$? Suppose I discovered some person so constituted that, when I told him that whenever I grunted in a special way I wanted him to blush or to incur some physical malady, thereafter whenever he recognized the grunt (and with it my intention), he did blush or incur the malady. Should we then want to say that the grunt meant$_{NN}$ something? I do not think so. This points to the fact that for x to have meaning$_{NN}$, the intended effect must be something which in some sense is within the control of the audience, or that in some sense of "reason" the recognition of the intention behind x is for the audience a reason and not merely a cause. It might look as if there is a sort of pun here ("reason for believing" and "reason for doing"), but I do not think this is serious. For though no doubt from one point of view questions about reasons for believing are questions about evidence and so quite different from questions about reasons for doing, nevertheless to recognize an utterer's intention in uttering x (descriptive utterance), to have a reason for believing that so-and-so, is at least quite like "having a motive for" accepting so-and-so. Decisions "that" seem to involve decisions "to" (and this is why we can "refuse to believe" and also be "compelled to believe"). (The "cutting" case needs slightly different treatment, for one cannot in any straightforward sense "decide" to be offended; but one can refuse to be offended.) It looks, then, as if the intended effect must be something within the control of the audience, or at least the *sort* of thing which is within its control.

One point before passing to an objection or two. I think it follows that from what I have said about the connection between meaning$_{NN}$ and recognition of intention that (insofar as I am right) only what I may call the primary intention of an utterer is relevant to the meaning$_{NN}$ of an utterance. For if I utter x, intending (with the aid of the recognition of this intention) to induce an effect E, and intend this effect E to lead to a further effect F, then insofar as the occurrence of F is thought to be dependent solely on E, I cannot regard F as in the least dependent on recognition of my intention to induce E. That is, if (say) I intend to get a man to do something by giving him some information, it cannot be regarded as relevant to the meaning$_{NN}$ of my utterance to describe what I intend him to do.

Now some question may be raised about my use, fairly free, of such words as "intention" and "recognition." I must disclaim any intention of peopling all our talking life with armies of complicated psychological occurrences. I do not hope to solve any philosophical puzzles about intending, but I do want briefly to argue that no special difficulties are raised by my use of the word "intention" in connection with meaning. First, there will be cases where an utterance is accompanied or preceded by a conscious "plan," or explicit formulation of intention (e.g. I declare how I am going to use x, or ask myself how to "get something across"). The presence of such an explicit "plan" obviously counts fairly heavily in favor of the utterer's intention (meaning) being as "planned"; though it is not, I think, conclusive; for example, a speaker who has declared an intention to use a familiar expression in an unfamiliar way may slip into the familiar use. Similarly in nonlinguistic cases: if we are asking about an agent's intention, a previous expression counts heavily; nevertheless, a man might plan to throw a letter in the dustbin and yet take it to the post; when lifting his hand, he might "come to" and say *either* "I didn't intend to do this at all" *or* "I suppose I must have been intending to put it in."

Explicitly formulated linguistic (or quasilinguistic) intentions are no doubt comparatively rare. In their absence we would seem to rely on very much the same kinds of criteria as we do in the case of nonlinguistic intentions where there is a general usage. An utterer is held to intend to convey what is normally conveyed (or normally intended to be conveyed), and we require a good reason for accepting that a particular use diverges from the general usage (e.g. he never knew or had forgotten the general usage). Similarly in nonlinguistic cases: we are presumed to intend the normal consequences of our actions.

Again, in cases where there is doubt, say, about which of two or more things an utterer intends to convey, we tend to refer to the context (linguistic or otherwise) of the utterance and ask which of the alternatives would be relevant to other things he is saying or doing, or which intention in a particular situation would fit in with some purpose he obviously has (e.g. a man who calls for a "pump" at a fire would not want a bicycle pump). Nonlinguistic parallels are obvious: context is a criterion in settling the question of why a man who has just put a cigarette in his mouth has put his hand in his pocket; relevance to an obvious end is a criterion in settling why a man is running away from a bull.

In certain linguistic cases we ask the utterer afterward about his intention, and in a few of these cases (the very difficult ones, such as a philosopher being asked to explain the meaning of an unclear passage in one of his works), the answer is not based on what he remembers but is more like a decision, a decision about how what he said is to be taken. I cannot find a nonlinguistic parallel here; but the case is so special as not to seem to contribute a vital difference.

All this is very obvious; but surely to show that the criteria for judging linguistic intentions are very like the criteria for judging non-linguistic intentions is to show that linguistic intentions are very like nonlinguistic intentions.

15

The Causal Theory of Perception

1

The Causal Theory of Perception (CTP) has for some time received comparatively little attention, mainly, I suspect, because it has been generally assumed that the theory either asserts or involves as a consequence the proposition that material objects are unobservable, and that the unacceptability of this proposition is sufficient to dispose of the theory. I am inclined to regard this attitude to the CTP as unfair or at least unduly unsympathetic and I shall attempt to outline a thesis which might not improperly be considered to be a version of the CTP, and which is, if not true, at least not too obviously false.

What is to count as holding a causal theory of perception? (1) I shall take it as being insufficient merely to believe that the perception of a material object is always to be causally explained by reference to conditions the specification of at least one of which involves a mention of the object perceived; that, for example, the perception is the terminus of a causal sequence involving at an earlier stage some event or process in the history of the perceived object. Such a belief does not seem to be philosophical in character; its object has the appearance of being a very general contingent proposition; though it is worth remarking that if the version of the CTP with which I shall be primarily concerned is correct, it (or something like it) will turn out to be a necessary rather than a contingent truth. (2) It may be held that the elucidation of the notion of perceiving a material object will include some reference to the role of the material object perceived in the causal ancestry of the perception or of the sense-impression or sense-datum involved in the perception. This contention is central to what I regard as a standard version of the CTP. (3) It might be held that it is the task of the philosopher of perception not to elucidate or characterize the ordinary notion of perceiving a material object, but to provide a rational reconstruction of it, to replace it by some concept more appropriate to an ideal or scientific language: it might further be suggested that such a redefinition might be formulated in terms of the effect of the presence of an object upon the observer's sense-organ and nervous system or upon his behavior or "behavior-tendencies" or in terms of both of these effects. A view of this kind may perhaps deserve to be called a causal theory of perception; but I shall not be concerned with theories on these lines. (4) I shall distinguish from the adoption of a CTP the attempt to provide for a wider or narrower range of propositions ascribing properties to material objects a certain sort of causal analysis: the kind of analysis which I have in mind is that which, on *one* possible interpretation, Locke could be taken as suggesting for ascriptions of, for example, color and temperature; he might be understood to be holding that such propositions assert that an object would, in certain standard conditions, cause an observer to have certain sorts of ideas of sense-impressions.

In Price's *Perception*,[1] there appears a preliminary formulation of the CTP which would bring it under the second of the headings distinguished in the previous paragraph. The CTP is specified as maintaining (1) that in the case of all sense-data (not merely visual and tactual) "belonging to" simply means *being caused by,* so that "M is present to my senses" will be equivalent to "M causes a sense-datum with which I am acquainted"; (2) that consciousness is fundamentally an inference from effect to cause. Since it is, I think, fair to say[2] that the expression "present to my senses" was introduced by Price as a special term to distinguish one of the possible senses of the verb "perceive," the first clause of the quotation above may be taken as propounding the thesis that "I am perceiving M" (in one sense of that expression) is to be regarded as equivalent to "I am having (or sensing) a sense-datum which is caused by M." (The second clause I shall for the time being ignore.) I shall proceed to consider at some length the feature which this version of the CTP shares with other noncausal

---

1. Steven Davis, ed., *Causal Theories of Mind: Action, Knowledge, Memory, Perception, and Reference* (Berlin, N.Y., 1983), p. 66. All references are to page numbers in this book.
2. Cf. ibid., pp. 21–25.

theories of perception, namely, the claim that perceiving a material object involves having or sensing a sense-datum; for unless this claim can be made out, the special features of the CTP become otiose.

2

The primary difficulty facing the contention that perceiving involves having or sensing a sense-datum is that of giving a satisfactory explanation of the meaning of the technical term "sense-datum." One familiar method of attempting this task is that of trying to prove, by means of some form of the Argument from Illusion, the existence of objects of a special sort for which the term "sense-datum" is offered as a class-name. Another method (that adopted in a famous passage by Moore) is that of giving directions which are designed to enable one to pick out items of the kind to which the term "sense-datum" is to be applied. The general character of the objections to each of these procedures is also familiar, and I shall, for present purposes, assume that neither procedure is satisfactory.

Various philosophers have suggested that though attempts to indicate, or demonstrate the existence of, special objects to be called sense-data have all failed, nevertheless the expression "sense-datum" can (and should) be introduced as a technical term; its use would be explicitly defined by reference to such supposedly standard locutions as "So-and-so looks φ (e.g., blue) to me," "It looks (feels) to me as if there were a φ so-and-so," "I seem to see something φ," and so on. Now as the objection to such proposals which I have in mind is one which might be described as an objection in principle, it is not to my present purpose to consider how in detail such an explicit definition of the notion of a sense-datum might be formulated. I should, however, remark that this program may be by no means so easy to carry through as the casual way in which it is sometimes proposed might suggest; various expressions are candidates for the key role in this enterprise, such as "looks" ("feels," etc.), "seems," "appears," and the more or less subtle differences between them would have to be investigated; and furthermore, even if one has decided on a preferred candidate, not all of its uses would be suitable; if, for example, we decide to employ the expressions "looks," etc., are we to accept the legitimacy of the sentence "It looks indigestible to me" as providing us with the sense-datum sentence "I am having an indigestible visual sense-datum"?

A general objection to the suggested procedure might run as follows: When someone makes such a remark as "It looks red to me," a certain implication is carried, an implication which is disjunctive in form. It is implied either that the object referred to is known or believed by the speaker not to *be* red, *or* that it has been denied by someone else to be red, *or* that the speaker is doubtful whether it is red, *or* that someone else has expressed doubt whether it is red, *or* that the situation is such that though no doubt has actually been expressed and no denial has actually been made, some person or other might feel inclined toward denial or doubt if he were to address himself to the question whether the object is actually red. This may not be an absolutely exact or complete characterization of the implication, but it is perhaps good enough to be going on with. Let us refer to the condition which is fulfilled when one or the other of the limbs of this disjunction is true as the D-or-D condition ("doubt or denial" condition). Now we may perhaps agree that there is liable to be something odd or even absurd about employing an "It looks to me" locution when the appropriate D-or-D condition is fairly obviously not fulfilled; there would be something at least prima facie odd about my saying "That looks red to me" (not as a joke) when I am confronted by a British pillar-box in normal daylight at a range of a few feet. At this point my objector advances a twofold thesis (*a*) that it is a feature of the use, perhaps of the meaning, of such locutions as "looks to me" that they should carry the implication that the D-or-D condition is fulfilled, and that if they were uttered by a speaker who did not suppose this condition was fulfilled, he would be guilty of a misuse of the locutions in question (unless of course he were intending to deceive his audience into thinking that the condition was fulfilled), and (*b*) that in cases where the D-or-D condition is unfulfilled, the utterance employing the "looks to me" locution, so far from being uninterestingly true, is neither true nor false. Thus armed, my objector now assails the latter-day sense-datum theorist. Our everyday life is populated with cases in which the sensible characteristics of the things we encounter are not the subject of any kind of doubt or controversy; consequently there will be countless situations in which the employment of the "looks to me" idiom would be out of order and neither true nor false. But the sense-datum theorist wants his sense-datum statements to be such that some one or more of them is true whenever a perceptual statement is true; for he wants to go on to give a *general* analysis of perceptual statements in terms of the notion of sense-data. But this goal must be unattainable if "looks to me" statements (and so sense-datum statements) can be truly made only in the *less* straightforward perceptual situations; and if the goal is unattainable, the CTP collapses.

It is, of course, possible to take a different view of the linguistic phenomena outlined in my previous paragraph. One may contend that if I were to say "it looks red to me" in a situation in which the D-or-D condition is not fulfilled, what I say is (subject to certain qualifications) true, not "neuter"; while admitting that, though true, it might be very misleading and that its truth might be very boring and its misleadingness very important, one might still hold that its *suggestio falsi* is perfectly compatible with its literal truth. Furthermore, one might argue that though perhaps someone who, without intent to deceive, employed the "it looks to me" locution when he did not suppose the D-or-D condition to be fulfilled would be guilty in some sense of a misuse of *language,* he could be said not to be guilty of a misuse of the particular locution in question; for, one might say, the implication of the fulfillment of the D-or-D condition attaches to such locutions not as a special feature of the meaning or use of these expressions, but in virtue of a general feature or principle of the use of language. The mistake of supposing the implication to constitute a "part of the meaning" of "looks to me" is somewhat similar to, though more insidious than, the mistake which would be made if one supposed that the so-called implication that one believes it to be raining was "a part of the meaning" of the expression "it is raining." The short and literally inaccurate reply to such a supposition might be that the so-called implication attaches because the expression is a propositional one, not because it is the particular propositional expression which it happens to be.

Until fairly recently it seemed to me to be very difficult indeed to find any arguments which seemed at all likely to settle the issue between these two positions. One might, for example, suggest that it is open to the champion of sense-data to lay down that the sense-datum sentence "I have a pink sense-datum" should express truth if and only if the facts are as they would have to be for it to be true, *if it were in order,* to say "Something looks pink to me," even though it may not actually be in order to say this (because the D-or-D condition is unfulfilled). But this attempt to bypass the objector's position would be met by the reply that it begs the question; for it assumes that there is some way of specifying the facts in isolation from the implication standardly carried by such a specification; and this is precisely what the objector is denying. As a result of frustrations of this kind, I was led to suspect that neither position should be regarded as right or wrong, but that the linguistic phenomena *could* be looked at in either way, though there might be reasons for preferring to adopt one way of viewing them rather than the other; that there might be no proofs or disproofs, but only inducements. On this assumption I was inclined to rule against my objector, partly because his opponent's position was more in line with the kind of thing I was inclined to say about other linguistic phenomena which are in some degree comparable, but mainly because the objector's short way with sense-data is an even shorter way with skepticism about the material world; and I think a skeptic might complain that though his worries may well prove dissoluble, he ought at least to be able to state them; if we do not allow him to state them, we cannot remove the real source of his discomfort. However, I am now inclined to think that the issue is a decidable one, and that my objector's position is wrong and that of his opponent right. I shall attempt to develop a single argument (though no doubt there are others) to support this claim, and as a preliminary, I shall embark on a discursus about certain aspects of the concept or concepts of implication, using some more or less well-worn examples.

3

[This section is here omitted, since the material which it presents is substantially the same as that discussed in Essay 2, under the title "Logic and Conversation." Under the general heading of "Implication," I introduced four main examples, one exemplifying what is commonly called the notion of "presupposition," the other three being instances of what I later called "implicature," in one case of conventional implicature and in the other two of nonconventional implicature. With regard to the selected examples I raised four different questions, on the answers to which depended some important distinctions between the examples. These questions were whether the truth of what is implied is a necessary condition of the original statement's possessing a truth-value, what it is that is properly regarded as the vehicle of implication, whether the implication possesses one or both of the features of detachability and cancelability, and whether the presence of the implication is or is not a matter of the meaning of some particular word or phrase. I also raised the question of the connection, in some cases, of the implication and general principles governing the use of language, in particular with what I later called the first maxim of Quality. On the basis of this material I suggested the possibility of the existence of a class of nonconventional implications which I later called conversational implicatures.]

4

(The Objection Reconsidered)

Let us now revert to the main topic of this section of my paper. Let us call a statement of the type expressible by such a sentence as "it looks red to me" an *L*-statement. What are we to say of the relation between an *L*-statement and the corresponding *D*-or-*D* condition, in terms of the ideas introduced in the previous subsection? Or, rather, since this might be controversial, what would my objector think it correct to say on this subject? As I have represented his position, he is explicitly committed to holding that the fulfillment of the appropriate *D*-or-*D* condition is a necessary precondition of an *L*-statement's being either true or false. He is also more or less explicitly committed to holding that the implication that the *D*-or-*D* condition is fulfilled is a matter of the meaning of the word "looks" (or of the phrase "looks to me"); that, for example, someone who failed to realize that there existed this implication would *thereby* show that he did not fully understand the meaning of the expression or phrase in question. It is conceivable that this last-mentioned thesis is independent of the rest of his position, that he could, if necessary, abandon it without destroying the remainder of his position. I shall not, therefore, in what follows address myself directly to this point, though I have hopes that it may turn out to be *solutum ambulando*. Next, he would, I think, wish to say that the implication of the fulfillment of the *D*-or-*D* condition is neither detachable nor cancelable; but even if he should wish to say this, he certainly *must* say it if his objection is to be of any importance. For if the implication is detachable or cancelable, all that the sense-datum theorist needs to do is to find some form of words from which the implication is detached or in which it is canceled, and use this expression to define the notion of a sense-datum. It is not enough that *some* ways of introducing sense-data should be vulnerable to his objection; it is essential that *all* should be vulnerable. Finally, it is not obvious that he is committed either to asserting or to denying any of the possibilities as regards what may be spoken of as being the vehicle of implication, so I shall not at the moment pursue this matter, though I shall suggest later that he can only maintain his position by giving what in fact is certainly a wrong answer to this question.

It is now time for the attack to begin. It seems to me that the contention that the fulfillment of the *D*-or-*D* condition is a necessary condition of the truth or falsity of an *L*-statement cannot be upheld (at any rate in its natural interpretation). For an *L*-statement can certainly be false, even if the *D*-or-*D* condition is unfulfilled. Suppose that I am confronted in normal daylight by a perfectly normal pillar-box; suppose further that I am in the presence of a normal unskeptical companion; both he and I know perfectly well that the pillar-box is red. However, unknown to him, I suffer chronically from Smith's Disease, attacks of which are not obvious to another party; these attacks involve, among other things perhaps, the peculiarity that at the time red things look some quite different color to me. I know that I have this disease, and I am having (and know that I am having) an attack at the moment. In these circumstances I say, "That pillar-box looks red to me." I would suggest that here the *D*-or-*D* condition is not fulfilled; my companion would receive my remark with just that mixture of puzzlement and scorn which would please my objector; and yet when he learned about my attack of Smith's Disease, he would certainly think that what I had said had been false.

At this point it might perhaps be suggested that though I have succeeded in producing an example of an *L*-statement which would be false, I have not succeeded in producing an example of an *L*-statement which is false when the *D*-or-*D* condition is unfulfilled; for in fact the *D*-or-*D* condition is fulfilled. For the speaker in my little story, it might be said, *has* some reason to doubt whether the pillar-box before him is red, and this is enough to ensure the fulfillment of the condition, *even though* the speaker also has information (e.g., that this is the pillar-box he has seen every day for years, and that it has not been repainted, and so on) which enables him entirely to discount this *prima facie* reason for doubt. But this will not do at all. For what is this *prima facie* reason for doubting whether the pillar-box really is red? If you like, it is that it looks blue to him. But this is an unnecessarily specific description of his reason; its looking blue to him only counts against its really being red because its looking blue is a way of failing to look red; there need be nothing specially important about its looking blue as distinct from looking any other color, except red. So this rescue attempt seems to involve supposing that one way of fulfilling the precondition of an *L*-statement's having a truth-value at all consists in its having the truth-value *F*, or at least in some state of affairs which entails that it has the truth-value *F*. But surely, that a statement should be false cannot be one way of fulfilling a precondition of that statement's having a truth-value; the mere fulfillment of a precondition of a statement's having a truth-value ought to leave it open (to be decided on other grounds) *which* truth-value it has.

Let us assume that this rearguard action has been disposed of. Then it is tempting to argue as follows: Since the objector can no longer maintain that fulfillment of the *D*-or-*D* condition is a prerequisite of an *L*-statement's having a truth-value, he will have to admit that fulfillment is *at most* a *partial truth*-condition, albeit of a special kind (i.e., is *one* of the things which have to be the case if the statement is to be true). It cannot be the *only* truth-condition, so there must be another truth-condition; indeed, we can say what this is in the light of the preceding argument; it consists in the nonfulfillment of the statement's falsity-condition or falsity-conditions (which have just been shown to be independent of the *D*-or-*D* condition); to put it less opaquely, it consists in there being nothing to make the *L*-statement false. But now, it may be thought, all is plain sailing for the sense-datum theorist; he can simply lay down that a sense-datum sentence is to express a truth if and only if the second truth-condition of the corresponding *L*-statement is fulfilled, regardless of whether its first truth-condition (the *D*-or-*D* condition) is fulfilled. It will be seen that the idea behind this argument is that, once the objector has been made to withdraw the contention that the fulfillment of the *D*-or-*D* condition is a condition of an *L*-statement's having a truth-value, he can be forced to withdraw also the contention that the implication that the *D*-or-*D* condition is fulfilled is nondetachable; and this destroys his position.

So far so good, perhaps, but unfortunately not yet good enough. For the objector has a powerful-looking reply at his disposal. He may say: "Once again you are covertly begging the question. You are assuming, quite without justification, that because one can, in some sense, distinguish the second truth-condition from the first, it is therefore the case that the implication of the fulfillment of the first (*D*-or-

D) condition is detachable; that is, that there must be a way of specifying the second condition which does not carry the implication that the first condition is fulfilled. But your argument has certainly not proved this conclusion. Consider a simple parallel: it is perfectly obvious that objects which are not vermilion in color may or may not be red; so being red is not a necessary falsity-condition of being vermilion. It is also true that being red is only a partial truth-condition of being vermilion if what this means is that to establish that something is red is not enough to establish that it is vermilion. But it does not follow (and indeed it is false) that there is any way of formulating a supplementary truth-condition for an object's being vermilion which would be free from the implication that the object in question is red. This *non sequitur* is very much the same as the one of which you are guilty; the fulfillment of the D-or-D condition may perfectly well be only a *truth*-condition of an L-statement, and only *one* of a pair of truth-conditions at that, without its being the case that the implication of its fulfillment is detachable." He may also add the following point: "Though the contention that the fulfillment of the D-or-D condition is a precondition of the truth or falsity of the corresponding L-statement cannot be upheld under the interpretation which you have given to it, it can be upheld if it is given another not unnatural interpretation. I cannot, in view of your counterexample, maintain that for an L-statement to be true, or again for it to be false, the D-or-D condition must be fulfilled. But I can maintain that the D-or-D condition's fulfillment is a condition of truth or falsity of an L-statement in the following sense, namely that if the D-or-D condition *is* fulfilled, then T and F are the two possibilities between which, on other grounds, the decision lies (i.e., N is excluded): whereas if the D-or-D condition is *not* fulfilled, then one has to decide not between these possibilities, but between the possibilities N and F (i.e., T is excluded.)"

This onslaught can, I think, be met, though at the cost of some modification to the line of argument against which it was directed. I think that the following reply can be made: "There is a crucial difference between the two cases which you treat as parallel. Let us endeavor to formulate a supplementary truth-condition for the form of statement "x is vermilion"; we might suggest the condition that x has the feature which differentiates vermilion things from other red things. But to suppose that x satisfies this condition, but does not satisfy the first truth-condition, namely that x should be red, would be to commit a logical absurdity; x cannot logically differ from red things which are not vermilion in *just* the way in which vermilion things differ from red things which are not vermilion, without being red. Consequently one cannot assert, in this case, that the second truth-condition is fulfilled without its being implied that the first is fulfilled, nor can one go on to cancel this implication. But in the case of an *L*-statement there is no kind of *logical* implication between the second truth-condition and the first. For one thing, if there were such a logical connection, there would also have to be such a logical connection between the *L*-statement itself and the fulfillment of the *D*-or-*D* condition; and if this were so, the implication that the *D*-or-*D* condition is fulfilled would have to be carried by *what was said* or *asserted* by the utterance of an *L*-statement. But that this is not so can be seen from the unacceptability of such a hypothetical as 'If this pillar-box looks red to me, then I or someone else is, or might be, inclined to deny that it is red or to doubt whether it is red.' For another thing, it is surely clear that if I were now to say 'Nothing is the case which would make it false for me to say that the palm of this hand looks pink to me, though I do not mean to imply that I or anyone else is or might be inclined to deny that, or doubt whether, it is pink,' this would be a perfectly intelligible remark even though it might be thought both wordy and boring. Indeed, I am prepared actually to say it. Consequently, although you may be right in claiming that it has not been shown that the implication of the fulfillment of the *D*-or-*D* condition is *detachable* (and indeed it may well be non-detachable), you must be wrong in thinking that this implication is not *cancelable*. Admittedly there is at least one case in which an implication which is not logical in character is at least in a sense noncancelable; we found one in considering example (2) 'She was poor but she was honest.' But if we look a little more closely, we can see that the reason why the implication here is, in a sense, not cancelable is just that it *is* detachable (by the use of 'and'). More fully, the reason why it would be peculiar to say 'She was poor but she was honest, though I do not mean to imply that there is any contrast' is that anyone who said this would have *first* gone out of his way to find a form of words which introduced the implication, and *then* would have gone to some trouble to take it out again. Why didn't he just leave it out? The upshot is that if you say that the implication of the fulfillment of the *D*-or-*D* condition is (*a*) not logical in character and (*b*) not detachable, then you must allow that it is cancelable. And this is all that the sense-datum theorist needs." If there is an answer to this argument, I do not at present know what it is.

I will conclude by making three auxiliary points.

(1) If I am right in thinking that my objector has gone astray, then I think I can suggest a possible explanation of his coming to make his mistake. His original resistance to attempts to distinguish between the facts stated by an L-statement and the fulfillment of the D-or-D condition arose, I think, from a feeling that if the D-or-D condition were unfulfilled, there would be no facts to state; and this feeling is, I suspect, the result of noticing the baffling character that the utterance of an L-statement would have in certain circumstances. But precisely *what* circumstances? I think the sort of imaginary example the objector has in mind may be the following: I and a companion are standing in front of a pillar-box in normal daylight. Each of us has every reason to suppose that the other is perfectly normal. In these circumstances he says out of the blue "This pillar-box looks red to me," and (it is assumed) I am not allowed to take this as a joke. So I am baffled. I do not know what to make of his utterance. But surely the reason why I am baffled is that I cannot see what communication-function he intends his utterance to fulfill; it has the form of an utterance designed to impart information, but what information could he possibly imagine would be imparted to me which I do not already possess? So of course this utterance is baffling. But what the objector may not have noticed is that if in these circumstances my companion had said not "This pillar-box looks red to me" but "This pillar-box is red," his utterance would have been equally baffling, if not *more* baffling. My point can be stated more generally. The objector wants to attribute to L-statements certain special features (e.g., that of being neither T nor F in certain circumstances) which distinguish them from at least some other statements. If so, he cannot derive support for his thesis from the fact that the utterance of an L-statement would be baffling in certain circumstances, when those circumstances are such that (*mutatis mutandis*) they would make *any statement whatever* baffling. He ought to take as his examples not L-statements made about objects which both speaker and audience can see perfectly clearly, but L-statements made about objects which the speaker can see but the audience cannot. But when the examples are thus changed, his case seems much less plausible.

(2) If I am asked to indicate what it would be *right* to say about L-statements and the implications involved in these utterances, I shall

answer: very much the same sort of thing as I have earlier in this essay suggested as regards disjunctive statements. I do not want to duplicate my earlier remarks, so I will deal with this very briefly. (i) The fulfillment of the relevant *D*-or-*D* condition is not a condition either of the truth *or* of the falsity of an *L*-statement, though if this condition is not fulfilled the utterance of the *L*-statement may well be extremely misleading (in its implication). (ii) Like my examples (3) and (4) above, we may speak either of the speaker or of his saying what he did say as vehicles of the implication; the second of these possibilities is important in that, if I am right about it, it leads to point (iii). (iii) The implication is not detachable in any official sense. For if the implication can be regarded as being carried by his saying that (rather than something else), for example, his mentioning *this* fact or putative fact rather than some other fact or putative fact, then it seems clear that any other way of stating the same fact or putative fact would involve the same implication as the original way of stating the fact in question. (iv) Comparably with examples (3) and (4), the implication is detachable in the further possible nonofficial sense which I referred to earlier in connection with (4); there will be *some* conditions of utterance in which the implication is no longer carried, for example, if I am talking to my oculist about how things look to me. (v) The implication is cancelable (I need say no more about this). (vi) As in the case of example (4), the reason why the implication is *standardly* carried is to be found in the operation of some such general principle as that giving preference to the making of a stronger rather than a weaker statement in the absence of a reason for not so doing. The implication therefore is not of a part of the meaning of the expression "looks to me." There is, however, here an important difference between the case of *L*-statements and that of disjunctives. A disjunctive is weaker than either of its disjuncts in a straightforward logical sense, namely, it is entailed by, but does not entail, each of its disjuncts. The statement "It looks red to me" is not, however, weaker than the statement "it is red" in just this sense; neither statement entails the other. I think that one has, nevertheless, a strong inclination to regard the first of these statements as weaker than the second; but I shall not here attempt to determine in what sense of "weaker" this may be true.

(3) The issue with which I have been mainly concerned may be thought rather a fine point, but it is certainly not an isolated one. There are several philosophical theses or dicta which would, I think,

need to be examined in order to see whether or not they are sufficiently parallel to the thesis which I have been discussing to be amenable to treatment of the same general kind. Examples which occur to me are the following: (1) You cannot see a *knife* as a knife, though you may see what is not a knife as a knife. (2) When Moore said he *knew* that the objects before him were human hands, he was guilty of misusing the word "know." (3) For an occurrence to be properly said to have a cause, it must be something abnormal or unusual. (4) For an action to be properly described as one for which the agent is responsible, it must be the sort of action for which people are condemned. (5) What is actual is not also possible. (6) What is known by me to be the case is not also believed by me to be the case. I have no doubt that there will be other candidates besides the six which I have mentioned. I must emphasize that I am not saying that all these examples *are* importantly similar to the thesis which I have been criticizing, only that, for all I know, they *may* be. To put the matter more generally, the position adopted by my objector seems to me to involve a type of maneuver which is characteristic of more than one contemporary mode of philosophizing. I am not condemning this kind of maneuver; I am merely suggesting that to embark on it without due caution is to risk collision with the facts. Before we rush ahead to exploit the linguistic nuances which we have detected, we should make sure that we are reasonably clear what sort of nuances they are.

5

I hope that I may have succeeded in disposing of what I have found to be a frequently propounded objection to the idea of explaining the notion of a sense-datum in terms of some member or members of the suggested family of locutions. Further detailed work would be needed to find the most suitable member of the family and to select the appropriate range of uses of the favored member when it is found; and, as I have indicated, neither of these tasks may be easy. I shall, for present purposes, assume that some range of uses of locutions of the form "It looks (feels, etc.) to X as if" has the best chance of being found suitable. I shall furthermore assume that the safest procedure for the Causal Theorist will be to restrict the actual occurrences of the term "sense-datum" to such classificatory labels as "sense-datum statement" or "sense-datum sentence"; to license the introduction of a "sense-datum terminology" to be used for the re-expression of sentences incorporating the preferred locutions seems to me both unnecessary and dangerous. I shall myself, on behalf of the CTP, often for brevity's sake talk of sense-data or sense-impressions; but I shall hope that a more rigorous, if more cumbrous, mode of expression will always be readily available. I hope that it will now be allowed that, interpreted on the lines which I have suggested, the thesis that perceiving involves having a sense-datum (involves its being the case that some sense-datum statement or other about the percipient is true) has at least a fair chance of proving acceptable.

I turn now to the special features of the CTP. The first clause of the formulation quoted above from Price's *Perception* may be interpreted as representing it to be a necessary and sufficient condition of its being the case that X perceives M that X's sense-impression should be causally dependent on some state of affairs involving M. Let us first enquire whether the suggested condition is necessary. Suppose that it looks to X as if there is a clock on the shelf; what more is required for it to be true to say that X sees a clock on the shelf? There must, one might say, actually be a clock on the shelf which is in X's field of view, before X's eyes. But this does not seem to be enough. For it is logically conceivable that there should be some method by which an expert could make it look to X as if there were a clock on the shelf on occasions when the shelf was empty: there might be some apparatus by which X's cortex could be suitably stimulated, or some technique analogous to posthypnotic suggestion. If such treatment were applied to X on an occasion when there actually was a clock on the shelf, and if X's impressions were found to continue unchanged when the clock was removed or its position altered, then I think we should be inclined to say that X did not see the clock which was before his eyes, just because we should regard the clock as playing no part in the origination of his impression. Or, to leave the realm of fantasy, it might be that it looked to me as if there were a certain sort of pillar in a certain direction at a certain distance, and there might actually be such a pillar in that place; but if, unknown to me, there were a mirror interposed between myself and the pillar, which reflected a numerically different though similar pillar, it would certainly be incorrect to say that I saw the first pillar, and correct to say that I saw the second; and it is extremely tempting to explain this linguistic fact by saying that the first pillar was, and the second was not, causally irrelevant to the way things looked to me.

There seems, then, a good case for allowing that the suggested condition is necessary; but as it stands it can hardly be sufficient. For in any particular perceptual situation there will be objects other than that which would ordinarily be regarded as being perceived, of which some state or mode of functioning is causally relevant to the occurrence of a particular sense-impression: this might be true of such objects as the percipient's eyes or the sun. So some restriction will have to be added to the analysis of perceiving which is under consideration. Price[3] suggested that use should be made of a distinction between "standing" and "differential" conditions: as the state of the sun and of the percipient's eyes, for example, are standing conditions in that (roughly speaking) if they were suitably altered, all the visual impressions of the percipient would be in some respect different from what they would otherwise have been; whereas the state of the perceived object is a differential condition in that a change in it would affect only some of the percipient's visual impressions, perhaps only the particular impression the causal origin of which is in question. The suggestion, then, is that the CTP should hold that an object is perceived if and only if some condition involving it is a differential condition of some sense-impression of the percipient. I doubt, however, whether the imposition of this restriction is adequate. Suppose that on a dark night I see, at one and the same time, a number of objects each of which is illuminated by a different torch; if one torch is tampered with, the effect on my visual impressions will be restricted, not general; the objects illuminated by the other torches will continue to look the same to me. Yet we do not want to be compelled to say that each torch is perceived in such a situation; concealed torches may illuminate. But this is the position into which the proposed revision of the CTP would force us.

I am inclined to think that a more promising direction for the CTP to take is to formulate the required restriction in terms of the way in which a perceived object contributes toward the occurrence of the sense-impression. A conceivable course would be to introduce into the specification of the restriction some part of the specialist's account, for example to make a reference to the transmission of light waves to the retina; but the objection to this procedure is obvious; if we are attempting to characterize the ordinary notion of perceiving, we should not explicitly introduce material of which someone who is perfectly capable of employing the ordinary notion might be igno-

---

3. *Perception*, p. 70.

rant. I suggest that the best procedure for the Causal Theorist is to indicate the mode of causal connection by examples; to say that, for an object to be perceived by X, it is sufficient that it should be causally involved in the generation of some sense-impression by X in the kind of way in which, for example, when I look at my hand in a good light, my hand is causally responsible for its looking to me as if there were a hand before me, or in which . . . (and so on), *whatever that kind of way may be;* and to be enlightened on that question, one must have recourse to the specialist. I see nothing absurd in the idea that a nonspecialist concept should contain, so to speak, a blank space to be filled in by the specialist; that this is so, for example, in the case of the concept of seeing is perhaps indicated by the consideration that if we were in doubt about the correctness of speaking of a certain creature with peculiar sense-organs as *seeing* objects, we might well wish to hear from a specialist a comparative account of the human eye and the relevant sense-organs of the creature in question. We do not, of course, ordinarily need the specialist's contribution; for we may be in a position to say that the same kind of mechanism is involved in a plurality of cases without being in a position to say what that mechanism is. It might be thought that we need a further restriction, limiting the permissible degree of divergence between the way things appear to X and the way they actually are. But objects can be said to be seen even when they are looked at through rough thick glass or distorting spectacles, in spite of the fact that they may then be unrecognizable.

At this point an objection must be mentioned with which I shall deal only briefly, since it involves a maneuver of the same general kind as that which I discussed at length earlier in this paper. The CTP as I have so expounded it, it may be said, requires that it should be linguistically correct to speak of the causes of sense-impressions which are involved in perfectly normal perceptual situations. But this is a mistake; it is quite unnatural to talk about the cause, say, of its looking to X as if there were a cat before him unless the situation is or is thought to be in some way abnormal or delusive; this being so, when a cause can, without speaking unnaturally, be assigned to an impression, it will always be something other than the presence of the perceived object. There is no natural use for such a sentence as "The presence of a cat caused it to look to X as if there were a cat before him"; yet it is absolutely essential to the CTP that there should be.

In reply to this objection I will make three points. (1) If we are to deal sympathetically with the CTP we must not restrict the Causal Theorist to the verb 'cause'; we must allow him to make use of other members of the family of causal verbs or verb-phrases if he wishes. This family includes such expressions as "accounts for", "explains," "is part of the explanation of", "is partly responsible for", and it seems quite possible that some alternative formulation of the theory would escape this objection. (2) If I regard myself as being in a position to say "There is a cat," or "I see a cat," I naturally refrain from making the weaker statement "It looks to me as if there were a cat before me," and so, *a fortiori,* I refrain from talking about the cause of its looking to me thus. But if I was right earlier in this paper, to have made the weaker statement would have been to have said something linguistically correct and true, even if misleading; is there then any reason against supposing that it could have been linguistically correct and true, even if pointless or misleading, to have ascribed to a particular cause the state of affairs reported in the weaker statement? (3) X is standing in a street up which an elephant is approaching; he thinks his eyes must be deceiving him. Knowing this, I could quite naturally say to X, "The fact that it looks to you as if there is an elephant approaching is accounted for by the fact that an elephant is approaching, not by your having become deranged." To say the same thing to one's neighbor at the circus would surely be to say something which is true, though it might be regarded as provocative.

I have extracted from the first clause of the initial formulation of the CTP an outline of a causal analysis of perceiving which is, I hope, at least not obviously unacceptable. I have of course considered the suggested analysis only in relation to seeing; a more careful discussion would have to pay attention to nonvisual perception; and even within the field of visual perception the suggested analysis might well be unsuitable for some uses of the word "see," which would require a stronger condition than that proposed by the theory.

6

Is the CTP, as so far expounded, open to the charge that it represents material objects as being in principle unobservable, and in consequence leads to skepticism about the material world? I have some difficulty in understanding the precise nature of the accusation, in that it is by no means obvious what, in this context, is meant by "unobservable."

(1) It would be not unnatural to take "unobservable" to mean "incapable of being perceived." Now it may be the case that one could, without being guilty of inconsistency, combine the acceptance of the causal analysis of perceiving with the view that material objects cannot in principle be perceived, if one were prepared to maintain that it is in principle impossible for material objects to cause sense-impressions but that this impossibility has escaped the notice of common sense. This position, even if internally consistent, would seem to be open to grave objection. But even if the proposition that material objects cannot be perceived is consistent with the causal analysis of perceiving, it certainly does not appear to be a consequence of the latter; and the exposition of the CTP has so far been confined to the propounding of a causal analysis of perceiving.

(2) The critic might be equating "unobservable" with "not directly observable"; and to say that material objects are not directly observable might in turn be interpreted as saying that statements about material objects lack that immunity from factual mistake which is (or is supposed to be) possessed by at least some sense-datum statements. But if "unobservable" is thus interpreted, it seems to be *true* that material objects are unobservable, and the recognition of this truth could hardly be regarded as a matter for reproach.

(3) "Observation" may be contrasted with "inference" as a source of knowledge, and so the critic's claim may be that the CTP asserts or implies that the existence of particular material objects can only be a matter of inference. But in the first place, it is not established that the acceptance of the causal analysis of perceiving commits one to the view that the existence of particular material objects is necessarily a matter of inference (though this view is explicitly asserted by the second clause of Price's initial formulation of the CTP); and second, many of the critics have been phenomenalists, who would themselves be prepared to allow that the existence of particular material objects is, in some sense, a matter of inference. And if the complaint is that the CTP does not represent the inference as being of the right kind, then it looks as if the critic might in effect be complaining that the Causal Theorist is not a Phenomenalist. Apart from the fact that the criticism under discussion could now be made only by someone who not only accepted Phenomenalism but also regarded it as the only means of deliverance from skepticism, it is by no means clear that to accept a causal analysis of perceiving is to debar oneself from accepting Phenomenalism; there seems to be no patent absurdity in the idea

that one could, as a first stage, offer a causal analysis of "X perceives M," and then re-express the result in phenomenalist terms. If the CTP is to be (as it is often regarded as being) a rival to Phenomenalism, ·the opposition may well have to spring from the second clause of the initial formulation of the theory.

There is a further possibility of interpretation, related to the previous one. If someone has seen a speck on the horizon which is in fact a battleship, we should in some contexts be willing to say that he has seen a battleship; but we should not, I think, be willing to say that he has observed a battleship unless he has recognized what he has seen as a battleship. The criticism leveled at the CTP may then be that it asserts or entails the impossibility in principle of *knowing*, or even of being reasonably assured, that one is perceiving a particular material object, even if one is in fact perceiving it. At this point we must direct our attention to the second clause of the initial formulation of the CTP, which asserted that "perceptual consciousness is fundamentally an inference from effect to cause." I shall assume (I hope not unreasonably) that the essence of the view here being advanced is that anyone who claims to perceive a particular material object M may legitimately be asked to justify his claim, and that the only way to meet this demand, in the most fundamental type of case, is to produce an acceptable argument to the effect that the existence of M is required, or is probably required, in order that the claimant's current sense-impressions should be adequately accounted for. A detailed exposition of the CTP may supplement this clause by supplying general principles which, by assuring us of correspondences between causes and effects, are supposed to make possible the production of satisfactory arguments of the required kind.

It is clear that, if the Causal Theorist proceeds on the lines which I have just indicated, he cannot possibly be accused of having *asserted* that material objects are unobservable in the sense under consideration; for he has gone to some trouble in an attempt to show how we may be reasonably assured of the existence of particular material objects. But it may be argued that (in which is perhaps a somewhat special sense of "consequence") it is an unwanted consequence of the CTP that material objects are unobservable: for if we accept the contentions of the CTP (1) that perceiving is to be analyzed in causal terms, (2) that knowledge about perceived objects depends on causal inference, and (3) that the required causal inferences will be unsound unless suitable general principles of correspondence can be provided, then we shall have to admit that knowledge about perceived objects is unobtainable: for the general principles offered, apart from being dubious both in respect of truth and in respect of status, fail to yield the conclusions for which they are designed; and more successful substitutes are not available. If this is how the criticism of the CTP is to be understood, then I shall not challenge it, though I must confess to being in some doubt whether this is what actual critics have really meant. My comment on the criticism is now that it is unsympathetic in a way that is philosophically important.

There seem to me to be two possible ways of looking at the CTP. One is to suppose an initial situation in which it is recognized that, while appearance is ultimately the only guide to reality, what appears to be the case cannot be assumed to correspond with what is the case. The problem is conceived to be that of exhibiting a legitimate method of arguing from appearance to reality. The CTP is then regarded as a complex construction designed to solve this problem; and if one part of the structure collapses, the remainder ceases to be of much interest. The second way of looking at the CTP is to think of the causal analysis of perceiving as something to be judged primarily on its intrinsic merits and not merely as a part of a solution to a prior epistemological problem, and to recognize that some version of it is quite likely to be correct; the remainder of the CTP is then regarded as consisting (1) of steps which appear to be forced upon one if one accepts the causal analysis of perceiving, and which lead to a skeptical difficulty, and (2) a not very successful attempt to meet this difficulty. This way of looking at the CTP recognizes the possibility that we are confronted with a case in which the natural dialectic elicits distressing consequences (or rather apparent consequences) from true propositions. To adopt the first attitude to the exclusion of the second is both to put on one side what may well be an acceptable bit of philosophical analysis and to neglect what might be an opportunity for deriving philosophical profit from the exposure of operations of the natural dialectic. This, I suggest, is what the critics have tended to do; though, no doubt, they might plead historical justification, in that the first way of looking at the CTP may have been that of actual Causal Theorists.

It remains for me to show that the CTP can be looked upon in the second way by exhibiting a line of argument, skeptical in character, which incorporates appropriately the elements of the CTP. I offer the following example. In the fundamental type of case, a *bona fide* claim to perceive a particular material object M is based on sense-datum statements; it is only by virtue of the occurrence of certain sense-impressions that the claimant would regard himself as entitled to assert the existence of M. Since the causal analysis of perceiving is to be accepted, the claim to perceive M involves the claim that the presence of M causally explains the occurrence of the appropriate sense-impressions. The combination of these considerations yields the conclusion that the claimant accepts the existence of M *on the grounds that* it is required for the causal explanation of certain sense-impressions; that is, the existence of M is a matter of causal inference from the occurrence of the sense-impressions. Now a model case of causal inference would be an inference from smoke to fire; the acceptability of such an inference involves the possibility of establishing a correlation between occurrences of smoke and occurrences of fire, and this is only possible because there is a way of establishing the occurrence of a fire otherwise than by a causal inference. But there is supposed to be no way of establishing the existence of particular material objects except by a causal inference from sense-impressions; so such inferences cannot be rationally justified. The specification of principles of correspondence is of course an attempt to avert this consequence by rejecting the smoke-fire model. [If this model is rejected, recourse may be had to an assimilation of material objects to such entities as electrons, the acceptability of which is regarded as being (roughly) a matter of their utility for the purposes of explanation and prediction; but this assimilation is repugnant for the reason that material objects, after having been first contrasted, as a paradigm case of uninvented entities, with the theoretical constructs or *entia rationis* of the scientist, are then treated as being themselves *entia rationis*.]

One possible reaction to this argument is, of course, "So much the worse for the causal analysis of perceiving"; but as an alternative, the argument itself may be challenged, and I shall conclude by mentioning, without attempting to evaluate, some ways in which this might be done. (1) It may be argued that it is quite incorrect to describe many of my perceptual beliefs (such as that there is now a table in front of me) as "inferences" of any kind, if this is to be taken to imply that it would be incumbent upon me, on demand, to justify by an argument (perhaps after acquiring further data) the contention that what appears to me to be the case actually is the case. When, in normal circumstances, it looks to me as if there were a table before me, I am entitled to say flatly that there is a table before me, and to reject any demand that I should justify my claim until specific grounds for doubting it have been indicated. It is essential to the skeptic to assume that any perceptual claim may, without preliminaries, be put on trial and that innocence, not guilt, has to be proved; but this assumption is mistaken. (2) The allegedly "fundamental" case (which is supposed to underlie other kinds of case), in which a perceptual claim is to be establishable purely on the basis of some set of sense-datum statements, is a myth; any justification of a particular perceptual claim will rely on the truth of one or more further propositions about the material world (for example, about the percipient's body). To insist that the "fundamental" case be selected for consideration is, in effect, to assume at the start that it is conceptually legitimate for me to treat as open to question all my beliefs about the material world at once; and the skeptic is not entitled to start with this assumption. (3) It might be questioned whether, given that I accept the existence of M on the evidence of certain sense-impressions, and given also that I think that M is causally responsible for those sense-impressions, it follows that I accept the existence of M *on the grounds that* its existence is required in order to account for the sense-impressions. (4) The use made of the smoke-fire model in the skeptical argument might be criticized on two different grounds. *First,* if the first point in this paragraph is well made, there are cases in which the existence of a perceived object is not the conclusion of a causal inference, namely those in which it cannot correctly be described as a matter of inference at all. *Second,* the model should never have been introduced; for whereas the proposition that fires tend to cause smoke is supposedly purely contingent, this is not in general true of propositions to the effect that the presence of a material object possessing property P tends to (or will in standard circumstances) make it look to particular persons as if there were an object possessing P. It is then an objectionable feature of the skeptical argument that it first treats noncontingent connections as if they were contingent, and then complains that such connections cannot be established in the manner appropriate to contingent connections. The noncontingent character of the proposition that the presence of a red (or round) object tends to make it look to particular people as if there were something red (or round) before them does not, of course, in itself preclude the particular fact that it looks to me as if there were something red before me from being explained by the presence of a particular red object; it is a noncontingent matter that corrosive substances tend to destroy surfaces to which they are applied; but it is quite legitimate to account for a particular case of surface damage by saying that it was caused by some corrosive substance. In each case the effect might have come about in some other way.

7

I conclude that it is not out of the question that the following version of the CTP should be acceptable: (1) It is true that X perceives M if, and only if, some present-tense sense-datum statement is true of X which reports a state of affairs for which M, in a way to be indicated by example, is causally responsible, and (2) a claim on the part of X to perceive M, if it needs to be justified at all, is justified by showing that the existence of M is required if the circumstances reported by certain true sense-datum statements, some of which may be about persons other than X, are to be causally accounted for. Whether this twofold thesis deserves to be called a Theory of Perception I shall not presume to judge; I have already suggested that the first clause neither obviously entails nor obviously conflicts with Phenomenalism; I suspect that the same may be true of the second clause. I am conscious that my version, however close to the letter, is very far from the spirit of the original theory; but to defend the spirit as well as the letter would be beyond my powers.

16

Some Remarks
about the Senses

A claim to the effect that certain creatures possess a faculty which should be counted as a sense, different from any of those with which we are familiar, might be met in more than one way, without actual repudiation of the alleged facts on which the claim is based.[1] It might be said that this faculty, though possibly in some way informative about the world, was not a faculty of perceiving; or it might be admitted that the exercise of the faculty constituted perception, and maintained that no new sense was involved, but only one of the familiar ones operating, perhaps, in some unfamiliar way.

About the first alternative I shall not say a great deal. It embraces a number of subalternatives:

(1) The faculty might be assimilated to such things as a moral sense, or a sense of humor. These are dubiously informative; and even if treated as informative, could not be regarded as telling (in the first instance) only about conditions of the world spatially and temporally present to the creature who is exercising them.

(2) The faculty might be held to be some kind of power of divination. This line might be adopted if the creature seemed to have direct (noninferential) knowledge of certain contemporary states or events in the material world, though this knowledge was not connected with the operation of any sense-organ. We should, of course, be very reluctant to accept this subalternative. We should so far as possible cling to the idea that such knowledge must be connected with the operation of a sense-organ, even if we could not identify it.

---

1. I am indebted to Rogers Albritton for a number of extremely helpful criticisms and suggestions concerning this essay.

(3) The exercise of the faculty—let us call it x-ing—might be denied the title of perception because of its analogy with the having of sensations. It might be held that x-ing consisted in having some sort of experience generated by material things or events in the x-er's environment by way of some effect on his nervous system, though it did not qualify as perceiving the things or events in question. The kind of situation in which this view might be taken may perhaps be indicated if we consider the assaults made by physiologists and psychologists on the so-called "sense of touch." They wish, I think on neurological grounds, to distinguish three senses: a pressure-sense, a warm-and-cold sense, and a pain-sense. Would we be happy to accept their pain-sense as a sense in the way in which sight or smell is a sense? I think not; for to do so would involve regarding the fact that we do not "externalize" pains as a mere linguistic accident. That is to say, it would involve considering as unimportant the following facts: (*a*) that we are ready to regard "malodorous," as distinct from "painful" or "sharply painful," as the name of a relatively abiding characteristic which material things in general either possess or do not possess; we are as a general rule prepared to regard questions of the form 'Is M (a material thing) malodorous?' as being at least in principle answerable either affirmatively or negatively, whereas we should very often wish to reject questions of the form "Is M painful?" or "Is M sharply painful?"; and (*b*) that we speak of smells but not of pains as being in the kitchen.

Very briefly, the salient points here seem to me as follows:

(*a*) Pains are not greatly variegated, except in intensity and location. Smells are.

(*b*) There is no standard procedure for getting a pain: one can be cut, bumped, burned, scraped, and so on. There is a standard procedure for smelling, namely, inhaling.

(*c*) Almost any type of object can inflict pain upon us, often in more than one way.

In consequence of these facts, our pains are on the whole very poor guides to the character of the things that hurt us. Particular kinds of smells, on the other hand, are in general characteristic of this or that type of object. These considerations I hope constitute a partial explanation of the fact that we do not, in general, attribute pain-qualities to things: we may in a special case speak of a thumbscrew, for example, as being a painful instrument, but this is because there is a standard way of applying thumbscrews to people.

We do not speak of pains as being in (say) the kitchen; and the reason for this is, I think, that if a source of pain moves away from a given place, persons arriving in this place after the removal do not get hurt. Smells, on the other hand, do linger in places, and so are "detachable" from the material objects which are their source. Though pains do not linger in places, they do linger with individuals after the source of pain has been removed. In this again they are unlike smells.

I shall now turn to discussion of the second possible way of meeting the claim of x-ing to be the exercise of a new sense. This, you will remember, took the form of arguing that x-ing, though perceiving, is merely perceiving by one of the familiar senses, perhaps through an unfamiliar kind of sense-organ. At this point we need to ask by what criteria senses are to be distinguished from one another. The answer to this question, if obtainable, would tell us how x-ing must differ from the exercise of familiar senses in order to count as the operation of a distinct sense. Four seemingly independent ideas might be involved:

I. It might be suggested that the senses are to be distinguished by the differing features that we become aware of by means of them: that is to say, seeing might be characterized as perceiving (or seeming to perceive) things as having certain colors, shapes, and sizes; hearing as perceiving things (or better, in this case, events) as having certain degrees of loudness, certain determinates of pitch, certain tone-qualities; and so on for the other senses.

II. It might be suggested that two senses, for example, seeing and smelling, are to be distinguished by the special introspectible character of the experiences of seeing and smelling; that is, disregarding the differences between the characteristics we learn about by sight and smell, we are entitled to say that seeing is itself different in character from smelling.

III. Our attention might be drawn to the differing general features of the external physical conditions on which the various modes of perceiving depend, to differences in the "stimuli" connected with different senses: the sense of touch is activated by contact, sight by light rays, hearing by sound waves, and so on.

IV. Reference might be made to the internal mechanisms associated with the various senses—the character of the sense-organs, and their mode of connection with the brain. (These suggestions need not of course be regarded as mutually exclusive. It is possible—perhaps indeed likely—that there is no one essential criterion for distinguishing the senses; that there is, rather, a multiplicity of criteria.)

One procedure at this point (perhaps the most desirable one) would be to consider, in relation to difficult cases, the applicability of the suggested criteria and their relative weights. But a combination of ignorance of zoology with poverty of invention diverts me to perhaps not uninteresting questions concerning the independence of these criteria, and in particular to the relation between the first and the second. The first suggestion (that differing senses are to be distinguished by the differing features which we perceive by means of them) may seem at first sight attractive and unmystifying; but difficulties seem to arise if we attempt to make it the sole basis of distinction between the senses. It looks as if, when we try to work out suggestion (I) in detail we are brought round to some version of the second suggestion (that the senses are to be distinguished by the special introspectible characters of their exercise).

There is a danger that suggestion (I) may incorporate from the start, in a concealed way, suggestion (II): for instance, to adopt it might amount to saying "Seeing is the sort of experience that we have when we perceive things as having certain colors, shapes, etc." If we are to eliminate this danger, I think we must treat suggestion (I) as advancing the idea that, starting with such sense-neutral verbs as "perceive," "seem," we can elucidate the notion of seeing in terms of the notion of perceiving things to have such-and-such features, smelling in terms of perceiving things to have such-and-such other features, and so on. In general, special perceptual verbs are to be explained in terms of general perceptual verbs together with names of special generic features which material things or events may be perceived to have. At this point an obvious difficulty arises: among the features which would presumably figure in the list of tactual qualities (which are to be used to distinguish feeling from other modes of perceiving) is that of warmth; but to say that someone perceives something to have a certain degree of warmth does not entail that he is *feeling* anything at all, for we can *see* that things are warm, and things can *look* warm.

To extricate the suggestion from this objection, it looks as if it would be necessary to introduce some such term as "directly perceive" (and perhaps also the term "directly seem," the two terms being no doubt definitionally linked). How precisely these terms would have to be defined I do not propose to inquire, but the definition would have to be such as to ensure that someone who saw that something was blue might be directly perceiving that it was blue, while someone who saw that something was warm could not be directly perceiving that it was warm. We then might try to define "see" and its congeners (and primary uses of "look" and its congeners) in terms of these specially introduced verbs. We might put up the following as samples of rough equivalences, without troubling ourselves too much about details, since all we require for present purposes is to see the general lines on which the initial suggestion will have to be developed:

(1) X sees M (material object) = X directly perceives M to have some color and some spatial property.

(2) X feels M = X directly perceives M to have some spatial property and degrees of one or more of such properties as warmth (coldness), hardness (softness), etc.

(3) M looks (primary sense) φ to X = M directly seems to X to have certain spatial and color properties, one of which is φ.

(4) M looks (secondary sense) φ to X = M directly seems to X to have certain spatial and color properties, one or more of which indicate to X that M is or may be φ.

Analogous definitions could be provided for primary and secondary uses of "feel" (with a nonpersonal subject).

This maneuver fails, I think, to put suggestion (I) in the clear. Some might object to the definitions of verbs like "see" (used with a direct object) in terms of "perceive that"; and there would remain the question of defining the special terms "directly perceive" and "directly seem." But a more immediately serious difficulty seems to me to be one connected with the seemingly unquestionable acceptability of the proposition that spatial properties may be directly perceived to belong to things both by sight and by touch. Suppose a man to be resting a half-crown on the palm of one hand and a penny on the palm of the other: he might (perhaps truthfully) say, "The half-crown looks to me larger than the penny, though they feel the same size." If we apply the rough translations indicated above, this statement comes out thus: "The half-crown and the penny directly seem to me to have certain spatial and color properties, including (in the case of the half-crown) that of being larger than the penny: but they also directly seem to me to have certain properties, such as certain degrees of roughness, warmth, etc., and spatial properties which include that of being equal in size."

The facts stated by this rigmarole seem to be (differently ordered) as follows:

(1) The coins directly seem to have certain spatial and color properties.

(2) The coins directly seem to have certain properties drawn from the "tactual" list.

(3) The half-crown directly seems larger than the penny.

(4) The coins directly seem to be of the same size.

But there is nothing in this statement of the facts to tell us whether the coins *look* different in size but *feel* the same size, or alternatively *feel* different in size but *look* the same size.

At this point two somewhat heroic courses suggest themselves. The first is to proclaim an ambiguity in the expression "size," distinguishing between visual size and tactual size, thus denying that spatial properties are really accessible to more than one sense. This more or less Berkeleian position is perhaps unattractive independently of the current argument; in any case the introduction of the qualifications "visual" and "tactual," in the course of an attempt to distinguish the senses from one another without invoking the special character of the various modes of perceiving, is open to the gravest suspicion. The second course is to amend the accounts of looking and feeling in such a way that, for example, "A looks larger than B" is re-expressible more or less as follows: "A directly seems larger than B in the kind of way which entails that A and B directly seem to have certain color-properties." But this seems to introduce a reference to special kinds or varieties of "direct seeming," and this brings in what seems to be only a variant version of suggestion (II).

But there is a rather more subtle course to be considered.[2] In addition to the link (whatever that may be) which may join certain *generic* properties (e.g., color, shape, size) so as to constitute them as members of a group of properties associated with a particular sense (e.g., as visual properties), another kind of link may be indicated which holds between specific properties (e.g., specific colors and shapes, etc.), and which might be of use in dealing with the difficulty raised by this current example. Suppose that A_1 is a specific form of some generic property which occurs only in the visual list (e.g., a particular color), that B_1 is a specific form of some generic property occurring in only the tactual list (e.g., a particular degree of warmth), and that X_1 and X_2 are specific forms of a generic property occurring in both the visual and the tactual lists (e.g., are particular shapes). Suppose

2. This idea was suggested to me by O. P. Wood.

further that someone simultaneously detects or seems to detect the presence of all these properties (A_1, B_1, X_1, X_2) in a given object. Now the percipient might find that he could continue to detect or seem to detect A_1 and X_1 while no longer detecting or seeming to detect B_1 and X_2; and equally that he could detect or seem to detect B_1 and X_2 while no longer detecting or seeming to detect A_1 and X_1; but on the other hand that he could not retain A_1 and X_2 while eliminating B_1 and X_1, or retain B_1 and X_1 while eliminating A_1 and X_2. There would thus be what might be called a "detection-link" between A_1 and X_1, and another such link between B_1 and X_2. On the basis of this link between X_1 and a purely visual property it might be decided that X_1 was here being visually detected, and analogously it might be decided that X_2 was being tactually detected. Similarly in the example of the coins one might say that there is a detection-link between inequality of size and certain purely visual properties the coins have or seem to have (e.g., their real or apparent colors) and a detection-link between equality of size and certain purely tactual properties the coins have or seem to have (e.g., their coldness): and thus the difficulty may be resolved.

There are three considerations which prevent me from being satisfied with this attempt to make suggestion (I) serviceable. I put them in what I regard as the order of increasing importance:

(1) Consider the possible case of a percipient to whom the two coins *look* equal in size when only seen, *feel* equal in size when only felt, but look unequal and feel equal when *both* seen *and* felt. This case is no doubt fantastic, but nevertheless it *seems* just an empirical matter whether or not the way things appear to one sense is affected in this sort of way by the operation or inoperation of another sense. If such a case were to occur, then the method adumbrated in my previous paragraph would be quite inadequate to deal with it: for equality of size would be codetectable *both* with visual properties alone *and* with tactual properties alone, whereas inequality in size would be codetectable neither with visual properties alone nor with tactual properties alone. So the percipient would, so far as this test goes, be at a loss to decide by which sense he detected (or seemed to detect) inequality. But I doubt whether this conclusion is acceptable.

(2) If it were possible for a creature to have two different senses by each of which he detected just the same generic properties, then the test suggested could not be applied in the case of those senses; for it depends on these being properties accessible to one but not both of

two senses with regard to which it is invoked. It is far from clear to me that it is inconceivable that just the same set of generic properties should be detectable by either one of two different senses. (I touch again on this question later.)

(3) Whether or not the suggested test, if applied, would always rightly answer the question whether a given spatial property is on a given occasion being detected by sight or touch, it seems quite certain that we never do employ this method of deciding such a question. Indeed there seems something peculiar about the idea of using *any* method, for the answer to such a question, asked about ourselves, never seems in the slightest doubt. And it seems rather strange to make the difference between detecting (or seeming to detect) a given property by sight and detecting (or seeming to detect) it by touch turn on what would be the result of an experiment which we should never in any circumstances perform.

Suggestion (I) has a further unattractive feature. According to it, certain properties are listed as visual properties, certain others as tactual properties, and so forth; and to say that color is a visual property would seem to amount to no more than saying that color is a member of a group of properties the others of which are . . . This leaves membership of the group as an apparently arbitrary matter. I now wish to see if some general account of the notion of a visual (tactual, etc.) property could be given if (as suggestion (II) would allow) we make unhampered use of special perceptual verbs like "see" and "look." I shall go into this question perhaps rather more fully than the immediate purposes of the discussion demand, since it seems to me to be of some intrinsic interest. I doubt if such expressions as "visual property" and "tactual property," have any clear-cut accepted use, so what follows should be regarded as a preliminary to deciding upon a use, rather than as the analysis of an existing one. I shall confine myself to the notion of a visual property, hoping that the discussion of this could be adapted to deal with the other senses (not, of course, necessarily in the same way in each case).

First, I suggest that we take it to be a necessary (though not a sufficient) condition of a property P being a visual property that it should be linguistically correct to speak of someone as *seeing* that some material thing M is P, and also (with one qualification to be mentioned later) of some thing M as *looking* P to someone. Within the class of properties which satisfy this condition I want to make some distinctions which belong to two nonindependent dimensions, one of which I shall call "determinability," the other "complexity":

(1) There are certain properties (for example, that of being blue) such that if P is one of them there is no better way (though there may be an equally good way) for me to make sure that a thing M is P than to satisfy myself that, observational conditions being optimal, M looks P to me. Such properties I shall label "directly visually determinable."

(2) It seems to me that there might be a case for labeling some properties as visually determinable, though indirectly so. I have in mind two possible kinds of indirectness. First, it might be the case that a primary (noninferior) test for determining whether M is P would be not just to ensure that M looked P in the most favorable conditions for observation, but to ensure, by scrutiny, that certain parts (in a wide sense) or elements of M had certain characteristics and were interrelated in certain ways; it being understood that the characteristics and relations in question are to be themselves *directly* visually determinable. For me, though no doubt not for a Chinese, the property of being inscribed with a certain Chinese character might be of this kind; and for everyone no doubt the property of having a chiliagonal surface would be of this kind. Second, a characteristic might be such that its primary test involved comparison of M (or its elements) with some standard specimen. Under this head I mean to take in both such properties as being apple-green, for which the primary test involves comparison with a color chart, and such a property as that of being two feet seven inches long, the primary test for which is measurement by a ruler. It is to be understood that the results of such comparison or measurement are to be describable in terms of properties which are directly visually determinable.

It seems to me possible that "visual characteristic" might be used in such a way that P would qualify as a visual characteristic only if it were directly visually determinable, or in such a way that it would so qualify if it were visually determinable either directly or indirectly. But there also seems to be a different, though I think linked, basis of classification, which might also be employed to fix the sense of the expression "visual characteristic." There will be some values of P such that an object M may be said to look P, with regard to which the question, "What is it about the way that M looks that makes it look P?" has no answer. More generally, it will be impossible to specify anything about the way things look, when they look P, which will account for or determine their looking P. One cannot, for example, specify anything about the way things look when they look blue, which makes them look blue. Characteristics for which this rough condition is satisfied I will call "visually simple." But with regard to those values of P which are such that a thing may look P, but which are not visually simple, there are various possibilities:

(1) The specification of what it is about the way a thing looks which makes it look P, or determines it to look P, may consist in specifying certain characteristics (of the visually determinable kind) which M has or looks to have, the presence of which indicates more or less reliably that M is P. Warmth is such a characteristic. In this kind of case P will not be visually determinable, and I should like to say that P is not a visual characteristic, and is neither visually simple nor visually complex. P will be merely "visually indicable."

(2) The specification of what it is about the way a thing M looks which makes it look P or determines it to look P might take the form of specifying certain properties (of a visually determinable or visually simple kind or both) the possession of which constitutes a logically sufficient condition for being P. The property of being lopsided might be of this kind. A man's face could perhaps be said to be made to look lopsided by his looking as if he had (and perhaps indeed his actually having) one ear set lower than the other; and his actually having one ear set lower than the other would perhaps be a logically sufficient condition of his face's being lopsided. Characteristics belonging to this class I will label "visually tightly complex."

(3) Consider such examples as "X's face looks friendly" or "X looks tough." Certainly friendliness and toughness are not themselves visually determinable: and certainly the questions "What is there about the way his face looks that makes it look friendly?" and "What is there about the way he looks that makes him look tough?" are in order. Nevertheless there may be considerable difficulty in answering such questions; and when the answer or partial answer comes, it may not amount to saying what it is about the look of X's face (or of X) which indicates more or less reliably that X is friendly (or tough). In such cases one might be inclined to say that though toughness is not a visual characteristic, being tough-looking is. The following remarks seem in point:

(4) It might be thought necessary, for this type of characteristic, to relax the initial condition which visual characteristics were required to satisfy, on the grounds that one cannot speak of someone as "looking tough-looking." But as Albritton has pointed out to me, it does

not seem linguistically improper to say of someone that (for example) he looked tough-looking when he stood in the dim light of the passage, but as soon as he moved into the room it could be seen that really he looked quite gentle.

(*a*) Being tough-looking is in some way dependent on the possession of visually determinable characteristics: there would be a logical absurdity in saying that two people were identical in respect of all visually determinable characteristics, and yet that one person was tough-looking and the other was not.

(*b*) Even if one has specified to one's full satisfaction what it is about the way X looks that make him look tough, one has not given a logically sufficient condition for being tough-looking. If I just produced a list of X's visually determinable characteristics, the possession of which does *in fact* make him look tough, no one could strictly *deduce* from the information given that X looks tough; to make quite sure, he would have to look at X himself.

(*c*) Though the primary test for determining whether X is tough-looking is to see how he looks in the most favorable observational conditions, this test may not (perhaps cannot) be absolutely decisive. If, after examination of X, I and my friends say that X is tough-looking, and someone else says that he is not, it need not be the case that the last-mentioned person is wrong or does not know the language; he may for example be impressed by some dissimilarity between X and standard tough customers, by which I and my friends are not impressed, in which case the dissident judgment may perhaps be described as eccentric, but not as wrong. In the light of this discussion one might say that such characteristics as being tough-looking are "visually near-determinable"; and they might also be ranked as visually complex (in view of their dependence on visually determinable characteristics), though "loosely complex" (in view of the nonexistence of logically sufficient conditions of their presence).

(5) The logical relations between the different sections of the determinability range and those of the simplicity-complexity range may need detailed examination. For instance, consider the statement "The sound of the explosion came from my right" (or "The explosion sounded as if it were on my right"). It may be impossible to specify anything about the way the explosion sounded which determined its sounding as if it were on my right, in which case by my criterion being on my right will qualify as an auditory simple property. Yet certainly the explosion's sounding, even in the most favorable observational

conditions, as if it were on my right is a secondary (inferior) test for the location of the explosion. So we would have an example of a property which is auditorily simple without being auditorily determinable. This may be of interest in view of the hesitation we may feel when asked if spatial characteristics can be auditory.

I should like to emphasize that I have not been trying to legislate upon the scope to be given to the notion of a visual characteristic, but have only been trying to provide materials for such legislation on the assumption that the special character of visual experience may be used to distinguish the sense of sight, thus allowing a relatively unguarded use of such words as "look."

Let us now for a moment turn our attention to suggestion (II), the idea that senses are to be distinguished by the special character of the experiences which their exercise involves. Two fairly obvious difficulties might be raised. First, that such experiences (if experiences they be) as seeing and feeling seem to be, as it were, diaphanous: if we were asked to pay close attention, on a given occasion, to our seeing or feeling as distinct from what was being seen or felt, we should not know how to proceed; and the attempt to describe the differences between seeing and feeling seems to dissolve into a description of what we see and what we feel. How then can seeing and feeling have the special character which suggestion (II) requires them to have, if this character resists both inspection and description? The second difficulty is perhaps even more serious. If to see is to detect by means of a special kind of experience, will it not be just a contingent matter that the characteristics we detect by means of this kind of experience are such things as color and shape? Might it not have been the case that we thus detected characteristic smells, either instead of or as well as colors and shapes? But it does not seem to be just a contingent fact that we do not see the smells of things. Suggestion (I), on the other hand, seems to avoid both these difficulties; the first because the special character of the experiences connected with the various senses is not invoked, and the second because since the smell of a thing is not listed among the properties the (direct) detection of which counts as seeing, on this view it emerges as tautological that smells cannot be seen.

We seem now to have reached an impasse. Any attempt to make suggestion (I) work leads to difficulties which seem soluble only if we bring in suggestion (II), and suggestion (II) in its turn involves difficulties which seem avoidable only by adopting suggestion (I). Is it the case, then, that the two criteria should be combined; that is, is the right answer that, for anything to count as a case of seeing, two conditions must be fulfilled: first, that the properties detected should belong to a certain group, and second, that the detection should involve a certain kind of experience? But this does not seem to be a satisfactory way out; for if it were, then it would be logically possible to detect smells by means of the type of experience characteristically involved in seeing, yet only to do this would not be to *see* smells, since a further condition (the property qualification) would be unfulfilled. But surely we object on logical grounds no less to the idea that we might detect smells through visual experiences than to the idea that we might see the smells of things: indeed, the ideas seem to be the same. So perhaps the criteria mentioned in suggestions (I) and (II) are not distinguishable; yet they *seem* to be distinct.

Maybe all is not yet lost, for there still remains the possibility that something may be achieved by bringing into the discussion the third and fourth suggestions. Perhaps we might save suggestion (I), and thus eliminate suggestion (II), by combining the former with one or both of the last two suggestions. For if to see is to detect certain properties (from the visual list) by means of a certain sort of mechanism (internal or external or both), then the arguments previously advanced to show the need for importing suggestion (II) seem to lose their force. We can now differentiate between the case in which two coins look different in size but feel the same size and the case in which they feel different in size but look the same size: we shall say that in the first case by mechanism A (eyes and affection by light waves) we detect or seem to detect difference in size while by mechanism B (hands and pressure) we detect or seem to detect equality of size: whereas in the second case the mechanisms are transposed. We can also characterize the visual list of properties as those detectable by mechanism A, and deal analogously with other lists of properties. In this way the need to invoke suggestion (II) seems to be eliminated.

Promising as this approach may appear, I very much doubt if it succeeds in eliminating the need to appeal to the special character of experiences in order to distinguish the senses. Suppose that long-awaited invasion of the Martians takes place, that they turn out to be friendly creatures and teach us their language. We get on all right, except that we find no verb in their language which unquestionably corresponds to our verb "see." Instead we find two verbs which we decide to render as "x" and "y": we find that (in their tongue) they speak of themselves as x-ing, and also as y-ing, things to be of this and that color, size, and shape. Further, in physical appearance they are more or less like ourselves, except that in their heads they have, one above the other, two pairs of organs, not perhaps exactly like one another, but each pair more or less like our eyes: each pair of organs is found to be sensitive to light waves. It turns out that for them x-ing is dependent on the operation of the upper organs, and y-ing on that of the lower organs. The question which it seems natural to ask is this: Are x-ing and y-ing both cases of seeing, the difference between them being that x-ing is seeing with the upper organs, and y-ing is seeing with the lower organs? Or alternatively, do one or both of these accomplishments constitute the exercise of a new sense, other than that of sight? If we adopt, to distinguish the senses, a combination of suggestion (I) with one or both of suggestions (III) or (IV), the answer seems clear: both x-ing and y-ing are seeing, with different pairs of organs. But *is* the question really to be settled so easily? Would we not in fact want to ask whether x-ing something to be round was like y-ing it to be round, or whether when something x-ed blue to them this was like or unlike its y-ing blue to them? If in answer to such questions as these they said, "Oh no, there's all the difference in the world!" then I think we should be inclined to say that either x-ing or y-ing (if not both) must be something other than seeing: we might of course be quite unable to decide *which* (if either) was seeing.

(I am aware that here those whose approach is more Wittgensteinian than my own might complain that unless something more can be said about how the difference between x-ing and y-ing might "come out" or show itself in publicly observable phenomena, then the claim by the supposed Martians that x-ing and y-ing are different would be one of which nothing could be made, which would leave one at a loss how to understand it. *First,* I am not convinced of the need for "introspectible" differences to show themselves in the way this approach demands (I shall not discuss this point further); *second,* I think that if I *have* to meet this demand, I can. One can suppose that one or more of these Martians acquired the use of the lower y-ing organs at some comparatively late date in their careers, and that at the same time (perhaps for experimental purposes) the operation of the upper x-ing organs was inhibited. One might now be ready to allow that a difference between x-ing and y-ing would have shown itself if in such a situation the creatures using their y-ing organs for the first time were unable straightaway, without any learning process, to use their "color"-words fluently and correctly to describe what they detected through the use of those organs.)

It might be argued at this point that we have not yet disposed of the idea that the senses can be distinguished by an amalgam of suggestions (I), (III), and (IV); for it is not clear that in the example of the Martians the condition imposed by suggestion (I) is fulfilled. The thesis, it might be said, is only upset if x-ing and y-ing are accepted as being the exercise of different senses; and if they are, then the Martians' color-words could be said to have a concealed ambiguity. Much as "sweet" in English may mean "sweet-smelling" or "sweet-tasting," so "blue" in Martian may mean "blue-x-ing" or "blue-y-ing." But if this is so, then the Martians after all do not detect by x-ing just those properties of things which they detect by y-ing. To this line of argument there are two replies:

(1) The defender of the thesis is in no position to use this argument; for he cannot start by making the question whether x-ing and y-ing are exercises of the same sense turn on the question (*inter alia*) whether or not a single group of characteristics is detected by both, and then make the question of individuation of the group turn on the question whether putative members of the group are detected by one, or by more than one, sense. He would be saying in effect, "Whether, in x-ing and y-ing, different senses are exercised depends (*inter alia*) on whether the same properties are detected by x-ing as by y-ing; but whether a certain x-ed property is the same as a certain y-ed property depends on whether x-ing and y-ing are or are not the exercise of a single sense." This reply seems fatal. For the circularity could only be avoided by making the question whether "blue" in Martian names a single property depend *either* on whether the kinds of experience involved in x-ing and y-ing are different, which would be to reintroduce suggestion (II), *or* on whether the mechanisms involved in x-ing and y-ing are different (in this case whether the upper organs are importantly unlike the lower organs): and to adopt this alternative would, I think, lead to treating the differentiation of the senses as being solely a matter of their mechanisms, thereby making suggestion (I) otiose.

(2) Independently of its legitimacy or illegitimacy in the present context, we must reject the idea that if it is accepted that in x-ing and y-ing different senses are being exercised, then Martian color-words will be ambiguous. For *ex hypothesi* there will be a very close correlation between things x-ing blue and their y-ing blue, far closer than that between things smelling sweet and their tasting sweet. This being

so, it is only to be expected that x-ing and y-ing should share the position of arbiters concerning the color of things: that is, "blue" would be the name of a single property, determinable equally by x-ing and y-ing. After all, is this not just like the actual position with regard to shape, which is doubly determinable, by sight and by touch?

While I would not wish to quarrel with the main terms of this second reply, I should like briefly to indicate why I think that this final quite natural comparison with the case of shape will not do. It is quite conceivable that the correlation between x-ing and y-ing, in the case supposed, might be close enough to ensure that Martian color-words designated doubly determinable properties, and yet that this correlation should break down in a limited class of cases: for instance, owing to some differences between the two pairs of organs, objects which transmitted light of a particular wavelength might (in standard conditions) x blue but y black. If this were so, then for these cases the conflict would render decision about the real color of the objects in question impossible. (I ignore the possibility that the real color might be made to depend on the wavelength of the light transmitted, which would involve depriving color of its status as a purely sensibly determinable property.)

I am, however, very much inclined to think that a corresponding limited breakdown in the correlation between sight and touch with regard to shape is not conceivable. The nature of the correlation between sight and touch is far too complicated a question to be adequately treated within the compass of this essay; so I shall attempt only to indicate, in relation to two comparatively simple imaginary cases, the special intimacy of this correlation. Both cases involve medium-sized objects, which are those with regard to which we are most willing to accept the equality of the arbitraments of sight and touch. The question at issue in each case is whether we can coherently suppose both (*a*) that, in a world which in general exhibits the normal correlation between sight and touch, some isolated object should standardly feel round but standardly look square, and also (*b*) that it should be undecidable, as regards that object, whether preference should be given to the deliverance of sight or to that of touch.

Case A. In this case I do not attribute to the divergent object the power of temporarily upsetting the correlation of sight and touch with regard to other normal objects while they are in its vicinity. Suppose that, feeling in my pocket, I were to find an object which felt as if it were round and flat like a penny, I take it out of my pocket and throw it on the table, and am astonished to see what looks like a square flat object: I find, moreover, that when surveyed by myself (and others) from various points, it continues to look as a square object should look. I now shut my eyes and "frame" the object by running my finger round its edge; my finger feels to me as if it were moving in a circle. I then open my eyes, and, since we are supposing that other objects are not affected by the divergent one, my finger also feels to me as if it were tracing a circular path, but not, of course, as if it were "framing" the visible outline of the object. One possibility is that my finger is seen to cut through the corners of the visible outline of the divergent object; and I think that such a lack of "visual solidity" would be enough to make us say that the object is really round, in spite of its visual appearance. Another possibility is that the visible path of my finger should be a circle within which the visible outline of the object is inscribed, and that, if I try, I fail to establish visible contact between my finger and the object's outline, except at the corners of that outline. I suggest that if the object's outline were visually unapproachable in this kind of way, this would very strongly incline us to say that the object was really round; and I suspect that this inclination could be decisively reinforced by the application of further tests of a kind to be mentioned in connection with the second case.

Case B. In this case I do attribute to the object the power of "infecting" at least some other objects, in particular my finger or (more strictly) the path traced by my finger. Suppose that, as before, when I trace the felt outline of the divergent object, it feels to me as if my finger were describing a circle, and also that, as before, the object looks square; now, however, the visible path of my moving finger is not circular but square, framing the visible outline of the object. Suppose also that I find a further object which is indisputably round, the size of which feels equal to the size which the divergent object is felt as having, and which (we will suppose) is not infected by proximity to the divergent object; if I place this unproblematic object behind the divergent one, as I move my finger around the pair of objects, it *feels* as if I am continuously in contact with the edges of both objects, but it *looks* as if I am in continuous contact with the divergent object, but in only occasional contact with the normal object. (I am taking the case in which the corners of the visible outline of the divergent object overlap the visible outline of the normal object.) Given this information alone, I think that it cannot be decided what the real shape of the divergent object is; but there are various further tests which I can make. One of these would be to put the two objects on the table, the divergent object being on top, to place my finger and thumb so that they are in felt contact with both objects but are visually in contact only with opposed corners of the visible outline of the divergent object, and then raise my hand; if thereby I lift both objects, the divergent object is really round; if I lift only the divergent object, it is really square.

A test closely related to the foregoing would be to discover through what sorts of aperture the divergent object could be made to pass, on the general principle that it is square pegs which fit into square holes and round pegs which fit into round holes. For example, suppose I find an aperture the real shape and size of which is such that, according to tactual comparison, it ought to accommodate the divergent object, while according to visual comparison it ought not to do so; then (roughly speaking) if the object can be made to pass through the aperture it is really round; if it cannot, it is really square. It seems to me that the decisiveness of this test can be averted only if we make one of two suppositions. We might suppose our fantasy-world to be such that apertures of a suitable real shape are not available to us; for this supposition, however, to be of interest, it would have to amount to the supposition of a *general* breakdown of the correlation of sight and touch as regards shape, which is contrary to the terms of our discussion, which is concerned only with the possibility of a limited breakdown in this respect. Alternatively, we might suppose that when we attempt to make the divergent object pass through a suitably chosen aperture which is really round, it feels as if the object passes through, but it looks as if the object fails to pass through. On this supposition there is some prospect that the real shape of the divergent object should remain undecidable. But we must consider the consequences of this supposition. What, for example, happens to my finger when it is pushing the divergent object tactually, though not visually, through the aperture? In order to keep the question of the real shape undecidable, I think we shall have to suppose that the finger tactually moves into the aperture, but visually remains outside. Given this assumption, it seems reasonable to conclude that it will have become a practical possibility, with regard to any object whatsoever, or at least any movable object, to divorce its tactual location from its visual location. Imagine, for example, that the divergent object is just outside one end of a suitably selected cylinder, and is attached to my waist by a string which passes through the cylinder; now I set myself the task of drawing the object through the cylinder by walking away. If I do not tug too hard, I can ensure that tactually my body, together with any objects attached to it, will move away from the cylinder, while visually it will not. And one might add, where shall *I* be then?

I suggest, then, that given the existence of an object which, for the Martians, standardly x-ed blue but y-ed black (its real color being undecidable), no conclusion could be drawn to the effect that other objects do, or could as a matter of practical possibility be made to, x one way and y another way either in respect of color or in respect of some other feature within the joint province of x-ing and y-ing; given, on the other hand, the existence of an object which, for us, standardly felt one shape and looked another, then *either* its real shape would be nonetheless decidable, *or* it would be practically possible to disrupt in the case of at least some other objects the correlation between sight and touch as regards at least one feature falling within their joint domain, namely spatial location; at least some objects could be made standardly to feel as if they were in one place and standardly to look as if they were in another. Whether such notions as those of a material object, of a person, and of human action could apply, without radical revision, to such a world, and whether such a world could be coherently supposed to be governed by any system of natural laws, however bizarre, are questions which I shall not here pursue.

(6) Compare the Molyneux problem. It has been properly objected against me that, in comparing the possibility of a limited breakdown in the correlation between x-ing and y-ing with the possibility of a corresponding limited breakdown in the correlation between sight and touch, I have cheated. For whereas I consider the possibility that a certain *class* of objects might x blue but y black, I consider only the possibility that a certain *isolated* object should standardly feel round but look square: I have failed to consider the possibility that, for example, objects of a particular felt size which feel round should look square and that there should therefore be no normal holes to use for testing divergent objects.

I can here do no more than indicate the lines on which this objection should be met. (1) The supposed limited breakdown cannot be restricted to objects of particular shapes, since the dimensions of objects and of holes can be measured both tactually and visually by measuring rods: and what happens when a divergent measuring rod is bent double? (2) Any shape-divergent object would be tolerated tactually but not visually (or vice versa) by normal holes (if available) of more than one specifically different size. Consequently, since we are ruling out a *general* breakdown of the correlation between sight and touch as regards the shapes in question, there must be *at least some* normal holes which will tolerate tactually but not visually (or visually but not tactually) *at least some* divergent objects: and this is enough for my purpose.

To return to the main topic, I hope that I have put up a fair case for supposing that suggestion (II) cannot be eliminated. How then, are we to deal with the difficulties which seemed to lead us back from suggestion (II) to suggestion (I), with a consequent impasse? The first of these was that such an alleged special experience as that supposedly involved in seeing eluded inspection and description. I think that this objection conceals an illegitimate demand. We are being asked to examine and describe the experience we have when we see, quite without reference to the properties we detect or think we detect when we see. But this is impossible, for the description of the experiences we have when we see involves the mention of properties we detect or seem to detect. More fully, the way to describe our visual experiences is in terms of how things look to us, and such a description obviously involves the employment of property-words. But in addition to the specific differences between visual experiences, signalized by the various property-words employed, there is a generic resemblance signalized by the use of the word "look," which differentiates visual from nonvisual sense-experience. This resemblance can be noticed and labeled, but perhaps not further described. To object that one cannot focus one's attention, in a given case, on the experience of seeing, as distinct from the properties detected, is perhaps like complaining that one cannot focus one's attention on the color of an object, ignoring its particular color. So the initial assumption of the independence of suggestions (I) and (II) has broken down: how extensive the breakdown is could be determined only by going on to consider how far differences in character between things reduce to differences between the experiences which people have or would have in certain circumstances. This would involve a discussion of traditional theories of perception for which at the moment I have neither time nor heart.

The second difficulty is that of explaining why, if sight is to be distinguished from other senses by the special character of the experiences involved in seeing, there is a logical objection to the idea that we might detect (say) the smells of things by means of experience of the visual type. Why can we not see the smell of a rose? Well, in a sense we can; a rose can (or at any rate conceivably might) look fragrant. But perhaps the objector wants us to explain why a rose cannot look fragrant in the same sense of "look" in which it may look red. The answer here is presumably that had nature provided a closer correlation between the senses of sight and smell than in fact obtains, the word "fragrant" might have been used to denote a doubly determinable property: in which case roses could have been said to look fragrant in just the sense of "look" in which they now look red. But of course the current rules for the word "fragrant" are adapted to the situation actually obtaining. If, however, the objector is asking us to explain why, on our view, given that fragrance is *merely* an olfactorily determinable property, it is not also at the same time a visually determinable property, then perhaps we may be excused from replying.

17

Presupposition and Conversational Implicature

I want in this essay to consider, from a certain point of view, whether the theory of descriptions could, despite certain familiar objections, be accepted as an account of *the* phrases, and whether the kind of linguistic phenomena that prompted the resort to the theory of presupposition as a special sort of logical relation (with all the ramifications which that idea would involve) could be dealt with in some other way.[1] One might consider three objections which have at one time or another been advanced by this or that philosopher.

The first is the kind of objection that primarily prompted Strawson's (1950) revolt against the theory of descriptions,[2] namely, that when one is asked such a question as whether the king of France is, or is not, bald, one does not feel inclined to give an answer; one does not feel very much inclined to say either that it is true that he is bald or that it is false that he is bald, but rather to say things like *The question does not arise* or *He neither is nor is not bald,* etc. There is, indeed, something unnatural about assigning a truth-value, as far as ordinary discourse is concerned, to statements made by means of sentences containing vacuous descriptions.

The second objection was also made by Strawson, namely, that if you take an ordinary conversational remark, such as *The table is covered with butter,* it seems a somewhat unacceptable translation to

---

1. This essay is intended as a tribute to the work, in this and other philosophical domains, of my friend, former pupil, and former Oxford colleague and collaborator Sir Peter Strawson.

2. B. Russell, "On Denoting," *Mind* 14 (1905): 479–499; P. F. Strawson, "On Referring," *Mind* 59 (1950): 320–344.

offer in its stead, *There exists one and only one table and anything which is a table is covered with butter.* To make this kind of remark is not to be committed, as seems to be suggested by the Russellian account, to the existence of a unique object corresponding to a phrase, *the so-and-so;* to suggest that one is so committed is quite unjustified.

The third objection (voiced by Searle, among others) is that one gets into trouble with the Russellian theory where one considers moods other than the indicative. To say, for example, *Give these flowers to your wife* does not look as if it translates into something like *Make it the case that there is one and only one person who is married to you, who is female, and who is given these flowers by you.* And, *Was your wife at the party?*, again does not seem as if it would be properly represented by *Was it the case that you have at least one wife and not more than one wife and that no one is both your wife and not at the party?* There does not seem to be the feeling that the person who asks whether your wife was at the party is, among other things, inquiring whether you are nonbigamously married.

I shall start by considering whether one could use, to deal with such difficulties, the notion of conversational implicature I characterized in Essay 2, and I shall attempt to apply this notion to Definite Descriptions. Now, what about *the present king of France?* As far as I could see, in the original version of Strawson's truth-gap theory, he did not recognize any particular asymmetry, as regards the presupposition that there is a king of France, between the two sentences, *The king of France is bald* and *The king of France is not bald;* but it does seem to be plausible to suppose that there is such an asymmetry. I would have thought that the implication that there is a king of France is clearly part of the conventional force of *The king of France is bald;* but that this is not clearly so in the case of *The king of France is not bald.* Let us abbreviate *The king of France is not bald* by $\bar{K}$. An implication that there is a king of France is often carried by saying $\bar{K}$, but it is tempting to suggest that this implication is not, inescapably, part of the conventional force of the utterance of $\bar{K}$, but is rather a matter of conversational implicature. So let us apply the tests of cancelability and detachment.

First, the implication seems to be explicitly cancelable. If I come on a group of people arguing about whether the king of France is bald, it is not linguistically improper for me to say that the king of France is not bald, since there is no king of France. Of course, I do not have to put it that way, but I perfectly well can. Second, the implication seems to be contextually cancelable, that is, cancelable by circumstances attending the utterance, $\bar{K}$. If it is a matter of dispute whether the government has a very undercover person who interrogates those whose loyalty is suspect and who, if he existed, could be legitimately referred to as the loyalty examiner; and if, further, I am known to be very skeptical about the existence of such a person, I could perfectly well say to a plainly loyal person, *Well, the loyalty examiner will not be summoning you at any rate,* without, I would think, being taken to imply that such a person exists. Further, if I am well known to disbelieve in the existence of such a person, though others are inclined to believe in him, when I find a man who is apprised of my position, but who is worried in case he is summoned, I could try to reassure him by saying *The loyalty examiner won't summon you, don't worry.* Then it would be clear that I said this because I was sure there is no such person.

Furthermore, the implicature seems to have a very high degree of nondetachability. Many of what seem to be other ways of saying, approximately, what is asserted by $\bar{K}$ also carry the existential implicature, for example, *It is not the case the king of France is bald, It is false that the king of France is bald, It is not true that the king of France is bald.* Of course, if the truth-gap theory is wrong, then there will be a way of asserting just what is asserted by $\bar{K}$ that lacks this implicature, namely, a Russellian expansion of it, for example, *It is not the case that there is one and only one person who is the king of France ...* But all that this breakdown of nondetachability would show would be that the presence of the implicature depends on the manner of the expression, in particular on the presence of the definite description itself. No implicature, however, could be finally established as conversational unless the explanation of its presence has been given and been shown to be of the right kind, as involving conversational maxims in an appropriate way. That is what I shall try to deal with next.

Before we go further, it would be expedient to define the task somewhat more precisely. If we are looking for a possible formal counterpart for such a sentence as *The king of France is bald,* we have two candidates to consider: (*a*) $(\iota x.Fx)\ Gx$, in which the iota-operator is treated as being syntactically analogous to a quantifier; and (*b*) G $(\iota x.Fx)$, in which the iota-operator is treated as a device for forming a term. If we select (*a*), then, when we introduce negation, we have two semantically distinguishable ways of doing so; $\sim((\iota x.Fx)\, Gx)$ and $(\iota x.Fx)\sim Gx$. The second will, and the first will not, entail the existence of an x that is uniquely F. But if we select the latter, there is only one place (prefixing) for the introduction of negation: and in consequence $\sim G(\iota x.Fx)$ will be an ambiguous structure (unless we introduce a disambiguating scope convention): on one reduction to primitive notation the existence of a unique F will be entailed, on the other it will not. (Call these respectively the strong and the weak readings.) Now if there were a clear distinction in sense (in English) between, say, *The king of France is not bald* and *It is not the case that the king of France is bald* (if the former demanded the strong reading and the latter the weak one), then it would be reasonable to correlate *The king of France is bald* with the formal structure that treats the iota-operator like a quantifier. But this does not seem to be the case; I see no such clear semantic distinction. So it seems better to associate *The king of France is bald* with the formal structure that treats the iota-operator as a term-forming device. We are then committed to the structural ambiguity of the sentence *The king of France is not bald*. The proposed task may now be defined as follows: On one reading *The king of France is not bald* entails the existence of a unique king of France, on the other it does not; but in fact, without waiting for disambiguation, people understand an utterance of *The king of France is not bald* as implying (in some fashion) the unique existence of a king of France. This is intelligible if on one reading (the strong one), the unique existence of a king of France is entailed, on the other (the weak one), though not entailed, it is conversationally implicated. What needs to be shown, then, is a route by which the weaker reading could come to implicate what it does not entail.

If one looks for some prima-facie plausibility for the idea of regarding the definite description as carrying an implicature of a nonconventional and conversational kind, where is one to find it? Well, one would have to select, first (and the case would have to be argued for), one or another of the different Russellian expansions as being that for which such an expression as *The king of France is bald* (or *The king of France is not bald*) is to be regarded as a definitional contraction. And I think there will be some case for selecting one particular one, namely, the one that would run *There is at least one king of France, there is not more than one king of France, and nothing which is the king of France is not bald*. It seems to have a particular feature that recommends it and might fit in with some general principle of discourse; namely, there are no conjunctions occurring in it within the scope of quantifiers. That is to say, it sets out separately three distinct clauses, and each one of these can be false while both of the others are true. I think this is perhaps appropriate because it may well have some connection with something that I am going to mention in a moment, namely, that this particular expansion is constructed in a way that makes it particularly suitable for denial on the part of somebody (a hearer) to whom it might be uttered. I would be inclined to suggest that we add to the maxims of Manner which I originally propounded some maxim which would be, as it should be, vague: "Frame whatever you say in the form most suitable for any reply that would be regarded as appropriate"; or, "Facilitate in your form of expression the appropriate reply." It is very clear that one of the appropriate replies to something that you have asserted is the denial of what you say. If your assertions are complex and conjunctive, and you are asserting a number of things at the same time, then it would be natural, on the assumption that any one of them might be challengeable, to set them out separately and so make it easy for anyone who wanted to challenge them to do so. So, let us make the assumption that we accept some such maxim and also agree that denial is a natural and suitable form of response to an assertion. Let us also adopt the following abbreviational scheme: "A" is to represent *There is at least one king of France,* "B" is to represent *There is at most one king of France,* "C" is to represent *Whatever is king of France is bald,* "ABC" is to represent the conjunction of A, B, and C, which we are taking as the favored Russellian expansion of "D," which represents *The king of France is bald.*

Now we may hope to reach the conclusion that the production of this abbreviation (D) would violate our newly introduced maxim of Manner unless one could assume that the speaker thought he was within his rights, in that he did not consider that a distinct denial of A or of B would be appropriate (that this was a response not to be looked for, in his view). As a start, given that *some* kind of denial has to be thought of as appropriate, as that is a natural response to any form of assertion, we might claim that one who employs the abbreviated form D ought *either* to be thinking it likely that, if there is to be a denial, it will be a wholesale denial, *or else,* to be thinking that, though the hearer may be going to reject one conjunct, one particular conjunct is, in some way, singled out as the one that is specially likely to be denied. It must, indeed, be the second possibility that is to be seriously considered, as the conjuncts cannot all be denied together consistently. If it is false that there exists at least one king of France, then it is vacuously true that whatever is king of France is bald (that nothing is both king of France and not bald). So that leaves us with the demand to show that, in some way, one particular conjunct is singled out. Now this would be the case if it would be reasonable to suppose that the speaker thinks, and expects his hearer to think, that some subconjunction of A and B and C has what I might call common-ground status and, therefore, is not something that is likely to be challenged. One way in which this might happen would be if the speaker were to think or assume that it is common knowledge, and that people would regard it as common knowledge, that there is one and only one *F*. But that would be only one way in which it could arise.

For instance, it is quite natural to say to somebody, when we are discussing some concert, *My aunt's cousin went to that concert,* when we know perfectly well that the person we are talking to is very likely not even to know that we have an aunt, let alone know that our aunt has a cousin. So the supposition must be not that it is common knowledge but rather that it is noncontroversial, in the sense that it is something that we would expect the hearer to take from us (if he does not already know). That is to say, I do not expect, when I tell someone that my aunt's cousin went to a concert, to be questioned whether I have an aunt and, if so, whether my aunt has a cousin. This is the sort of thing that I would expect him to take from me, that is, to take my word for. So, we have now got into the position that we might well be in the clear, as far as concerns representing the existential implication as a conversational implicature, if we could show that, in general, there should be a reasonable expectation, other things being equal, that, in the favored Russellian expansion of a definite description, two of the clauses (in fact, the first and the second) would be matters that would have this common-ground status, and so not be controversial or likely to be open to challenge. We might, then, assume that, so far, it looks as if the hearer would be justified in concluding that two of the items must be given common-ground status, the only question is which two. Now the third clause (C) is general in form. And we can think of a general statement as being either something the establishment of which depends on the complete enumeration of a set of instances, or as something to be an inductive step.

Let us take the first possibility. Let us suppose it is enumeratively based. That is, we are to think of *Nothing that is F is not G* as to be reached by finding the instances of *F* and seeing that none of them fail to be *G*. For it to be possible to establish this enumeratively if the whole sentence (D) is true, it must be the case that there exists just one *F* which is the basis of the enumeration. And so we have, in effect, a conjunctive statement that tells us there are a certain number of cases (just one) that would test a certain generalization, and then gives us the generalization. It would seem to be very peculiar to imagine that anybody could be in the situation in which he was prepared to speak of C, but not as being common ground, because he would have to be put in the position of saying something like, "I can accept that nothing is *F* but not *G*, that 'what is *F* is *G*' is true, and is also to be established by complete enumeration. But what I am uncertain about is whether you are right about whether there are any instances of *F*, or, if so, how many." It is not necessary that it should be *impossible* for somebody to be in that position, but that it is certainly not to be expected; and what is to be generally assumed may depend, not on something being universally the case, but merely on its being expectable.

Again, we can take the other possibility. Suppose we take the last clause, C, not as being an enumerative generalization, but as an open one. And there may be some cases in which that is how it is to be thought of. Even so, it is prima facie not to be expected that you would find somebody in the position of being prepared to concede the generalization but being concerned about whether and how often that generalization is instantiated. Again, I am not saying that that is not possible. But that would certainly be not the kind of situation that one would think of as being the natural one; and the implicature depends on what is to be expected, not on what is universally true.

If this line of argument (or something like it) goes through, then we could perhaps explain why it is that somebody who says it is not the *case* that the present king of France is bald (someone who denies what is expressed by D) would also be implicating, though not explicitly stating, that there is a unique king of France. It is as if he is countering a remark which might be made to him, in which the speaker has indicated that he is expecting the challenge to come, if at all, in a particular direction, namely, to C; and he just says, "No, that is not so." He denies that the present king of France is bald, and so naturally he will be taken to be going along with the expected restriction of comment that is implicitly carried by the presentation of the original statement in the abbreviated form (D), rather than in the full form in which each clause would have been set up for him to object to if he wants to. The position that I am outlining might be presented, in summary fashion, as follows:

A speaker S, who utters D (the affirmative form of a sentence having as subject a definite description) might expect a hearer H to reflect (or intuit) as follows:

"1. (By the conversational 'tailoring' principle) S has uttered D rather than its Russellian expansion; so there is one particular Russellian conjunct that S expects me (if I reject anything) to reject, while accepting the other conjuncts.

2. That is, all but a particular one of the Russellian conjuncts are thought of by him as likely to possess common-ground status (to be treated as noncontroversial).

3. The first two conjuncts would, in most natural circumstances, be items which anyone would have to know or accept in order to have a good ground for accepting the third.

4. So the first two conjuncts are the ones to which he attributes common-ground status."

A speaker S', who utters D̄ (the negation of D) might expect a hearer H' to reflect (or intuit) as follows:

"1. Speaker S' has uttered the negation of D; so he is speaking as if he were responding negatively to S (above), that is, to one who utters D.

2. So S' is fulfilling the expectations that S would have had about H, that is, he is accepting the first two conjuncts and rejecting the third."

We may note, before moving on, that for a very large range of cases a different account of the existential implication carried by the negative forms of statements involving descriptions might be available. Consider utterances of such a sentence as *The book on the table is not open.* As there are, obviously, many books on tables in the world, if we are to treat such a sentence as being of the form *The F is not G* and as being, on that account, ripe for Russellian expansion, we might do well to treat it as exemplifying the more specific form *The F' which is φ is not G,* where "φ" represents an epithet to be identified in a particular context of utterance ("φ" being a sort of quasi-demonstrative). Standardly, to identify the reference of "φ" for a particular utterance of *The book on the table is (not) open,* a hearer would proceed via the identification of a particular book as being a good *candidate* for being the book meant, and would identify the reference of "φ" by finding in the candidate a feature, for example, that of *being in this room,* which could be used to yield a composite epithet ("book on the table in this room"), which would in turn fill the bill of being an epithet which the speaker had in mind as being uniquely satisfied by the book selected as candidate. If the hearer fails to find a suitable reference for "φ" in relation to the selected candidate, then he would, normally, seek another candidate. So determining the reference of "φ" would standardly involve determining what feature the speaker might have in mind as being uniquely instantiated by an actual object, and this in turn would standardly involve satisfying oneself that some particular feature actually is uniquely satisfied by a particular actual object (e.g. a particular book). So utterances both of *The book on the table is open* and of *The book on the table is not open* would alike imply (in one way or another) the existence of a particular book on a table.

We might, indeed, if we regard this apparatus as reasonably well set up, try to use it to deal with the difficulty raised in the third main objection mentioned, namely, the difficulty about applying the Russellian expansion to moods other than the indicative. First, I think a distinction is needed. I think that the objection, as I presented it, is put in a bad form. I think it is important to notice a distinction between what I might call *causing* something to be the case and what I might call *ensuring* that it is the case. If I tell somebody to cause it to be the case that a particular person has somewhere to live and enough to live on, it looks certainly as if I am thinking that he has to operate in order to promote both clauses; I mean, that he will have to find him somewhere to live and give him enough to live on. And it seems possible that he could hardly claim to have caused him to have somewhere to live and to have enough to live on unless he had done both of these things. But, if I merely tell somebody to ensure that the person has somewhere to live and enough to live on, then I think he could also, afterward, claim that he had ensured this, even though, in fact, when he got onto the scene, he found that the man already had somewhere to live and that all he needed was something to live on. All he has to do, so to speak, is to bring the state of affairs up to completion, if that is required. What exactly one is entitled to say if one finds not only that the man has somewhere to live, but also has enough to live on, after one has been told to ensure that he has both of these things, perhaps is not quite so clear.

So to the question of the imperatives: part of the paradoxical character of the suggested Russellian account comes from the fact that I began with *Make it the case that,* which suggests that if I were to say *Give these flowers to your wife,* the expansion of that imperative must begin *Make it the case that* . . . And then, when you put in the full Russellian expansion, it looks as if I am instructing you to make three changes, one corresponding to each clause. But if I put in *Ensure that* . . . instead, then there would not be this implication. All that would be required is that you should bring the thing to completion, so to speak, insofar as there is a gap. And so it may well turn out, also (indeed, in some cases it turns out as a matter of logical fact or something like it), that you *cannot* do anything about some of the clauses.

You cannot now make it the case that you are now married to one and only one person. Either you are or you are not. That is outside your control; so, in many cases, the only clause left with respect to which you can act is the one covered by *Make it the case that she has the flowers.* But, of course, there will be some cases where this particular provision would not work. If I tell somebody who is not presently married and, as far as I know, has no immediate prospect of getting married, *See that your next wife looks after you properly,* I do not necessarily think that he is going to get married. Nor, I think, am I instructing him to get married. It would be possible, presumably, on a Russellian account, for him to take my instruction as telling him to select a wife, first, and then, second, to make sure that she looks after him properly. So we would need something to ensure that it was not taken this way.

At this point, if one supposed that it is being taken as an assumption by me, as common ground between us, as not to be questioned, that he will at some time or other have another wife (and the point is that when the time comes she should look after him properly), then he will not take the imperative force, so to speak, as attaching to the selection of a particular wife. So, if it is a conversational implicatum that he will at some time or other have a wife, then this will be excerpted from the instructions. I am inclined to think that this particular dodge works reasonably well for the range of cases considered; but I am not wholly happy about it, as it stands, because this general phenomenon of presupposition (or cases that look like presupposition) is one that occurs in a large number of places. In recent years, linguists have made it increasingly difficult for philosophers to continue to keep their eyes glued to a handful of stock examples of (alleged) presupposition, such as the king of France's baldness and the inquiry whether you have left off beating your wife.

There is, in fact, an enormous range of cases in which the questions about presuppositions arise, not least in connection with psychological verbs. One can distinguish, perhaps, a number of such cases in connection with psychological verbs. Let us take, first, *think*. If I say that somebody thinks (or believes) that such-and-such, there is no indication that what he thinks or believes is true. Supposing, however, I take the verb *discover,* and I say *Somebody discovered that the roof was leaking.* Here, it is not logically possible to discover that one's roof is leaking unless one's roof is leaking. On the other hand, I do not think (though, perhaps, this is doubtful) that so-and-so did not discover *P* also implies that *P* is true. I think I can say that some explorer went off to someplace expecting to discover that the natives were very interesting in certain respects, but he did not discover that because they were not. So here we have a case where there is a logical implication on the part of the affirmative, but not on the part of its denial. (That looks like a case of entailment.)

Then there is a third case, which perhaps is exemplified by the word *know,* in which to say that somebody did know that so-and-so was the case and to say that he did not know that so-and-so was the case both imply that it was the case. This is a specimen, I think, of the kind of verb that has been called *factive.* There is a distinction between this and a fourth case, because, though both the affirmation and denial of statements about particular people knowing that *P* carries with it a commitment to *P,* you can weaken the verb in such a way that this implication is lost. *He knew that P* and *He didn't know that P* both carry this implication, but *He thought he knew that P* does not. When I say *He thought he knew that P,* I am not committing myself to its being the case that *P,* but there are some verbs in which even the weakened forms also seem to carry this implication, particularly, perhaps, a verb like *regret* (i.e., *He thought he regretted his father's death, but it afterwards turned out that he didn't,* as far as it makes sense, would, I think, still imply the committal to his father's death). I am not sure about the last distinction, and I think perhaps it does not matter very much. These are cases where there is some kind of a commitment on the part of a normal speaker, by using both the affirmative and the negative forms, to some common element's being true; and I do not see that it is going to be particularly easy to represent the implication in the case of *regret* as being one of a conversational kind. It does not look as attractive as the Russellian case. So, I would be interested in having recourse to a conventional device which would be a substitute in standard cases for an original conversational implicature. To this end I deploy a revised and slightly more complicated version of the square brackets device which was introduced in Essay 4. The new version may be used to reinterpret the original device. The revised rules would read:

1. (*a*) If expression *A* is of the denominated type *T,* then *A*[*B*]*C* is rewritten as *BABC*.
   (*b*) If expression *A* is not of type *T,* or is null, then *A*[*B*]*C* is rewritten as *ABC*.
2. In rewriting, nested brackets are eliminated, seriatim, from exterior to interior.
3. If no connective directly precedes a closing (right-hand) square bracket, "&" is supplied in rewriting, where needed, to preserve syntactical admissibility.
4. Any opening (left-hand) parentheses introduced in rewriting are closed terminally.
5. In preposing an expression containing a bound variable, the variable is changed.

Using the revised version, $\sim([P{\supset}]Q)$ will be rewritten as $P{\supset}\sim(P{\supset}Q)$, which is equivalent to $P{\supset}\sim Q$ (the rewrite of $\sim([P{\supset}]Q)$ on the original version). We could use the revised version to handle the alleged existential presuppositions of *some* and *every, every F is G* could be represented as $\sim[(\exists x)(Fx\ \&]\sim Gx)$, with the rewrite $(\exists y)\ (Fy\ \&\sim(\exists x)(Fx\ \&\sim Gx))$. We may also use the revised device in the formal representation of such a factive verb as *regret*.

Accordingly, *x regrets* φ (e.g., that Father is ill) is defined as:

1. [*x* knows* φ &] *x* is anti φ
   *x knows** φ is defined as *x thinks* [φ]
   So, *x regrets* φ emerges as
2. [*x* thinks [φ] & [*x* is anti φ]

So, *x does not regret* φ would be expressible as:

1. $\sim$([*x* thinks [φ] &] *x* is anti φ)
   Replacing exterior square brackets, we get

2. x thinks [φ] & ~ (x thinks [φ] & x is anti φ)
   Replacing remaining square brackets, we get
3. φ & x thinks φ & φ & ~ (x thinks φ & x is anti φ)
   Eliminating redundant occurrence of φ, we get
4. φ & x thinks φ & ~(x thinks φ & x is anti φ)
   which is equivalent to
5. φ & x thinks φ & ~(x is anti φ)

We may, finally, consider the employment of the square brackets device to handle the possible difficulties for the Russellian account connected with the appearance of definite descriptions in sentences couched in a mood other than the indicative:

1. *Arrest the intruder*
   could be thought of as representable (using "!" as an imperative operator) as
2. ! ([[($\exists_1 x$) (x is an intruder) &] ($\forall y$) (y is an intruder $\supset$ you will arrest y))
   Provided "!" is treated as belonging to the denominated type *T*, (2) will be rewritten (on the original version of the square bracket device) as
3(a). ($\exists_1 x$) (x is an intruder) & ! ($\forall y$) (y is an intruder $\supset$ you will arrest y) and (on the revised version) as
3(b). ($\exists_1 z$) (z is an intruder) & ! (($\exists_1 x$) (x is an intruder & ($\forall y$) (y is an intruder $\supset$ you will arrest y))

Since the first clause of 3(b) STATES that there is just one intruder, the imperatival clause cannot be taken as enjoining that the addressee see to it that there be just one intruder.

In conclusion, let me briefly summarize the course of this essay, primarily in order to distinguish what I have been attempting to do from what I have not. I have endeavored to outline, without aligning myself with it, an exposition of the thesis that the existential presuppositions seemingly carried by definite descriptions can be represented within a Russellian semantics, with the aid of a standard attachment of conversational implicature; I paid attention both to the possibility that such implicata are cancelable and detachable and also to the availability of more than one method of deriving them from the operation of conversational principles. Promising though such an account may seem, I have suggested that it may run into trouble when it is observed that the range of cases of presupposition extends far beyond the most notorious examples, and that perhaps not the whole of this range would prove amenable to the envisaged mode of treatment. At this point I took up the idea of a minimal strengthening of a Russellian pattern of analysis by the addition of a purely syntactical scope device, which could at the same time be regarded as a conventional regimentation of a particular kind of nonconventional implicature. I have not, in this essay, given any consideration at all to what might well turn out to be the best treatment of definite descriptions, namely to the idea that they are, in the first instance at least, to be regarded as being, semantically, a special subclass of referential expressions.

18

Meaning Revisited

I am going to treat informally some topics connected with meaning. Rather than trying to say something particularly new, I have the idea of putting one or two of the thoughts I have had at various times into some kind of focus, so that there might emerge some sense about not merely what kind of view about the nature of meaning I am, or was, inclined to endorse, but also why it should be antecedently plausible to accept this kind of view. When I say "antecedently plausible," I mean plausible for some reasons other than that the view in question offers some prospects of dealing with the intuitive data: the facts about how we use the word "mean," and so on. So I shall be digging just a little bit into the background of the study of meaning and its roots in such things as philosophical psychology; but I hope without any very formidable detail.

The main theme will be matters connected with the relation between speaker's meaning and meaning in a language, or word meaning, sentence meaning, expression meaning, and so on. In the course of this account, I shall make reference to something like the definitions or analyses that I have previously offered; I do not guarantee that any that I use will be quite the same, but this does not worry me because I am not here concerned with the details. It seems to me that with regard to the possibility of using the notion of intention in a nested kind of way to explicate the notion of meaning, there are quite a variety of plausible, or at least not too implausible, analyses, which differ to a greater or lesser extent in detail, and at the moment I am not really concerned with trying to adjudicate between the various versions.

The essay will be in three sections. In the first, I shall try to sketch three kinds of correspondence which one might be justified in looking for, or even demanding, when thinking about thought, the world, and language. I hope this will provide some sort of a framework within which to set views about meaning; it may in fact offer some sort of impetus toward this or that view. In the second section, which will again involve an attempt to fit things into a wider framework, I shall provide some discussion of what I once called the distinction between natural and nonnatural meaning. Here I am interested not so much in the existence of that distinction, which has now, I think, become pretty boringly common ground (or mutual knowledge), but rather in the relationship between the two notions, the connections rather than the dissimilarities between them. I shall announce the contents of the third section when I come to it; we'll keep it as a mystery package.

I. Language, Thought, and Reality

The first of the three correspondences which one might expect to find when thinking in largish terms about the relationships between reality, thought, and language or communication devices, is a correspondence between thought and reality: what I shall call, for some kind of brevity, psychophysical correspondence. This has obvious connections with the general idea of truth in application to beliefs or analogous notions describing physical states. The point I want to get at is that it is not just that there *are* such correspondences, or that it is intuitively plausible to think there are, but rather that their presence is *needed,* or *desirable,* if one looks at the ways in which human beings and other sentient creatures get around and stay alive, as well as perhaps doing more ambitious things than that. This leads to a view, which I have held for some time, of a battery of psychological concepts which we use both about ourselves and about what one might think of as lower creatures, as having the function of providing an explanatory bridge between the appearance of a creature in a certain kind of physical situation and its engaging in certain sorts of behavior.

For instance, suppose we have a creature C that is in the presence of a certain object, let's say a piece of cheese, and we get a situation in which the creature eats the object. In certain circumstances, we might want to invoke the contents of a psychological theory in order to explain the transition from the creature's being in the presence of the object to its eating it. The "bridgework" which would be done in these terms can be put in a rather schematic and unrealistic way, which again does not worry me since I am not trying to provide a proper explanation, but merely a rough idea of what the pattern of a proper explanation would be.

First, let us suppose that the creature believes (or thinks, if it is not advanced enough to have beliefs) that the object is a bit of cheese, and that it also believes that the object is nearby. Second, let us suppose that the creature believes, or thinks, that cheese is something to eat; and third, that the creature is hungry, that it wants to eat. All this looks relatively unexciting, just as it should. Then by virtue of what I would think of as a vulgar, vernacular, psychological law, the operation of which is the reason for the introduction of the concepts of believing and wanting, we get our first psychological law for the creature or type of creature in question. This is that for any particular object X and for any feature F and for any activity or type of behavior A, if the creature C believes that the object X both has the feature F and is nearby, or within reach, and that things of type F are suitable for activity A, then the creature wants to A with respect to the object X. In other words, the law harnesses the object to the type of activity.

Applying the law to the three initial premises given above, we reach a further stage: namely, that the creature C wants to eat the object X, that is, the piece of cheese. We might then invoke a second psychological law for this creature, this time a psychophysical law: that for any type of activity A, if a creature C, wants to A with respect to some particular object X, and if it is not prevented in one or another of a set of ways which might or might not be listable, then creature C does produce the activity A with respect to X. And with the application of the second law, we get to our final step, which is that the creature C eats the object X. We now have our explanation, a bridge between the initial situation, the creature's being in the presence of a piece of cheese, and the final behavior, the creature's eating it.

The laws I have mentioned are vulgar laws. The kind of theory in which I think of them appearing would not be a specialist or formalized psychological theory, if indeed there are such things; I am perhaps not very comfortable with the word "theory" being applied to it. It would be the rough kind of system with which we all work, and the laws in it are to be thought of as corrigible, modifiable and *ceteris paribus* in character.

Now the creature C may be frustrated if certain psychophysical correspondences do not obtain. For instance, if C believes *wrongly* that the object in front of it is a piece of cheese, or thinks *wrongly* of cheese as being from its point of view something to eat, then at the very least, C may get indigestion when it consumes the object. For this reason, psychophysical correspondences are required (things like beliefs have to be true, and so on) for the operation of the psychological mechanisms which I have sketched to be *beneficial* to the creature in question.

In a similar way, if the creature's desire to eat the object is for some reason not fulfilled, the creature stays hungry. Here again we need some kind of correspondences, parallel to those between beliefs and reality, between desires, wants, states of will and so on, and reality. Desires, etc. need to correspond to reality in order to be fulfilled: that is, in order for the psychological mechanism to operate in a beneficial way.

Finally, if C is a rational or reflective creature (which I have not so far been assuming), it may recognize the kind of facts about itself that I have just sketched, may recognize that correspondences between psychological states and the world are in general required for the psychological mechanism to be useful, and may also recognize that subject to this proviso of correspondence, the psychological mechanism is conducive to survival or to the attainment of other of its objectives. If it recognizes all this, then it will presumably itself think of such correspondences as being desirable things to have around from its own point of view: that is, the correspondences will not only *be* desirable but will be regarded by C as desirable.

In the first place, then, we have psychophysical correspondences, and they seem to be the kind of things that one would want to have. But there are further correspondences too. There is, as it were, a triangle consisting of reality, thought, and language or communication devices, and we now have, I hope, one hookup, between thought and reality. However, I think there is also a hookup of a different kind, which would also be desirable, between thought and communication devices. This would again involve correspondences of a relatively simple and obvious kind, along the following lines.

First, the operation of such creatures as I have been talking about is at least in certain circumstances going to be helped and furthered if there is what one might think of as shared experience. In particular, if psychological states which initially attach to one creature can be transmitted or transferred or reproduced in another creature (a process which might be called ψ-transmission), that would be advantageous. Obviously, the production of communication devices is a resource which will help to effect such transfers.

If one accepts this idea, then one could simply accept that for the process to be intelligible, understandable, there will have to be correspondences between particular communication devices or utterances on the one hand, and psychological states on the other. These correspondences may be achieved either directly, or (more likely) indirectly, via the *types* to which the particular utterances belong: the sentences which the particular utterances are utterances of, the gesture-types which the particular gestures are productions of, and so on. Whether direct or indirect, the correspondence would be between utterances or utterance-types on the one hand, and *types* of psychological states on the other, where these would include, for example, the belief-types to which the beliefs of particular people belong: not *Jones's* belief that such-and-such, but *a* belief that such-and-such.

If there exist these correspondences between utterances or utterance-types on the one hand, and psychological types on the other, we can say that it is in general, and subject to certain conditions, *desirable* for there to occur, in the joint or social lives of creatures of the kind in question, sequences of the following sort: a certain psychological state ψ^1 in certain circumstances is followed by a certain utterance U, made in certain circumstances, which in turn, if the circumstances are right, is followed by a particular instance of a further psychological type ψ^2, a state not now in the communicating creature but in the creature who is communicated to. And it might be a matter of desirability for ψ^1 and ψ^2 to be states of one and the same, rather than of different sorts, so that when these sequences ψ^1, U, ψ^2 occur, they involve utterances and psychological states between which these psycholinguistic correspondences obtain.

Of course, transfers can occur without these correspondences obtaining. A creature may choose the wrong utterance to express its psychological state, and then there will probably be a misfire in the utterance, and the psychological state induced in the second creature will not be the same as the one present in the first. Alternatively, the first creature may operate all right, but the second creature may, as it were, misunderstand the device that was produced, and so pick up the wrong belief or desire, one that does not correspond to the utterance produced by the first creature.

The general condition, or at least the most salient general condition, for the desirability or beneficial character of transfers of this sort is connected with the obtaining of the first kind of correspondence. That is, if all these transfers were to involve the transmission of mistaken beliefs, it is not clear that one would regard this communication mechanism as beneficial, even if the appropriate psycholinguistic correspondences held. I do think it is in some sense inconceivable that all the transfers should involve mistaken beliefs, but at least such a state of affairs can be contemplated. So a general condition would be that soul-to-soul transfers, so to speak, are beneficial provided that the states transmitted are ones which correspond with the world.

It looks now as if we have got to a point at which we have in outline, presented in a sort of general, semitheological way, a rough prototype of a notion of truth in application to beliefs and such-like things. That would give the first kind of correspondence. In the second kind of correspondence, we have what is at least a promising candidate for being a rough prototype of the notion of meaning, for it looks as though it is not implausible to suggest that to explain, with respect to some particular utterance or utterance-type what type of psychological state it corresponds to, in such a way that transfers of this kind are characteristically a feature of creatures' lives, would be a first approximation to explaining the meaning of the utterances or utterance-types in question. We have thus hooked up all three corners: corner number one, reality, has been hooked up with corner number two, thought, and we have hooked up thought, corner number two, with language or communication devices, corner number three. This of course yields a derivative link between corner number three, utterances or sentences, and corner number one, reality, via the beliefs or other psychological states with which they are themselves connected. But it is perhaps also worthwhile to ask whether in addition to such an indirect connection between language and reality, one which proceeds through the intermediation of psychological states, there is an arguable possibility of a direct link: a direct line between language and reality as well as a line through thought. And I think it is at least arguable that there is, though of course one of a kind which we will have to harmonize with the links that have already been introduced.

If I ask the question "What are the conditions for a specified belief (for instance a belief that snow is white) corresponding with the world?" I can give answers for individual cases without much difficulty. For instance, I can say that a belief that snow is white will correspond to the world just in case snow is white, and I can say that a belief that cheese is blue will correspond to the world just in case cheese is blue; and you can see perfectly well what the rather dreary routine is that I use in these particular cases. However, it has been noticed by philosophers that there are difficulties about explicitly generalizing the individual bits of communication of which I have just spouted one or two samples. That is because to generalize from them would presumably be to omit reference to the particular objects and the particular beliefs, and to state in general what the conditions are for beliefs corresponding to objects. That is to say, a general condition of correspondence between beliefs and the world would have to begin something like: "For any item which one believes, that item corresponds with the world if . . ."; but then how does one go on? In the particular cases, I had a sentence which I had cited or referred to in the antecedent on the left-hand side, which I then produced on the right-hand side; but since I have eliminated all reference to particular beliefs or sentences, I no longer have a sentence available with which to complete the general condition.

It looks as if I should want to say something like: "For any item P, if one believes that P, then one's belief that P corresponds with the world just in case P." Unfortunately that involves difficulties, because by the ordinary account of quantification, I am talking about objects or items, so I might just as well use the letter x, characteristic of objects, and say: "For any item x, if x is believed, then x corresponds with the world just in case x." But that seems rather like producing the generalization that if any object x is a pig, then x: and that is not an intelligible form of statement, because "x" is not a variable for which one can substitute sentences. In fact, something seems to have got left out somewhere, and we have not got an intelligible specification of truth-conditions. Moreover, this is difficult to remedy, because without getting into tortures over shifts between thinking of propositions or propositional expressions as sometimes like names (with the form of *that*-clauses) and sometimes like sentences (the result of detaching the word "that" from these *that*-clauses), it is difficult to know what to do.

It looks as though, to avoid this difficulty, if I want to produce a generalization of the idea of correspondences between psychological states and the world which I have already in some sense provided for, I might well have to use some form like the following: "If a certain sentence S is an expression of a certain particular belief, then the belief which the sentence S expresses corresponds with the world just in case S is true." That is to say, to remedy this difficulty in generalization, I now bring into play a notion of truth in application to sentences, and I do this in order to have a way of stating generally the conditions for the correspondence of beliefs and the world. Thus, in trying to safeguard the characterization of what it is for beliefs to correspond with the world, I have introduced another correspondence, a correspondence between utterances or sentences and the world, signalized by the appearance of the word "true."

It looks, then, as if in order to achieve a characterization of the first kind of correspondence, between beliefs and the world, one has to make use of a parallel kind of correspondence between utterances or sentences and the world. Hence these latter correspondences may be not only possible but needed if one is to be able to state, in a general way, that correspondences of the psychophysical kind actually obtain.

However, though they may be required for expository purposes, as I have sketched, it might still be the case that in order to show that correspondences between sentences and the world were desirable, not just for purposes of theoretical exposition but from the point of view of creatures who operate with such utterances or utterance-types, one still has to bring in the psychological states in specifying the conditions of suitability, desirability, or whatever. That is, it might be that one can certainly formulate or characterize some notion of direct correspondence between utterances and the world, and this might have a certain limited teleological justification because it is needed to provide a general way of expressing the conditions for other types of correspondence, but if one wants to provide a more general teleological justification, one would need to make reference to beliefs and other psychological states. In other words, for a more general justification of the idea of truth in application to sentences, one might have to bring in all three corners, including the missing one.

II. Natural and Nonnatural Meaning

I have now, as it were, smuggled in some sort of preliminary version of the kind of view about meaning which I have gone on record as holding; but that is qualified by the fact that I have also smuggled in versions of the kind of views that other people have gone in for too. Let me now try to advance the case a little further, in a way which might support my sort of view as opposed to certain other views.

I do not think it is too controversial to advance the idea that there is a reasonably clear intuitive distinction between cases where the word "mean" has what one might think of as a natural sense, a sense in which what something means is closely related to the idea of what it is a natural sign for (as in "Black clouds mean rain"), and those where it has what I call a nonnatural sense, as in such contexts as "His remark meant so-and-so," "His gesture meant that he was fed up," and so on (cf. Essay 14).

I have offered one or two recognition tests which might enable one to tell which of these, natural or nonnatural meaning, one was actually dealing with in a given case. The tests were, roughly speaking, that the nonnatural cases of meaning, cases which are related to communication, are what we might call nonfactive, whereas the natural cases are factive. That is, anyone who says "Those black clouds mean rain," or "Those black clouds meant that it would rain," would presumably be committing himself to its being the case that it will rain, or that it did rain. However, if I say "His gesture meant that he was fed up," under an interpretation of a nonnatural kind, one specially connected with what we think of as communication, then to say that does not commit you to his actually being fed up. I also noted that the specification of the nonnatural meaning of items can be comfortably done via the use of phrases in quotation marks, whereas it would seem rather odd to say that those black clouds meant "It will rain": it does not look as if one can replace the *that*-clause here by a sentence in quotation marks.

Assuming for the moment that these tests are roughly adequate, what I want to do now is not to emphasize the differences between these cases, because that has already been done, but rather to look at what they have in common. Is this double use of the word "mean" just like the double use of the word "vice" to refer sometimes to something approximating to a sin and sometimes to a certain sort of instrument used by carpenters? One is pretty much inclined in the latter case to say that there are two words which are pronounced and written the same.

On general grounds of economy, I am inclined to think that if one can avoid saying that the word so-and-so has this sense, that sense, and the other sense, or this meaning and another meaning, if one can allow them to be variants under a single principle, that is the desirable thing to do: don't multiply senses beyond necessity. And it occurs to me that the root idea in the notion of meaning, which in one form or adaptation or another would apply to both of these cases, is that if x means that y, then this is equivalent to, or at least contains as a part of what it means, the claim that y is a consequence of x. That is, what the cases of natural and nonnatural meaning have in common is that, on some interpretation of the notion of consequence, y's being the case is a consequence of x.

Of course one will expect there to be differences in the kind of consequence involved, or the way in which the consequence is reached. So what I want to do now is look to see if one would represent the cases of nonnatural meaning as being descendants from, in a sense of "descendant" which would suggest that they were derivative from and analogous to, cases of natural meaning. I shall also look a little at what kind of principles or assumptions one would have to make if one were trying to set up this position that natural meaning is in some specifiable way the ancestor of nonnatural meaning.

In the case of natural meaning, among the things which have natural meaning, besides black clouds, spots on the face, and symptoms of this or that disease, are certainly forms of behavior: things like groans, screeches, and so on, which mean, or normally mean, that someone or something is in pain or some other state. Thus special cases of natural meaning are cases in which bits of things like bodily behavior mean the presence of various elements or states of the creature that produces them. In the natural case, the production of these pieces of behavior, or at least the presence in those pieces of behavior of the particular features which, as it were, do the meaning for one, is nonvoluntary. Thus we have as a sort of canonical pattern that some creature X nonvoluntarily produces a certain piece of behavior α, the production of which means, or has the consequence, or evidences, that X is in pain. That is the initial natural case. Let us now see if we could in one or more stages modify it so as to end up with something which is very much like nonnatural meaning.

Stage one in the operation involves the supposition that the creature actually voluntarily produces a certain sort of behavior which is such that its nonvoluntary production would be evidence that the creature is, let us say, in pain. The kinds of cases of this which come most obviously to mind will be cases of faking or deception. A creature normally voluntarily produces behavior not only when, but *because*, its nonvoluntary production would be evidence that the creature is in a certain state, with the effect that the rest of the world, other creatures around, treat the production, which is in fact voluntary, as if it were a nonvoluntary production. That is, they come to just the same conclusion about the creature's being in the state in question, the signaled state. The purpose of the creature's producing the behavior voluntarily would be so that the rest of the world should think that it is in the state which the nonvoluntary production would signify.

In stage two not only does creature X produce this behavior voluntarily instead of nonvoluntarily, as in the primitive state, but we also assume that it is *recognized* by another creature Y, involved with X in some transaction, as being the voluntary production of a certain form of behavior the nonvoluntary production of which evidences, say, pain. That is, creature X is now supposed not only to simulate pain-behavior, but also to be recognized as simulating pain-behavior. The import of the recognition by Y that the production is voluntary undermines, of course, any tendency on the part of Y to come to the conclusion that creature X is in pain. So, one might ask, what would be required to restore the situation: what could be added which would be an antidote, so to speak, to the dissolution on the part of Y of the idea that X is in pain?

A first step in this direction would be to go to what we might think of as stage three. Here, we suppose that creature Y not only recognizes that the behavior is voluntary on the part of X, but also recognizes that X *intends* Y to recognize his behavior as voluntary. That is, we have now undermined the idea that this is a straightforward piece of deception. Deceiving consists in trying to get a creature to accept certain things as signs of something or other without knowing that this is a faked case. Here, however, we would have a sort of perverse faked case, in which something is faked but at the same time a clear indication is put in that the faking has been done.

Creature Y can be thought of as initially baffled by this conflicting performance. There is this creature, as it were, simulating pain, but announcing, in a certain sense, that this is what it is doing: what on earth can it be up to? It seems to me that if Y does raise the question of why X should be doing this, it might first come up with the idea that X is engaging in some form of play or make-believe, a game to which, since X's behavior is seemingly directed toward Y, Y is expected or intended to make some appropriate contribution. Cases susceptible of such an interpretation I regard as belonging to stage four.

But, we may suppose, there might be cases which could not be handled in this way. If Y is to be expected to be a fellow-participant with X in some form of play, it ought to be possible for Y to recognize what kind of contribution Y is supposed to make; and we can envisage the possibility that Y has no clue on which to base such recognition, or again that though some form of contribution seems to be suggested, when Y obliges by coming up with it, X, instead of producing further play-behavior, gets cross and perhaps repeats its original, and now problematic, performance.

We now reach stage five, at which Y supposes not that X is engaged in play, but that what X is doing is trying to get Y to believe or accept that X is in pain: that is, trying to get Y to believe in or accept the presence of that state in X which the produced behavior, when produced nonvoluntarily, is in fact a natural sign of, naturally means. More specifically, one might say that at stage five creature Y recognizes that creature X in the first place intends that Y recognize the production of the sign of pain (of what is usually the sign of pain) to be voluntary, and further intends that Y should regard this first intention as being a sufficient reason for Y to believe that X is in pain; and that X has these intentions because he has the additional further intention that Y should not merely have sufficient reason for believing that X is in pain, but should actually believe it.

Whether or not in these circumstances Y will not merely recognize that X intends, in a certain rather queer way, to get Y to believe that X is in pain, whether Y not only recognizes this but actually goes on to believe that X is in pain, would presumably depend on a further set of conditions which can be summed up under the general heading that Y should regard X as trustworthy in one or another of perhaps a variety of ways. For example, suppose Y thinks that, either in general or at least in this type of case, X would not want to get Y to believe that X is in pain unless X really were in pain. Suppose also (this would perhaps not apply to a case of pain but might apply to the communication of other states) that Y also believes that X is trustworthy, not just in the sense of not being malignant, but also in the sense of being, as it were, in general responsible, for example, being the sort of creature who takes adequate trouble to make sure that what he is trying to get the other creature to believe is in fact the case, and who is not careless, negligent, or rash. Then, given the general fulfillment of the idea that Y regards X either in general or in this particular case as being trustworthy in this kind of competent, careful way, one would regard it as rational not only for Y to recognize these intentions on the part of X, that Y should have certain beliefs about X's being in pain, but also for Y actually to pass to adopting these beliefs.

So far I have been talking about the communication of the idea that something is the case, for example, that X is in pain or some other state, by means of a nondeceptive simulation on the part of the communicating creature of the standard signs or indices of such a state. But the mechanism that has been used, involving the interchange of beliefs or intentions of different orders, really does not require that what is taken as the communication vehicle should be initially a natural expression or sign of the state of affairs being communicated. If we now relax this requirement, we get to stage six, the road to which may be eased by the following reflection, for which I am indebted to Judith Baker.

In relation to the particular example which I have been using, to reach the position ascribed to it in stage five, Y would have to solve, bypass, or ignore a possible problem presented by X's behavior: why should X produce what is not a genuine but a faked expression of pain if what X is trying to get Y to believe is that X is *in pain?* Why not just let out a natural bellow? Possible answers are not too hard to come by: for example, that it would be unmanly, or otherwise uncreaturely, for X to produce *naturally* a natural expression of pain, or that X's nonnatural production of an expression of pain is not to be supposed to indicate *every* feature which would be indicated by a natural production (the nonnatural emission, for example, of a loud bellow might properly be taken to indicate pain, but not that degree of pain which would correspond with the decibels of the particular emission). This problem would not, however, arise if X's performance, instead of being something which, in the natural case, would be an *expression* of that state of X which (in the nonnatural case) it is intended to get Y to believe in, were rather something more loosely connected with the state of affairs (not necessarily a state of X) which it is intended to convey to Y; X's performance, that is, would be suggestive, in some recognizable way, of the state of affairs without being a natural response of X to that state of affairs.

We reach, then, a stage in which the communication vehicles do not have to be, initially, natural signs of that which they are used to communicate; provided a bit of behavior could be expected to be seen by the receiving creature as having a discernible connection with a particular piece of information, then that bit of behavior will be usable by the transmitting creature, provided that that creature can place a fair bet on the connection being made by the receiving creature. Any link will do, provided it is detectable by the receiver, and the looser the links creatures are in a position to use, the greater the freedom they will have as communicators, since they will be less and less restricted by the need to rely on prior natural connections. The widest possible range is given where creatures use for these purposes a range of communication devices which have no antecedent connections at all with the things that they communicate or represent, and the connection is simply made because the knowledge, or supposition, or assumption, of such an artificial connection is prearranged and foreknown. Here creatures can simply cash in, as it were, on the stock of semantic information which has already been built into them at some previous stage.

In some cases, the artificial communication devices might have certain other features too, over and above the one of being artificial: they might, for example, involve a finite number of fundamental, focal, elementary, root devices and a finite set of modes or forms of combination (combinatory operations, if you like) which are capable of being used over and over again. In these cases, the creatures will have, or be near to having, what some people have thought to be characteristic of a language: namely, a communication system with a finite set of initial devices, together with semantic provisions for them, and a finite set of different syntactical operations or combinations, and an understanding of what the functions of those modes of combination are. As a result, they can generate an infinite set of sentences or complex communication devices, together with a correspondingly infinite set of things to be communicated, as it were.

So, by proceeding in this teleological kind of way, we seem to have provided some rationale both for the kind of characterization of speaker's meaning which I went in for long ago, and also for the characterization of various kinds of communication systems, culminating in things which have features which are ordinarily supposed (more or less correctly, I would imagine) to be the features of a fully developed language. I say that we *seem* to have provided a rationale; for there is, I think, a large residual question of a methodological kind. My succession of stages is not, of course, intended to be a historical or genetic account of the development of communication and language; it is a myth designed, among other things, to exhibit the conceptual link between natural and nonnatural meaning. But how can such a link be explained by a *myth*? This question is perhaps paralleled, as was recently suggested to me, by the question how the nature and validity of political obligation (or perhaps even of moral obligation) can possibly be explained by a *mythical* social contract. While the parallel may be suggestive and useful, one might be pardoned for wondering how much more it does besides match one mystery with another. But that is a problem for another day.

III. The Mystery Package

Well, this is the mystery package. First, a small anecdote. My sometimes mischievous friend Richard Grandy once said, in connection with some other occasion on which I was talking, that to represent my remarks, it would be necessary to introduce a new form of speech act, or a new operator, which was to be called the operator of *quessertion*. It is to be read as "It is perhaps possible that someone might assert that . . .", and is to be symbolized "?⊢"; possibly it might even be iterable. I treasure this suggestion to just about the same degree as I treasure his dictum, delivered on another occasion, that I "can always be relied upon to rally to the defense of an 'under-dogma.'" Everything I shall suggest here is highly quessertable. I shall simply explore an idea; I do not know whether I want to subscribe to it or not. In what follows, then, I am not to be taken as making any ground-floor assertions at all: except for the assertion that something is quesserted.

The general idea that I want to explore, and which seems to me to have some plausibility, is that something has been left out, by me and perhaps by others too, in the analyses, definitions, expansions, and so on, of semantic notions, and particularly various notions of meaning. What has been left out has in fact been left out because it is something which everyone regards with horror, at least when in a scientific or theoretical frame of mind: the notion of value.

Though I think that in general we want to keep value notions out of our philosophical and scientific inquiries (and some would say out of everything else), we might consider what would happen if we relaxed this prohibition to some extent. If we did, there is a whole range of different kinds of value predicates or expressions which might be admitted in different types of case. To avoid having to choose between them, I am just going to use as a predicate the word "optimal": the meaning of which could of course be more precisely characterized later.

The reason why I am particularly interested in this general idea is that my own position, which I am not going to try to state or defend in any detail at the moment, is that the notion of value is absolutely crucial to the idea of rationality, or of a rational being. There are many ways in which one can characterize what it is to be a rational being. Some of them may turn out to be equivalent to one another in some sense: they may turn out to apply to exactly the same cases. However, it may be that even though they are equivalent, there is one that is particularly fruitful from a deductive-theoretical point of view. I have strong suspicions that the most fruitful idea is the idea that a rational creature is a creature which evaluates, and that the other possible characterizations may turn out to be co-extensive with this, though in some sense less leading. I do not know whether it follows from this, but at any rate I think it is true, that all naturalistic attempts at the characterization of rationality are doomed to failure. Value is in there from the beginning, and one cannot get it out. This is not something to be argued about here, but it should give some indication of the kind of murky framework in which I shall now start to operate.

It seems to me that there are two different problems connected with meaning in which questions of value might arise. I call them the minor problem and the major problem. The minor problem has to do with the relation between what, speaking generally, I may call word meaning and speaker meaning. It seems plausible to suppose that to say that a sentence (word, expression) means something (to say that "John is a bachelor" means that John is an unmarried male, or whatever it is) is to be somehow understood in terms of what particular users of that sentence (word, expression) mean on particular occasions. The first possible construal of this is rather crude: namely, that usually people do use this sentence, etc., in this way. A construal which seems to me rather better is that it is conventional to use this sentence in this way; and there are many others.

Now I do not think that even the most subtle or sophisticated interpretation of this construal will do, because I do not think that meaning is essentially connected with convention. What it is essentially connected with is some way of fixing what sentences mean: convention is indeed one of these ways, but it is not the only one. I can invent a language, call it Deutero-Esperanto, which nobody ever speaks. That makes me the authority, and I can lay down what is proper. Notice that we are immediately arriving at some form of evaluative notion: namely, what it is proper to do.

The general suggestion would therefore be that to say what a word means in a language is to say what it is in general optimal for speakers of that language to do with that word, or what use they are to make of it; what particular intentions on particular occasions it is proper for them to have, or optimal for them to have. Of course, there is no suggestion that they *always* have to have those intentions: it would merely be optimal, *ceteris paribus,* for them to have them. As regards what is optimal in any particular kind of case, there would have to be a cash value, an account of why this is optimal. There might be a whole range of different accounts. For example, it might be that it is conventional to use this word in this way; it might be that it is conventional among some privileged class to use it in this way—what some technical term in biology means is not a matter for the general public but for biologists; it might be, when an invented language is involved, that it is what is laid down by its inventor. However, what we get in every case, as a unification of all these accounts, is the optimality or propriety of a certain form of behavior. That concludes my discussion of the minor problem.

The major problem in which questions of value arise has to do not with attempts to exhibit the relation between word meaning and speaker meaning, but with attempts to exhibit the anatomy of speaker meaning itself. At this point, my general strategy was to look for the kind of regresses which Schiffer and others have claimed to detect concealed beneath the glossy surface of my writings on meaning: infinite and vicious regresses which they propose to cast out, substituting another regressive notion, such as mutual knowledge, instead; raising somewhat the question why their regresses are good regresses and mine are bad ones.

However, as I tried, by looking at Schiffer, to disentangle exactly what the alleged regresses are, I found it almost impossible to do so. That is, someone who alleges an infinite regress ought surely to provide a general method for generating the next stage of the regress out of the previous one, and I could see no general way of doing this: the connections between one stage and another seemed to be disparate. That is not to say that there is no way of doing this. I used to think when talking to Schiffer that there was one, and that I understood it, but now I do not. However, since the actual nature of the regress, or regressive accusation, does not matter very much, what I have done is to invent my own, which I will call a pseudo-Schiffer regress; and so far from trying to make it leaky or creaky at the joints, on the contrary, I would like it to be as strong as I can make it, and if it is not strong enough, I am going to pretend that it is.

The regress can be reconstructed along the following lines. One might start with the idea that when some speaker S utters some sentence to a hearer A, meaning by it that p, he does this wanting A to think 'p'. That is, at stage one we have "S wants A to think 'p,'" where p represents the content of A's thought or intended thought. However, for reasons that came up long ago, having to do with the distinction between natural and nonnatural meaning, we cannot stop at stage one. We have to proceed to stage two, at which we get "S wants A to think 'p, on the strength of the idea that S wants A to think "p"'"; and so on.

We have now reached a curious situation, in that there is a certain sort of disparity between what S wants A to think: namely "p, on the strength of S wanting A to think that p," and the accounts that are given, so to speak, in the subclause of this as to what it is that S wants A to think. That is, S wants A to think not just "p," but "p on the grounds that S wants A to think that p"; but when we are stating what the grounds are, what A is supposed to think, we find that he is only supposed to think "p." In other words, what we specify A as intended to think of as the reason for thinking "p" is always one stage behind what the speaker envisages as the reason why he wants A to think "p."

We thus arrive at something of the form "S wants A to think 'p, because S wants A to think "p, because S wants . . ."'" and so on. We put in the extra clause in order to catch up, but we never do catch up, because by putting in the extra clause we merely introduce another thing to catch up with. It is like moving from stage one to stage two: we start with stage one, we add the move from stage one to stage two, but by the time we get to stage two, the place we have to get to is stage three, and so on.

I have chosen this regress because it is rather colorful, but it is not the only one I could have used. What I am looking for is an infinite regress which combines the two following characteristics: first, like all infinite regresses, it cannot be realized: that is, a completion, a situation in which S has an intention which is infinitely expanded in this kind of way, cannot actually exist; and second, the idea that it should exist is a desideratum. That is, what I am looking for is a situation in which a certain highly complex intention is at one and the same time logically impossible and also desirable. That is not in itself, it seems to me, an unreasonable goal: it certainly can happen that things are logically impossible but desirable, and if it does, I can make use of it.

The pattern of analysis which I would now suggest as the primary interpretant for speaker's meaning would be that S is in that state with respect to whatever he wishes to communicate or impart (p) which is optimal for somebody communicating p. It then turns out that when you cash the value of what it is that is optimal, you find that the optimal state is a state that is in fact logically impossible. That in itself seems to me to be not in the least objectionable so far, although there are some points that would have to be argued for. The whole idea of using expressions which are explained in terms of ideal limits would seem to me to operate in this way. The ideal limits might not be realizable in any domain, or they might be realizable in certain domains but not in the domain under consideration; for instance, the fact that they are not realizable might be contingent, or it might be non-contingent. It might be for one reason or another (let us pretend for simplicity) that there cannot be in the sublunary world any things that are, strictly speaking, circular. Nevertheless, that does not prevent us from applying the word "circular' in the sublunary world, because we apply it in virtue of approach to, or approximation to, the ideal limit which is itself not realized. All we need is a way of so to speak measuring up actual particulars against the unrealizable quality of the perfect particular. Indeed, maybe something like this is what Plato went in for.

It seems to me that the notion of knowledge might be explicable in this way. This is a notion which might be, is conceivably, realizable in a certain domain but not in others. Here we look to the people in the past who have suggested that the standard, or crucial, feature of knowledge is that if you know something, you cannot be wrong. Some people then went on to say that it follows that the only things we can know are necessary truths, because there, in some sense of "cannot", we cannot be wrong; and there are various familiar objections to this. Now I might want to say that those people are right, if what they meant was that *strictly speaking* the only things that can be known are necessary truths. However, that does not restrict us to supposing that people who talk about knowing other things are using the word "know" improperly: all it requires is that there should be some license to apply the word nonstrictly to things which in some way approach or approximate to the ideal cases.

It is not my business on this occasion to suggest exactly, or in any detail, what the demands for approach or approximation might be. I will only say that, whatever they are, they ought to be ones which justify us in *deeming* certain cases to satisfy a given ideal even though they do not, in fact, strictly speaking exemplify it; just as in Oxford on one occasion, there was a difficulty between an incoming provost and a college rule that dogs were not allowed in college: the governing body passed a resolution deeming the new provost's dog to be a cat. I suspect that crucially we do a lot of deeming, though perhaps not always in such an entertaining fashion.

Let me summarize the position we have now reached. First, on this account of speaker meaning, as a first approximation to what we mean by saying that a speaker, by something he says, on a particular occasion, means that p, is that he is in the optimal state with respect to communicating, or if you like, to communicating that p. Second, that the optimal state, the state in which he has an infinite set of intentions, is in principle unrealizable, so that he does not *strictly speaking* mean that p. However, he is in a situation which is such that it is legitimate, or perhaps even mandatory, for us to deem him to satisfy this unfulfillable condition.

Finally, there is the question of how this relates to the regresses which people have actually found: regresses, or prolongations of the set of conditions, which actually exist. Certain ingenious people, such as Strawson and Dennis Stampe, and ending up with Schiffer, who moves so fast and intricately that one can hardly keep up with him, have produced counterexamples to my original interpretant in an analysis of meaning, counterexamples which are supposed to show that my conditions, or any expansion of them, are insufficient to provide an account of speaker meaning. The alleged counterexample is always such that it satisfies the conditions on speaker meaning as set forward so far, but that the speaker is nevertheless supposed to have what I might call a sneaky intention. That is, in the first and most obvious case, his intention is that the hearer should in fact accept p on such and such grounds, but should *think* that he is supposed to accept p not on those grounds but on some other grounds. That is, the hearer is represented, at some level or other of embedding, as having, or being intended to have, or being intended to think himself intended to have (or . . .), a misapprehension with regard to what is expected of him. He thinks he is supposed to proceed in one way, whereas really he is supposed to proceed in another. I would then want to say that the effect of the appearance of a sneaky intention, the function that such a sneaky intention would have in the scheme I am suggesting, would simply be to cancel the license to deem what the speaker is doing to be a case of meaning on this particular occasion: that is, to cancel the idea that this is to be allowed to count as a sublunary performance, so to speak, of the infinite set of intentions which is only celestially realizable.

In a way, what this suggestion does, or would do if it were otherwise acceptable, is to confer a rationale upon a proposal which I actually did make in an earlier paper, to the effect that what was really required in a full account of speaker meaning was the *absence* of a certain kind of intention. This may very well be right, but the deficiency in that proposal was that it gave no explanation of *why* this was a reasonable condition to put into an account of speaker meaning. I think, if we accepted the framework I have just outlined, this arbitrariness, or *ad hocness,* would be removed, or at least mitigated.

19

Metaphysics, Philosophical Eschatology, and Plato's *Republic*

I. Metaphysics and Philosophical Eschatology

Some time ago the idea occurred to me that there might be two distinguishable disciplines each of which might have some claim to the title of, or a share of the title of, Metaphysics. The first of these disciplines I thought of as being categorial in character, that is to say, I thought of it as operating at or below the level of categories. Following leads supplied primarily by Aristotle and Kant, I conceived of it as concerned with the identification of the most general attributes or classifications, the *summa genera*, under which the various specific subject-items and/or predicates (predicate-items, attributes) might fall, and with the formulation of metaphysical principles governing such categorial attributes (for example some version of a Principle of Causation, or some principle regulating the persistence of substances). The second discipline I thought of as being supracategorial in character; it would bring together categorially different subject-items beneath single classificatory characterizations, and perhaps would also specify principles which would have to be exemplified by items brought together by this kind of supracategorial assimilation. I hoped that the second discipline, which I was tempted to label "Philosophical Eschatology," might provide for the detection of affinities between categorially different realities, thus protecting the principles associated with particular categories from suspicion of arbitrariness. In response to a possible objection to the effect that if a pair of items were really categorially different from one another, they could not be assimilated under a single classificatory head (since they would be incapable of sharing any attribute), I planned to reply that even should it be impossible for categorially different items to share a single attribute, this objection might be inconclusive since assimilation might take the form of ascribing to the items assimilated not a common attribute but an analogy. Traditionally, in such disciplines as theology, analogy has been the resort of those who hoped to find a way of comparing entities so radically diverse from one another as God and human beings. Such a mode of comparison would of course require careful examination; such examination I shall for the moment defer, as I shall also defer mention of certain further ideas which I associated with philosophical eschatology.

For a start, then, I might distinguish three directions as being ones in which a philosophical eschatologist might be expected to deploy his energies:

(1) The provision of generalized theoretical accounts which unite specialized metaphysical principles which are separated from one another by category-barriers.

(2) Fulfillment of such an undertaking might involve an adequate theoretical characterization of a relation of Affinity, which, like the more familiar relation of similarity, offers a foundation for the generalization of specialized regularities, but which, unlike similarity, is insensitive, or has a high degree of insensitivity, to the presence of category-barriers. To suggest the possibility of such a relation is not, of course, to construct it, nor even to provide a guarantee that it can be constructed.

(3) An investigation of the notion of Analogy, and a delineation of its links with other seemingly comparable notions, such as Metaphor and Parable. Can this list be expanded?

At this point I turn to a paper by Judith Baker, entitled "'Another Self': Aristotle On Friendship" (as yet unpublished). On the present occasion my concern is focused on methodological questions; so I propose first to consider the ideas about methodology, in particular Aristotle's methodology, which find expression in her paper, and then to inquire whether these ideas suggest any additions to the prospective subject matter of philosophical eschatology.

(1) Judith Baker suggests that Aristotle's philosophical method, which is partially characterized in the *Nicomachean Ethics* itself as well as in other works of Aristotle, treats the existence of a common consensus of opinion with respect to a proposition as conferring at

least provisional validity (validity *ceteris paribus*) upon the proposition in question; in general, no external justification of the acceptance of the objects of universal agreement is called for. This idea has not always been accepted by philosophers; to take just one famous example, Moore's attachment to the authority of Common Sense seems to be attributed by Moore himself to the acceptability of some principle to the effect that the Common Sense view of the world is in certain fundamental respects unquestionably correct. Unfortunately Moore does not formulate the principle in question, nor does he identify the relevant aspects. If my perception of Moore is correct, he would in Aristotle's view have been looking for an external justification for the acceptance of the deliverances of Common Sense where none is required, and so where none exists.

(2) Though no external justification is required for accepting the validity of propositions which are generally or universally believed, the validity in question is only provisional; for a common consensus may be undermined in either of two ways. First, there may be a common consensus that proposition A is true; but there may be two mutually inconsistent propositions, B_1 and B_2, where while there is a common consensus that either B_1 or B_2 is true, there is no common consensus concerning the truth of B_1 or the truth of B_2; there are, so to speak, two schools of thought, one favoring B_1 and one favoring B_2. Furthermore (we may suppose), the combination of B_1 with A will yield C_1, whereas the combination of B_2 with A will yield C_2; and C_1 and C_2 are mutually inconsistent. In such a situation it becomes a question whether the acceptability of A is left intact; if it is, a method will have to be devised for deciding between B_1 and B_2. (The preceding schematic example is constructed by me, not by Aristotle or Judith Baker.) Second, to cope with problems created by the appearance on the scene of conflicts or other stumbling blocks the theorist may be expected to systematize the data which are vouched for by common consensus by himself devising general propositions which are embedded in his theory. Such generalities will not be directly attested by a consensus, but their acceptability will depend on the adequacy of the theory in which they appear to yield propositions which are directly matters of general agreement. When an impasse (aporia) arises, the aim of the theorist will be to eliminate the impasse with minimal disturbance to the material regarded as acceptable before the impasse, including the theoretical generalities of the theorist. Judith Baker claims that a typical example of such an impasse is recognized

by Aristotle as arising in connection with friendship; the threefold proposition that in the good life no good is lacking, that the good life is self-sufficient, and that the possession of friends is a good, each element in which is a matter of general agreement. This seems to validate the inconsistent proposition that the good life both will and will not involve the possession of friends. It is Judith Baker's suggestion that Aristotle's characterization of a friend as another self (another me) is a serious theoretical proposal which is designed to eliminate the impasse with minimal disturbance.

(3) Judith Baker mentions also a certain kind of criticism, an example of which, leveled at Socrates's treatment of justice in *The Republic,* was produced about twenty years ago by David Sachs. Sachs complained that in response to a request from Glaucon and Adeimantus to show that the just life is a happy life, Socrates first recharacterizes the just life in terms of the conception of a soul in which all elements maximally fulfill their function and then argues that a life so characterized will be a happy life. This response on the part of Socrates is guilty of an *ignoratio elenchi;* what Glaucon and Adeimantus want Socrates to show to be happy is the just life as understood to be the life to which the word "just" applies in its ordinary sense, but what Socrates does is in effect to redefine the notion of the just life as that life which exemplifies justice* where justice* is defined in terms of fulfillment of function. But that the just* life is happy is not what Socrates was asked to show; what is wanted from him is a demonstration not that the just* life is happy but that the just life is happy; and this he fails to provide. There seems plainly to be something wrong with this line of criticism; Sachs calls Socrates to task for exhibiting in his rejoinder just those capacities which have earned him his reputation as an eminent ethical theorist, which are indeed the very capacities the presence of which has marked him out as a specially suitable person to respond to the skepticism of Thrasymachus. Surely he cannot be debarred from using just those talents which he has been more or less invited to use. There is the further point that the mode of criticism with which Sachs assailed Socrates could be adapted for use against any theorist of a certain very general kind, which could embrace many theorists who have no connection at all with philosophy; in fact, I suspect that any theorist whose theoretical activity is directed toward rendering explicit knowledge which is already implicitly present would be vulnerable to this kind of charge of having "changed the subject." So it seems to me that a detailed anal-

ysis of the illegitimacy of this kind of criticism would be both desirable and at the same time by no means easy to attain.

The reflections in which I have just been engaged, then, suggest to me two further items which might be added to a prospective subject matter of philosophical eschatology, should such a discipline be allowed as legitimate. One would be a classification of the various kinds of impasse or aporia by theorists who engaged in the Aristotelian undertaking of attempting to systematize material with which they are presented by lay inquirers, together with a classification of the variety of responses which might be effective against such impasses. The other would be a thoroughgoing analysis of the boundary between legitimate and illegitimate imputations to a theorist of the sin of "having changed the subject." Beyond these additions I have at the moment only one further suggestion. Sometimes the activities of the eschatologist might involve the suggestion of certain principles and some of the material embodied in those principles might contain the potentiality of independent life, a potentiality which it would be theoretically advantageous to explore. This further exploration might be regarded as being itself a proper occupation for the eschatologist. One example might be a further examination of the theoretical notion of an *alter ego*, already noted as a notion which might be needed to surmount an impasse in the philosophical theory of friendship. Another example might be the kind of abstract development of such notions as movement, that which moves, and that which is moved, which is prominent in Book λ of Aristotle's *Metaphysics*, which forms a substantial part of what is thought of as Aristotle's Theology.

I shall not, however, at this point attempt to expand further the shopping list for philosophical eschatology. I shall turn instead to a different but related topic, namely the possibility that in Plato's *Republic* we find a discussion of justice which does as it stands, or would after a certain kind of reconstruction, serve as an example of an application of philosophical eschatology. I shall first develop this idea, and then at the conclusion of my presentation furnish a summary account of its argument.

II. The Actual Debate between Socrates and Thrasymachus in the *Republic*

We should bear in mind that the purpose of looking at the discussion of Justice in the *Republic* is to see if the course of that discussion could be looked on as a conscious, subconscious, or unconscious venture by Socrates or Plato into the discipline of philosophical eschatology.

(1) The discussion begins with a pressing invitation to Socrates to take part in an examination of the question "What is Justice?" It is clear that despite the intrusion of distractions Socrates has not lost sight of this focus.

(2) Two preliminary answers are put forward; that of Cephalus ("to tell the truth and pay one's debts"); and that of his son Polemarchus ("to give every man his due"). The first of these answers seems to be an attempt to exhibit the nature of Justice by means of its paradigmatic rules, while the second attempts to provide a general characterization or definition. Socrates points out that even paradigmatic rules allow of exceptions, with the consequence that a practical principle will be needed to identify the exceptions; while Polemarchus's suggested definition is faulted on the grounds that counterintuitively it allows Justice on occasion to be exhibited in causing harm. It seems to be open to Polemarchus to reply to Socrates that the connection of Justice with punishment makes it questionable whether it is counterintuitive to suppose that Justice sometimes involves causing harm. Indeed we might inquire why the answers suggested by Cephalus and Polemarchus are given house-room at all if they are going to be so cursorily handled.

(3) The debate with Thrasymachus. A number of different factors to my mind raise serious questions about the role of this debate in the general scheme for the treatment of Justice in the *Republic*.

(a) The quality of Thrasymachus's dialectical apparatus seems to be (to put it mildly) not of the highest order.

(b) Socrates himself remarks that in the course of the debate the original question ("What is Justice?") becomes entangled in a confused way with a number of other seemingly different questions such as whether the just life is the happiest life (or is more, or less, happy than the unjust life), whether the just life is worthy of choice, etc. What does Thrasymachus achieve beyond the generation of confusion?

(c) Socrates' replies to Thrasymachus are by no means always intellectually impeccable; yet so far as I can see, this fact is not pointed out.

(d) Glaucon and Adeimantus are dissatisfied with the upshot of this debate and call upon Socrates to show that the just life is the happy life, not making it clear what the connection is between this demand and the answering of the original question about the nature of Justice.

(e) Socrates endeavors to meet the demands of Plato's older brothers, but to do this, he resorts to the elaborate presentation of an analogy between the soul and the state. What justifies the presentation, in the current context, of the nature of this analogy?

(4) Blow-by-blow details of the debate with Thrasymachus.

Round 1. Thrasymachus at the outset couples the thesis that "justice is the interest of the stronger" with the admission that rulers are not infallible in their estimates of where the interest of the stronger lies. As the comments of Socrates, Polemarchus, and Cleitophon make clear, this leads Thrasymachus into an intolerable tension between the idea that the edicts of the ruler command obedience because they spring from a belief on the part of the ruler that obedience is in the interest of the stronger, and the idea that obedience is demanded if, but only if, it would in fact be conducive to the interest of the stronger. Thrasymachus seeks to repair his position by distinguishing between (a) what the ruler commands and (b) what the ruler commands qua ruler; the latter cannot but be conducive to the interest of the stronger, though no such assurance attends the former. Though no one points this out, the attempted escape seems to carry the consequence that whether the ruler's commands do or do not call for obedience may be, and may continue to be, shrouded in obscurity.

But apart from this initial confusion, the debate in Round 1 is characterized by a number of further disfigurements or blemishes, responsibility for which may attach not only to Thrasymachus but, by association, to Socrates. Some of these disfigurements or blemishes may indeed also be visible in subsequent rounds.

(a) It is not made clear, nor indeed is the question raised, whether the kind of justice under discussion is political (or politico-legal) justice, or moral justice. The general tenor of Thrasymachus's remarks would suggest that his concern is with political or politico-legal justice. Indeed it seems not impossible that it is part of Thrasymachus's position that there is no such thing as moral justice, that the concept of moral justice is chimerical and empty. If this were his position, he could be characterized as a certain sort of skeptic; but whether or not it is his position should surely not be left in doubt.

(b) Thrasymachus nowhere makes it clear whether he regards the popular application of the term "just," which Thrasymachus may not himself endorse, as a positive or a negative commendation. Are just acts supposed to be acts which fulfill some condition which acts should fulfill, or acts which are free from an imputation that they fulfill some condition which acts should not fulfill?

(c) It is not clear whether Thrasymachus's thesis that justice is the interest of the stronger is to be taken as a thesis about the "nominal essence" or about the "real essence" of justice. Is Thrasymachus suggesting that the right way to conceive of justice, the correct interpretation of the term "just," is as signifying that which is in the interest of the stronger? Or is he suggesting that whatever content we attach to the concept of justice, the characteristic which explains why just acts are done and why they have the effects which standardly attend them, is that of being in the interest of the stronger?

(d) Thrasymachus seems uninterested in distinguishing between the use of the word "just" ("right") as part of a sentential operator which governs sentences which refer to possible actions (e.g., "it is just (right) that a person who has contracted a debt should repay it at the appointed time," "it is just for a juror to refuse offers of bribes") and its use as an epithet which applies to actually performed actions (e.g., "he distributed payments, for the work done, justly"). The two uses are no doubt intimately connected with one another, but they are surely distinguishable.

(e) Thrasymachus is not at pains to make it clear whether the phrase "the stronger" refers to the ruler or government (the *official* boss) or to the person or persons who wield political power (the *real* boss). These persons might or might not be identical.

As a result of these obscurities the precise character of Thrasymachus's position is by no means easy to discern.

Round 2. At the end of Round 1, as it seems to me, Socrates seeks to counter Thrasymachus's reliance on a distinction between what the practitioner of an art ordains *simpliciter* and what the practitioner ordains qua practitioner of that art, by suggesting that if we take this distinction seriously, we shall be led to suppose that when the practitioner acts qua practitioner, his concern is not with his own well-being but with the well-being of the subject matter which the art controls; so rulers qua rulers will be concerned with the well-being of their subjects rather than of themselves. This contention seems open to the response that there is nothing to prevent the well-being of the subject matter from being, on occasion, that state of the subject matter which is congenial to the interest of the practitioner. This indeed may be the tenor of Thrasymachus's outburst comparing the treatment of subjects by rulers with the treatment of sheep by shepherds. If so, Socrates does not seem to have any better reply than to suggest that the dominance of concern on the part of rulers to obtain compensation for their operations hardly supports the idea that it is common practice for them to use their offices to feather their own nests; a response to which Socrates adds an obscurely relevant demand for a distinction between the practice of an art which is typically not directed toward the interests of the practitioner, and the special case of a concomitant exercise of the art of profit-making, which is so directed.

Thrasymachus, however, complicates matters by introducing a new line of attack against the merits of justice vis-à-vis injustice. He suggests that in the private citizen justice (devotion to the interest of the stronger, that is, of the ruler) is folly, while injustice (devotion to his own interest) is sensible even if dubiously effective; while the grand-scale injustice of rulers, as exhibited in tyranny, has everything to recommend it. It is not clear that this manifesto is legitimate, since it is not clear that, on his own terms, Thrasymachus is entitled to count tyranny as injustice; the tyrant is not preferring his own interests to the interests of someone stronger than himself, since no one is stronger than he. It is true, of course, that while Thrasymachus may not be entitled to call tyranny injustice, he may be equally not entitled to call it justice, since though the tyrant may be the strongest person around, he is certainly not stronger than himself. So perhaps Thrasymachus's plea for injustice may turn out to be a misfire.

Round 3. In response to a query from Socrates, Thrasymachus recapitulates his position, which is not that injustice is a good quality and justice a bad quality, nor (exactly) the reverse position, but is rather that justice is *folly* or extreme simplicity, whereas injustice is *good sense*. With this contention there is also associated Thrasymachus's view that injustice implies strength, and that the unjust life rather than the just life is the happy life.

Socrates' reply to Thrasymachus invokes arguments which seem weak to the point of feebleness. In his first argument he gets Thrasymachus to agree that the just man seeks to compete with, or outdo only the unjust man, whereas the unjust man competes both with the just and with the unjust. Reflection on the arts, however, prompts the observation that in general the expert competes only with the inexpert, whereas the nonexpert competes alike with the inexpert and with the expert, so it is the just man, not the unjust man, who runs parallel to the general case of the expert, and who therefore must be regarded as possessing not only expertise but also good sense. Among the flaws in this argument one might point particularly to the dubious analogy between the province of justice and the province of the arts, and also to a blatant equivocation with the word "compete," which might mean either "try to perform better than" or "try to get the better of."

In the succeeding argument against the alleged strength of injustice, Socrates remarks that injustice breeds enmity, observes that efficient and thoroughgoing injustice requires "honor among thieves," and concludes that a fully unjust man would in real life be weaker than one who was less fully unjust. Maybe this argument shows that the unjust man cannot, with maximum effectiveness, literally "go the whole hog" in injustice; but this is far from showing that he should never have started on any part of the hog.

Finally, Socrates counters Thrasymachus's claim that the unjust life, rather than the just life, is the happy life, by getting Thrasymachus to agree that at least for certain kinds of things the best state of a thing of that kind lies in the fulfillment of the function of that kind, which will also constitute an exhibition of the special and peculiar excellence of things of that kind; and also that justice is in the required sense the special excellence of the soul; from which he concludes that justice is the best state of the soul and as a consequence gives rise to the happy life. This argument, perhaps, palely foreshadows Socrates' strategy in the main part of the dialogue; but at this point it seems ineffective, since no case has been made out why Thrasymachus should agree to what one would expect him to regard as the quite uncongenial suggestion that justice is the special excellence of the soul.

(5) Transition to the main body of the Dialogue. Glaucon and Adeimantus express dissatisfaction with Socrates' handling of Thrasymachus. Glaucon invokes a distinction between three classes of goods: those which are desirable only for their own sake, those which are desirable both in themselves and for the sake of their consequences, and those which are desirable only for the sake of their consequences. He remarks that it is the view of Socrates, shared by himself and Adeimantus, that justice belongs to the second class of goods, those which are doubly desirable; but he wishes to see the truth of

this view demonstrated, particularly as the generally received opinion seems to be that justice belongs to the third class of goods which are desirable only for the sake of their consequences and have no intrinsic value. He wishes Socrates to show that justice is desirable in respect of its effect on those who possess it, independently of any rewards or consequences to which it may lead. He wishes Socrates to show that it is reasonable to desire to be just rather than merely to seem just, and, indeed, that the life of the just man is happy even if his reputation is bad. Otherwise it will remain feasible:

(a) that the institutions of justice are acceptable only because they secure for us the greater good of protection from the inroads of others at the cost of the lesser evil of blocking our inroads upon others, and

(b) that if the possession of Gyges's ring would enable our inroads upon others to remain undiscovered, no reasonable person would deny himself this advantage.

Adeimantus reinforces the demands expressed by Glaucon by drawing attention to the support lent by the prevailing education and culture to the received opinion about justice as distinct from the view of it taken by Socrates, Glaucon, and himself. Apart from the tendency to represent the rewards associated with justice as really attending not justice itself but the reputation for justice, Adeimantus observes that even when the rewards are thought of as attending not merely the semblance of justice but justice itself, the rewards are conceived of as material and consequential rather than as consisting in the fact that justice is its own reward. He also points to the fact that even when recognition that it is injustice rather than justice which pays leads to the pursuit of injustice and thereby to the incurring of divine wrath, the prevailing culture and education teach that the gods can be bought off. So unless Socrates follows the course proposed by Glaucon, he will be saddled with the charge that really he agrees with Thrasymachus, that so-called justice is really pursuit of the interest of the stronger, the strength of whose case lies in his command of the big battalions, and that the so-called injustice involved in the alternative pursuit of one's own interests is really inhibited only by the threat of *force majeure*.

In his attempt to accede to the demands of Glaucon and Adeimantus, Socrates embarks on his elaborate analogy between the state and the soul. The details of this presentation lie outside the scope of my present inquiry, which is concerned only with the structural aspects of Socrates' procedure.

III. Does Thrasymachus Have a Coherent Position?

(1) When we operate as moral philosophers in the borderland between Ethics and Political Theory, one of the salient questions which we encounter is whether there is a distinction between moral and political concepts and how such a distinction, if it exists, should be characterized. In this connection it will be of great importance to consider the viewpoint of a philosopher, if such a philosopher can be found, who maintains that there is no distinction, or at least no genuine distinction, between moral and political concepts in this area or in some significant part of this area. If it were possible without undue distortion to exhibit Thrasymachus as a kind of moral skeptic—as someone who holds, for example, that while political justice, or politico-legal justice, is an intelligible notion with real application, the same cannot be said of moral justice, which can be seen to be ultimately an illusion—then it might be philosophically advantageous to regard Thrasymachus in that way. We should examine, therefore, the prospects of success for such an interpretation of Thrasymachus's position. Can he be viewed as one who regards political justice, but not moral justice, as a viable concept?

(2) If we attempt to proceed further in this direction, we encounter a difficulty at the outset, in that it is unclear just what concept it is which the friends of moral justice suppose to be the concept of moral justice. Is the term "moral justice" to be thought of as referring to moral value in general, as distinct from other kinds of value? Or is the notion of moral justice to be conceived as possessing some more specific content, so that, while both fairness and loyalty are morally admirable qualities, only the first can be properly regarded as a form of moral justice? And if the notion of moral justice is to be supposed to cover only a part of the domain of moral value, to which part of that domain is its application restricted? To the region of fairness? To that of equality of opportunity? To that of respect for natural rights? Rival candidates seem to abound.

In the case of Plato's Thrasymachus it seems that he, perhaps like Plato himself, is not disposed to engage in the kind of conceptual sophistication practised by Aristotle and by some philosophers since Aristotle; for Thrasymachus, the friends of moral justice (on the assumption that the representation of Thrasymachus as a kind of moral skeptic is legitimate) will be philosophers who treat the term "moral justice" as one which refers to morality, or to moral virtue in general, a usage which Aristotle also recognizes as legitimate, alongside the usage in which "justice" is the name of one or more specific virtues.

(3) If our program requires that we try to represent Thrasymachus as a certain sort of moral skeptic, obviously one part of his position will be that the concept of moral justice is unacceptable. One or both of two forms of unacceptability might be in question, namely alethic unacceptability and semantic unacceptability. The suggestion might be that positive ascriptions of moral justice are never in fact true, and so are always alethically unacceptable, or that such ascriptions, together perhaps with their negations, suffer from some form of unintelligibility, and so are semantically unacceptable. Some indeed might contend that general alethic unacceptability generates semantic unacceptability, that if a certain kind of characterization is always false, that implies that that kind of characterization is in some way unintelligible. Let us assume that the revised presentation of Thrasymachus will be one which, for one reason or another, ascriptions of moral justice are semantically unintelligible. This assumption will leave open a considerable range of possibilities with regard to the more precise interpretation of the notion of semantic unacceptability, ranging perhaps from the extreme suggestion that ascriptions of moral justice are just gibberish, to the suggestion that they admit no fully successful rational elucidation.

(4) Within the boundaries of this position, the new Thrasymachus might perhaps hold that, though the concept of moral justice is semantically unacceptable, a related concept, which we may call "moral justice∗," is fully admissible. Moral justice∗ is to be supposed to have precisely the same *descriptive* content as moral justice; ascriptions, however, of moral justice∗ will entirely lack the ingredient of favorable valuation or endorsement which is carried by the term "moral justice." It might, however, be objected that the proposed separation of the descriptive content of moral justice from its evaluative content is quite inadmissible; if we are looking for predicates which from an ascriptive point of view are specifications of the general descriptive condition for moral justice, but which at the same time lack the evaluative element which attaches to the term "moral justice," we shall need predicates which are considerably more specific than "morally just∗." Indeed, some might claim that it is pure fantasy to suppose that any predicate, however specific, could signify a descriptive character which falls within the general character signified by the term "moral justice" after detachment of the term's eval-

uative signification. Description cannot be thus severed from evaluation.

(5) Whatever may be the final upshot of debate about the possibility of separating the descriptive and the evaluative significations of the term "morally just," it is clear that a further element in the position of the new Thrasymachus will be that whatever semantic unacceptability may attach to moral justice, there is a further kind of justice, namely political (or politico-legal) justice, which is free from this defect. Political justice is a concept which is both intelligible and has application. The old Thrasymachus, however, wished to combine this recognition of the intelligibility and the applicability of the concept of political justice with the contention that the applicability of the concept of political justice to a particular line of actual or possible action provided a basis not for the commendation but rather for the discommendation of that line of action; the wise, prudent, or sensible man would be led away from rather than toward the adoption of a certain course of action, would become less rather than more favorably disposed toward the idea of his becoming engaged in it, if he were told, perfectly correctly, that political justice required his engagement in it. This further contention has the air of paradox; how could the fact that political justice, or indeed any kind of justice, requires a man to undertake a particular course of action, be in the eyes of that man a bad mark against doing the action in question? Can the new Thrasymachus align himself in this matter with the old? It can fairly easily be seen that the idea that the position of the old Thrasymachus involves paradox is ill-founded. That this is so can best be shown by the introduction of one or two fairly simple distinctions. First, a value (or disvalue) may be either intrinsic or extrinsic. Roughly speaking, the value (or disvalue) of x will be intrinsic if it attaches to x in virtue of some element in the character of x; it will be extrinsic if it depends on the nature of some effect of x. To present the distinction somewhat more accurately, a value or disvalue of x will be intrinsic if its presence is dependent on some property of x which may indeed be a causal property, but if it is a causal property, it is one whose value or disvalue does not depend on the value or disvalue of that which is caused. The property of causing raised eyebrows is a causal property and may be one with which value or disvalue is associated; but if the eyebrow-raising is something with which value or disvalue is associated, this is not because of the antecedent value or disvalue of elevated eyebrows, but rather because of a connection between raised eyebrows and sur-

prise. A value or disvalue will be extrinsic if it attaches to x in virtue of a causal property the value or disvalue of which depends upon the antecedent value or disvalue of that which is caused. Second, a value or disvalue may be either direct or indirect. A value which is a direct value of x must rest, if it rests on other features at all, on features of x which, at least on balance, are values rather than disvalues; similarly, a direct disvalue of x, if it rests on other features of x, must rest on features which are at least on balance disvalues. An indirect value of x may rest on a prior disvalue of x, provided that this disvalue is less than that which would attach to any alternative state of x. The disvalue of being beheaded may be indirectly a value, provided that (for example) it is less than the disvalue which would attach to the only other option, namely to being burned at the stake. The least of a number of possible evils may thus be indirectly a good. The old Thrasymachus, then, was perfectly entitled to deny that political justice is *directly* a kind of good, provided he was willing to allow (as he was) that *indirectly* it is, or may be, a good. There is then no conceptual barrier to incorporating in the position of the new Thrasymachus the thesis that political justice is only indirectly a good; it is acceptable only as a way of averting the greater evil of being at the mercy of predators.

(6) This would perhaps be an appropriate moment to consider a little more closely what I have been speaking of as Thrasymachus's combination of rejection of the concept of moral justice and acceptance of the concept of political justice. There are two ways of looking at this matter. One, which is, I think, suggested by my discussion, is that there are two distinct concepts, which some philosophers regard as being both parallel and viable, namely moral justice and political justice. The special characteristic of Thrasymachus is supposed to be that he allows the second concept while rejecting the first. I shall call this approach the "two-concept" view of justice, according to which the unqualified term "justice" might be used to refer to either of two distinct concepts. The second way of looking at things I shall call the "one-concept" view of justice, according to which the least misleading account of the difference between moral justice and political justice will be not that two different concepts are involved, but that two different kinds of reason or backing may be relied upon in determining the application of a single concept, namely that expressed simply by the word "justice" without the addition of any adjectival modification. The term "justice" will always ultimately refer to a system of practical rules for the regulation of conduct, perhaps not just any and

every such system but one which conforms to certain restrictions—
for example, perhaps, one which is limited to the regulation of certain
kinds of conduct or regions of conduct. The difference between moral
and political justice might be thought of as lying in the fact that in
the case of moral justice the system of rules is to be accepted on account of the intrinsic desirability that conduct of a certain sort should
be governed by practical rules or by practical rules of a certain sort,
where a system of rules of political justice rests on the desirability of
the consequences of making conduct subject to rules, or to those particular rules. This possibly more Kantian conception of the relation
between moral and political justice will perhaps carry the consequence that the view of Socrates and his friends that moral justice is
desirable independently of the consequences of acting justly is no accident, but is a constitutive feature of moral justice; without it, moral
justice would not be moral. It should of course be recognized that the
idea that there is only one concept of justice, though there may be
different kinds of reason for accepting a system of rules of justice,
does not entail that one and the same system of rules of justice may
be acceptable for radically different kinds of reasons; there might be
a single concept of justice without its ever being true that different
sorts of reason could ever justify the acceptance of a single system of
rules of justice. We may, of course, if we wish to treat a one-concept
view of justice as in fact invoking two concepts of justice; but if we
do, we should recognize that the two concepts of justice are higher-
order concepts, each relating to different kinds of reasons governing
the applicability of a single lower-order concept of justice.

(7) Let us take stock. We seem to have reached a position in which
(a) we have failed to detect any incoherence in the views of the old
Thrasymachus, and (b) it seems to be a live possibility that intrinsic
desirability is not an accidental feature but is a constitutive feature of
moral justice. We should now inquire what considerations, if any,
would be grounds for dissatisfaction with the viewpoint of Thrasymachus.

IV. Moral Justice and Skepticism

(1) The claim that what I am presenting is a reconstruction of Socrates' original defense of moral justice rests on my utilization of some
of Socrates' leading ideas, notably on the idea that the presence of
moral justice in a subject x depends upon a feature or features of
components of x, that the relevant feature or features of the compo-

nents is that individually each of them fulfills its role or plays its part, whatever that role or part may happen to be (or, perhaps better, taken all together, their overall state is one which realizes most fully their various separate roles), that in satisfying this condition, they, the components, enable x to realize the special and peculiar virtue of excellence of the type to which x essentially belongs, that this fact entitles us to regard x as a good or well-conditioned T (where "T" refers to the type in question), and this in turn, if membership of T consists in being a soul, ensures that the life of x is happy, in an appropriate sense of "happy." My account also resembles the original account given by Socrates in that it deploys the notion of analogy which was a prominent ingredient in Socrates' story, though it seeks to improve on Socrates' presentation by making it clear just why the notion of analogy should be brought into this discussion, and by making its appearance something more than an expository convenience. My presentation seeks also to link the idea of maximal or optimal fulfillment of function not merely with the concept of moral injustice but more centrally and more directly with the more widely applicable concept of what one might call "health." This change carries with it an increase in the number of stages to be considered from two (the political and the moral) to three (the physiological, the political, and the moral). My presentation also introduces the suggestion that the very same factors which determine whether a particular entity x, belonging to a certain type T, merits the accolade of being a T which is healthy, well-conditioned, or in good shape, *also* by their presence (in lower degrees) determine the difference between the existence (or survival) of x, rather than its nonexistence (or nonsurvival). The same features, for example, which at the physiological stage determine whether a body is or is not well-conditioned, also determine by their appearance or nonappearance in lower degrees whether that body does or does not exist or survive. (This example in fact calls for a more careful formulation.) I shall proceed to a more detailed discussion of the three stages recognized in my account. The complications are considerable, and intelligibility of presentation may call for omissions and convenient distortions.

(2) Stage 1. At this stage (the physiological stage) there appear a number of different items or types of item, namely:

(a) physiological things, such as human and animal bodies (ϕ-thing$_1$, ϕ-thing$_2$, ϕ-thing$_n$;

(b) physiological components (ϕ-components or bodily organs).

These will include both distinct types of φ-component or organ, like the Liver and the Heart, and distinct instances or tokens of these types, like my liver and my heart, or my liver and your heart. Entry (b) will distribute a number of different types of bodily organ one apiece among human or animal bodies. For these purposes sets of teeth and pairs of human legs will have to count as single organs.

(c) Functional properties of physiological components or organs. These correspond to the jobs or functions which the various organs crucially fulfill in the life of the φ-thing or body to which they belong, such as walking, eating, achieving, and digestion. For convenient oversimplification I assume that each organ has just one functional property, which will be variable in degree.

(d) Certain properties of φ-things (bodies) ("global properties") which will be dependent on the functional properties exhibited by the arrays of physiological components or organs which belong to the things in question. The properties under this head which presently concern me are two in number: one, which will not be variable in degree, will be the property of existence or survival, which will depend on the array of physiological components belonging to a particular φ-thing achieving a minimal level with respect to the functional properties of the members of the array, that is to say, a level which is sufficient to ensure that the array of physiological components continues to exhibit some positive degree of the functional properties of that array. The other φ-thing property which will concern me is one which will be variable in degree; it is the property of well-being, or well-being as a φ-thing of the sort to which it belongs. Maximal well-being will depend on an optimal combined exemplification of the functional properties of a φ-thing's physiological components. The higher levels of this latter property are commonly known as "bodily health" (without qualification), or as "bodily healthiness." At all levels the phrase "bodily health" may be used to signify the dimension within which variation takes place between one level and another.

(3) Before I embark on a consideration of the details of subsequent stages, perhaps I should amplify the account of my intended procedure, including the general structure of my strategy for the characterization and defense of moral justice:

(a) The items involved in the stage 1 (physiological entities or bodies, their components or organs, the functional properties, and certain overall features of bodies, such as existence and being in good shape, which are dependent on the functional properties of organs) exist or are exemplified quite naturally and without the aid of analogy at this level. The stage therefore may be regarded as providing paradigms which may be put to work in the specification of related items which appear in subsequent stages and into the constitution of which analogy does enter.

(b) Those members of the list of items, mentioned in 3(a) as appearing in later stages, which are *properties* as distinct from things, may be specified in two different ways. One way will be to make use of abstract nouns or phrases which are peculiar and special to properties belonging to that stage, and which do not incorporate any reference to more generic properties specifications of which are found also at stages other than the one to which the property under discussion itself belongs. The other way is to build the specifications from what at least seem to be more generic properties, together with a differentiating feature which singles out the particular stage at which the specified properties apply. Leaving on one side for a moment the second mode of specification, I shall comment briefly on the first. This may be expected to yield for us, at the political stage, such properties as those expressed by the phrases "political justice" and "political existence," and by whatever epithets are appropriate for the expression of the features of this or that part of a state on which the global properties of political justice and political existence will depend. Again, at the psychological stage, the first method will give us, unless the state is beset by illusion, expressions for the psychological properties of moral justice and psychological existence, and for the particular features of parts of the soul (whatever these parts may be) on which the presence of moral justice and psychological existence will depend. It will be noted that more than one important issue has so far been passed over; I have ignored the possibility that political and moral justice might be different specifications of a more general feature for which the name "justice," without added qualification, might be appropriate; I have left it undetermined whether "parts of the state" are to be regarded, as they were by Socrates, as particular political classes or in some other way, perhaps as political offices or departments; and I have so far ducked the question of the objects of reference of the phrase "parts of the soul." Such matters obviously cannot be indefinitely left on one side.

(c) I turn now to the considerably more complicated second mode of specification of the relevant range of properties. As already remarked, this mode of specification will incorporate references to seemingly generic properties the appearance of which are not restricted to just one stage, a fact which perhaps entitles us to talk here about "multistage" epithets (predicates) and properties. Examples of second-mode specification will be such epithets as "is in good shape as a body" and "is in good shape as a state," both of which incorporate the more generic epithet "is in good shape" which seemingly applies to objects belonging to different stages, namely to animal bodies and to states. In addition to such "holistic" epithets which apply to subjects which inhabit different stages, there will also be "meristic" epithets, like "part" itself, which apply to parts of such aforementioned subjects. One of my main suggestions is that the multistage epithets which are characteristically embedded in second-mode specifications always, or at least in all but one kind of cases, apply only analogically to the subjects to which they do apply. I may remark that we shall need to exercise considerable care not to become entangled with our own bootlaces when we talk about analogical epithets, the analogical application of epithets, and analogical properties. Such care is particularly important in view of the fact that it is also one of my contentions that there will be properties the possession of which may be nonanalogically conveyed by use of the first mode, and analogically conveyed by use of the second mode.

It should be observed that although I have claimed that there are two different modes of property-specification, I have not claimed that for each individual property, at least within a certain range of properties, a specimen of each mode of specification will be available for use; it may be that in certain cases the vocabulary would provide only for a second-mode specification, or that a first-mode specification can be made available only via a stipulative definition based initially on a preexisting second-mode specification. Since in my view most of the difficulties experienced by philosophers concerning this topic have arisen from doubts and discomforts about the applicability and consequences of second-mode specifications, gaps which appear in the ranks of first-mode specifications might be expected to favor neo-Socrates rather than neo-Thrasymachus, unless neo-Thrasymachus can make out a good case in favor of the view that where first-mode specifications are lacking, second-mode specifications will also be lacking; in which case the onus of proof will lie on the skeptic rather than on his opponent. It should also be observed that further discussion of the relation between second-mode and first-mode specifications might make a substantial contribution to two distinct philosophical questions, namely:

(i) whether it is sometimes true that description presupposes valuation (since second-mode specification seems only too often to rely on ideas about how things should go or ought to go);

(ii) whether it is sometimes or always true that valuation presupposes Teleology or Finality, since second-mode specifications characteristically introduce references to functions and purposes.

(d) I shall now recapitulate the main features which I am supposing to attach to first-mode and second-mode specifications, with a view to raising some further questions about the two modes:

(i) Properties which will be specified, when one uses first-mode specifications by single-stage epithets (properties like bodily health, political justice, and, perhaps controversially, moral justice) may also be specified by the use of second-mode specifications which will incorporate references to seemingly multistage properties such as well-being and existence. The property of bodily health, for example, may also be referred to as the property of well-being as a physiological entity, the property of political justice as the property of well-being as a political entity (or state), and the property of moral justice (perhaps) as the property of well-being as a psychological entity (or soul).

(ii) The global properties of well-being as this or that type of entity will depend on a maximal (or optimal) degree of fulfillment, by the various parts of the subjects of those global properties, of a sequence of meristic properties associated with the jobs or functions of those parts.

(iii) The very same meristic properties on which the various forms of well-being depend will also determine, at a lower degree of realization, the difference between the existence and the nonexistence of the entities which inhabit a particular stage.

(iv) It might be possible, by a move which would be akin to that of "Ramsification," to redescribe the things which inhabit a certain stage, their components or parts, the jobs or functions of such components, the property of well-being and the property of existence as being just those items which, *in a certain realm,* are *analogical counterparts* to the *prime* items, in *the physiological realm,* respectively, of bodies, organs, bodily functions, health, and life (survival).

(v) These proposals might achieve a combination of generalization and justification (validation) of the items to which they relate, given the assumption that the proposed redescriptions are semantically and alethically acceptable.

Among the questions which most immediately clamor for consideration will be the following:

(Q1) How are we to validate my intuitive judgment that second-mode specifications which involve multistage epithets will always, or at least sometimes, be analogical in character?

(Q2) How are we to elucidate the phrase used in (iv) "in a certain realm"?

(Q3) How is it to be shown that the proposed redescriptions are not merely semantically but also alethically acceptable?

I will take these questions in turn.

(e) Question (Q1) calls for the justification of a thesis which, without offering arguments in its support, I suggested as being correct, namely that if there are multistage epithets, that is to say, epithets which apply sometimes to objects belonging to one stage and also sometimes to objects belonging to another stage, the application of such an epithet to one, and possibly to both, of these segments of its extension must be analogical rather than literal. It seems to me that, before such a thesis can be defended or justified, it needs to be emended, since as it stands it seems most unlikely to be true. Consider first the epithet "healthy"; there would, I think, be intuitive support for the idea that when we talk, for example, of "a healthy mind in a healthy body," at least one of these applications of the epithet "healthy" must be analogical rather than literal, since only a body can be said to be *literally* healthy. But if we turn to the epithets "sound" and "in good order," though I think there will be intuitive support for the idea that both bodies and minds may be said to be sound or to be in good order, and indeed for the idea that bodies and minds can truly be said to be sound or in good order just in case they can truly be said to be healthy, there will not, I think, be intuitive support for the idea that the application of the epithets "sound" and "in good order" to either bodies or minds, or to both, is analogical rather than literal. I would in fact be inclined to regard the application of each of these epithets to both kinds of entity as being literal. I would suggest that the needed emendation, while it allowed that the literal application of epithets may straddle the division between its applicability to subjects that belong to one stage and to subjects that belong to another, would insist that, when such literal cross-stage applications occur, they depend upon prior cross-stage applications of some other epithet, where one or even both of the segments of application are analogical rather than literal.

How should the emended thesis be supported? My idea would be that the barriers separating the applications of an epithet to objects belonging to one stage from its application to objects belonging to another will in fact be category-barriers, and that there are good grounds for supposing that objects which differ from one another in category cannot genuinely possess common properties, and so cannot ultimately, at the most fundamental level, be items to which a single epithet will literally and nonanalogically apply. If objects x and y are categorically debarred from sharing a single property, then they are also debarred from falling, literally and nonanalogically, within the range of application of an epithet whose function is to signify just that property. There is nothing to prevent a body and a mind from being, each of them, literally in good order, provided that the condition needed for being literally in good order is that of being either literally healthy (in the case of a body) or (in the case of a mind) (analogically speaking) healthy. Perhaps the first matter to which we should attend in an endeavor to form a clear conception of (for example) the place of being (analogically speaking) healthy, a feature which may attach to minds, within a generalized notion of being in good order, or (perhaps) of being healthy, is the consideration that the question whether the application of a certain epithet to certain things is literal or analogical, is by no means the same question as the question whether its application to those things is or is not to be taken seriously. It may, for example, remain an importantly serious question whether John Stuart Mill is properly to be regarded as a friend of the working classes long after it has been decided that, if the epithet "friend of the working classes" does apply to John Stuart Mill, it applies to him analogically rather than literally; it does not apply to him in at all the same kind of way as that in which the epithet "friend of Mr. Gladstone" may have applied or, perhaps, failed to apply to him. The question whether a particular person is in good shape may be a question an important aspect of which is expressed by the question "Is his mind (analogically speaking) healthy?"; if so, given that the first question is, as it may be, one to be taken seriously, the same would be true of the second question.

A second consideration, which we should not allow ourselves to lose sight of, is one which has already been briefly mentioned in the first part of this essay. We are operating in an area in which, not infrequently perhaps, we shall be under pressure from what Aristotle would have called an Aporia. We find ourselves confronted by a number of seemingly distinct kinds of items, and by a number of features each of which is special to one of these kinds. If we heed intuition— also, perhaps, if we heed the way we talk—we shall be led to suppose that these features are all specifications of some more general feature which is manifested, with specific variations, throughout the range formed by the kinds in question, a putative general feature for which ordinary language may even provide us with a candidate's name. Furthermore, if we heed intuition, we shall be led to suppose that the members of this range of special features have a common explanation, a further general feature which accounts for the first general feature, and also, with the aid of specific variations, for the original range of special features. To follow this route would seemingly be just to follow the procedures which we constantly employ in describing and accounting for the phenomena which the world lays before us. In the present case, the application of this method would be to a range of items which includes bodies, states, and (perhaps) souls and also to such special features of these items as (respectively) bodily health, political justice, and (perhaps) moral justice.

Unfortunately, at this point, we encounter a major difficulty. The items which are the subjects to which the members of the range of special features attach, namely bodies, states, and souls, insofar as they are genuine objects at all, seem plainly to belong to different categories from one another; and these categorial differences would be such as to preclude, if widely received views about categories are to be accepted, the possibility that there are any properties which are shared by items which differ from one another with respect to the kinds to which they belong. It looks, then, as if the possibility that there is a generic property of which the special properties are differentiations, and the possibility that there is a further generic property which serves to account for the first generic property, have both been eliminated. I have in fact not attempted to set out a theory of categories which would carry this consequence, and it would certainly be necessary to attempt to fill this lacuna. But the prospects that this undertaking would remove the difficulty do not at first sight seem encouraging. If, then, we are not to abandon all hope of rational solution, we shall be forced to do one of three things:

(i) Relinquish the idea of applying here procedures for description and explanation which are operative in examples which are not bedeviled by category difference.

(ii) Argue that the category differences which seem only too prominent on the present occasion are only apparent and not real.

(iii) Devise a less restrictive theory of the effect of category differences on the sharing of properties.

In the light of these problems, we should obviously be at pains to consider whether attention to the notion of analogical application would have any chance of providing relief.

I propose to leave this problem on one side for a moment, returning to consideration of it at a later point; immediately, I shall address myself to a possible response to the suggestion that the question whether the possible application of a given epithet to a certain subject is an issue which it is proper to take seriously, is quite distinct from the question whether such application, if it existed, would be analogical or literal. The response would be that the distinction between the two questions does not have to be a simple black-or-white matter; it might be that, while the fact that if such application existed at all it would be an analogical application is not a universal obstacle to the idea that the application is one which should be taken seriously, it is also not true that there is no connection between the two questions; if the inquiry into the application of the epithet is one of a certain sort or one which is conducted with certain purposes in view, then the idea that such application would be analogical stands in the way of the idea that the application is one to be taken seriously; if, however, the character and purposes of the inquiry are of some other sort, then the two questions may be treated as distinct.

It might, for example, be held that if the inquiry about the application of an epithet is one which aims at reaching scientific truth, at laying bare the true nature of reality, then the fact that the application of the epithet would be analogical conflicts with the idea that it should be taken seriously; if, however, the inquirer's concern is not with scientific truth but rather with the acceptability, either in general or in a particular case, of some practical principle (or principle of conduct), then the two questions may be treated as distinct. Something like this "halfway" position is perhaps discernible in Kant; in, for example, his claim that Ideas of Pure Reason, with regard to which no transcendental proofs are available, admits of "regulative" but not of "constitutive" employment, a suggestion which is perhaps repeated in his demand for a nondogmatic kind of teleology, a teleology which somehow guides our steps without adding to our stock of beliefs. The situation, however, is vastly complicated by the fact that the notion of what is "practical" is susceptible to more than one interpretation; on a wider interpretation, any principles or precepts would count as practical provided that they relate to questions about how one should proceed. On a second interpretation of "practical," only those examples of principles and precepts which are "practical" in the first sense will count as "practical" which relate not just to some form of procedure but to procedure in the world of action as distinct from procedure in the world of thought. Imperatives which are practical in the second and narrower sense will, as Kant himself seems to have thought, include those which tell us how to act but will not include those which tell us how to think; they will be concerned with the conduct of the business of life but not with the conduct of the business of thought. This ambiguity leaves principles and precepts which concern conduct of the business of thought in a somewhat indeterminate position; they will be practical in the wider sense since they are concerned with questions about how we should conduct ourselves; however, what is given with one hand seems to be swiftly taken away by the other when we observe that the conduct they prescribe is conduct which is specifically involved in arriving at decisions about scientific truths and the nature of reality. For me the issue is made even more complicated by the fact that I have instinctive sympathy toward the idea that so-called transcendental proofs should be thought of as really consisting in reasoned presentation of the necessity, in inquiries about knowledge and the world, of thinking about the world in certain very general ways. This viewpoint would introduce interconnections between what we are to believe and how we are to proceed which will be by no means easy to accommodate.

I return now to discussion of the quandary which I propounded a little while ago, and the severe limitations on explanation seemingly imposed by category-differences between features which need to be explained. As I see it, my task will be to provide a somewhat more formalized characterization of the phenomenon of analogical application than has yet been offered, perhaps a logico-metaphysical characterization, which will at the same time be one which both preserves those category-differences and their consequential features, and at the same time avoids undue restrictions on the application of standard procedures for the construction of explanations. This may seem like a tall order, but I think it can be met.

Let us first look at the notion of instantiation and at one or two related notions. If I am informed that x instantiates y (that x is an instance of y), and also that y specifies z (that y is a specification of z, that being y is a way of being z, that y is a form of z), then I am entitled to infer that x instantiates z. If, however, instead of being informed that y specifies z, I am informed that y instantiates z, the situation is different; I cannot infer from the information that x instantiates y and y instantiates z, that x instantiates z. The relation of instantiation is not transitive, since if azure specifies blue, and blue specifies color, then it looks as if azure must specify color. Let us now define a relation of "subinstantiation"; x will subinstantiate z just in case there is some item or other, y, such that x instantiates y and y instantiates z. We might perhaps offer, as a slightly picturesque representation of the foregoing material, the statements that if x specifies y, then x and y belong to the same level or order of reality as one another, if x instantiates y, then x belongs to a level which is one step lower than that of y, and that if x subinstantiates y, then x belongs to a level which is two steps lower than that of y. Now it seems natural to suppose that when a number of more specialized explanations are brought under a single more general and so more comprehensive explanation, this is achieved through representing the various features, which are separately accounted for in the original specialized explanations, as being different specifications of a single more general feature. If, however, we were entitled to say that the crucial relation connecting the more specialized explicanda with a generalized explicandum is not, or at least is not in those cases in which the specialized explicanda are categorically different from one another, that of specification but rather of subinstantiation, then we shall be able to avoid the uncomfortable conclusion that the admissibility of generalized explicanda involves the admissibility of the idea that categorically different subject items may be instances of common properties. An item need not, indeed perhaps cannot, instantiate that which it subinstantiates.

To conclude my treatment of the quandary, I need to show, as best I can, that a systematic replacement of references to the relation of specification by references to the relation of instantiation would have no ill effect on the standard procedure for generalizing a set of specialized explanations, with which we have provided ourselves, of the presence of discriminated specialized properties. To fulfill this undertaking, I must consider two cases, one involving the application of a procedure for generalization which is characterized in terms which involve reference to the relation of specification, and the other in which all references to specification are replaced by references to additional and "higher-level" occurrences of the relation of instantiation.

Case I. (i) We start with a group of particulars (x_1 through x_n), with regard to each of which we are informed that it possesses property D; and with two further groups of particulars (y_1 through y_m and z_1 through z_k) instantiating, respectively, properties E and F.

(ii) The generalization procedure begins when we find further properties A, B, C, such that x_1 through x_n, y_1 through y_m and z_1 through z_k instantiate, respectively, A, B, and C; *and* (as we know or legitimately conjecture) A implies D, B implies E, and C implies F.

(iii) We next find the more general properties P, Q, such that A and D, specify in way 1, respectively, P and Q; B and E, specify in way 2, respectively P and Q; and C and F, specify in way 3, respectively, P and Q.

(iv) We are now, it seems, in a position to predict that whatever instantiates property P, will, *in a corresponding way*, instantiate property Q; that is to say, to predict for example that anything which has A will have D; and though I would hesitate to say that provision of the materials for systematic prediction is the same thing as explanation, I would suggest that, at least in the context which I am considering, it affords sufficient grounds for supposing that explanation has in fact been achieved.

Case II. Case II begins to differ from Case I only when we reach stage (iii). In Case II stage (iii), instead of saying that A and D specify in way 1, respectively, P and Q, we shall say something to the effect that A and D are "first group" instances, respectively, of P and Q; and precisely parallel changes, introducing, instead of the phrase "first-group instance" either the phrase "second-group instance" or "third-group instance" will be made in what we say about properties B and E and properties C and F.

Though I would not claim to have a wholly clear head in the matter, it seems to me that the difference between Case II and Case I generates no obstacle to the attribution of legitimacy of the procedure for generalization with which I am currently concerned. The scope for systematic prediction, and so for explanation, will be quite unaffected. If I am right in this suggestion I shall, I think, have succeeded in providing what was mentioned in Part I of this essay as a desideratum, namely a development of a concept of Affinity, which would be less impeded by category-barriers than the more familiar notion of Similitude.

(f) I now turn briefly to question Q2. This is the question how to interpret the expression "in respect to a certain realm" within such phrases as in "an analogical extension, in a certain realm, of the property of health, in the primary physiological realm to which animal and human bodies are central." I should make clear the problem of ambiguity which prompts this question; there is one way of looking at things, one conception, according to which there is a certain realm, which is that to which souls are central, and into which there is projected an analogical extension of the property of health. In this conception the notion of souls is logically prior to the notion of the psychological realm to which souls are central, and both are logically prior to the property which is the analogical extension of the property of health, which in the primary physiological realm is the property of bodies. But there is another conception which might particularly appeal to those who regard souls as being, initially at least, somewhat dubious entities, according to which souls are introduced into the psychological realm to be the subjects or bearers of a property in that realm which is an analogical extension of the property of health, which in the physiological realm belongs to bodies. According to this conception, fairly plainly, the conception of souls is logically posterior both to the notion of the psychological realm and to the analogical extension of the property of health which exists in that realm. Question Q2 is in effect an accusation: it suggests that the two conceptions are mutually inconsistent, since souls cannot be at one and the same time both logically prior to and logically posterior to both the concept of the realm to which they are supposedly central and to a certain property, analogous to bodily health which exists in that world; it further suggests that Socrates (or neo-Socrates) need both of these conceptions, but, of course, cannot have both of them.

To meet this objection, I would suggest that a promising line to take would be to deny that we start with a certain realm, the psychological realm, the nature of which is determined either by the subject-items, namely souls, which are central to it, or by the properties, such as a certain analogue of bodily health, which characterize things in it; and that we then proceed at a later point to add to it the remaining members of these two classes of elements. Rather, we start off with analogues of two of the elements in the primary physiological realm, souls which are analogues of bodies and a class of properties one of which is an analogue of bodily health, and call the realm to which these analogues belong the psychological realm. In this way the incoherence covertly imputed by question Q2 will be dissolved, since neither of these psychological elements (souls and properties like the analogue of bodily health) will be logically prior to the other. What in fact has been done is to introduce, first, a double analogical extension of two types of items which belong to the primary physiological realm and, second, the notion of a psychological realm for use in a convenient way of talking about what has initially been done.

No doubt more than this will need to be said in a full treatment of the topic; but perhaps for present purposes, which are primarily directed toward defusing a certain criticism, what has been said will be sufficient.

V. Prospects for Ethical Theory (Question Q3)

Question Q3 might be expanded in the following way; we can imagine ourselves encountering someone who addresses us in the following way: "You have certainly achieved something. There is one class of philosophers who would be inclined to deny that the notion of moral justice can be regarded as an acceptable and legitimate concept, because there is no way in which the intuitive idea of moral justice can be coherently presented in a rigorous manner. What you have said has shown that such a philosopher's position is untenable; for you have shown that if we allow the possibility of representing moral justice as a certain sort of analogical extension of a basic notion, namely health, which is a property of bodies, items which belong to a basic or primary realm of objects, you have succeeded in characterizing in a sufficiently articulated way the possession of moral justice to which the philosopher in question is opposed on the grounds of its incoherence. That is no small achievement, but it is not, nevertheless, from your point of view, good enough. For there will be another class of philosophers who find no incoherence in the notion of moral justice, but claim that lack of incoherence is a necessary condition but not a sufficient condition for accepting moral justice as a genuine feature of anything in the world. The uses that we make of our characterizations of moral justice and other such items must be as part of an as it were encyclopedic picture of the fundamental ingredients and contents of the rational world; and if, of the two would-be encyclopedic accounts, one contains everything which the other contains together with something which the other does not contain, while the other account contains nothing beyond a certain part of what the first account contains, it will be rational, in selecting the optimum encyclopedic volume, to prefer the smaller to the larger volume, unless it can be shown that what is contained in the larger volume but omitted in the smaller one is something which should be present in a comprehensive picture of the rational world. To be fit for inclusion in an account of the rational world, a contribution must be not only coherent but also something which is needed. This demand you have not fulfilled."

To this critic I should be inclined to reply in the following manner. "I agree with you that more is required to justify the incorporation of moral justice within the conceptual furniture of the world than a demonstration that the notion of moral justice is one which is capable of being coherently and rigorously presented; and I agree that I have not met this additional demand, in whatsoever it may consist. But I think it can be met; and indeed I think I can not only say what is required in order to meet it but also bring off the undertaking of actually meeting it. The required supplementation will, I suggest, involve two elements; first, a demonstration of the value, in some appropriate sense of "value," of the presence in the world of moral justice, and second, a demonstration that it is, again in the same appropriate sense, up to us whether or not the notion of moral justice does have application in the world." I shall now enlarge upon the two ingredients of this proposed response.

First Supplementation. A person who is concerned about the realization in the world of moral or political justice will encounter at a number of points alternative options relating to such realization which he may have to take into account. The number of such options will vary according to whether a "two-concept" view or a "one-concept" view is taken of justice; the number will be larger if a two-concept view is taken, and I shall begin with that possibility.

(1) On a two-concept view, there will be two properties the realization of which has to be considered, moral justice and political justice. One who is concerned about the application of these properties, and who is unhampered by any skeptical reservations, will have to consider the application of each of these properties to a particular individual, standardly himself, and also to a general subject-item, such as a particular totality of individuals each of whom might consider the

application to himself as an individual of each of the initial properties. There will also be a variety of distinct motivational appeals which the application of one of these forms of justice has to a particular subject-item, the consequential appeal of that realization (e.g. its payoff), or both. If we go beyond Plato, we might have to add such forms of motivational appeal as that which arises from subscriptions to some principle governing the realization of the initial property.

(2) On a one-concept view the initial array of options will be considerably reduced, though it is perhaps questionable whether such reduction will correspond to any reduction in genuinely distinct and authentic options. On the assumption that it would not, I shall temporarily go along with the idea that a one-concept view is the correct one. On this view a distinction between moral and political justice will reappear as the difference between concern for the application of a single property, that of justice, when it is motivated by the intrinsic appeal of its realization in a given subject-item (one might perhaps say its moral appeal) or alternatively, when it is motivated by the idea of the consequence of such a realization (one might say by its political appeal). One should perhaps be careful to allow that the idea that a single concept or property may exert different forms of motivational appeal does not carry with it the idea that one and the same body of precepts will reflect that concern, regardless of the question whether the motivational foundation is moral or political.

It is crucially important to recognize that situations which are only subtly different from one another may exert quite different forms of motivational appeal. Nothing has so far been said to rule out the possibility that while Socrates and other such persons may each be concerned that people in general should value the realization of justice in themselves because of its intrinsic appeal, that is to say, for moral reasons, nevertheless their concern that people in general should value for moral reasons the realization in themselves of justice is based at least in part on consequential or political grounds rather than on any intrinsic or moral appeal. It is possible to be concerned that people be sensitive to the moral appeal of being just, and at the same time for that concern to be at least partly founded on political rather than on moral considerations. If that is so, then the concern for a widespread realization of moral justice might itself have a non-moral foundation. Such considerations as these might be sufficient to ensure that the realization of moral justice in a community is of value to that community. This value might consist in the fact that if the members of a community are morally concerned for the realization of justice in themselves, their manifestation of socially acceptable behavior will not be dependent on the real or threatened operations of law-enforcers, to the advantage of all.

Second Supplementation. If we were to leave things as they are at the end of the first supplementation, though we should perhaps have shown that the realization of moral justice in the world was of value to inhabitants of the world and possibly also absolutely, we should not have escaped the suggestion that this alone is not adequate to our needs; it would leave open the possibility that all one could do would be to pray that moral justice is realized in the world, and then when we have found out whether this is or is not the case, to jubilate or to wail as the case might be. To make good our defense of moral justice, we should need to be able to show that in some sense the realizability of moral justice in the world is up to us. At this point it seems to me we move away from the territory of Socrates and Plato and nearer to the territory of Kant; it also seems to me that at this point the problems become immensely more difficult, and partly because of that, I shall not attempt to devise here a solution to them, but only to provide a few hints about how such a solution might be attained. As we have been interpreting the notion of moral justice, its realizability is an idea which is very close to that of the validity of Morality; and if we were to follow Kant's lead, we should be on our way to a supposition which is close to his idea that the validity of Morality depends upon the self-imposition of law, an idea which, though obscure, seems to suggest that what secures the validity of Morality is something which, in some sense or other of the word "do," is something that we ourselves do, and so perhaps in some sense or other "could," we could avoid doing. What kind of "doing" this might be, and how it might be expected to support Morality, to my mind remain shrouded in darkness even after one has read what Kant has to say; there seems little reason to expect that it would closely resemble the kind of doing with which we are familiar in the ordinary conduct of life. There is also important uncertainty about the proper interpretation of the word "could"; it might refer to some kind of psychological or natural possibility, something which some would be inclined to call a kind of causal possibility; or it might refer to some kind of "rational" possibility, the existence of which would require the availability of a reason or possible reason for doing whatever is said to be rationally possible. Not everything which is psychologically possible is also rationally possible; and I think it might be strategically advantageous if it could be held that the Kantian view assigns psychological possibility but not rational possibility to the avoidance of the institutive act which underlies Morality; but whether this is Kant's view, and how, if it is his view, it is to be made good, are problems which I do not know how to solve.

VI. The *Republic* and Philosophical Eschatology

Let me first present what I see as the background to the reconstructed debate between Thrasymachus and Socrates, or rather perhaps between neo-Thrasymachus and neo-Socrates. Neo-Thrasymachus is a Minimalist and a Naturalist who has affinities with Hume; he rejects the concept of moral justice on the grounds that it would be at one and the same time a nonnatural and psychologistic feature and also an evaluative feature. At this point we may suppose that neo-Socrates, who is not committed to any form of Naturalism, will have retorted to neo-Thrasymachus that a blanket rejection of psychologistic and evaluative features will totally undermine philosophy. This part of the debate is not recorded, but we may imagine neo-Thrasymachus to have responded that neo-Socrates is in no better shape; for he can make sense of the notion of moral justice only by representing it as a special case of a favorable feature, namely well-being, which spans category-barriers between radically different sorts of entities, such as bodies, political states, and persons. But neo-Socrates himself will be committed to holding a view of universals which will prohibit any such crossing of category-barriers by a single universal. To this charge neo-Socrates may resort to two forms of defense, one less radical than the other. The less radical form would involve the claim that while there have to be category-barriers, these do not have to be as severe and restrictive as the accusation suggests. The more radical form of defense would refrain from relying on a more permissive account of category-barriers even though it allowed that such increased permissiveness would be in order. It would rely rather on a distinction between concepts which may span category-barriers, whether these are more or less severe in nature, and universals which may not span such barriers. A closely parallel distinction between (i) an expression's having a single meaning and (ii) its being used to signify a single universal can, I think, be found in Aristotle. This distinction would be made possible by making concepts rest on a foundation of affinities as distinct from the foundation of similarities which underlies universals; affinities may, while similarities may not, be characterizable purely in analogical terms. The working out of such a distinction would be one of a variety of concerns which would be the province of a special discipline of philosophical eschatology. The key to its success would lie in the observance of a distinction between instantiation and subinstantiation. The latter notion would permit generalization and explanation to cross category-barriers and would undermine the charges of incoherence brought by neo-Thrasymachus against neo-Socrates and his favored notion of moral justice. At some level of reinterpretation, then, Socrates's appeal to an analogy between the Soul and the State would be at least partly aimed at showing that the concept of Moral Justice, which Thrasymachus would like to banish as theoretically unintelligible, is analogically linked with the concept of bodily health, admitted by everyone, including Thrasymachus, as a legitimate concept, in such a way that, despite radical categorial differences between the two concepts, if the concept of bodily health is intelligible, the concept of Moral Justice is also intelligible.

However, to exhibit Moral Justice as a feature which is really applicable to items in the world, such as persons and actions, more is needed than to show that its ascription to such items is free from incoherence. It will be necessary to show that such ascription, if it were allowed, would serve a point or purpose, and also that it is in some important way up to us to ensure that such ascription is admissible. The fulfillment of the last undertaking might force us to leave the territory of Socrates and Plato and to enter that of Kant.

Retrospective Epilogue

I shall devote this Epilogue to a detailed review of the deeper aspects of the unity which I believe the essays in this volume to possess. These deeper aspects are three in number, and I shall now enumerate them separately. The first is that the connections between the topics discussed are sometimes stronger and more interesting than the essays themselves make clear: partly this is due to the fact that these connections were not, I think, seen by me at the time at which the essays were written, and it is only in retrospect that I begin to see their number and their importance. The second aspect, on which I think the first is dependent, is that the various topics which interested me at the time at which these essays were written seem to be ones which are, first of all, important and second, topics which still interest me, and some of them, perhaps all of them, are matters which I still feel that I need to make up my mind about more thoroughly and clearly. Consequently these essays can perhaps be regarded as the first word but not the last word in a number of directions in which it is important that philosophers should go. The third and last of these deeper aspects is one that has already been remarked upon in the preface as providing the methodological theme which runs through the contents of this volume. It consists in the application of or illustration of a certain sort of way of doing philosophy, one which was one of the many ways in which philosophy was done in Oxford at the time at which I was there and which are connected with the application to philosophy of a particular kind of interest in language, particularly ordinary language. Such interest took more than one form, and I do not think that in any of the forms it has been very well articulated or expressed or described by those who practised it; and I think it is of fundamental importance to philosophizing. The last part of this epilogue will be devoted to an attempt to make its character more clear.

I shall begin by listing the persistent or recurrent thematic strands which it seems to me I can discern in the essays appearing in this volume, and I shall then return after having listed them to consider them one by one in varying degrees of detail. I think I can detect eight such strands though some of them have more than one component and the components do not necessarily have to be accepted as a block. The first of these main strands belongs to the philosophy of perception; it involves two theses; first that the general notion of perception, the concept expressed by the verb "perceive," is properly treatable by means of causal analysis; and second that in the more specific notions connected with perception like those involving different modalities of perception like "seeing" and "hearing," various elements have to be considered but one which cannot be ignored or eliminated is the experiential quality of the sense-experiences perception involves. A third question, about the analysis of statements describing objects of perception like material objects, was also prominent in my thinking at the time at which these essays were written but does not figure largely in these pages. The second strand is a concern to defend the viability of an analytic/synthetic distinction together perhaps with one or more of such closely related distinctions as that between necessary and contingent or between a priori and a posteriori. A third strand is a defense of the rights of the ordinary man or common sense vis-à-vis the professional philosopher, the idea being that for reasons which have yet to be determined and accurately stated the ordinary man has a right to more respect from the professional philosopher than a word of thanks for having got him started.

The fourth strand relates to meaning; it consists in two theses: first, that it is necessary to distinguish between a notion of meaning which is relativized to the users of words or expressions and one that is not so relativized; and second, of the two notions the unrelativized notion is posteriori to, and has to be understood in terms of, the relativized notion; what words mean is a matter of what people mean by them.

The fifth strand is the contention that in considering the notion of meaning we should pay attention to two related distinctions. First, a distinction between those elements of meaning which are present by virtue of convention and those which are present by virtue of something other than convention; and second, between those elements of meaning which standardly form part of what a word or form of words asserts (or its user asserts), and those elements of meaning which rather form part of what the words or their users imply or otherwise convey or are committed to. A distinction, that is to say, (a) between conventional and nonconventional meaning and (b) between assertive and nonassertive meaning. Strand six is the idea that the use of language is one among a range of forms of rational activity and that those rational activities which do not involve the use of language are in various ways importantly parallel to those which do. This thesis may take the more specific form of holding that the kind of rational activity which the use of language involves is a form of rational cooperation; the merits of this more specific idea would of course be independent of the larger idea under which it falls.

Strands seven and eight both relate to the real or apparent opposition between the structures advocated by traditional or Aristotelian logic, on the one hand, and by modern or mathematical logic, on the other. In a certain sense these strands pull in opposite directions. Strand seven consists in the contention that it is illegitimate to represent, as some modern logicians have done, such grammatical subject phrases as "the King of France," "every schoolboy," "a rich man," and even "Bismarck" as being only ostensibly referential; that they should be genuinely referential is required both for adequate representation of ordinary discourse and to preserve a conception of the use of language as a rational activity.

Strand eight involves the thesis that, notwithstanding the claims of strand seven, genuinely referential status can be secured for the subject phrases in question by supplementing the apparatus of modern logic in various ways which would include the addition of the kind of bracketing devices which are sketched within the contents of this volume.

Strand One

I now turn to a closer examination of the first of these eight thematic strands, the strand, that is, which relates to the analysis of perception.[1] The two essays involving this strand seem to me not to be devoid of merit; the essay on the Causal Theory of Perception served to introduce what later I called the notion of Conversational Impli-

1. Cf. esp. Essays 15–16.

cature which has performed, I think, some useful service in the philosophy of language, and also provided an adequate base for the rejection of à bad, though at one time popular, reason for rejecting a causal analysis of perception; and the essay called "Some Remarks about the Senses," drew attention, I think, to an important and neglected subject, namely the criteria by which one distinguishes between one modality of sense and another. But unfortunately to find a way of disposing of one bad reason for rejecting a certain thesis is not the same as to establish that thesis, nor is drawing attention to the importance of a certain question the same as answering that question. In retrospect it seems to me that both these essays are open to criticisms which so far as I know have not been explicitly advanced.

In "The Causal Theory of Perception" I reverted to a position about sense-datum statements which was originally taken up by philosophers such as Paul and Ayer and some others; according to it, statements to the effect that somebody was having a sense-datum, or had a sense-datum or was having a sense-datum of a particular sort, are to be understood as alternative ways of making statements about him which are also expressible in terms of what I might call phenomenal verbs like "seem" or, more specifically, like "looks," "sounds," and "feels."

This position contrasted with the older kind of view, according to which statements about sense-data were not just alternative versions of statements which could be expressed in terms of phenomenal verbs but were items which served to account for the applicability of such a range of verbs. According to the older view, to say that someone had a sense-datum which was red or mouselike was not just an outlandish alternative way of saying it looked to him as if there was a mouse or something red before him, but was rather to specify something which explained why it looked to him as if there was something red before him or as if there were a mouse before him. The proponents of the newer view of sense-data would have justified their suggestion by pointing to the fact that sense-data and their sensible characteristics are mysterious items which themselves stand in need of explanation, and so cannot properly be regarded as explaining rather than as being explained by the applicability of the phenomenal verb-phrases associated with them. It is not clear that these criticisms of the older view are justified; might it not be that while in one sense of the word "explained" (that which is roughly equivalent to "rendered intelligible") sense-data are explained in terms of phenomenal verbs, in another sense of "explained" (that which is roughly equivalent to "accounted for") the priority is reversed, and the applicability of phenomenal verbs is explained by the availability of sense-data and their sensible feature. The newer view, moreover, itself may run into trouble. It seems to me to be a plausible view that the applicability of phenomenal verbs is itself to be understood as asserting the presence or occurrence of a certain sort of experience, one which would explain and in certain circumstances license the separate employment of a verb phrase embedded in the phenomenal verb-phrase; for it to look or seem to me as if there is something red before me is for me to have an experience which would explain and in certain unproblematic circumstances license the assertion that there is something red before me. It will be logically incoherent at one and the same time to represent the use of phenomenal verbs as indicating the existence of a basis, of some sort or other, for a certain kind of assertion about perceptible objects and as telling us what that basis is. The older view of sense-data attempted to specify the basis; the newer view, apparently with my concurrence, seems to duck this question and thereby to render mysterious the interpretation of phenomenal verb-phrases.

Second, in "Some Remarks about the Senses" I allow for the possibility that there is no one criterion for the individuation of a sense, but I do not provide for the separate possibility that the critical candidates are not merely none of them paramount but are not in fact independent of one another. For example, sense organs are differentiated not by their material character, but by their function. Organs that are just like eyes would in fact be not eyes but ears if what they did was, not to see, but to hear; again, real qualities of things are those which underlie or explain various causal mechanisms, such as our being affected by vibrations or light rays. So criterial candidates run into one another; and indeed the experiential flavor or quality of experience to which I attach special importance is in fact linked with the relevant ranges of what Locke called secondary qualities which an observer attributes to the objects which he perceives; so we might end up in a position that would not have been uncongenial to Locke and Boyle, in which we hold that there are two ways of distinguishing between senses, one of which is by the character of their operations (processes studied by the sciences rather than by the ordinary citizen), and the other would be by the difference of their phenomenal character, which would be something which would primarily be of interest to ordinary people rather than to scientists. These reflections suggest to me two ideas which I shall here specify but not argue for. The first is that, so far from being elements in the ultimate furniture of the world, sense-data are items which are imported by theorists for various purposes; such purposes might be that one should have bearers of this or that kind of relation which is needed in order to provide us with a better means for describing or explaining the world. Such relations might be causal or spatial where the space involved is not physical space but some other kind of space, like visual space, or it might be a system of relations which in certain ways are analogous to spatial relations, like relations of pitch between sounds. This idea might lead to another, namely that consideration of the nature of perception might lead us to a kind of vindication of common sense distinct from those vindications which I mention elsewhere in this epilogue, for if sense-data are to be theoretical extensions introduced or concocted by theorists, theorists will need common sense in order to tell them what it is to which theoretical extensions need to be added. Philosophers' stories derive their character and direction from the nonphilosophical stories which they supplement,

Strand Two

The second of these eight strands[2] consists in a belief in the possibility of vindicating one or more of the number of distinctions which might present themselves under the casual title of "The analytic/synthetic distinction." I shall say nothing here about this strand not because I think it is unimportant; indeed I think it is one of the most important topics in philosophy, required in determining, not merely the answers to particular philosophical questions, but the nature of philosophy itself. It is rather that I feel that nothing less than an adequate treatment of the topic would be of any great value, and an adequate treatment of it would require a great deal of work which I have not yet been able to complete. This lacuna, however, may be somewhat mitigated by the fact that I provided some discussion of this topic in "Reply to Richards" contained in *Philosophical Grounds of Rationality* and by the fact that at the conclusion of this epilogue I shall also advance a slightly skittish hint of the direction in which I have some inclination to go. I hope that this treatment will serve as an interim indication of what my final position might be.

2. Cf. esp. Essay 13.

Strand Three

The third strand[3] consists in a disposition on my part to uphold in one form or another the rights of the ordinary man or of common sense in the face of attacks which proceed from champions of specialist philosophical or scientific theory. All parties would, I think, agree that specialist theory has to start from some basis in ordinary thought of an informal character; the question at issue is whether the contents and views contained in that thought have to continue to be respected in some measure or other by the specialist theorist even after the specialist theorist has embarked on his own work.

According to some, at that point, the contribution of ordinary thought and speech can be ignored, like a ladder to be kicked away once the specialist has got going. My support for common sense is not eroded by the failure of many attempts made by philosophers to give a justification or basis for such support; indeed the negative part of my contribution to the subject consists in the rejection of a number of such attempts. Some of these rejections appear in discussions contained in this volume, others in other places. One form of defense of common sense is one propounded by Moore in the famous paper on that subject. This seems to consist in the presumed acceptability of the obvious; it seems to consist in that because so far as I can see no other reason is given for the acceptance of what Moore counts as propositions of common sense. If I have read Moore aright I find this form of defense of common sense unsatisfactory on the grounds that the conception of the obvious is not in an appropriate sense an objective conception. This is pointedly illustrated by the famous story of the British mathematician G. H. Hardy, who in a lecture announced that a certain mathematical proposition was obvious, at which point one of his audience demurred and said that it was not obvious to him. Hardy then halted the lecture, paced outside the lecture room for a quarter of an hour, returned, and said "It is obvious." The trouble is that obviousness requires consent, on the part of the parties concerned, in the obviousness of what is thought of as obvious.

A second and different line of defense of common sense comes from Thomas Reid, who points to the need for first principles of human knowledge. Once these are secured, then various forms of derivation and deduction and inference can account for the accumulation of

3. Cf. esp. Essays 8–10.

known propositions which are as it were theorems in the system of knowledge; but theorems need to look back to axioms and these axioms are things which Reid regards as matters which it is the function of common sense to provide. The fault which I find here is a conflation of the notion of axioms as being organizational items from which nonaxiomatic propositions are supposed to be derivable with an epistemic interpretation of axioms as providing the foundations of human knowledge; whereas it seems to me arguable and indeed plausible to suppose that the grounds for the acceptance of the contents of this or that system do not lie in the prior evidence or self-evidence of the axioms of the system but in the general character of the system in containing what one thinks it ought to contain in the way of what is knowable.

From an epistemic point of view the justifiability of the system lies in its delivering, in general, what one wants it to deliver and thinks it should deliver, rather than in the availability of a range of privileged intuitions which, happily, provide us with a sufficiency of starting points for rational inference. If common sense comes into the picture at all in this connection it seems to me that it should be with regard to a recognition in some degree or other of what the system ought to be expected to deliver to us rather than as a faculty which assures us of starting points which form the axioms of the system.

A third attempt to justify common sense is that provided by Malcolm in his interpretation of Moore; Malcolm suggested that Moore's point should be thought of as being that standard descriptions of certain sorts of situations cannot be incorrect since the standards of correctness are set by the nature of the descriptions which are standardly used to describe those situations. The trouble with this line, to my mind, is that it confuses two kinds of correctness and incorrectness. Correctness of use or usage, whether a certain expression is properly or improperly applied, gives us one kind of correctness, that of proper application, but that an expression is correct in that sense does not guarantee it against another sort of incorrectness, namely logical incoherence.

The final form of an attempt to justify common sense is by an appeal to Paradigm or Standard Cases; cases, that is, of the application of an expression to what are supposedly things to which that expression applies if it applies to anything at all; for example, if the expression "solid" applies to anything at all it applies to things like "desks" and "walls" and "pavements." The difficulty with this attempt is that it contains as an assumption just what a skeptic who is querying common sense is concerned to deny: no doubt it may be true that if the word "solid" applies to anything at all it applies to things like "desks," but it is the contention of the skeptic that it does not apply to anything, and therefore the fact that something is the strongest candidate does not mean that it is a successful candidate for the application of that expression. On the positive side I offered as an alternative to the appeals I have just been discussing, a proposed link between the authority of common sense and the theory of meaning. I suggested roughly that to side with the skeptic in his questioning of commonsense beliefs would be to accept an untenable divorce between the meaning of words and sentences on the one hand, and the proper specification of what speakers mean by such words and sentences on the other. This attempt to link two of the eight strands to one another now seems to me open to several objections, at least one of which I regard as fatal.

I begin with two objections which I am inclined to regard as nonfatal; the first of these is that my proposed reply to the skeptic ignores the distinction between what is propounded as, or as part of, one's message, thus being something which the speaker intends, and on the other hand what is part of the background of the message by way of being something which is implied, in which case its acceptance is often *not* intended but is rather assumed. That there is this distinction is true, but what is, given perfect rapport between speaker and hearer, something which a speaker implies, may, should that rapport turn out to be less than perfect, become something which the speaker is committed to asserting or propounding. If a speaker thinks his hearer has certain information which in fact the hearer does not, the speaker may, when this fact emerges, be rationally committed to giving him the information in question, so what is implied is at least potentially something which is asserted and so, potentially, something the acceptance of which is intended.

A second (I think, nonfatal) objection runs as follows: some forms of skepticism do not point to incoherences in certain kinds of message; they rely on the idea that skeptical doubts sometimes have to have been already allayed in order that one should have the foundations which are needed to allay just those doubts. To establish that I am not dreaming, I need to be assured that the experiences on which I rely to reach this assurance are waking experiences. In response to this objection, it can be argued, first, that a defense of common sense does not have to defend it all at once, against *all* forms of skeptical doubts, and, second, it might be held that with regard to the kinds of skeptical doubts which are here alluded to, what is needed is not a well-founded assurance that one's cognitive apparatus is in working order but rather that it should *in fact* be in working order whatever the beliefs or suppositions of its owner may be.

The serious objection is that my proposal fails to distinguish between the adoption, at a certain point in the representation of the skeptic's proposed position, of an extensional and of an intensional reading of that account. I assumed that the skeptic's position would be properly represented by an intensional reading at this point, in which case I supposed the skeptic to be committed to an incoherence; in fact, however, it is equally legitimate to take not an intensional reading but an extensional reading in which case we arrive at a formulation of the skeptic's position which, so far as has been shown, is reasonable and also immune from the objection which I proposed. According to the intensional reading, the skeptic's position can be represented as follows: that a certain ordinary sentence s does, at least in part, mean that p, second, that in some such cases, the proposition that p is incoherent, and third, that standard speakers intend their hearers incoherently to accept that p, where "incoherently" is to be read as specifying part of what the speaker intends. That position may not perhaps be strictly speaking incoherent, but it certainly seems wildly implausible. However, there seems to be no need for the skeptic to take it and it can be avoided by an extensional interpretation of the appearance in this context, of the adverb "incoherently." According to this representation it would be possible for s to mean (in part) that p and for p to be incoherent and also for the standard speaker to intend the hearer to accept p which would be to accept something which is *in fact* incoherent though it would be no part of the speaker's intention that in accepting p the hearer should be accepting something which is incoherent. To this reply there seems to me to be no reply.

Despite this failure, however, there seem to remain two different directions in which a vindication of common sense or ordinary speech may be looked for. The first would lie in the thought that whether or not a given expression or range of expressions applies to a particular situation or range of situations is simply determined by whether or not it is standardly applied to such situations; the fact that in its application those who apply it may be subject to this or that form of intellectual corruption or confusion does not affect the validity of the claim that the expression or range of expressions does apply to those situations. In a different line would be the view that the attributions and beliefs of ordinary people can only be questioned with due cause, and due cause is not that easy to come by; it has to be shown that some more or less dire consequences follow from *not* correcting the kind of belief in question; and if no such dire consequences can be shown then the beliefs and contentions of common sense have to be left intact.

Strand Four[4]

This strand has already been alluded to in the discussion of Strand 3, and consists in my views about the relation between what might roughly be described as word-meaning and as speaker's-meaning. Of all the thematic strands which I am distinguishing this is the one that has given me most trouble, and it has also engendered more heat, from other philosophers, in both directions, than any of its fellows. I shall attempt an initial presentation of the issues involved.

It has been my suggestion that there are two distinguishable meaning concepts which may be called "natural" meaning and "nonnatural" meaning and that there are tests which may be brought to bear to distinguish them. We may, for example, inquire whether a particular occurrence of the verb "mean" is factive or nonfactive, that is to say whether for it to be true that so and so means that p it does or does not have to be the case that it is true that p; again, one may ask whether the use of quotation marks to enclose the specification of what is meant would be inappropriate or appropriate. If factivity is present and quotation marks would be inappropriate, we would have a case of natural meaning; otherwise the meaning involved would be nonnatural meaning. We may now ask whether there is a single overarching idea which lies behind both members of this dichotomy of uses to which the word "mean" seems to be subject. If there is such a central idea it might help to indicate to us which of the two concepts is in greater need of further analysis and elucidation and in what direction such elucidation should proceed. I have fairly recently (in Essay 18) come to believe that there is such an overarching idea and that it is indeed of some service in the proposed inquiry. The

4. Cf. esp. Essays 5–6, 7, 12.

idea behind both uses of "mean" is that of consequence; if x means y then y, or something which includes y or the idea of y, is a consequence of x. In "natural" meaning, consequences are states of affairs; in "nonnatural" meaning, consequences are conceptions or complexes which involve conceptions. This perhaps suggests that of the two concepts it is "nonnatural" meaning which is more in need of further elucidation; it seems to be the more specialized of the pair, and it also seems to be the less determinate; we may, for example, ask how conceptions enter the picture and whether what enters the picture is the conceptions themselves or their justifiability. On these counts I should look favorably on the idea that if further analysis should be required for one of the pair the notion of "nonnatural" meaning would be first in line.

There are factors which support the suitability of further analysis for the concept of "nonnatural" meaning. "Meaning$_{NN}$" ("nonnatural meaning") does not look as if it names an original feature of items in the world, for two reasons which are possibly not mutually independent: (a) given suitable background conditions, meaning$_{NN}$ can be changed by *fiat*; (b) the presence of meaning$_{NN}$ is dependent on a framework provided by a linguistic, or at least a communication-engaged community.

It seems to me, then, at least reasonable and possibly even mandatory, to treat the meaning of words, or of other communication vehicles, as analyzable in terms of features of word users or other communicators; nonrelativized uses of "meaning$_{NN}$" are posterior to and explicable through relativized uses involving reference to word users or communicators. More specifically, what sentences mean is what (standardly) users of such sentences mean by them; that is to say, what psychological attitudes toward what propositional objects such users standardly intend (more precisely, M-intend) to produce by their utterance. Sentence-meaning then will be explicable either in terms of psychological attitudes which are standardly M-intended to produce in hearers by sentence utterers or to attitudes taken up by hearers toward the activities of sentence utterers.

At this point we begin to run into objections. The first to be considered is one brought by Mrs. J. Jack,[5] whose position I find not wholly clear. She professes herself in favor of "a broadly 'Gricean' enter-

---

5. In an as yet unpublished paper entitled "The Rights and Wrongs of Grice on Meaning."

prise" but wishes to discard various salient elements in my account (we might call these "narrowly Gricean theses"). What, precisely, is "broad Griceanism"? She declares herself in favor of the enterprise of giving an account of meaning in terms of psychological attitudes, and this suggests that she favors the idea of an analysis, in psychological terms, of the concept of meaning, but considers that I have gone wrong, perhaps even radically wrong, in my selection of the ingredients of such an analysis.

But she also reproves me for "reductionism," in terms which suggest that whatever account or analysis of meaning is to be offered, it should not be one which is "reductionist," which might or might not be equivalent to a demand that a proper analysis should not be a proper reductive analysis. But what kind of analysis is to be provided? What I think we cannot agree to allow her to do is to pursue the goal of giving a *lax* reductive analysis of meaning, that is, a reductive analysis which is unhampered by the constraints which characteristically attach to reductive analysis, like the avoidance of circularity; a goal, to which, to my mind several of my opponents have in fact addressed themselves. ((In this connection I should perhaps observe that though my earlier endeavors in the theory of meaning were attempts to provide a reductive analysis, I have never (I think) espoused *reductionism,* which to my mind involves the idea that semantic concepts are unsatisfactory or even unintelligible, unless they can be provided with interpretations in terms of some predetermined, privileged, and favored array of concepts; in this sense of "reductionism" a felt ad hoc need for reductive analysis does not have to rest on a reductionist foundation. Reductive analysis might be called for to get away from unclarity not to get to some predesignated clarifiers.)) I shall for the moment assume that the demand that I face is for a form of *reductive* analysis which is less grievously flawed than the one which I in fact offered; and I shall reserve until later consideration of the idea that what is needed is *not* any kind of reductive analysis but rather some other mode of explication of the concept of meaning.

The most general complaint, which comes from Strawson, Searle, and Mrs. Jack, seems to be that I have, wholly or partially, misidentified the intended (or M-intended) effect in communication; according to me it is some form of acceptance (for example, belief or desire), whereas it should be held to be understanding, comprehension, or (to use an Austinian designation) "uptake." One form of the cavil (the more extreme form) would maintain that the *immediate* intended target is *always* "uptake," though this or that form of acceptance may be an ulterior target; a less extreme form might hold that the immediate target is sometimes, but not invariably, "uptake." I am also not wholly clear whether my opponents are thinking of "uptake" as referring to an understanding of a sentence (or other such expression) as a sentence or expression in a particular *language,* or as referring to a comprehension of its occasion-meaning (what the sentence or expression means on *this* occasion in this speaker's mouth). But my bafflement arises primarily from the fact that it seems to me that my analysis already invokes an analyzed version of an intention toward some form of "uptake" (or a passable substitute therefor), when I claim that in meaning$_{NN}$ a hearer is intended to recognize himself as intended to be the subject of a particular form of acceptance, and to take on such an acceptance for that reason. Does the objector reject this analysis and if so why? And in any case his position hardly seems satisfactory when we see that it involves attributing to speakers an intention which is specified in terms of the very notion of meaning which is being analyzed (or in terms of a dangerously close relative of that notion). Circularity seems to be blatantly abroad.

This question is closely related to, and is indeed one part of, the vexed question whether, in my original proposal, I was right to embrace a self-denial of the use of semantic concepts in the specification of the intentions which are embedded in meaning$_{NN}$, a renunciation which was motivated by fear of circularity. A clear view of the position is not assisted by the fact that it seems uncertain what should, or should not, be *counted* as a deployment of semantic notions.

So far we seem to have been repelling boarders without too much difficulty; but I fear that intruders, whose guise is not too unlike that of the critics whom we have been considering, may offer, in the end at least, more trouble. First, it might be suggested that there is a certain arbitrariness in my taking relativized meaning as tantamount to a speaker's meaning something *by* an utterance; there are other notions which might compete for this spot, in particular the notion of something's meaning something *to* a hearer. Why should the claims of "meaning *to,*" that is of passive or recipient's meaning, be inferior to those of "meaning *by*" (that is, of acting or agent's meaning)? Indeed a thought along these lines might lie behind the advocacy of "uptake" as being sometimes or even always the target of semantic intention.

A possible reply to the champion of passive meaning would run as follows: (1) If we maintain our present program, relativized meaning is an intermediate analytic stage between nonrelativized meaning and a "semantics-free" ("s-free") paraphrase of statements about meaning. So, given our present course, the fact (if it should be a fact) that there is no obviously available s-free paraphrase for "meaning *to*" would be a reason against selecting "meaning to" as an approved specimen of relativized meaning. (2) There does however seem in fact to be an s-free paraphrase for "meaning to," though it is one in which is embedded that paraphrase which has already been suggested for "meaning by"; "s means p to X" would be interpreted as saying "X knows what the present speaker does (*alternatively* a standard speaker would) mean by an utterance of s"; and at the next stage of analysis we introduce the proffered s-free paraphrase for "meaning by." So "meaning to" will merely look back to "meaning by," and the cavil will come to naught.

At least in its present form. But an offshoot of it seems to be available which might be less easy to dispose of. I shall first formulate a sketch of a proposed line of argument against my analysis of meaning, and then consider briefly two ways in which this argumentation might be resisted.

First, the argument.

(1) In the treatment of language, we need to consider not only the relation of language to communication, but also, and concurrently, the relation of language to thought.

(2) A plausible position is that, for one reason or another, language is indispensable for thought, either as an instrument for its expression or, even more centrally, as the vehicle, or the material, in which thought is couched. We may at some point have to pay more attention to the details of these seeming variants, but for the present let us assume the stronger view that for one reason or another the occurrence of thought requires, either invariably or at least in all paradigmatic cases, the presence of a "linguistic flow."

(3) The "linguistic flows" in question need to attain at least a certain level of comprehensibility from the point of view of the thinker; while it is plain that not all thinking (some indeed might say that *no* thinking) is entirely free from confusion and incoherence, too great a departure of the language-flow from comprehensibility will destroy its character as (or as the expression of) thought; and this in turn will undermine the primary function of thought as an explanation of bodily behavior.

(4) Attempts to represent the comprehensibility, to the thinker, of the expression of thought by an appeal to either of the relativized concepts of meaning$_{NN}$ so far distinguished encounter serious, if not fatal, difficulties. While it is not impossible to mean something by what one says to oneself in one's head, the occurrence of such a phenomenon seems to be restricted to *special* cases of self-exhortation ("what I kept telling myself was. . . . . ."), and not to be a *general* feature of thinking as such. Again, recognition of a linguistic sequence as meaning something *to me* seems appropriate (perhaps) when I finally catch on to the way in which I am *supposed to take* that sequence, and so to instances in which I am being addressed by another not to those in which I address myself; such a phrase as "I couldn't get myself to understand what I was telling myself" seems dubiously admissible.

(5) So an admission of the indispensability of language to thought carries with it a commitment to the priority of nonrelativized meaning to either of the designated relativized conceptions; and there are no other promising relativized candidates. So nonrelativized meaning is noneliminable.

The foregoing resistance to the idea of eliminating nonrelativized meaning by reductive analysis couched in terms of one or the other variety of relativized meaning might, perhaps, be reinforced by an attempt to exhibit the invalidity of a form of argument on which, it might be thought, the proponent of such reduction might be relying. While the normal vehicles of interpersonal communication are words, this is not exclusively the case; gestures, signs, and pictorial items sometimes occur, at times even without linguistic concomitants. That fact might lead to the supposition that nonlinguistic forms of communication are *pre*-linguistic, and do not depend on linguistic meaning. A closely related form of reflection would suggest that if it is the case (as it seems to be) that sometimes the elements of trains of thought are nonlinguistic, then prelinguistic thinking is a genuine possibility. (This was a live issue in the latter part of the nineteenth century.) But, it may be said, both of these lines of argument are inconclusive, for closely related reasons. The fact that on occasion the vehicles of communication or of thought may be wholly nonlinguistic does not show that such vehicles are prelinguistic; it may well be that such vehicles could only fulfill their function as vehicles against a background of linguistic competence without which they would be lost. If, for example, they operate as *substitutes* for language, language for which they are substitutes needs perhaps to be available to their users.

We now find ourselves in a serious intellectual bind. (1) Our initial attention to the operation of language in communication has provided powerful support for the idea that the meaning of words or other communication devices should be identified with the potentiality of such words or devices for causing or being caused by particular ranges of thought or psychological attitudes. When we are on this tack we are inexorably drawn toward the kind of psychological reductionism exhibited in my own essays about Meaning. (2) When our attention is focused on the appearance of language in thinking we are no less strongly drawn in the opposite direction; language now seems constitutive of thought rather than something the intelligibility of which derives from its relation to thought.

We cannot have it both ways at one and the same time. This dilemma can be amplified along the following lines. (1) States of thought, or psychological attitudes cannot be prelinguistic in character. (2) Thought states therefore presuppose linguistic thought-episodes which are constitutive of them. (3) Such linguistic thought-episodes, to fulfill their function, must be intelligible sequences of words or of licensed word-substitutes. (4) Intelligibility requires appropriate causal relation to thought states. (5) So these thought states in question, which lie behind intelligibility, cannot themselves be built up out of linguistic sequences or word-flows. (6) So some thought states are prelinguistic (a thesis which contradicts thesis 1).

It appears to me that the seemingly devastating effect of the preceding line of argument arises from the commission by the arguer of two logical mistakes—or rather, perhaps, of a single logical mistake which is committed twice over in substantially similar though superficially different forms. The first time round the victim of the mistake is myself, the second time round the victim is the truth. In the first stage of the argument it is maintained that the word-flows which are supposedly constitutive of thought will have to satisfy the condition of being significant or meaningful and that the interpretation of this notion of meaningfulness resists expansion into a relativized form, and resists also the application of any pattern of analysis proposed by me. The second time round the arguer contends that any word-flow which is held to be constitutive of an instance of thinking will have to be supposed to be a significant word-flow and that the fulfillment of this condition requires a certain kind of causal connection with admissible psychological states or processes and that to fulfill their function at this point neither the states in question nor the processes connected with them can be regarded as being constituted by further word-flows; the word-flows associated with thinking in order to provide for meaningfulness will have to be extralinguistic, or prelinguistic, in contradiction to the thesis that thinking is *never* in any relevant sense prelinguistic.

At this point we are surely entitled to confront the propounder of the cited argument with two questions. (1) Why should he assume that I shall be called upon to identify the notion of significance, which applies to the word-flows of thought, directly with any favored locution involving the notion of meaning which can be found in my work, or to any analysis suggested by me for such a locution? Why should not the link between the significance of word-flows involved in thinking and suggestions offered by me for the analysis of meaning be much less direct than the propounder of the argument envisages? (2) With what right, in the later stages of the argument, does the propounder of the argument assume that if the word-flows involved in thought have to be regarded as significant, this will require not merely the provision at some stage of a reasonable assurance that this will be so but also the incorporation within the defining characterization of thinking of a special condition explicitly stipulating the significance of constitutive word-flows, despite the fact that the addition of such a condition will introduce a fairly blatant contradiction?

While, then, we shall be looking for reasonable assurance that the word-flows involved in thinking are intelligible, we shall not wish to court disaster by including a requirement that may be suggested as a distinct stipulated condition governing their admissibility as word-flows which are constitutive of thinking; and we may even retain an open mind on the question whether the assurance that we are seeking is to be provided as the conclusion of a deductive argument rather than by some other kind of inferential step.

The following more specific responses seem to me to be appropriate at this point.

(1) Since we shall be concerned with a language which is or which has been in general use, we may presume the accessibility of a class of mature speakers of that language, who by practice or by precept can generate for us open ranges of word-sequences which are, or again are not, admissible sentences of that language.

(2) A favorable verdict from the body of mature speakers will establish particular sentences both as significant and, on that account, as expressive of psychological states such as a belief that Queen Anne is dead or a strong desire to be somewhere else. But the envisaged favorable verdicts on the part of mature speakers will only establish particular sentences as expressive of certain psychological states in general; they will not confer upon the sentences expressiveness of psychological states relative to particular individuals. For that stage to be reached some further determination is required.

(3) Experience tells us that any admissible sentence in the language is open to either of two modes of production, which I will call "overt" and "sotto voce." The precise meaning of these labels will require further determination, but the ideas with which I am operating are as follows. (a) "Overt" production is one or another of the kinds of production, which will be characteristic of communication. (b) "Sotto voce" production which has some connection with, though is possibly not to be identified as, "unspoken production," is typically the kind of production involved in thinking. (c) Any creature which is equipped for the effective overt production of a particular sequence is also thereby equipped for its effective sotto voce production.

(4) We have reached a point at which we have envisaged an indefinite multitude of linguistic sequences certified by the body of mature speakers not merely as legitimate sentences of their language but also as expressive of psychological states in general, though not of psychological states relevant to any particular speaker. It seems then that we need to ask what should be added to guarantee that the sentences in the repertoire of a particular speaker should be recognized by him not merely as expressive of psychological states in general but as expressive of *his* psychological states in particular. I would suggest that what is needed to ensure that he recognizes a suitable portion of his repertoire of sentences as being expressive relative to himself is that he should be the center of a life story which fits in with the idea that he, rather than someone else, is the subject of the attributed psychological states. If this condition is fulfilled, we can think of him, perhaps, not merely as linguistically fluent but also as linguistically proficient; he is in a position to apply a favored stock of sentences to himself. It would of course be incredible, though perhaps logically conceivable, for someone to be linguistically fluent without being linguistically proficient.

It is of course common form, as the world goes, for persons who are linguistically fluent and linguistically proficient to become so by natural methods, that is to say, as a result of experience and training, but we may draw attention to the abstract possibility that the attributes in question might be the outcome not of natural but of artificial processes; they might, for example, be achieved by some sort of physiological engineering. Are we to allow such a fantasy as being conceivable, and if not, why not?

I shall conclude the discussion of Strand Four with two distinct and seemingly unconnected reflections.

(A) We might be well advised to consider more closely the nature of representation and its connection with meaning, and to do so in the light of three perhaps not implausible suppositions.

(1) That representation by means of verbal formulations is an artificial and noniconic mode of representation. (2) That to replace an iconic system of representation by a noniconic system will be to introduce a new and more powerful extension of the original system, one which can do everything the former system can do and more besides. (3) That every artificial or noniconic system is founded upon an antecedent natural iconic system.

Descriptive representation must look back to and in part do the work of prior iconic representation. That work will consist in the representation of objects and situations in the world in something like the sense in which a team of Australian cricketers may represent Australia; they do on behalf of Australia something which Australia cannot do for itself, namely engage in a game of cricket. Similarly our representations (initially iconic but also noniconic) enable objects and situations in the world to do something which they cannot do for themselves, namely govern our actions and behavior.

(B) It remains to inquire whether there is any reasonable alternative program for the problems about meaning other than of the provision of a reductive analysis of the concept of meaning. The only alternative which I can think of would be that of treating "meaning" as a theoretical concept which, together perhaps with other theoretical concepts, would provide for the primitive predicates involved in a semantic system, an array whose job it would be to provide the laws and hypotheses in terms of which the phenomena of meaning are to be explained. If this direction is taken, the meaning of particular expressions will be a matter of hypothesis and conjecture rather than of intuition, since the application of theoretical concepts is not generally thought of as reachable by intuition or observation. But some of those like Mrs. Jack who object to the reductive analysis of meaning are also anxious that meanings should be intuitively recognizable. How this result is to be achieved I do not know.

Strand Five

Strand Five is perhaps most easily approached through an inquiry whether there is any kind, type, mode, or region of signification which has special claims to centrality, and so might offer itself as a core around which more peripheral cases of signification might cluster, perhaps in a dependent posture. I suggest that there is a case for the supposition of the existence of such a central or primary range of cases of signification; and further that when the question of a more precise characterization of this range is raised, we are not at a loss how to proceed. There seem to be in fact not merely one, but two ways of specifying a primary range, each of which has equally good claim to what might be called "best candidate status." It is of course a question which will await final decision whether these candidates are distinct from one another. We should recognize that at the start we shall be moving fairly large conceptual slabs around a somewhat crudely fashioned board and that we are likely only to reach sharper conceptual definition as the inquiry proceeds.

We need to ask whether there is a feature, albeit initially hazy, which we may label "centrality, " which can plausibly be regarded as marking off primary ranges of signification from nonprimary ranges. There seems to be a good chance that the answer is "Yes." If some instances of signification are distinguishable from others as relatively direct rather than indirect, straightforward rather than devious, plain rather than convoluted, definite rather than indefinite, or as exhibiting other distinguishing marks of similar general character, it would seem to be not unreasonable to regard such significations as belonging to a primary range. Might it not be that the capacity to see through a glass darkly presupposes, and is not presupposed by, a capacity at least occasionally to achieve full and unhampered vision with the naked eye?

But when we come to ask for a more precise delineation of the initially hazy feature of centrality, which supposedly distinguishes primary from nonprimary ranges of signification, we find ourselves confronted by two features, which I shall call respectively "formality" and "dictiveness," with seemingly equally strong claims to provide for us a rationally reconstructed interpretation of the initially hazy feature of centrality.

Our initial intuitive investigation alerts us to a distinction within the domain of significations between those which are composite or complex and those which are noncomposite or simple; and they also suggest to us that the primary range of significations should be thought of as restricted to simple or noncomposite significations; those which are complex can be added at a later stage. Within the field left by this first restriction, it will be appealing to look for a subordinate central range of items whose signification may be thought of as being in some appropriate sense direct rather than indirect, and our next task will be to clarify the meaning, or meanings, in this context of the word "direct." One class of cases of signification with a seemingly good claim to centrality would be those in which the items or situations signified are picked out as such by their falling under the conventional meaning of the signifying expression rather than by some more informal or indirect relationship to the signifying expression. "The President's advisers approved the idea" perhaps would, and "those guys in the White House kitchen said 'Heigh Ho'" perhaps would not, meet with special favor under this test, which would without question need a fuller and more cautious exposition. Perhaps, however, for present purposes a crude distinction between conventional or formal signification and nonconventional or informal signification will suffice.

A second and seemingly not inferior suggestion would be that a special centrality should be attributed to those instances of signification in which what is signified either is, or forms part of, or is specially and appropriately connected with what the signifying expression (or its user) *says* as distinct from implies, suggests, hints, or in some other less than fully direct manner conveys. We might perhaps summarily express this suggestion as being that special centrality attaches to those instances of signification in which what is signified is or is part of the "dictive" content of the signifying expression. We should now, perhaps, try to relate these suggestions to one another.

Is the material just sketched best regarded as offering two different formulations of a single criterion of centrality, or as offering two distinct characterizations of such centrality? It seems fairly clear to me that, assuming the adequacy for present purposes of the formulation of the issues involved, two distinct criteria are in fact being offered. One may be called the presence or absence of *formality* (whether or not the relevant signification is part of the conventional meaning of the signifying expression); the other may be called the presence or absence of *dictive* content, or *dictiveness* (whether or not the relevant signification is part of what the signifying expression *says*); and it seems that formality and informality may each be combined with dictiveness or again with nondictiveness. So the two distinctions seem to be logically independent of one another. Let us try to substantiate this claim.

(1) If I make a standard statement of fact such as "The chairman of the Berkeley Philosophy Department is in the Department office.", what is signified is, or at least may for present purposes be treated as being, the conventional meaning of the signifying expression; so formality is present. What is signified is also what the signifying expression says; so dictiveness is also present.

(2) Suppose a man says "My brother-in-law lives on a peak in Darien; his great aunt, on the other hand, was a nurse in World War I," his hearer might well be somewhat baffled; and if it should turn out on further inquiry that the speaker had in mind no contrast of any sort between his brother-in-law's residential location and the one-time activities of the great aunt, one would be inclined to say that a condition conventionally signified by the presence of the phrase "on the other hand" was in fact not realized and so that the speaker had done violence to the conventional meaning of, indeed had misused, the phrase "on the other hand." But the nonrealization of this condition would also be regarded as insufficient to falsify the speaker's statement. So we seem to have a case of a condition which is part of what the words conventionally mean without being part of what the words say; that is, we have formality without dictiveness.

(3) Suppose someone, in a suitable context, says "Heigh-ho." It is possible that he might thereby mean something like "Well that's the way the world goes." Or again if someone were to say "He's just an evangelist," he might mean, perhaps, "He is a sanctimonious, hypocritical, racist, reactionary, money-grubber." If in each case his meaning were as suggested, it might well be claimed that what he meant was in fact what his words said; in which case his words would be dictive but their dictive content would be nonformal and not part of the conventional meaning of the words used. We should thus find dictiveness without formality.

(4) At a Department meeting, one of my colleagues provides a sustained exhibition of temperamental perversity and caprice; at the close of the meeting I say to him, "Excuse me, madam," or alternatively, I usher him through the door with an elaborate courtly bow. In such a case perhaps it might be said that what my words or my bow convey is that he has been behaving like a prima donna; but they do not say that this is so, nor is it part of the conventional meaning of any words or gestures used by me that this is so. Here something is conveyed or signified without formality and without dictiveness.

There seems then to be a good prima-facie case for regarding formality and dictiveness as independent criteria of centrality. Before we pursue this matter and the questions which arise from it, it might be useful to consider a little further the details of the mechanism by which, in the second example, we achieve what some might regard as a slightly startling result that formality may be present independently of dictiveness. The vital clue here is, I suggest, that speakers may be at one and the same time engaged in performing speech-acts at different but related levels. One part of what the cited speaker in example two is doing is making what might be called ground-floor statements about the brother-in-law and the great aunt, but at the same time as he is performing these speech-acts he is also performing a higher-order speech-act of commenting in a certain way on the lower-order speech-acts. He is *contrasting* in some way the performance of some of these lower-order speech-acts with others, and he signals his performance of this higher-order speech-act in his use of the embedded enclitic phrase, "on the other hand." The truth or falsity and so the dictive content of his words is determined by the relation of his ground-floor speech-acts to the world; consequently, while a certain kind of misperformance of the higher-order speech-act may constitute a semantic offense, it will not touch the truth-value, and so not the dictive content, of the speaker's words.

We may note that a related kind of nonformal (as distinct from formal) implicature may sometimes be present. It may, for example, be the case that a speaker signals himself, by his use of such words as "so" or "therefore," as performing the speech-act of *explaining* will be plausible only on the assumption that the speaker accepts as true one or more further unmentioned ground-floor matters of fact. His acceptance of such further matters of fact has to be supposed in order to rationalize the explanation which he offers. In such a case we may perhaps say that the speaker does not formally implicate the matters of fact in question.

A problem which now faces us is that there seem to be two "best candidates," each of which in different ways suggests the admissibility of an "inner/outer" distinction, and we need to be assured that there is nothing objectionable or arbitrary about the emergence of this seemingly competitive plurality. The feature of formality, or conventional signification, suggests such a distinction, since we can foresee a distinction between an inner range of characteristics which belong directly to the conventional meaning of a signifying expression, and an outer range of characteristics which, although not themselves directly part of the conventional meaning of a given signifying expression, are invariably, perhaps as a matter of natural necessity, concomitant with other characteristics which do directly belong to the conventional meaning of the signifying expression. Again, if there is an inner range of characteristics which belong to the dictive content of a signifying expression as forming part of what such an expression says, it is foreseeable that there will be an outer range of cases involving characteristics which, though not part of what a signifying expression says, do form part of what such an expression conveys in some gentler and less forthright manner—part, for example, of what it hints or suggests.

To take the matter further, I suspect that we shall need to look more closely at the detailed constitution of the two "best candidates." At this point I have confined myself to remarking that dictiveness seems to be restricted to the ground-floor level, however that may be determined, while formality seems to be unrestricted with regard to level. But there may well be other important differences between the two concepts. Let us turn first to formality, which, to my mind, may prove to be in somewhat better shape than dictiveness. To say this is not in the least to deny that it involves serious and difficult problems; indeed, if some are to be believed—for example, those who align themselves with Quine in a rejection of the analytic/synthetic distinction—these problems may turn out to be insuperable, and may drive us into a form of skepticism. But one might well in such an event regard the skepticism as imposed by the intractability of the subject-matter, not by the ineptitude of the theorist. He may well have done his best.

Some of the most pressing questions which arise concerning the concept of formality will be found in a fourfold list, which I have compiled, of topics related to formality. First and foremost among these is the demand for a theoretically adequate specification of conditions which will authorize the assignment of truth conditions to suitably selected expressions, thereby endowing those expressions with a conventional signification. It is plain that such provision is needed if signification is to get off the ground; meanings are not natural growths and need to be conferred or instituted. But the mere fact that they are needed is insufficient to show that they are available; we might be left in the skeptic's position of seeing clearly what is needed, and yet being at the same time totally unable to attain it. We should not, of course, *confuse* the suggestion that there is, strictly speaking, no such thing as the exercise of rationality with the suggestion that there is no rationally acceptable theoretical account of what the exercise of rationality consists in; but though distinct these suggestions may not be independent; for it is conceivably true that the *exercise* of rationality can exist only if there is a theoretically adequate account, accessible to human reason, of what it is that constitutes rationality; in which case an acceptance of the second suggestion will entail an acceptance of the first suggestion. These remarks are intended to raise, but not to settle, the question whether our adoption of linguistic conventions is to be explained by appeal to a general capacity for the adoption of conventions (the sort of explanation offered by Stephen Schiffer in *Meaning*), here I intend neither to endorse nor to reject the possibility of such an explanation. Similar troubles might attend a superficially different presentation of the enterprise, according to which what is being sought and, one hopes, legitimately fixed by fiat would be not conventional meanings for certain expressions, but a solid guarantee that, in certain conditions, in calling something a so-and-so, one would not be miscalling it a so and so. The conditions in question would of course have to be conditions of truth.

Inquiries of the kind just mentioned might profitably be reinforced by attention to other topics contained in my fourfold list. Another of these would involve the provision of an inventory which will be an example of what I propose to call a "semi-inferential sequence." An example of such a sequence might be the following:

(I) It is, speaking extensionally, general practice to treat ϕ as signifying F.

(II) It is, speaking intensionally, general practice to treat ϕ as signifying F.

(III) It is generally accepted that it is legitimate to treat φ as signifying F.

(IV) It is legitimate to treat φ as signifying F.

(V) φ does signify F.

Explanatory Remarks

(1) What is involved in the phenomenon of treating φ (an expression) as signifying F has not been, and would need to be, explicitly stated.

(2) A "semi-inferential sequence" is not a sequence in which each element is entailed or implied by its predecessor in the sequence. It is rather a sequence in which each element is entailed or implied by a *conjunction* of its predecessor with an identifiable and verifiable *supplementary condition,* a condition which however has not been explicitly specified.

(3) Some semi-inferential sequences will be "concept-determining" sequences. In such sequences the final member will consist of an embedded occurrence of a structure which has appeared previously in the sequence, though only as embedded within a larger structure which specifies some psychological state or practice of some rational being or class of rational beings.

(4) It is my suggestion that, for certain valuational or semantic concepts, the institution of truth-conditions for such concepts is possible only *via* the mediation of a semi-inferential concept-determining sequence.

(5) To speak extensionally is to base a claim to generality on actual frequencies.

(6) To speak intensionally is to base a claim to generality on the adoption of or adherence to a rule the observance of which may be expected to generate, approximately, a certain actual frequency.

(7) The practical modalities involved in (III) and (IV) may be restricted by an appended modifier, such as "from a logical point of view" or "from the point of view of good manners."

It might also be valuable to relate the restricted field of inferences connected with semantic proprieties to the broader and quite possibly analogous field of inferences connected with practical proprieties in general, which it would be the business of ethics to systematize. If skepticism about linguistic proprieties could not be prevented from expanding into skepticism about improprieties of any and every kind, that might be a heavier price than the linguistic skeptic would be prepared to pay.

It would be unwise at this point to neglect a further direction of inquiry, namely proper characterization of the relation between words on the one hand, and on the other the sounds or shapes which constitute their physical realizations. Such reflections may be expected to throw light on the precise sense in which words are instruments, and may well be of interest both in themselves and as a needed antidote to the facile acceptance of such popular but dubiously well founded hypotheses about language as the alleged type-token distinction. It is perhaps natural to assume that in the case of words the fundamental entities are particular shapes and sounds (word tokens) and that words, in the sense of word-types are properly regarded as classes or sets of mutually resembling word tokens. But I think that such a view can be seen to be in conflict with common sense (to whatever extent that is a drawback). John's rendering of the word "soot" may be indistinguishable from James's rendering of the word "suit"; but it does not follow from this that when they produce these renderings, they are uttering the same word, or producing different tokens of the same word-type. Indeed there is something tempting about the idea that, in order to allow for all admissible vagaries of rendering, what are to count for a given person as renderings of particular words can only be determined by reference to more or less extended segments of his discourse; and this in turn perhaps prompts the idea that particular audible or visible renderings of words are only established as such by being conceived by the speaker or writer as realizations of just those words. One might say perhaps the words come first and only later come their realizations.

Together with these reflections goes a further line of thought. Spades are commonly and standardly used for such purposes as digging garden beds; and when they are so used, we may speak indifferently of using a spade to dig the bed and of using a spade (simpliciter). On a windy day when I am in the garden, I may wish to prevent my papers from blowing away, and to achieve this result, I may put my spade on top of them. In such a case I think I might be said to be using a spade to secure the papers but not to be using a spade (simpliciter) unless perhaps I were to make an eccentric but regular use of the spade for this purpose. When it comes, however, to the use for this or that purpose of words, it may well be that my freedom of speech is more radically constrained. I may be the proud possessor of a brass plaque shaped as a written representation of the word "mother." Maybe on a windy day I put this plaque on top of my papers to secure them. But if I do so, it seems to be wrong to speak of me as having used the word "mother" to secure my papers. Words may be instruments but if so, they seem to be *essentially* confined to a certain region of employment, as instruments of communication. To attempt to use them outside that region is to attempt the conceptually impossible. Such phenonema as this need systematic explanation.

On the face of it, the factors at work in the determination of the presence or absence of dictiveness form a more motley collection than those which bear on the presence of formality. The presence or absence of an appropriate measure of ardor on behalf of a thesis, a conscientious reluctance to see one's statements falsified or unconfirmed, an excessive preoccupation with what is actually or potentially noncontroversial background material, an overindulgence in caution with respect to the strength to be attributed to an idea which one propounds, and a deviousness or indirectness of expression which helps to obscure even the identity of such an idea, might well be thought to have little in common, and in consequence to impart an unappealing fragmentation to the notion of dictive content. But perhaps these factors exhibit greater unity than at first appears; perhaps they can be viewed as specifying different ways in which a speaker's alignment with an idea or thesis may be displayed or obscured; and since in communication in a certain sense all must be public, if an idea or thesis is too heavily obscured, then it can no longer be regarded as having been propounded. So strong support for some idea, a distaste for having one's already issued statements discredited, an unexciting harmony the function of which is merely to establish a reference, and a tentative or veiled formulation of a thesis may perhaps be seen as embodying descending degrees of intensity in a speaker's alignment to whatever idea he is propounding. If so, we shall perhaps be in line with those philosophers who, in one way or another, have drawn a distinction between "phrastics" and "neustics," philosophers, that is to say, who in representing the structure of discourse lay a special emphasis on (a) the content of items of discourse whose merits or demerits will lie in such features as correspondence or lack of correspondence with the world and (b) the mode or manner in which such items are advanced, for example declaratively or imperatively, or (perhaps one might equally well say) firmly or tentatively.

In this connection it would perhaps be appropriate to elaborate somewhat the characters of tentativeness and obliqueness which are specially visible in cases of "low commitment." First "suggestion." Suggesting that so-and-so seems to me to be, with varying degrees of obviousness, different from (a) stating or maintaining that so-and-so (b) asserting it to be likely or probable that so-and-so (c) asserting it to be possible that so-and-so, where presumably "it is possible" means "it is not certain that it is not the case that so-and-so." Suggesting that so-and-so is perhaps more like, though still by no means exactly like, asserting there to be some evidence that so-and-so. Standardly, to suggest that so-and-so invites a response, and, if the suggestion is reasonable, the response it invites is to meet in one way or another the case which the maker of the suggestion, somewhat like a grand jury, supposes there to be in favor of the possibility that so-and-so. The existence of such a case will require that there should be a truthful fact or set of facts which might be explained by the hypothesis that so-and-so together with certain other facts or assumptions, though the speaker is not committed to the claim that such an explanation would in fact be correct. Suggesting seems to me to be related to, though in certain respects different from, hinting. In what seem to me to be standard cases of hinting one makes, explicitly, a statement which does, or might, justify the idea that there is a case for supposing that so-and-so; but what there might be a case for supposing, namely that so-and-so, is not explicitly mentioned but is left to the audience to identify. Obviously the more devious the hinting, the greater is the chance that the speaker will fail to make contact with his audience, and so will escape without having committed himself to anything.

Strand Six[6]

Strand Six deals with Conversational Maxims and their alleged connection with the Cooperative Principle. In my extended discussion of the properties of conversational practice I distinguished a number of maxims or principles, observance of which I regarded as providing standards of rational discourse. I sought to represent the principles or axioms which I distinguished as being themselves dependent on an overall super-principle enjoining conversational cooperation. While the conversational maxims have on the whole been quite well received, the same cannot, I think, be said about my invocation of

6. Cf. esp. Essays 2, 4.

a supreme principle of conversational cooperation. One source of trouble has perhaps been that it has been felt that even in the talk-exchanges of civilized people browbeating disputation and conversational sharp practice are far too common to be offenses against the fundamental dictates of conversational practice. Another source of discomfort has perhaps been the thought that, whether its tone is agreeable or disagreeable, much of our talk-exchange is too haphazard to be directed toward any end cooperative or otherwise. Chitchat goes nowhere, unless making the time pass is a journey.

Perhaps some refinement in our apparatus is called for. First, it is only certain aspects of our conversational practice which are candidates for evaluation, namely those which are crucial to its rationality rather than to whatever other merits or demerits it may possess; so, nothing which I say should be regarded as bearing upon the suitability or unsuitability of particular issues for conversational exploration; it is the rationality or irrationality of conversational conduct which I have been concerned to track down rather than any more general characterization of conversational adequacy. So we may expect principles of conversational rationality to abstract from the special character of conversational interests. Second, I have taken it as a working assumption that whether a particular enterprise aims at a specifically conversational result or outcome and so perhaps is a specifically conversational enterprise, or whether its central character is more generously conceived as having no special connection with communication, the same principles will determine the rationality of its conduct. It is irrational to bite off more than you can chew whether the object of your pursuit is hamburgers or the Truth.

Finally we need to take into account a distinction between solitary and concerted enterprises. I take it as being obvious that insofar as the presence of implicature rests on the character of one or another kind of conversational enterprise, it will rest on the character of concerted rather than solitary talk production. Genuine monologues are free from speaker's implication. So since we are concerned as theorists only with concerted talking, we should recognize that within the dimension of voluntary exchanges (which are all that concern us) collaboration in achieving exchange of information or the institution of decisions may coexist with a high degree of reserve, hostility, and chicanery and with a high degree of diversity in the motivations underlying quite meager common objectives. Moreover we have to remember to take into account a secondary range of cases like cross-examination in which even the common objectives are spurious, apparent rather than real; the joint enterprise is a simulation, rather than an instance, of even the most minimal conversational cooperation; but such exchanges honor the cooperative principle at least to the extent of aping its application. A similarly degenerate derivative of the primary talk-exchange may be seen in the concerns spuriously exhibited in the really aimless over-the-garden-wall chatter in which most of us from time to time engage.

I am now perhaps in a position to provide a refurbished summary of the treatment of conversational implicature to which I subscribed earlier.

(1) A list is presented of conversational maxims (or "conversational imperatives") which are such that, in paradigmatic cases, their observance promotes and their violation dispromotes conversational rationality; these include such principles as the maxims of Quantity, Quality, Relation, and Manner.

(2) Somewhat like moral commandments, these maxims are prevented from being just a disconnected heap of conversational obligations by their dependence on a single supreme Conversational Principle, that of cooperativeness.

(3) An initial class of actual talk-exchanges manifests rationality by its conformity to the maxims thus generated by the Cooperative Principle; a further subclass of exchanges manifests rationality by simulation of the practices exhibited in the initial class.

(4) Implicatures are thought of as arising in the following way; an implicatum (factual or imperatival) is the content of that psychological state or attitude which needs to be attributed to a speaker in order to secure one or another of the following results; (a) that a violation on his part of a conversational maxim is in the circumstances justifiable, at least in his eyes, or (b) that what appears to be a violation by him of a conversational maxim is only a seeming, not a real, violation; the spirit, though perhaps not the letter, of the maxim is respected.

(5) The foregoing account is perhaps closely related to the suggestion made in the discussion of Strand Five about so-called conventional implicature. It was in effect there suggested that what I have been calling conversational implicature is just those assumptions which have to be attributed to a speaker to justify him in regarding a given sequence of lower-order speech-acts as being rationalized by their relation to a conventionally indexed higher-order speech-act.

I have so far been talking as if the right ground plan is to identify a supreme Conversational Principle which could be used to generate and justify a range of more specific but still highly general conversational maxims which in turn could be induced to yield particular conversational directives applying to particular subject matters, contexts, and conversational procedures, and I have been talking as if this general layout is beyond question correct; the only doubtful matter being whether the proffered Supreme Principle, namely some version of the Cooperative Principle, is the right selection for the position of supreme Conversational Principle. I have tried to give reasons for thinking, despite the existence of some opposition, that, provided that the cited layout is conceded to be correct, the Conversational Principle proposed is an acceptable candidate. So far so good; but I do in fact have some doubts about the acceptability of the suggested layout. It is not at all clear to me that the conversational maxims, at least if I have correctly identified them as such, do in fact operate as distinct pegs from each of which there hangs an indefinitely large multitude of fully specific conversational directives. And if I have misidentified them as the conversational maxims, it is by no means clear to me what substitutes I could find to do the same job within the same general layout, only to do it differently and better. What is primarily at fault may well be not the suggested maxims but the concept of the layout within which they are supposed to operate. It has four possible problems.

(1) The maxims do not seem to be coordinate. The maxim of Quality, enjoining the provision of contributions which are genuine rather than spurious (truthful rather than mendacious), does not seem to be just one among a number of recipes for producing contributions; it seems rather to spell out the difference between something's being, and (strictly speaking) failing to be, any kind of contribution at all. False information is not an inferior kind of information; it just is not information.

(2) The suggested maxims do not seem to have the degree of mutual independence of one another which the suggested layout seems to require. To judge whether I have been undersupplied or oversupplied with information seems to require that I should be aware of the identity of the topic to which the information in question is supposed to relate; only after the identification of a focus of relevance can such an assessment be made; the force of this consideration seems to be blunted by writers like Wilson and Sperber who seem to be disposed

to sever the notion of relevance from the specification of some particular direction of relevance.

(3) Though the specification of a direction of relevance is necessary for assessment of the adequacy of a given supply of information, it is by no means sufficient to enable an assessment to be made. Information will also be needed with respect to the degree of concern which is or should be extended toward the topic in question, and again with respect to such things as opportunity or lack of opportunity for remedial action.

(4) While it is perhaps not too difficult to envisage the impact upon implicature of a real or apparent undersupply of information, the impact of a real or apparent oversupply is much more problematic.

The operation of the principle of relevance, while no doubt underlying one aspect of conversational propriety, so far as implicature is concerned has already been suggested to be dubiously independent of the maxim of Quantity; the remaining maxim distinguished by me, that of Manner, which I represented as prescribing perspicuous presentation, again seems to formulate one form of conversational propriety, but its potentialities as a generator of implicature seem to be somewhat open to question.

Strands Seven and Eight[7]

These strands may be considered together, representing, as they do, what might be deemed a division of sympathy on my part between two different schools of thought concerning the nature and content of Logic. These consist of the Modernists, spearheaded by Russell and other mathematically oriented philosophers, and the Traditionalists, particularly the neo-Traditionalists led by Strawson in *An Introduction to Logical Theory*. As may be seen, my inclination has been to have one foot in each of these at least at one time warring camps. Let us consider the issues more slowly.

(A) Modernism

In their most severe and purist guise Modernists are ready to admit to the domain of Logic only first-order predicate logic with identity, though laxer spirits may be willing to add to this bare minimum some

7. Cf. esp. Essays 3, 17.

more liberal studies, like that of some system of modalities. It seems to me that a Modernist might maintain any one of three different positions with respect to what he thinks of as Logic.

(1) He might hold that what he recognizes as Logic reflects exactly or within an acceptable margin of approximation the inferential and semantic properties of vulgar logical connectives. Unless more is said, this position is perhaps somewhat low on initial plausibility.

(2) He might hold that though not every feature of vulgar logical connectives is preserved, all features are preserved which deserve to be preserved, all features that is to say, which are not irremediably vitiated by obscurity or incoherence.

(3) Without claiming that features which are omitted from his preferred system are ones which are marred by obscurity or incoherence he might claim that those which are not omitted possess, collectively, the economic virtue of being adequate to the task of presenting, in good logical order, that science or body of sciences the proper presentation of which is called for by some authority, such as Common Sense or the "Cathedral of Learning."

(B) Neo-Traditionalism

So far as I can now reconstruct it, Strawson's response to Modernism at the time of *An Introduction to Logical Theory*, ran along the following lines.

(1) At a number of points it is clear that the apparatus of Modernism does not give a faithful account of the character of the logical connectives of ordinary discourse; these deviations appear in the treatment of the Square of Opposition, the Russellian account of Definite, and also of Indefinite, Descriptions, the analysis of conditionals in terms of material implication, and the representation of universal statements by universal quantifiers. Indeed, the deviant aspects of such elements in Modernism are liable to involve not merely infidelity to the actual character of vulgar connectives, but also the obliteration of certain conceptions, like presupposition and the existence of truth-gaps, which are crucial to the nature of certain logically fundamental speech-acts, such as Reference.

(2) The aspects thus omitted by Modernists are not such that their presence would undermine or discredit the connectives in the analysis of which they would appear. Like Cyrano de Bergerac's nose, they are features which are prominent without being disfiguring.

(3) Though they are not, in themselves, blemishes, they do nevertheless impede the optimally comprehensive and compendious representation of the body of admissible logical inferences.

(4) We need, therefore, two kinds of logic; one, to be called the logic of language, in which in a relaxed and sometimes not fully determinate way the actual character of the connectives of ordinary discourse is faithfully represented; the other, to be called formal logic, in which, at some cost to fidelity to the actual character of vulgar logical connectives, a strictly regimented system is provided which represents with maximal ease and economy the indefinite multitude of admissible logical inferences.

(C) My Reactions to These Disputes

(1) I have never been deeply moved by the prospect of a comprehensive and compendious systematization of acceptable logical inferences, though the tidiness of Modernist logic does have some appeal for me. But what exerts more influence upon me is my inclination to regard propositions as constructed entities whose essential character lies in their truth-value, entities which have an indispensable role to play in a rational and scientific presentation of the domain of logical inference. From this point of view a truth-functional conception of complex propositions offers prospects, perhaps, for the rational construction of at least part of the realm of propositions, even though the fact that many complex propositions seem plainly to be non-truth-functional ensures that many problems remain.

(2) A few years after the appearance of *An Introduction to Logical Theory* I was devoting much attention to what might be loosely called the distinction between logical and pragmatic inferences. In the first instance this was prompted as part of an attempt to rebuff objections, primarily by followers of Wittgenstein, to the project of using "phenomenal" verbs, like "look" and "seem," to elucidate problems in the philosophy of perception, particularly that of explaining the problematic notion of sense-data, which seemed to me to rest on a blurring of the logical/pragmatic distinction. (That is not to say, of course, that there might not be other good reasons for rejecting the project in question.) It then occurred to me that apparatus which had rendered good service in one area might be equally successful when transferred to another; and so I canvassed the idea that the alleged divergences between Modernists' Logic and vulgar logical connectives might be

represented as being a matter not of logical but of pragmatic import.

(3) The question which at this point particularly beset not only me but various other philosophers as well was the question whether it is or is not required that a nonconventional implicature should always possess maximal scope; when a sentence which used in isolation standardly carries a certain implicature, is embedded in a certain linguistic context, for example appears within the scope of a negation-sign, must the embedding operator, namely the negation-sign, be interpreted only as working on the conventional import of the embedded sentence, or may it on occasion be interpreted as governing not the conventional import but the nonconventional implicatum of the embedded sentence? Only if an embedding operator may on occasion be taken as governing not the conventional import but the nonconventional implicatum standardly carried by the embedded sentence can the first version of my account of such linguistic phenomena as conditionals and definite descriptions be made to work. The denial of a conditional needs to be treated as denying not the conventional import but the standard implicatum attaching to an isolated use of the embedded sentence. It certainly does not seem reasonable to subscribe to an absolute ban on the possibility that an embedding locution may govern the standard nonconventional implicatum rather than the conventional import of the embedded sentence; if a friend were to tell me that he had spent the summer cleaning the Augean stables, it would be unreasonable of me to respond that he could not have been doing that since he spent the summer in Seattle and the Augean stables are not in Seattle. But where the limits of a license may lie which allows us to relate embedding operators to the standard implicata rather than to conventional meanings, I have to admit that I do not know.

(4) The second version of my mode of treatment of issues which, historically speaking, divide Modernists from Traditionalists, including neo-Traditionalists, offers insurance against the possibility that we do not have, or that we sometimes do not have, a license to treat embedding locutions as governing standard implicata rather than conventional import. It operates on the idea that even if it should prove necessary to supplement the apparatus of Modernist logic with additional conventional devices, such supplementation is in two respects undramatic and innocuous and does not involve a radical reconstruction of Modernist apparatus. It is innocuous and undramatic partly because the newly introduced conventional devices can be re-

garded simply as codification, with a consequently enlarged range of utility, of pre-existing informal methods of generating implicature; and partly because the new devices do not introduce any new ideas or concepts, but are rather procedural in character. This last feature can be seen from the fact that the conventional devices which I propose are bracketing or scope devices, and to understand them is simply to know how sentences in which they initially appear can be restructured and rewritten as sentences couched in orthodox modernistic terms from which the new devices have been eliminated. What the eye no longer sees the heart no longer grieves for.

Philosophical Method and Ordinary Language

I shall conclude this Epilogue by paying a little attention to the general character of my attitude to ordinary language. In order to fulfill this task, I should say something about what was possibly the most notable corporate achievement of my philosophical early middle age, namely the so-called method of linguistic botanizing, treated, as it often was in Oxford at the time, as a foundation for conceptual analysis in general and philosophical analysis in particular. Philosophers have not seldom proclaimed the close connection between philosophy and linguistic analysis, but so far as I know, the ruthless and unswerving association of philosophy with the study of ordinary language was peculiar to the Oxford scene, and has never been seen anywhere before or since, except as an application of the methods of philosophizing which originated in Oxford. A classic miniature example of this kind of procedure was Austin's request to Warnock to tell him the difference between playing golf correctly and playing golf properly. But also the method was commonly deployed not merely as a tool for reaching conceptual "fine-tuning" with regard to pairs of expressions or ideas, but in larger-scale attempts to systematize the range of concepts which appear in a certain conceptual region. It may well be the case that these concepts all fall under a single overarching concept, while it is at the same time true that there is no single word or phrase which gives linguistic expression to just this concept; and one goal of linguistic botanizing may be to make this concept explicit and to show how the various subordinate concepts fall under it. This program is closely linked with Austin's ideas about the desirability of "going through the dictionary." In some cases, this may be quite a long job, as for example in the case of the word "true"; for one feature of the method is that no initial assumptions are made about the subdivisions involved in subordinate lexical entries united by a single word; "true friends," "true statements," "true beliefs," "true bills," "true measuring instruments," "true singing voices" will not be initially distinguished from one another as involving different uses of the word "true"; that is a matter which may or may not be the outcome of the operation of linguistic botanizing; subordinations and subdivisions are not given in advance. It seems plausible to suppose that among the things which are being looked for are linguistic proprieties and improprieties: and these may be of several different kinds; so one question which will call for decision will be an identification of the variety of different ways in which proprieties and improprieties may be characterized and organized. Contradictions, incoherences, and a wealth of other forms of unsuitability will appear among the outcomes, not the starting points, of linguistic botanizing, and the nature of these outcomes will need careful consideration. Not only may single words involve a multitude of lexical entries, but different idioms and syntactical constructions appearing within the domain of a single lexical entry may still be a proper subject for even more specific linguistic botanizing. Syntax must not be ignored in the study of semantics.

At this point we are faced with two distinct problems. The first arises from the fact that my purpose here is not to give a historically correct account of philosophical events which actually took place in Oxford some forty years ago but rather to characterize and as far as possible to justify a certain distinctive philosophical methodology. Now there is little doubt that those who were engaged in and possibly even dedicated to the practice of the prevailing Oxonian methodology, such persons as Austin, Ryle, Strawson, Hampshire, Urmson, Warnock, and others (including myself) had a pretty good idea of the nature of the procedures which they were putting into operation; indeed it is logically difficult to see how anyone outside this group could have had a better idea than the members of the group since the procedures are identifiable only as the procedures which these people were seeking to deploy. Nevertheless there is still room for doubt whether the course of actual discussions in every way embodied the authentic methodology, for a fully adequate implementation of that methodology requires a good and clear representation of the methodology itself; the more fragmentary the representation the greater the chance of inadequate implementation; and it must be admitted that the ability of many of us to say at the time what it was that we were doing was fragmentary in the extreme. This may be an insoluble problem in the characterization of this kind of theoretical activity; to say what such an activity is presupposes the ability to perform the activity in question; and this in turn presupposes the ability to say what the activity in question is.

The second and quite different problem is that some of the critics of Oxonian philosophizing like Russell, Quine and others have exhibited strong hostility not indeed in every case to the idea that a study of language is a prime concern of philosophy, but rather to the idea that it should be a primary concern of philosophy to study *ordinary* language. Philosophy finds employment as part of, possibly indeed just as an auxiliary of, Science; and the thinking of the layman is what scientific thinking is supposed to supersede, not what it is supposed to be founded on. The issues are obscure, but whether or not we like scientism, we had better be clear about what it entails.

Part of the trouble may arise from an improperly conceived proposition in the minds of some self-appointed experts between "we" and "they"; between, that is, the privileged and enlightened, on the one hand, and the rabble on the other. But that is by no means the only possible stance which the learned might adopt toward the vulgar; they might think of themselves as qualified by extended application and education to pursue further and to handle better just those interests which they devise for themselves in their salad days; after all, most professionals begin as amateurs. Or they might think of themselves as advancing in one region, on behalf of the human race, the achievements and culture of that race which other members of it perhaps enhance in other directions and which many members of it, unfortunately for them perhaps, are not equipped to advance at all. In any case, to recognize the rights of the majority to direct the efforts of the minority which forms the cultured elite is quite distinct from treating the majority as themselves constituting a cultured elite.

Perhaps the balance might be somewhat redressed if we pay attention to the striking parallels which seem to exist between the Oxford which received such a mixed reception in the mid-twentieth century, and what I might make so bold as to call that other Oxford which, more than two thousand three hundred years earlier, achieved not merely fame but veneration as the cradle of our discipline. The following is a short and maybe somewhat tendentious summary of that earlier Athenian dialectic, with details drawn mostly from Aristotle but also to some extent from Plato and, through Plato, from Socrates himself. In Aristotle's writing the main sources are the beginning of the *Topics*, the beginning of the *Nicomachean Ethics*, and the end of the *Posterior Analytics*.

(1) We should distinguish two kinds of knowledge, knowledge of fact and knowledge of reasons, where what the reasons account for are the facts.

(2) Knowledge proper involves both facts to be accounted for and reasons which account for them; for this reason Socrates claimed to know nothing; when we start to research, we may or may not be familiar with many facts, but whether this is so or not we cannot tell until explanations and reasons begin to become available.

(3) For explanations and reasons to be available, they must derive ultimately from first principles, but these first principles do not come ready-made; they have to be devised by the inquirer, and how this is done itself needs explanation.

(4) It is not done in one fell swoop; at any given stage researchers build on the work of their predecessors right back to their earliest predecessors who are lay inquirers. Such progressive scrutiny is called "dialectic," starts with the ideas of the Many and ends (if it ever ends) with the ideas of the Wise.

(5) Among the methods used in dialectic (or "argumentation") is system-building, which in its turn involves higher and higher levels of abstraction. So first principles will be, roughly speaking, the smallest and most conceptually economical principles which will account for the data which the theory has to explain.

(6) The progress toward an acceptable body of first principles is not always tranquil; disputes, paradoxes, and obstructions to progress abound, and when they are reached, recognizable types of emendation are called upon to restore progress.

(7) So the continuation of progress depends to a large extent on the possibility of "saving the phenomena," and the phenomena consist primarily of what is said, or thought, by the Wise and, before them, the Many.

I find it tempting to suppose that similar ideas underlie the twentieth-century Oxonian dialectic; the appeal to ordinary language might be viewed as an appeal to the ultimate source of one, though not of every, kind of human knowledge. It would indeed not be surprising were this to be so, since two senior Oxonians (Ryle and Austin) were both skilled and enthusiastic students of Greek philosophy.

But this initially appealing comparison between what I have been calling Oxonian Dialectic and Athenian Dialectic encounters a serious objection, connected with such phrases as "what is said" (ta legomena, τα λεγόμεηα). The phrase "what is said" may be interpreted in either of two ways. (I) It may refer to a class of beliefs or opinions which are commonly or generally held, in which case it would mean much the same as such a phrase as "what is ordinarily thought." (II) It may refer to a class of ways of talking or locutions, in which case it will mean much the same as "ways in which ordinary people ordinarily talk." In the Athenian Dialectic we find the phrase used in both of these senses; sometimes, for example, Aristotle seems to be talking about locutions, as when he points out that while it is legitimate to speak of "running quickly" or "running slowly," it is not legitimate to speak of "being pleased quickly" or "being pleased slowly"; from which he draws the philosophical conclusion that running is, while pleasure is not (despite the opinions of some philosophers), a *process* as distinct from an *activity*. At other times he uses the phrase "what is said" to refer to certain generally or vulgarly held beliefs which are systematically threatened by a projected direction of philosophical theory, as the platitude that people sometimes behave incontinently seems to be threatened by a particular philosophical analysis of Will, or the near-platitude that friends are worth having for their own sake seems to be threatened by the seemingly equally platitudinous thesis that the Good Life is self-sufficient and lacking in nothing. In the Athenian Dialectic, moreover, though both interpretations are needed, the dominant one seems to be that in which what is being talked about is common opinions, not commonly used locutions or modes of speech. In the Oxonian Dialectic, on the other hand, precisely the reverse situation seems to obtain. Though some philosophers, most notably G. E. Moore, have maintained that certain commonly held beliefs cannot but be correct and though versions of such a thesis are discernible in certain Oxonian quarters, for example in Urmson's treatment of Paradigm Case Arguments, no general characterization of the Method of "Linguistic Botanizing" carries with it any claim about the truth-value of any of the specimens which might be subjected to Linguistic Botanizing; nor, I think, would any such characterization be improved by the incorporation of an emendation in this connection. So the harmony introduced by an assimilation of the two Dialectics seems to be delusive.

I am, however, reluctant to abandon the proposed comparison between Oxonian and Athenian Dialectic quite so quickly. I would begin by recalling that as a matter of historical fact Austin professed a strong admiration for G. E. Moore. "Some like Witters" he once said, "but Moore is *my* man." It is not recorded what aspects of Moore's philosophy particularly appealed to him, but the contrast with Wittgenstein strongly suggests that Moore primarily appealed to him as a champion of Common Sense, and of philosophy as the source of the analysis of Common Sense beliefs, a position for which Moore was especially famous, in contrast with the succession of less sharply defined positions about the role of philosophy taken up at various times by Wittgenstein. The question which now exercises me is why Moore's stand on this matter should have specially aroused Austin's respect, for what Moore said on this matter seems to me to be plainly inferior in quality, and indeed to be the kind of thing which Austin was more than capable of tearing to shreds had he encountered it in somebody else. Moore's treatments of this topic seem to me to suffer from two glaring defects and one important lacuna. The two glaring defects are: (1) he nowhere attempts to characterize for us the conditions which have to be satisfied by a generally held belief to make it part of a "Common Sense view of the world"; (2) even if we overlook this complaint, there is the further complaint that nowhere, so far as I know, does Moore justify the claim that the Common Sense view of the world is at least in certain respects unquestionably correct. The important lacuna is that Moore considers only one possible position about the relation between such specific statements as that "Here is one human hand and here is another" and the seemingly general philosophical statement that material objects exist. Moore takes it for granted that the statement about the human hands entails the general statement that material objects exist; but as Wittgenstein remarked, "Surely those who deny the reality of the material world do not wish to deny that underneath my trousers I wear underpants." Moore was by no means certainly wrong on this matter, but the question which comes first, interpretation or the assessment of truth-value, is an important methodological question which Moore should have taken more seriously.

My explanation of part of Austin's by no means wholly characteristic charity lies in my conjecture that Austin saw, or thought he saw, the right reply to these complaints and mistakenly assumed that Moore himself had also seen how to reply to them. I shall develop this suggestion with the aid of a fairy tale about the philosophical

Never-Never Land which is inhabited by philosophical fairy god-mothers. Initially we distinguish three of these fairy godmothers, M*, Moore's fairy godmother, A*, Austin's fairy godmother, and G*, Grice's fairy godmother. The common characteristic of fairy god-mothers is that they harbor explicitly all the views, whether explicit or implicit, of their godchildren. G* reports to Grice that A* mistak-enly attributes to M* a distinction between two different kinds of subjects of belief, a distinction between personal believers who are individual persons or groups of persons, and nonpersonal believers who are this or that kind of abstraction, like the spirit of a particular language or even the spirit of language as such, the Common Man, the inventor of the analytic/synthetic distinction (who is distinct from Leibniz) and so forth. A distinction is now suggested between the Athenian Dialectic, the primary concern of which was to trace the development of more and more accomplished personal believers, and a different dialectic which would be focused on nonpersonal believ-ers. Since nonpersonal believers are not historical persons, their be-liefs cannot be identified from their expression in any historical de-bates or disputes. They can be identified only from the part which they play in the practice of particular languages, or even of languages in general.

So what G* suggested to Grice ran approximately as follows. A*, with or without the concurrence of the mundane Austin, attributed to Moore the recognition of a distinction between personal and non-personal, common or general beliefs, together with the idea that a Common Sense view of the world contains just those nonpersonal beliefs which could be correctly attributed to some favored nonper-sonal abstraction, such as the Common Man. More would of course need to be said about the precise nature of the distinction between the Common Man and other abstractions; but once a distinction has been recognized between personal and nonpersonal believers, at least the beginnings are visible of a road which also finds room for (1) the association of nonpersonal beliefs, or a particular variety of nonper-sonal beliefs, with the philosophical tool or instrument called Com-mon Sense, and for (2) the appeal to the structure and content of languages, or language as such, as a key to unlock the storehouse of Common Sense, and also for (3) the demand for Oxonian Dialectic as a supplementation of Athenian Dialectic, which was directed to-ward personal rather than nonpersonal beliefs. G* conjectured that this represented Austin's own position about the function of Linguistic Botanizing, or even if this were not so, it would have been a good position for Austin to adopt about the philosophical role of Linguistic Botanizing; it would be a position very much in line with Austin's known wonder and appreciation with regard to the richness, subtlety, and ingenuity of the instrument of language. It was however also G*'s view that the attribution of such reflections to Moore would have involved the giving of credit where credit was not due; this kind of picture of ordinary language may have been Austin's but was certainly not Moore's; his conception of Common Sense was deserving of no special praise.

We also have to consider the strength or weakness of my second charge against Moore, namely that whether or not he has succeeded in providing or indeed has even attempted to provide a characterization of commonsense beliefs, he has nowhere offered us a justification of the idea that commonsense beliefs are matters of knowledge with certainty or indeed possess any special degree or kind of credibility. Apart from the production, on occasion, of the somewhat opaque suggestion that the grounds for questioning a commonsense belief will always be more questionable than the belief itself, he seems to do little beyond asserting (1) that he himself knows for certain to be true the members of an open-ended list of commonsense beliefs, (2) that he knows for certain that others know for certain that these beliefs are true. But this is precisely the point at which many of his opponents, for example Russell, would be ready to join issue with him. It might here be instructive to compare Moore with another perhaps equally uncompromising defender of knowledge with certainty, namely Cook Wilson. Cook Wilson took the view that the very nature of knowledge was such that items which were objects of knowledge could not be false; the nature of knowledge guaranteed, perhaps logically guaranteed, the truth of its object. The difficulty here is to explain how a state of mind can in such a way guarantee the possession of a particular truth-value on the part of its object. This difficulty is severe enough to ensure that Cook Wilson's position must be rejected; for if it is accepted no room is left for the possibility of thinking that we know p when in fact it is not the case that p. This difficulty led Cook Wilson and his followers to the admission of a state of "taking for granted," which supposedly is subjectively indistinguishable from knowledge but unlike knowledge carries no guarantee of truth. But this modification amounts to surrender; for what enables us to deny that all of our so-called knowledge is really only "taking for granted"? But while Cook Wilson finds himself landed with bad answers, it seems to me that Moore has no answers at all, good or bad; and whether nonanswers are superior or inferior to bad answers seems to me a question hardly worth debating.

It is in any case my firm belief that Austin would not have been sympathetic toward the attempts made by Moore and some of his followers to attribute to the deliverances of common sense, whatever these deliverances are supposed to be, any guaranteed immunity from error. I think, moreover, that he would have been right in withholding his support at this point, and we may notice that had he withheld support, he would have been at variance with some of his own junior colleagues at Oxford, particularly with philosophers like Urmson who, at least at one time, showed a disposition, which as far as I know Austin never did, to rely on so-called Arguments from Paradigm Cases. I think Austin might have thought, rightly, that those who espoused such arguments were attempting to replace by a dogmatic thesis something which they already had, which was, furthermore, adequate to all legitimate philosophical needs. Austin plainly viewed ordinary language as a wonderfully subtle and well-contrived instrument, one which is fashioned not for idle display but for serious (and nonserious) use. So while there is no guarantee of immunity from error, if one is minded to find error embedded in ordinary modes of speech, one had better have a solid reason behind one. That which must be assumed to hold (other things being equal) can be legitimately rejected only if there are grounds for saying that other things are not, or may not be, equal.

At this point, we introduce a further inhabitant of the philosophical Never-Never Land, namely R* who turns out to be Ryle's fairy godmother. She propounds the idea that, far from being a basis for *rejecting* the analytic/synthetic distinction, opposition to the idea that there are initially two distinct bundles of statements, bearing the labels "analytic" and "synthetic," lying around in the world of thought waiting to be noticed, provides us with the key to making the analytic/synthetic distinction *acceptable*. The proper view will be that analytic propositions are among the inventions of theorists who are seeking, in one way or another, to organize and systematize an initially undifferentiated corpus of human knowledge. Success in this area is a matter of intellectual vision, not of good eyesight. As Plato once remarked, the ability to see horses without seeing horseness is a mark of stupidity. Such considerations as these are said to lie behind reports that yet a fifth fairy godmother, Q*, was last seen rushing headlong out of the gates of Never-Never-Land, loudly screaming and hotly pursued (in strict order of seniority) by M*, R*, A*, and G*. But the narration of these stirring events must be left to another and longer day.

Index

文库索引

General Linguistics 普通语言学

Phonetics and Phonology 语音学与音系学

<u>Syntax 句法学</u>

Baltin, M. et al.（eds） *The Handbook of Contemporary Syntactic Theory*
当代句法理论通览

Chomsky, N. *Knowledge of Language：Its Nature，Origin，and Use*
语言知识:其性质、来源及使用

Cook, V. *Chomsky's Universal Grammar：An Introduction*
Second edition
乔姆斯基的普遍语法教程

Ouhalla, J. *Introducing Transformational Grammar：From Principles and Parameters to Minimalism* Second edition
转换生成语法导论:从原则参数到最简方案

Radford, A. *Syntax：A Minimalist Introduction*
句法学:最简方案导论

Radford, A. *Transformational Grammar：A First Course*
转换生成语法教程

Smith, N. *Chomsky：Ideas and Ideals*
乔姆斯基:思想与理想

<u>Semantics 语义学</u>

Lappin, S.（ed） *The Handbook of Contemporary Semantic Theory*
当代语义理论指南

Lyons, J. *Linguistic Semantics：An Introduction*
语义学引论

Saeed, J.I. *Semantics*
语义学

<u>Morphology 形态学</u>

Matthews, P.H. *Morphology* Second edition
形态学

Packard, J.L. *The Morphology of Chinese：A Linguistic and Cognitive Approach*
汉语形态学:语言认知研究法

<u>Pragmatics 语用学</u>

Mey, J.L. *Pragmatics：An Introduction* Second edition
语用学引论

Levinson, S.C. *Pragmatics*
语用学

396

Peccei, J.S.	*Pragmatics*
	语用学
Sperber, D. et al.	*Relevance*: *Communication and Cognition* Second edition
	关联性：交际与认知
Verschueren, J.	*Understanding Pragmatics*
	语用学新解

Discourse Analysis 话语分析

Brown, G. et al.	*Discourse Analysis*
	话语分析
Gee, J.P.	*An Introduction to Discourse Analysis*: *Theory & Method*
	话语分析入门：理论与方法

Philosophy of Language 语言哲学

Austin, J.L.	*How to Do Things with Words* Second edition
	如何以言行事
Grice, H.P.	*Studies in the Way of Words*
	言辞用法研究
Searle, J.R.	*Speech Acts*: *An Essay in the Philosophy of Language*
	言语行为：语言哲学论
Searle, J.R.	*Expression and Meaning*: *Studies in the Theory of Speech Acts*
	表述和意义：言语行为研究

Language Origin 语言起源

| Aitchison, J. | *The Seeds of Speech*: *Language Origin and Evolution* |
| | 言语的萌发：语言起源与进化 |

History of Linguistics 语言学史

| Robins, R.H. | *A Short History of Linguistics* Fourth edition |
| | 语言学简史 |

Lexicography 词典学

Bejoint, H.	*Modern Lexicography*: *An Introduction*
	现代词典学入门
Cowie, A.P.	*English Dictionaries for Foreign Learners*: *A History*
	英语学习词典史

| Hartmann, R.R.K. et al. | *Dictionary of Lexicography*
词典学词典 |

Stylistics 文体学

Leech, G. N.	*A Linguistic Guide to English Poetry* 英诗学习指南：语言学的分析方法
Leech, G. N. et al.	*Style in Fiction：A Linguistic Introduction to English Fictional Prose* 小说文体论：英语小说的语言学入门
Thornborrow, J. et al.	*Patterns in Language：Stylistics for Students of Language and Literature* 语言模式：文体学入门
Wright, L. et al.	*Stylistics：A Practical Coursebook* 实用文体学教程

Typology 语言类型学

| Croft, W. | *Typology and Universals*
语言类型学与普遍语法特征 |

Anthropological Linguistics 人类语言学

| Foley, W. | *Anthropological Linguistics：An Introduction*
人类语言学入门 |

Sociolinguistics 社会语言学

Coulmas, F.（ed）	*The Handbook of Sociolinguistics* 社会语言学通览
Crystal, D.	*English as a Global Language* 英语：全球通用语
Fasold, R.	*The Sociolinguistics of Language* 社会语言学
Hudson, R.A.	*Sociolinguistics* Second edition 社会语言学教程
Wardhaugh, R.	*Introduction to Sociolinguistics* Third edition 社会语言学引论

Psycholinguistics 心理语言学

| Aitchison, J. | *The Articulate Mammal：An Introduction to Psycholinguistics* Fourth edition
会说话的哺乳动物：心理语言学入门 |

398

Carroll, D. W.　　　　　*Psychology of Language* Third edition
　　　　　　　　　　　语言心理学

Intercultural Communication 跨文化交际

Samovar, L. A. et al.　　*Communication Between Cultures* Second edition
　　　　　　　　　　　跨文化交际

Scollon, R. et al.　　　　*Intercultural Communication: A Discourse Analysis*
　　　　　　　　　　　跨文化交际：语篇分析法

Translatology 翻译学

Baker, M.　　　　　　　*In Other Words: A Coursebook on Translation*
　　　　　　　　　　　换言之：翻译教程

Bell, R. T.　　　　　　　*Translation and Translating: Theory and Practice*
　　　　　　　　　　　翻译与翻译过程：理论与实践

Cognitive Linguistics 认知语言学

Taylor, J. R.　　　　　　*Linguistic Categorization: Prototypes in Linguistic Theory*
　　　　　　　　　　　Second edition
　　　　　　　　　　　语言的范畴化：语言学理论中的类典型

Ungerer, F. et al.　　　　*An Introduction to Cognitive Linguistics*
　　　　　　　　　　　认知语言学入门

Functional Linguistics 功能语言学

Bloor, T. et al.　　　　　*The Functional Analysis of English: A Hallidayan Approach*
　　　　　　　　　　　英语的功能分析：韩礼德模式

Halliday, M. A. K.　　　　*An Introduction to Functional Grammar* Second edition
　　　　　　　　　　　功能语法导论

Halliday, M. A. K.　　　　*Language as Social Semiotic: The Social Interpretation of Language and Meaning*
　　　　　　　　　　　作为社会符号的语言：从社会角度诠释语言与意义

Halliday, M. A. K. et al.　*Cohesion in English*
　　　　　　　　　　　英语的衔接

Thompson, G.　　　　　*Introducing Functional Grammar*
　　　　　　　　　　　功能语法入门

Historical Linguistics 历史语言学

Lehmann, W. P.　　　　　*Historical Linguistics: An Introduction* Third edition
　　　　　　　　　　　历史语言学导论

Trask, R. L.   *Historical Linguistics*
历史语言学

Corpus Linguistics 语料库语言学

Biber, D. et al.   *Corpus Linguistics*
语料库语言学

Kennedy, G.   *An Introduction to Corpus Linguistics*
语料库语言学入门

Statistics in Linguistics 语言统计学

Woods, A. et al.   *Statistics in Language Studies*
语言研究中的统计学

History of the English Language 英语史

Baugh, A. C. et al.   *A History of the English Language* Fourth edition
英语史

Freeborn, D.   *From Old English to Standard English* Second edition
英语史：从古代英语到标准英语

First Language Acquisition 第一语言习得

Foster-Cohen, S. H.   *An Introduction to Child Language Development*
儿童语言发展引论

Goodluck, H.   *Language Acquisition: A Linguistic Introduction*
从语言学的角度看语言习得

Peccei, J. S.   *Child Language* New edition
儿童语言

Second Language Acquisition 第二语言习得

Cohen, A. D.   *Strategies in Learning and Using a Second Language*
学习和运用第二语言的策略

Cook, V.   *Linguistics and Second Language Acquisition*
语言学和第二语言习得

Cook, V.   *Second Language Learning and Language Teaching*
Second edition
第二语言学习与教学

James, C.   *Erros in Language Learning and Use: Exploring Error Analysis*
语言学习和语言使用中的错误：错误分析探讨

Larsen-Freeman, D. et al.	*An Introduction to Second Language Acquisition Research* 第二语言习得研究概况
Nunan, D.	*Second Language Teaching and Learning* 第二语言教与学
Reid, J. M.	*Learning Styles in the ESL/EFL Classroom* ESL/EFL 英语课堂上的学习风格
Richards, J.C. et al.	*Reflective Teaching in Second Language Classrooms* 第二语言课堂教学反思

Language Education 语言教育

Brown, H.D.	*Principles of Language Learning and Teaching* Third edition 语言学习和语言教学的原则
Brown, H.D.	*Teaching by Principles: An Interactive Approach to Language Pedagogy* 根据原理教学：交互式语言教学
Brown, J.D.	*The Elements of Language Curriculum: A Systematic Approach to Program Development* 语言教学大纲要素：课程设计系统法
Harmer, J.	*How to Teach English* 怎样教英语
Hatch, E. et al.	*Vocabulary, Semantics and Language Education* 词汇、语义学和语言教育
Johnson, K.	*An Introduction to Foreign Language Learning and Teaching* 外语学习与教学导论
Richards, J. et al.	*Approaches and Methods in Language Teaching* 语言教学的流派
Trudgill, P. et al.	*International English* Third edition 英语：国际通用语
Ur, P.	*A Course in Language Teaching: Practice and Theory* 语言教学教程：实践与理论

Research Method 研究方法

| McDonough, J. et al. | *Research Methods for English Language Teachers*
英语教学科研方法 |
| Slade, C. | *Form and Style: Research Papers, Reports, Theses* Tenth edition
如何写研究论文与学术报告 |

Thomas, J. et al. (eds)   *Using Corpora for Language Research*
用语料库研究语言

Wray, A. et al.   *Projects in Linguistics: A Practical Guide to Researching Language*
语言学课题：语言研究实用指南

Testing 测试学

Alderson, J.C. et al.   *Language Test Construction and Evaluation*
语言测试的设计与评估

Bachman, L.F. et al.   *Interfaces between Second Language Acquisition and Language Testing Research*
第二语言习得与语言测试研究的接口

Davies, A. et al.   *Dictionary of Language Testing*
语言测试词典

Henning, G.   *A Guide to Language Testing: Development, Evaluation and Research*
语言测试指南：发展、评估与研究

Heaton, J.B.   *Writing English Language Tests* New edition
英语测试

Wood, R.   *Assessment and Testing: A Survey of Research*
评估与测试：研究综述

Academic Writing 学术写作

Roberts, W.H. et al.   *About Language: A Reader for Writers* Fifth edition
谈语言：写作读本

Course Design 课程设计

Yalden, J.   *Principles of Course Design for Language Teaching*
语言教学课程设计原理

English Grammar 英语语法

Biber, D. et al.   *Longman Grammar of Spoken and Written English*
朗文英语口语和笔语语法

Hopper, P.J. et al.   *Grammaticalization*
语法化学说

Dictionary 辞典

Bussmann, H.   *Routledge Dictionary of Language and Linguistics*
语言与语言学词典

Crystal, D.	*The Cambridge Encyclopedia of Language* Second edition 剑桥语言百科全书
Johnson, K. et al.	*Encyclopedic Dictionary of Applied Linguistics: A Handbook for Language Teaching* 应用语言学百科辞典：语言教学手册
Richards, J.C. et al.	*Longman Dictionary of Language Teaching & Applied Linguistics* 朗文语言教学及应用语言学辞典(英英·英汉双解)